The Fearless Judge

The Fearless Judge

The Life and Times of Justice A.M. Ahmadi

Insiyah Vahanvaty

JUGGERNAUT BOOKS
C-I-128, First Floor, Sangam Vihar, Near Holi Chowk,
New Delhi 110080, India

First published by Juggernaut Books 2024

Copyright © Insiyah Vahanvaty 2024

10 9 8 7 6 5 4 3 2 1

P-ISBN: 9789353457983
E-ISBN: 9789353456733

The views and opinions expressed in this book are the author's own.
The facts contained herein were reported to be true as on the date of publication
by the author to the publishers of the book, and the publishers are not
in any way liable for their accuracy or veracity.

All rights reserved. No part of this publication may be reproduced,
transmitted, or stored in a retrieval system in any form or by any means without the
written permission of the publisher.

Typeset in Adobe Caslon Pro by
R. Ajith Kumar, Noida

Printed at Thomson Press India Ltd

To my North Star, my beloved grandparents.

You fought the good fight,
You finished the race.
May you always fly free,
May you rest in eternal peace.

Contents

Foreword by Chief Justice D.Y. Chandrachud	ix
Foreword by Justice Rohinton F. Nariman	xiii
1. The Black Sheep of the Family	1
2. 'I Did Not Choose the Law; the Law Chose Me'	12
3. Ties that Bind, Ties that Break	24
4. From Bar to Bench	36
5. A Fork in the Road	59
6. The Citizen's Judge	81
7. Gavel and Grit	105
8. The Ayodhya Matter	137
9. Triumphs and Trials	162
10. The Chief's Chair	188
11. The Bhopal Gas Case: Courage Under Fire	225
12. Beyond the Bench	240
Epilogue	281
Notes	283
Author's Note	309
Acknowledgements	311
Index	313

Foreword

Chief Justice D.Y. Chandrachud

Justice Aziz Mushabber Ahmadi, whose legacy this book celebrates, was an institution builder and a mentor to many. His distinctions are numerous – more than any account of his life can exhaustively enlist. Insiyah Vahanvaty comes quite close as she skilfully crafts what is a doting account of her grandfather's life while authoring an objective narrative of the life of a public functionary in service of the Constitution. The book contains an encapsulation of events that shaped the country and formed the backdrop of Justice Ahmadi's life.

His journey to the office of the Chief Justice of India – the first to have ascended through the ranks, from the City Civil Court in Ahmedabad to the High Court and finally to the Supreme Court – is a testament to his service to the nation. Justice Ahmadi once dreamt of charting different seas and joining the Merchant Navy. Still a lawyer, an unassuming Justice Ahmadi was so overcome with surprise at the question of his elevation that he asked Justice Shelat, 'Does your Lordship know my age?' Eventually, at thirty-two years of age, he ascended to the Bench of the City Civil Court, Ahmedabad.

He was committed to the Gandhian talisman of contemplating the meaning of our actions for the weakest. A young Aziz would tiptoe in scorching heat to catch a glimpse of the Mahatma himself as he travelled across Surat. Later, perhaps a fleeting sight of Mahatma Gandhi and the years of following his father across the many districts and talukas of present-day Gujarat and Maharashtra would shape his judicial instincts as the citizen's judge.

We remember Justice Ahmadi as the judge who, while at the Supreme Court, was a part of 811 judgements, the author of 232 of them. In S.R. Bommai[1], he gave secularism in India a firm basis in the 'principles of accommodation and tolerance'. In Indra Sawhney[2], he couched affirmative action in equality rather than its exceptions. We see in Vahanvaty's adept narration how he was not only an astute, rights-upholding judge, but a force of nature whose work was his only sanctuary.

As Chief Justice of India, Justice Ahmadi pioneered transformative reforms, including computerization in filing, listing and allocation processes. He classified pending cases and allocated them to dedicated benches, which had by then developed a muscle to quickly dispose of them. He digitized these judgements for better access. Unsurprisingly, a pendency of 1,20,000 cases at the start of his tenure was reduced to 18,000 when he retired. Sir Harry Woolf's fitting nickname for Justice Ahmadi – 'the case cracker' – was richly earned.

Justice Ahmadi was also a judicial statesman, regularly consulted for his erudite inputs within and beyond the country. Intrigued by the system in the United States, he introduced the law clerks' programme at the Indian Supreme Court. He contributed immensely to legal education and training, as he led the High-Powered Committee on Legal Education and laid the foundation of the National Judicial Academy, Bhopal. Mentored by Justice M.P. Thakkar, who oversaw the first ever Lok Adalat in 1982 at Una, Gujarat, Justice Ahmadi was a firm believer in alternate dispute resolution. He tackled 98,000 land acquisition cases in a single day through the Lok Adalat. His initiatives in legal aid and ADR, including a reciprocal arrangement with the UK, earned him, in the words of the Lord Chief Justice of England and Wales, 'respect and admiration of the judiciary throughout the common law world'.

Justice Ahmadi championed gender sensitivity in the judiciary. He would not shy away from highlighting the possibility of bias in judicial opinions. In Madhukar Narayan Mardikar[3], he liberated women's credibility – as witnesses or survivors – from a searching inquiry of their history and character. His support for NGO Sakshi led to the establishment of the Asia Pacific Advisory Forum on Judicial Education on Equality Issues. The NGO's work, as the book notes, culminated in the landmark Vishakha Guidelines.

We find traces of Justice Ahmadi's contributions across the length and breadth of the profession. In July 1999, Justice Ahmadi was part of a three-member arbitral tribunal (also consisting of Justice V.D. Tulzapurkar and Justice M.H. Kania) before which I was appearing. On the last day, in Ottawa, I sought his advice on a personal conundrum I was facing, equally if not more compelling than the arbitration itself. Justice Ahmadi came to my rescue with sage advice. As I pitched to him the question of taking up judgeship, Justice Ahmadi said, with his distinct clarity, that it was 'absolutely worth it!' Like the countless aspects of the profession enriched by his wisdom, my life took a turn, empowered and emboldened by his words.

Justice Ahmadi and his spouse were (to use an expression fondly used by my sister and me for our parents) a 'package deal'. They were always together. On a monsoon flight from Delhi to Mumbai, I had a chance seat next to Justice Ahmadi. As the flight waded through clouds heavy with impending showers, he whispered with a glint in the eye, 'Just watch as she starts reading the Holy Quran'. In a moment, across the aisle, Mrs Ahmadi began her prayers for the safety of the aircraft and all of us. There is a memorable photograph of both of them drinking from a single tender coconut with two straws. That truly defines their relationship more than words can convey. At Ottawa, after work, they were together – Justice Ahmadi was full of stories about his travels as a young judge in Gujarat, driving his own Fiat. He regaled his co-arbitrator and us lawyers on both sides with his humour and tales of the judiciary.

Justice Ahmadi had an innate sense of justice based on a grasp of social reality. On one occasion in his court, I was appearing for the petitioner in a habeas corpus petition. Our client was seeking access to his friend and partner, who unfortunately reported that she wasn't interested in meeting him. Realizing that this was the end of the road for my client, Justice Ahmadi was conscious of the impact of parental coercion. He created conditions for the free exercise of her volition in the future. I quite lost touch with what happened in the case later. But this was just another example of the fact that sitting on the high bench of the highest court, he was never out of sync with the 'common touch'.

The book offers us a peek into the workings of his brilliant mind, waist-tall piles of books strewn across his residence and his immersion into the singular cause of providing justice. It is a promising account of the lesser-known aspects of his life, his aspirations for the profession and for the country at large. I hope we carry forward those hopes in our efforts as institutions and individuals.

Justice D.Y. Chandrachud
Chief Justice of India

Foreword

Justice Rohinton F. Nariman

The purest love known to man, namely the love of a granddaughter for her grandfather, has produced this remarkable book. Insiyah Vahanvaty has portrayed her grandfather exactly as he was, as far as I can remember, having appeared before him in many cases in the Supreme Court and having known him and his family intimately. Many things led to Justice Ahmadi's judgements in later life, such as a person of a lower caste being beaten-up; and having been attacked by the opposite side client in a criminal case, which made him give up practicing criminal law. His rise in the legal profession has truly been meteoric, from a government pleader to a city civil court judge at the young age of 32; then secretary-cum-legal remembrancer; then High Court judge at the relatively young age of 44; and Supreme Court judge at the relatively young age of 56, culminating in a glorious chief justiceship of India for over two years.

Justice Ahmadi stood rock solid for three constitutional values in particular: freedom of speech, personal liberty, and, above all, the secular character of the Constitution of India. Insiyah touches upon some of his High Court judgements and many of the extremely important Supreme Court judgements that have shaped this nation, including his judgements in the Mandal Commission Case, the judgement in S.R. Bommai's case, and the Third Judges Case of 1993, all of which were nine-judge bench judgements.

Apart from these, many other judgements are referred to, but what makes the judge stand out is not just his judgements but his all-round capacity to function as a judge. As the chief justice of India, he inherited an arrears burden of 1,20,000 cases and brought it down to 18,000 when he retired. He was almost solely responsible for alternative dispute resolution, leading to the enactment of Section 89 (amended) of the Code of Civil Procedure. He was also responsible for great strides in Lok Adalats, legal aid and mediation. A committee headed by him in 1994 led to the five-year law course being taught in 26 specialist law colleges.

After retirement, he was in great demand as an arbitrator and travelled on various committees and commissions to countries such as Liberia, East Timor, Zimbabwe and Bangladesh. He was even responsible, as Chairman of the Bhopal Memorial Hospital, for ensuring that many of the victims of the Union Carbide gas tragedy were rehabilitated both physically and otherwise. Not a very religious man, he dauntlessly fought for what he thought was right, till the end. He even took up the unpopular cause of a Mazoon claiming to be the successor to Syedna, who is the head of the Dawoodi Bohra community, which culminated (after a prolonged legal battle) in a single-judge judgement of the Bombay High Court against the cause that Justice Ahmadi was espousing.

He lived a life of courage and stuck to what he thought was right throughout his long judicial career, making him the 'Darling of the Bar', both in Gujarat and the Supreme Court. I recommend this book, not only to every lawyer but also to the general public at large, for the miracle that love can produce. The book is exceptionally well-written in simple English and grips the reader from start to finish.

Justice Rohinton F. Nariman
Retired Supreme Court Judge

1

The Black Sheep of the Family

'One paisa?' I asked, looking up at my *nana jaan* disbelievingly. 'Yes,' he said. 'One paisa.' A judge at the High Court of Gujarat at the time, my grandfather was already a busy man. But in the summer holidays, when the courts were closed, and my younger brother and I had been deposited at my grandparents' home in Ahmedabad for two months, he regaled us with stories of a magical childhood – full of adventures and mischief. He told us tales of himself running off with the other *mohalla* boys with a single paisa tightly clasped in one of their little fists. The precious paisa, given by an indulgent parent was equivalent to 3 *pais*, which fetched them a pair of *nankhattaies*, a measure of *namkeens* wrapped in a twist of newspaper and a tiny sweet wrapped in a banana leaf. Filled with anticipation and childish impatience, these goodies would rarely make it out of the shop – being gleefully devoured while standing at the shop counter itself.

He recalled in vivid detail the camps of American troops that would sometimes be stationed outside the cities, awaiting deployment. Young Aziz never questioned the presence of these soldiers until much later; at the time he was far too young to understand that the world was going through a terrible turmoil – World War II was being fought across multiple borders and the colony of India had been forced to participate. From the British stronghold of Bengal to the sun-drenched plains of the Deccan, military bases had sprung to life. India's vast landscape, abundant resources and strategic location made it a critical theatre for the Allies.

The British contributed substantial manpower and resources to the war effort, much of which was extracted from its colony, India. But the boys cared little for geopolitics. Almost every evening, Aziz and his friends waited impatiently for the school bell to ring so that they could run off to these camps and find the soldiers, most of whom were bored and gladly welcomed the company. More often than not, the boys would return with a little goodie – an imported biscuit or a coveted piece of imported chocolate that was gobbled up in one big greedy mouthful before other grubby hands could get to it. Sometimes, these excursions were cut short when he was discovered prematurely by his father's *patawaala* and dragged home.

Patawaalas were the orderlies that judges of the time were given, which Aziz's father, Mushabber Ahmadi as a sub-judge was entitled to. Named after the bright sash draped across their expansive bodies, these tall broad men dressed in white tunics and red sashes held together by big brass buckles, with magnificent *phetas* on their heads, were entrusted with all matters of the judges' home. Whether it was shopping for vegetables for dinner, lighting kerosene lamps at sundown or picking the kids up from school, the patawaalas did it all. But they were most visible when the judge was walking to court. Then it was a sight to behold . The patawaalas walked in a formation with some ahead of the judge and others behind, blowing their whistles to encourage people to get out of the way and clear the path for His Honour. Sometimes one patawaala walked ahead of the rest, carrying a large wooden box with a big padlock dangling from it, containing confidential records. So confidential that they couldn't be left in the courts overnight – after a few incidents of miscreants trying to break into the box, it was carried to and from the judges' home at the beginning and end of every day. So when school was let out and Aziz's younger sister had arrived home, but he was nowhere to be found, a patawaala was sometimes sent out in search of the mischievous boy.

When Aziz Ahmadi spoke of these times, it was with a wistful yearning – it was almost as if he could taste the nankhattaies and the simpler times of his boyhood on his tongue.

Born into a modest but well-educated Dawoodi Bohra family on 25 March 1932, young Aziz's earliest memories were of carefree days and simple times. Running around the courtyards of old Surat mansions, taking turns to jump off the highest *otlas* (quintessential Surat style porches) that were an architectural feature of every home of the times, and buying the cheapest sweets from the local shops, the Surat of Aziz's childhood was not the bustling township it is today; he described it as 'an underdeveloped township with open drains and non-flush latrines.' The Surtis[1] were a friendly, happy-go-lucky lot who lived at a leisurely pace and believed in enjoying life – and meals. Food was a big part of the Surti culture, as it remains to date, and the Surtis were more concerned with their daily menu than they were about Indian independence or world events. It is no wonder then that before it came to be known for diamonds, Surat was known for its baked goods, namkeens and *undhiyu*. As the old saying goes, '*Surat nu jaman, Kashi nu maran* (Come to Surat to eat, go to Kashi to die).'

The Bohras of Surat, especially, were an extremely wealthy community, accustomed to a soft, luxurious life funded by unending generational wealth. It was common for most families to own at least four properties – one, a mansion in Surat that served as the main family home; two, a bungalow on the Tapti River that was suitable for weekends with the family; three, a home in a nearby village called Gordhor when one wanted a change of scenery; and last, a vacation home in Dummas, by the beach. Of course, privately owned horse-drawn carriages and a large domestic staff to look after these properties were essentials. But these were the 'original' Surti Bohras – the few thousand families that had lived in the city for as long as history remembered. A vibrant and close-knit community, the Dawoodi Bohras are mainly known for three things – cuisine, business acumen and progressive thinking. They also boast of high levels of secular education and maintain a characteristic apolitical attitude. A well-travelled lot, Bohras are predominantly a trading community, but their members are to be found engaged in a diverse range of occupations.

With roots tracing back to the Fatimid dynasty in Egypt, the Dawoodi Bohras are followers of Islam's Shia branch. Although originating from Yemen, Bohras settled in Gujarat before spreading to different parts of the world. This is why the community speaks Gujarati with Persian references, and their food and traditions have Gujarati influences.

Women are distinctly identified through their traditional dress called a *rida*. Essentially a two-piece burqa that doesn't cover the face, the rida consists of an upper cape-like garment and a lower skirt, both embroidered and decorated with lace. They come in bright and vivid colours – hot pink, forest green, marigold yellow – everything except black. The men wear a three-piece white *kurta-pajama-saaya* (tunic, trousers, overcoat) set, with distinct white crocheted caps having gold embroidery, which sets them apart from other Muslims.

The Bohras also have several distinct customs, primary among them being the *misaaq*.[2] An oath that takes place at the time of puberty, misaaq is an acknowledgement of one's allegiance to Allah, his Prophet Mohammad,[3] Imam Ali as his successor and the *Dai*[4] as the representative of the Imam. It is also a promise to follow the tenets of the Islamic faith. Considered a rite of passage marking a child's entry into adulthood, this oath-taking ceremony is conducted with much celebration and congratulatory fanfare.

Mealtimes are characterized by members of the community (or family if at home) sitting on a carpet on the floor around a large metal plate called the *thaal*, which is placed on a stand. Each *thaal* can comfortably seat 6–8 individuals – a whole family. The number of courses, alternating between *mithaas* (sweet) and *kharaas* (savoury), varies based on the occasion and the family's affluence, but every meal will start, without fail, with a pinch of salt to awaken the palette. Usually creaking under the weight of the rich bohra *halwas*, biryanis, mutton samosas and steaming bowls of meat curries, these enormous *thaals* are a true testament to the Bohra's love for food. A large majority of Bohra families continue to eat this way, dining tables conspicuously absent from their homes.

Presiding over all matters of faith, and even secular ones, is the *Dai-e-Mutalaq* or high priest, believed to be the vice-regent of the Imam. Also known as the *Syedna*, this religious head is highly respected, almost worshipped. The Dai is also expected to engage with the community's social and economic progress besides looking after its weaker members. In modern times, Dais have ventured into the political sphere, sharing platforms with political leaders and encouraging their participation in Bohra functions. Despite this, the average Bohra tends to be insular and community-centric, steering clear of political affairs, preferring to focus on their businesses and the task of making money. Peace-loving and averse to violence, the community prides itself on being focused on education and entrepreneurship while maintaining strong ties with cultural practices and tradition. It is important to note that apart from spiritual wealth, the Bohra clergy is endowed – and entrusted – with immense material wealth. Although there are no definitive records to precisely gauge the extent of this wealth, it is certainly substantial. The clergy not only owns opulent private mansions all over the world but is also entrusted with public wealth, which is used to build and maintain community spaces, mosques, schools, hospitals, housing development projects, charitable foundations and welfare programmes. The enormous quantum of this wealth has allowed them to build institutions and infrastructure not only in India, but in most other countries where the Bohras have migrated.

In the small population of pre-Independence Surat, numbering around two or three lakhs, a sense of camaraderie thrived – a true community spirit. Modern-day communalism and bigotry were unheard of then; in fact, the Bohras from that era reminisce about their school days with affection. Educated at Hindu-dominated schools taught by Hindu teachers, these cultured, well-dressed and soft-spoken children were teachers' pets. Far removed from any kind of religious discrimination, these Surti residents would not experience any prejudice for some years still.

The 1940s saw a change in this demographic. Facing an imminent threat of Japanese invasion, Surat witnessed an influx of people, especially from Calcutta. Subhash Chandra Bose had formed the Azad Hind Fauj, further creating panic among the Calcutta Bohras. During and after Independence, others came to Surat too, seeing it as a safe haven, a place that was untouched by the violence. The city's population swelled with Hindus and Muslims alike, forever changing the dynamic of the local populations. What remained intact was the Gujarati enterprise, talent for business and resilience.

The Indian independence movement was at its zenith, a powerful wave of change sweeping across the nation. Aziz, too young to fully grasp the significance of the historical transformation unfolding before his eyes, held only fleeting memories of this time. But even he knew who Mohandas Karamchand Gandhi was. The Father of the Nation, affectionately known as Gandhiji, often embarked on train journeys through the heartlands of Gujarat and Maharashtra, passing through hordes of men, women and children who would gather for a glimpse of the remarkable man. Unperturbed by the sun beating down and the dust swirling around them, the children waited for the deafening screech of metal against metal, followed by the train rounding the corner and coming into view.

Standing on tiptoe, shoving each other to get a better view, the children's eyes searched the train to catch a glimpse of the nation's most beloved man who would sometimes appear in one of the train's open carriages. He stood there, his frail form silhouetted against the backdrop of the Indian landscape, his round glasses perched on his nose. With a gentle smile, he waved at the children scattered along the tracks, their faces smeared with a mixture of dust and anticipation. The children waved back excitedly, their small hands fervently reciprocating the friendly gesture. Too young to understand the historical changes taking place, their waving and cheering were simple acts of innocence. Aziz and his friends were completely unaware that the ordinary-looking man they were waving to would soon go on to negotiate an independent nation for them, shaping the destiny of India in ways they couldn't yet comprehend.

As a family, the Ahmadis invested in education; educating not only their sons but also their daughters to graduate and postgraduate levels. This was unusual for the times, as well as for the Bohra community. In fact, the first lady to earn a graduate degree in all of Ahmedabad was reportedly Rehana Ahmadi – Aziz Ahmadi's cousin. In a world of the landed and wealthy who preferred not to work if they could help it, the Ahmadis stood out as different. Aziz's grandfather, Imran Ali Ahmadi, who married twice (thereby giving Aziz several step-uncles), held the position of Deputy

Inspector of Education during the British Raj, which earned the family the generic nickname of 'Depoty' in the area. Aziz's father, with a double degree, BA LLB, was a sub-judge in the judiciary, which necessitated a lot of moving around for the family. A judge in pre-Independence India, when most similar positions were held by Englishmen, Mushabber Imran Ahmadi was a well-regarded gentleman, albeit not a wealthy one.

Often posted to remote districts and *talukas* – villages and one-horse towns within the states that are now Gujarat and Mumbai – this constant movement might have been taxing for some, but not for Aziz. To him, it only meant more places to have new, glorious adventures. An unfortunate fallout of these movements was the interrupted education of both siblings. Local schools typically imparted instruction in regional languages, which meant the children had to either travel long distances by train to get to a Gujarati or English medium school or skip a few months until their father was posted somewhere else again. But these postings were important for another reason – they allowed Aziz the opportunity to be confronted by the real grit and grime of India, including the ugly reality of bigotry, casteism and caste-based violence. These early experiences stayed with him throughout his life, shaping his understanding of the oppressed and powerless.

Because rural areas and smaller towns were considered safe enough for children to be let free to mosey about, Aziz often wandered off on his own, sometimes several miles away from home. One summer vacation, when Aziz was about 12 years old, his cousins had come to stay. On a rainy day when the girls were playing indoors, Aziz and his cousin decided to cross the paddy fields of what is currently the heavily constructed north-west Mumbai to find a makeshift theatre they knew was a mile away, hoping to watch a film – a rare treat. As the skies rumbled and opened up, dumping a deluge of water onto the fields, the boys took off. They raced through the paddy, splashing mud and sludge from the puddles over their shoes, legs and shorts until they finally came upon the theatre. What can only be described as a poorly constructed tin shed with wooden benches and sticky floors, presided over by a rather large, formidable-looking lady, the 'theatre' leaked water every time it rained. Undeterred by this minor inconvenience, the wet, bedraggled boys splashed through the puddles on the floor and dropped a couple of coins in the big lady's hand in exchange for a seat on the hard wooden benches. Surrounded by ashtrays and the kind of men that no respectable family would have allowed their sons to hobnob with, Aziz and his cousin squelched excitedly onto a wooden bench. Soon enough, a grainy, pirated print of the movie appeared, projected onto a bedsheet that acted as a screen. Watching the movie through a hazy pall of cigarette smoke, the odour of human sweat and the loud clattering of raindrops on the tin roof, the adventure was almost too delicious to endure. Despite barely being able to hear the film because of the racket created by the rain on the tin roof, the boys were wrapped in a cocoon of pure contentment.

On their way back, however, a rude shock awaited them. Walking through the village now that the rain had stopped, they came upon an old man being beaten ruthlessly by a group of younger men. The one being beaten was dark and skinny, dressed in a torn *lungi*. The ones doing the beating, were well-fed and dressed better. Stopping dead in their tracks, the cousins looked at each other. Afraid to go any closer, they simply turned around and ran home. Aziz later learned that the man was a lower caste individual and was being beaten as punishment for drawing water from a well that was reserved for the upper caste families. Over the years and many transfers to rural talukas, Aziz would witness other cruel practices, such as men being forced to tie broomsticks behind their backs when they walked to sweep away their footprints behind them, or being made to clang two metallic objects together in order to alert people of their arrival, allowing them time to move out of the way and avoid becoming contaminated by their shadows. These formative memories were significant – Justice Ahmadi would later remind his peers of these realities when discussing his ideas of equality, affirmative action and the upliftment of systematically oppressed communities. The insights gained during these years would resurface in numerous events throughout Justice Ahmadi's life, but their most significant manifestation would occur many decades later during the landmark Mandal Commission case.

Aziz's mother, Shirin Bensaab, was a tall, imposing woman with a commanding presence. Dressed in typical Gujarati *onna-ghagras*, she was often seen with the extra fabric of the *onna* tucked into the waistband of her *ghagra* and her hair tied into a tight, sensible bun as she went about household chores in a practical, business-like manner. A stern, no-nonsense woman who ran a tight ship, she was also no stranger to tragedy. After her entire family was wiped out during the Spanish flu of 1918, except for one elder sister and a father who was unable to look after her by himself, she was taken in and raised by a childless, wealthy neighbour. Her marriage to Mushabber was a union that required her to not only downgrade her lifestyle substantially, but also endure postings to remote areas where she knew nobody and had nothing to occupy herself with. These frustrations were not minor ones. And this did not bode well for her relationship with her son. A wild, uncontrollable child whose zest for adventure could not be contained, Aziz was well acquainted with the back of his mother's hand. Unable to understand her son's need to explore and his devil-may-care attitude, Shirin Ahmadi was simply destined for a difficult relationship with Aziz Ahmadi from the very beginning.

His father, a brilliant writer and highly intelligent man, was very proper and respectable in demeanour. A tall, lanky man with high cheekbones, a fashionable toothbrush moustache and a wizened appearance, he never left the house without a starched white shirt under an impeccably pressed safari suit and a *pheta* on his head. Although born to devout Muslim parents, M.I. Ahmadi was a non-practising Muslim and described himself as agnostic. Secular and progressive-minded, he maintained a deliberate distance from religious practices as well as the affairs of the Bohra community. While he held a mild disdain for overly religious displays, he approached matters of faith with respect, especially towards his wife, a practising Muslim who followed all the tenets of Islam. However, both of Aziz's parents were united in their disinclination towards the Dai and what they perceived as the clergy's interference in personal lives.

But more than anything else, Mushabber took his position as a judge extremely seriously and viewed his family's conduct as a reflection on his own esteemed reputation and respect in society. And Aziz's activities and interests did not meet his approval. Dismayed at his son's insistence on playing rough games, returning home in tattered clothes, caked with mud, sometimes with a black eye from a scuffle with another boy, his only hope lay in making sure the boy's career was well chosen. Towards this, Mushabber had his heart set on Aziz eventually becoming an engineer. Not in his wildest thoughts did he imagine the boy would follow in his own footsteps, nor did he have the slightest inkling of his son's brilliance at the time. So, constantly feeling like a misfit in his family, life at home was not harmonious for Aziz. His pain was compounded by the fact that the darling of the family, his sister Zulekha, understood her brother no better than his parents understood their son, laying the foundations for a lifelong chasm with Aziz on one side and his parents and sister on the other.

The black sheep of the family, young Aziz therefore took to spending more time outside the home than in it, seeking validation outside rather than inside. As he got to his teenage years, he rebelled. Taking to smoking excessively in his teenage years, Aziz was never home. On most days, he was to be found by the town *chowk*, smoking cheap unfiltered cigarettes and planning mischief with his friends or picking street fights by day and slinking into the home late at night.

An audacious prankster, trouble was Aziz's mischievous sidekick. One of his favourite pranks was to tease and provoke the local police in a battle of wits. In those days, bicycles came fitted with kerosene lanterns, which tended to go out on windy days. It also meant that the flame would last only as long as the oil did. At the time, traffic regulations required cyclists to have a functioning light when riding at night. Waiting patiently until *magrib* (sunset), the boys would then get on their cycles and start peddling towards the police *chowki* of Nanpura. Coasting through the town looking as innocent as the day they were born, the boys jangled their cycle bells to make sure the police chowki up ahead knew they were coming. Aziz, leading the pack, blew out his kerosene lamp, ears peeled for the sound they all knew was sure to follow. *Farrrrrrr* . . . the sound of a whistle. Leaping out of the shadows amid the charged air with a triumphant '*Light kidhar hai* (Where is the light)?' was a portly constable. Red faced and panting, he was sure he had finally caught up to the rascals. Aziz responded calmly, '*Bhai, tha . . . abhi batti olaayi gayi* (Brother, the lamp was on; it has only just blown out).' The constable, determined to get the gang of boys this time responded, '*Mein kem maanu* (How do I know this is true)?' '*Toh dekh* (Then look),' said Aziz, grabbing his hand and placing it firmly on the scalding hot lantern that was, indeed, alight a minute ago. Amid a cacophony of yells and profanities, the constable snatched his smarting hand back as the boys, in a symphony of jangling bicycle bells and kicking up a trail of dust, pedalled away as fast as they could, guffawing like impish daredevils.

On other occasions, they lay in wait on windy days, seeking out an unsuspecting policeman whose lantern had surrendered to the wind. Sweeping in as a group, they would force their bewildered captive to dismount and escort him to the police station, marching through the streets of Surat. Responding to the man's half-hearted bleats of protest, the boys would extract a promise of leniency for themselves the next time they were caught before setting the fellow free.

The family could not understand this brand of mischief – they were mortified at stories of their son being reprimanded by the police and disapproved of the company he kept – boys shrouded in an air of mystery, whose family backgrounds were not always known. Some were rough and prone to street scuffles, although almost all were bright. Every day when Aziz returned home, there were fireworks between him and his mother over dirty clothes, his smoking or the visible marks of scrapes and scuffles.

But life was carefree and without worry, despite having very little spending money. The availability or lack of resources was not a cause for anxiety for young Aziz, as indeed, it would not be throughout his life. Although rationed supplies, food shortages and the British Raj marked the young boy's childhood, yet he neither knew of nor cared for any of it. Possessing a rare zest for life, this time was for exploring and throwing caution to the winds.

Ambition, brilliance and greatness would not appear for some time yet. For now, he was simply the black sheep.

2

'I Did Not Choose the Law; the Law Chose Me'

It was the morning of 15 August 1947. The air was abuzz with promise, the trees appeared greener and the roses redder. A strange euphoria filled the lungs with every breath. India was, at last, free.

Fifteen-year-old Aziz Ahmadi woke up to the sounds of jubilation on the street below. Showering quickly and skipping breakfast, he grabbed a *khakhra* from the breakfast thaal his parents and Zulekha were sitting at and ran out. The streets of Ahmedabad had turned into one big carnival, and he didn't want to miss a minute of it. Today, his parents didn't stop him either; they intended to do the same as soon as they had finished breakfast. Tonight, the family planned to take a horse-carriage ride around town to see the lights that had been set up in celebration of this historic day.

It was a time of scarcity – supply chains had been disrupted and everyone was feeling the pinch. Food shortages meant wheat, a staple grain, was in short supply, affecting the daily sustenance of families. Even the wheat that was available was of low quality, requiring several rounds of cleaning before it could be consumed. Other essential items such as butter and sugar too were in limited supply. Electricity and kerosene were both rationed. Poor quality cloth had flooded the market, meaning the family had to go without new clothes this year. Families had to adapt their lifestyles to cope, learning to use these resources sparingly to make them last.

But today, all this was forgotten.

Straddling his rickety bicycle, Aziz noisily jangled his rusty bell impatiently, weaving through the winding lanes of the Dawoodi Bohra mohalla, which were unusually busy for this time of the day. Those cursing and hurriedly jumping out of his path wouldn't remain annoyed for long – the excitement in the air was irresistible. Schoolchildren marched along the main road under the supervision of class teachers, kicking up a cloud of dust and filling the air with patriotic songs sung in an off-key chorus. The flags they carried fluttered in the cool breeze – the fresh, cool air of independent India. People of all shapes and sizes thronged the streets, chai shops and the chowk. The din of the chatter was infectious. Stopping at the chowk, his usual hangout, Aziz overheard snippets of conversation. 'A Tryst with Destiny . . .' Yes, he had heard Nehru's speech at midnight on the family radio.

But the celebration was bittersweet. The city was swarming with police presence, reminding the locals that the country had been partitioned into two dominions. This carelessly executed partition of erstwhile India into two nations based on religious lines was one of the bloodiest events – and greatest calamities – in world history. It would also cause one of the biggest migrations in world history. For months before and after the Partition, Hindus and Muslims would clash in a brutal and senseless battle, wasting hundreds of thousands of lives. Historians estimate that a total of one million people lost their lives in the religious violence that characterized this period. This tumultuous time also triggered a mass exodus of hundreds of thousands of Muslims, who, fearing for their lives, left everything behind and sought refuge in Pakistan. Most of these migrations were acts of panic, fear and desperation.

A trading community, the Bohras are a pacifist group that tend to remain removed from political events – a deliberate detachment that has allowed them to live in peace and harmony as a minority community. Having migrated to India nearly 450 years ago, the Bohras had, over the centuries, developed deep-rooted connections in India, where they not only established religious centres but also flourishing businesses. This long-standing presence created a strong sense of loyalty and attachment to the country where they had lived in peace and harmony with their Hindu neighbours and friends.

This loyalty, coupled with cultural considerations and the desire to preserve their religious and business foundations, made the Bohras reluctant to leave and start afresh elsewhere. But ultimately, they would be guided by their leader.

In the crucial months preceding the Partition, the *Dai-e-Mutalaq*, the spiritual leader of the Bohra community, travelled to Delhi, spending several months engaging in talks with political leaders like Nehru and Gandhi, the architects of India's secular vision. He was seeking assurances that the Bohra community would be secure and remain unmolested if they opted to stay in India. After months of deliberations and assurances, the *Dai-e-Mutalaq* was satisfied and the Bohras made the choice to remain in India. In a tremendous show of trust, the Dai himself, and his family, chose not to leave, sending a powerful message not only to Bohras worldwide, but also to the political leadership of the time. Today, India is home to the largest population of Bohras in the world, a testament to the trust forged during those initial days.

But this was not true for all Muslims – many of Aziz's friends had already left with their families and several others would do the same over the next few months and years. In a wave of panic, hundreds of thousands of people would flee, terrified of becoming a religious minority at a time when the Indian subcontinent was engulfed in violent riots. Hindus from Pakistan would leave their homes, businesses, even family members behind to cross over to the Indian side, while Muslims in India did the same as they fled to Pakistan. This large-scale human migration and forced displacement would not only shape the broader narrative of the two nations, but also significantly affect the demographic of Ahmedabad – a city known for communal tensions even before Partition. While the border states of India bore the brunt, with almost every family having lost either property or family members to the brutal cleaving of the nation, the Bohra community stood largely insulated from these hardships.

But even so, these tensions existed, for the most part, outside the walls of the city, where a considerable population of refugees and internally displaced people had found settlement, alongside the working class from textile mills. The walled city of Ahmedabad, however, home to many of the city's older, wealthier families, remained relatively peaceful. On this historic day, the entire strength of the police force had been deployed to ensure peace and calm across the country. However, the true storm of violence would arrive a few months after, when the police were gradually withdrawn from their posts.

Aziz would remember these times vividly. On an ordinary afternoon as the sun cast long shadows across the uneven cobblestones of the streets, Aziz and his friends had wandered outside the gates of the walled city, as they often did. But today, an unfamiliar energy hung in the air. A curious unease stirred among the crowds with the growing sensation that something was brewing below the surface. Feeling strangely uneasy, the boys started to make their way back to the gates, only to find the grand entrance gates standing firmly shut with only the smaller ones granting access to pedestrians kept open. Confused, they looked at each other nervously. Their unspoken questions would soon be answered.

As if drawn by an unseen magnet, people started to converge, forming clusters that punctuated the once-quiet surroundings. And then, a glint of blades and metal prongs catching the rays of the sun as they were waved around in the air. Before their bewildered eyes, the numbers of men carrying swords and *trishuls* (tridents) swelled, their chants resonating with passionate fervour. This was no ordinary day. For weeks, communal tensions between Hindus and Muslims had been steadily escalating. On this particular day, the leaders of some of these communal factions had decided to breach the fortified walls of the walled city of Ahmedabad, bringing outside tensions into the city. In the midst of this charged atmosphere, an unbelievable sight – Aziz squinted, almost unable to believe his eyes – a fully grown enormous lumbering elephant emerged from the shadows, trumpeting its arrival amid loud cheers and fanfare. The very ground seemed to tremble under its colossal weight. The onlookers erupted into a cacophony of delighted roars. The mahout, perched firmly atop, displayed immaculate control over the animal as he guided the gigantic creature forward. The air crackled with tension.

A slow realization crept over the boys. What was going to happen was becoming terrifyingly clear.

Breaking into a run, the creature charged, its massive frame colliding against the gates with a resounding thud, nearly dislodging the mahout. The elephant's initial attempt to breach the gates fell short, yet this only seemed to stoke the excitement and fervour of the sword-wielding mob who had begun chanting and screaming with excitement. Undaunted, the mahout led the elephant a few steps backwards, preparing for a second, more forceful charge. Staring at the scene in disbelief, a chilling realization suddenly washed over the boys. They were the sole Muslims present. With hearts racing wildly in their chests, they began to quietly back away, slipping away from the mob and trying to blend into the crowd without drawing attention to themselves. Breaking into a run as soon as they were at a safe distance, they didn't stop until they reached the mohalla.[1] While the exact identity of the group attempting to breach the city walls remains unverified, it is likely that the incident occurred during the Jagannath Rath Yatra, a religious annual procession that features performers, boisterous participants and elephants. Over the years, Hindu–Muslim clashes during this yatra had become a recurring concern.

Later, news would trickle in. The elephant's formidable efforts had not succeeded in toppling the city's gates. Yet, the city's atmosphere had changed. No longer confined to the outskirts, communal clashes became increasingly common within the walls as well; neighbours who had coexisted peacefully for generations found themselves pitted against each other, hurling not just insults and animosity, but also sticks and stones. A divisive atmosphere had gripped the city.

This was the time Aziz became most aware of his Muslim identity, frequently encountering derogatory slurs and religiously charged taunts. Not one to walk away from these insults, Aziz, with his gang, often came away from them with bloodied noses and black eyes, much to the dismay of his father, who couldn't reconcile with the idea of his son engaging in street brawls, and the wrath of his mother, who was tasked with washing and mending his clothes.

Just as the nation grappled with the complexities of Independence,

Aziz, on the verge of adulthood, was entangled in his own quest for self-discovery.

Of all the pursuits that the Bohra community is engaged in, there is one field where there is almost no representation – the sports field. Regarded as an indulgent hobby for a bored afternoon at best, the Bohras consider playing sports not only far too strenuous for their luxury-loving constitutions, but also a waste of time. In this, Aziz was different. Borderline obsessive about sports, he embraced a wide variety of games – table tennis, football, cricket. Cricket, in particular, held a special place in his heart; no other activity could rival the temptation of a game in the mohalla or at the cricket club. Causing further distress to his parents was his habit of sneaking out of the house early in the mornings or bunking college classes to play the game. His father couldn't hide his exasperation – his constant derision included the prediction that Aziz would ultimately amount to nothing in life. A prediction which, happily, did not come true.

This deep enduring love for sports was to remain a constant in his life until his Supreme Court days where friendly cricket matches between the bar and bench were a common activity. But for now, it was frowned upon. His father, who dreamt of Aziz one day becoming a successful engineer, berated him on a daily basis. To Mushabber Ahmadi, engineering was not only a respectable professional choice, it also promised steady employment and income – a safe choice for his wayward son. It was to this end that Aziz was forced into the Science stream immediately after passing his matriculation exam, much to Mushabber's relief. But Mushabber's satisfaction was to be short lived.

One frosty winter afternoon when he was supposed to be in class, Aziz was, as usual, on the cricket field. As he sauntered home swinging his bat, he knew something was wrong. Glancing up as he turned into the street, he spotted his mother in the balcony, face black as thunder, eyes locked upon him. His heart sank. As he entered the house and slipped his shoes off in the foyer, he noticed his father standing in the living room, face flushed with rage and breathing heavily. An opened letter in his hand, envelope on the floor. Aziz's stomach twisted into knots. He knew instantly what had happened.

A few weeks earlier, during a leisurely moment at the chai shop, as he enjoyed a cup of hot tea and a cigarette, and idly flipped through the newspaper, he had stumbled upon an intriguing advertisement. The Merchant Navy was seeking applicants. Enthralled by the idea of a sailor's life at sea, full of freedom and adventure, Aziz had filled out the form and applied for the position immediately. He hadn't considered that they would send a letter home. But of course they had. Mushabber Ahmadi was furious. His eyes blazing like hot coals seared into Aziz, and the precious letter was torn up before his eyes and tossed into the dustbin.

Aziz waited for his father to leave the room before advancing up to his desk and fishing out the pieces of the letter from the wastepaper basket. Kneeling on the floor, he tried to piece it together. 'Dear Aziz Mushabber Ahmadi, we are pleased to inform you . . .' So, it was good news. He had been selected. But now, what did it matter? The bitterness of disappointment and anger at the cruelty with which the blow had been dealt enveloped the young man. Resentment crashed over the young teenager like a tsunami. Wave after wave of red-hot rage; then a decision. He had never cared for engineering; it was his father's dream. All he cared for was the allure of the cricket field, the camaraderie with his friends, the sheer joy of hitting the ball out of the field. He yearned to be unburdened by another's expectations.

And so, in his usual impulsive way, Aziz marched straight up to the administration office the very next day to request a change in streams. Now enrolled in Arts, he heaved a sigh of relief. Although he knew this would result in more berating when his father heard about it, he no longer cared. A while later, his decision to study law immediately upon finishing his intermediate level would be guided by the same detachment.

This sudden, reckless shift in Aziz's career trajectory would prove to be profoundly significant. It was a decision spurred by a headstrong and stubborn determination, made not for a newfound love of the law, but the distaste for science, fuelled by a singular obsession with cricket. Making no secret of his motivations, he would openly state that his reason for choosing law at that early stage was not a display of laziness; instead, it was a calculated move designed to carve out more free time for cricket.

As he would often joke in his later years, 'I did not choose the law, the law chose me.' It was a fact; the fates had deposited Aziz exactly where he needed to be.

Aziz was able to complete only one year at L.A. Shah Law College in Ahmedabad before Mushabber Ahmadi was transferred yet again back to Surat, where Aziz was born. Another disturbance in his education, requiring him to enrol in Sarvajanik Law College. Institutes of average repute, both colleges boasted of neither a great faculty nor illustrious alumni. They were simply convenient places to finish one's studies and receive an LLB degree. But this time of early adulthood was significant for Aziz, as he developed many enduring friendships – some of which would last him a lifetime. This is also where he would meet his future wife.

When Aziz returned to Surat, he found he had no friends left in the city. The handful of boys he used to know had moved on and he found himself faced with the daunting task of rebuilding a social circle from scratch. One day, as he was passing by the cinema house, he came upon a boy of his age, with a Barna table tennis bat in hand. Aziz's eyes lit up. Approaching the boy, he initiated a conversation. Having learnt that the boy was a Bohra and he played at the table tennis club, Aziz introduced himself as a Bohra and asked if he could play too. An obliging fellow, the boy took Aziz to the sports hall and introduced him to the other members. Aziz asked if he could play. A slow day at the club meant there weren't too many players waiting for a turn, so they willingly handed him a bat. Aziz had a good game and so his request to join the club was readily approved. He would show up every evening; delighted to be back in his comfort zone – playing sports. Gregarious and witty, he soon became popular. Of the regulars at the club, he became particularly close to two brothers, Taher and Yusuf Muchhala. Aziz soon learnt that the table tennis club was not the only Bohra sports club there was. They also had a cricket club and a soccer club. In addition, the Bohra Welfare Society, which hosted cultural events, was another opportunity to interact with people. Aziz and Taher, now thick as thieves, found themselves at odds with the organizers of the Welfare Society. Instead of submitting, they broke off and started their own show – the United Bohra Club of which Aziz was President, Taher,

Treasurer and Yusuf, Executive Member. The club became immensely successful and held some large-scale cultural events and mixers. Having thus entrenched himself in the Bohra social circuit of Surat, it was time for Aziz to leave again. Another transfer order for Mushabber Ahmadi, summoning him back to Ahmedabad.

Having cleared the bar exam in his first attempt, Aziz Ahmadi started his practice in 1954, appearing in the trial courts of Ahmedabad. Hoping to give Aziz the exposure that he needed, Mushabber Ahmadi approached Mahomedaali Jivaji Merchant, a senior lawyer well known for his prowess in criminal law. Merchant saab's colourful response was nothing short of characteristic. 'The boy is ready to swim. *Daal do andar. Thoda paani pee lega toh theek hai* (Throw him into the river, if he swallows a little water so be it).' Thus saying, he proceeded to take Aziz under his wing. A year into their work together, and Merchant was convinced. He remarked to his son Ishaq, 'Aziz has a brilliant legal mind – this boy will go places.' It was a statement of high regard, further demonstrated when Aziz started his own practice and inherited his mentor's chambers and law clerk. In later years, as Aziz's career began to soar, M.J. Merchant's pride in his protégé would only grow. As he proudly remarked several times, 'This boy learnt from me.' But young Ishaq's thoughts were not on Aziz at the time. Rather, his affections were directed towards his sister, Zulekha, whom he would eventually marry. Ishaq and Aziz liked each other well enough but never developed a truly deep friendship due to the complexities between Aziz and Zulekha. Nevertheless, the two men would always hold each other in high regard throughout their lives.

One of Aziz's dearest friends in Ahmedabad was his namesake, Aziz Munshi. Both sons of judges, the two boys had attended college classes together and played cricket together. After passing the bar exam, they started their practice together in Mofussil courts. However, much would change in the years following Independence – and Munshi eventually left for Pakistan. This was not new for Aziz, losing friends to the new border had become almost routine for him – most didn't even try to stay in touch. But Munshi did. Becoming successful very quickly, Munshi was Attorney General for Pakistan for four terms, and his services were solicited in almost every Indo-Pak dialogue of the time. Many years later, when Soli Sorabjee was on an official visit to Pakistan, he joked with Justice Aziz Ahmadi that while Urdu was a beautiful language, he missed speaking Gujarati on the trip. Justice Ahmadi promptly put him in touch with Munshi, setting the stage for the beginning of another warm friendship.

Niranjan Bhatt, another very close friend, would remain so until the day Justice Ahmadi breathed his last. At this point, they were playing cricket and planning mischief together, but as time wore on and Aziz Ahmadi became the Chief Justice of India, he would seek Bhatt's help in his mission to introduce judicial reforms.

A lawyer he might have become, with the weight of important and difficult cases on his shoulders, but Aziz's wit and mischief would remain intact. When Bejan Daruwala, another dear childhood friend, crossed paths with him many years later when Aziz was a High Court judge, Daruwala offered to read his horoscope. Aziz retorted in his classic sharp-witted way, 'All right. So, how much will you pay me if I allow you to?'

Over the years, Aziz would forget some of the cases he was involved in, but he would always remember his first court appearance vividly. Descending the library staircase one evening, he was accosted by a Bohra gentleman who also happened to be a family acquaintance. This gentleman offered Aziz an execution brief – one worth the staggering sum of Rs 12,000, a small fortune in those days. An execution brief is utilized in civil cases to enforce a decree issued after the final judgement. The process prescribed by the civil procedure code for executing the decree is typically initiated by the decree holder by filing an execution petition. Taken aback at the significant stakes, Aziz was nonetheless eager to embark upon his legal journey, and so he accepted the brief. To seek advice on how to tackle this case, Aziz turned to his senior, M.J. Merchant. Encouraging his protégé, Merchant saab reviewed the brief and then advised Aziz to take this opportunity to familiarize himself with the Code of Civil Procedure before the hearing. Next, Aziz approached his father who offered him further support. Armed with the support and encouragement of two stalwarts of the legal landscape of the time, young Aziz gathered the confidence to argue his case, ultimately achieving a successful outcome.

So successful, in fact, that the delighted client offered him an additional sum beyond his fees, a gesture Aziz respectfully declined. Having thus got off to a good start, Aziz embarked upon his legal journey with confidence and eagerness.

While Aziz Ahmadi was practising in the vibrant Mofussil courts of Ahmedabad, news about the bifurcation of the expansive bilingual state of Bombay was received. The state that so far had encompassed both Gujarat and Maharashtra was now to be divided on linguistic lines. The Bombay High Court, which had served as the apex legal authority for the vast region, had to be divided. Judges proficient in the Gujarati language were assigned to the newly established Gujarat High Court, an institution officially inaugurated on 1 May 1960. In parallel, the High Court of Bombay continued to serve the state of Maharashtra.[2] The legal fraternity braced itself for change, with many lawyers and judges relocating to their state of choice. Aziz, fluent in Gujarati, remained in Gujarat.

Shortly after the High Court of Gujarat commenced its operations in Ahmedabad, preparations were set in motion to establish a City Civil and Sessions Court in the city, a system modelled closely on the Bombay pattern. This court would be the highest in the district and the second highest in the state. This important endeavour was entrusted to Mr Nassarwanji Vakil, a prominent lawyer practising at the Surat Bar. Approaching the task with enthusiasm and vigour, Mr Vakil managed to complete the task in record time. It was under his guidance that the rules and regulations were drafted, readying the City Civil and Sessions Court for its inauguration on 4 November 1961.[3] Mr Vakil thus assumed the role of the first Principal Judge of the court he had helped set up, marking a historical moment in the legal landscape of Ahmedabad.

The very first case heard in this brand-new court was one argued by Mr Aziz Ahmadi before the Principal Judge himself.[4] A case that he won but would lead to an alarming incident years later. Furious at losing the case, the defendant did not forget the lawyer at whose hands he had suffered. At that time, the security arrangements in lower courts were far from robust, and individuals could freely access the court premises. Several years later, this disgruntled individual would storm Ahmadi's chambers in a fit of rage.

Aziz, although understandably perturbed, maintained a composed exterior. Thinking quickly, he discreetly pressed the alert bell, signalling his *Havildar* to rush to his aid. In the meantime, he continued to engage with the aggressive intruder, hoping to avert any violent intentions he might have. But the intruder would not calm down, growing more agitated at Aziz's attempts to calm him down. Fortunately, the Havildar was on his way to the chamber. Spotting him at a distance, the intruder turned around and fled, never to be seen by Aziz again.

It was at this time, during his career as a lawyer, that Aziz formed several lifelong friendships, notable among them being Justice Dhruvkumar Harshadrai Shukla, Mr Jayendra Mohanlal Thaker and Justice Manharlal Pranlal Thakkar. Shukla, a lawyer at the time, would soon be appointed as a judge of the City Civil and Sessions Court and eventually Gujarat High Court. He and Ahmadi would serve on several benches together. Eventually, Shukla would go on to become Gujarat's first Lokayukta. Jayendra and Aziz remained inseparable, as indeed, they had been through their college years. Fiercely loyal, Jayendra would stand by Aziz through all of life's ups and downs. He would inherit Aziz's criminal law practice when Aziz transitioned into civil law. Justice Thakkar, already an experienced judge in the City Civil Court, stood tall and imposing. A commanding figure and a decade older than Ahmadi, he towered over his peers by at least a head. His presence was accentuated by a booming voice that commanded attention and respect. Slowly but surely, he was becoming Ahmadi's mentor, with the two men spending long hours discussing matters of shared ideology and debating points of law. United by a common ideology and shared compassion for the weak, oppressed and marginalized, their conversations, when not focused on the technicalities of the law, revolved around the ways in which the legal system could be harnessed to protect those in greatest need. Staunch secularists, the two men would remain bound by their sheer distaste for any communal and religious influences in matters of governance and justice.

3

Ties that Bind, Ties that Break

At twenty-eight years old in 1960, Aziz was truly hitting his stride. His career was flourishing and the path ahead gleamed with promise that seemed well within reach. Yet, amid his professional success, he yearned for something more meaningful. Surrounded by friends who had already embraced marriage and parenthood, Aziz began to feel the weight of his solitude. The desire for a deeper connection and partnership grew stronger with each passing day. But Aziz wanted a true partner – someone who would walk beside him, not behind him.

And he knew who he hoped that would be.

Aziz's closest companions in Surat were the Muchhala brothers who resided within the walls of a grand ancestral mansion. Within its confines lived not only the Muchhala brothers, but also their grandparents, their widowed mother and their elder sister, Amena Muchhala. The opulent mansion, once a symbol of lavish abundance, now showed undeniable signs of age and lack of care. Its grand facade, adorned with intricate carvings and ornate balconies, was now chipped, the paint faded, revealing the gentle patina of age. Inside, the crystal chandeliers illuminated the dust-laden windows and luxurious Persian carpets alike. The building, a three-storey structure meant to house several generations at once, was sparsely populated, carrying the unmistakable aura of a home that was once filled with laughter, riches and hope, but now creaked under the weight of grief and heartache. Their family history echoed the highest highs and the lowest lows of life.

Once upon a time, the Muchhalas were synonymous with wealth and success, standing tall as one of the most prosperous Surti Bohra families. The source of their riches was the jute industry, which surged during the upheavals of World War I and II. The demand for jute-made products like tents, canvas and ropes was at an all-time high, sending the Muchhalas' investments skyrocketing. These investments, overseen by their shrewd grandmother, yielded dividends of monumental proportions. In the absence of a proper banking system, the dividends were received in cash. These bags full of cash were then stuffed into large wooden *sandooks*, chained and padlocked, awaiting reinvestment. Their yearly earnings were a staggering Rs 80,000 at a time when household expenses rarely crossed Rs 100 a month. Millionaires of their time, the Muchhalas lived lives of absolute luxury and comfort, convinced that the well of money would never run dry. They showered friends and family with extravagant gifts, shouldering the expenses of weddings and the education of loved ones, employees and less fortunate acquaintances. They contributed generously to philanthropic activities, earning a reputation as not just a wealthy family, but also a charitable one.

The siblings' father, Hatim Muchhala was still in college by the time all three of them were born. Born and bred in the lap of luxury, Hatim Muchhala attended college five miles away dressed in a dapper three-piece suit, a red Turkish cap and driving his vibrant red Morris – perhaps the first one Surat had seen. A few weeks after he started college, Hatim's mother, the brains behind the family's riches and de facto head of the family, announced that the five-mile journey was too lengthy and taxing on her darling son who had to drive back in the middle of the day for lunch and afternoon prayers. So, she acquired a three-storey building two miles from the college, christening it Hatim Manzil. Although Hatim still lived at home, Hatim Manzil was where he would enjoy his freshly cooked midday meal, offer his prayers and recharge before returning for the evening classes.

But the Muchhala siblings would see very little of this opulence. As extraordinary was their rise into wealth and success, so too would be their fall into near poverty.

When twenty-five-year-old Hatim Muchhala first began coughing, his young wife didn't think much of it. But within a few short weeks, he was burning up with fever, delirious and too weak to walk. The once-vibrant Hatim was now confined to his bed, eyes glazed over. Desperation led the family to consult various doctors, but opinions were conflicting. Typhoid was a rare, almost incurable disease at the time, and the doctors couldn't agree on what ailed Hatim. Several misdiagnoses and a few short months later, tragedy struck. Young Hatim was dead.

With him disappeared the family's fortunes, their happiness and hopes for the future. Before the family could recover from the devastating loss of their beloved son, husband and father, the winds of Partition swept through the nation, forever altering the fate of the Muchhalas. When the new borders were drawn on the map, the sprawling jute fields that supplied the mills now belonged to the new lands of East Pakistan, later Bangladesh. A crucial detail that tanked the family fortunes. For, the mills in India now fell silent, with no yarn to weave into fabric. East Pakistan refused to supply material to India, with the intention of setting up their own mills. As a result, the companies that once thrived on the golden threads of jute were now reduced to liquidation, and the family's income dipped to zero, overnight. It was a swift and bitter end.

Amena Muchhala, the eldest child and therefore the closest to her mother, was most aware of the shifting sands of her family's circumstances and familial relationships. In the absence of her father's protection, her mother was kept on a tight budget by her grandmother. The money gone, Amena watched as her mother's cherished collection of jewellery was gradually pawned off piece by piece in a desperate bid to cope with the mounting challenges of providing for three children without any means of income. She sat beside her grandmother on the huge Burma teak four-poster bed, as the wrinkled old lady negotiated the sale of their numerous properties and downgraded the size of their staff. She watched as streams of opportunistic men flowed through her grandmother's large imposing room, eyes sparkling at the prospect of acquiring a magnificent carpet, a priceless artefact or an exquisite piece of jewellery for mere pennies. Men who had once revered her grandmother, declining to even sit on the floor in her presence, now lounged comfortably on her antique chairs and plush velvet cushions. The vultures had descended, all at once.

By the time young Amena had grown into a woman of extraordinary beauty and elegance, her family's fortunes had crumbled to dust.

A slender woman with milky white skin, long black hair that fell down to her lower back, a high forehead and a sharp aristocratic nose, Amena was indeed a striking woman. The family may no longer have money, but they were still considered one of the most cultured and well-bred of their time, making Amena a highly sought after prospect.

So, when, at the age of twenty-one she received a marriage proposal from a cultured and prosperous family, she readily accepted. Although her fiancé was practically a stranger to her, she accepted this as characteristic of the times. Ideally, the Muchhalas would have preferred a longer engagement to allow the couple more time to get to know one another, but they were unable to withstand the pressures of the affluent family, which wanted to speed up the wedding. And so, Amena and the young man were married quickly, without fanfare or celebration, the *nikah* solemnised in a small room. Yet, the couple continued to live apart for many months, in separate towns, an arrangement that caused much confusion and anguish.

In time, the truth emerged – the young man was grappling with severe depression and other undiagnosed mental troubles – a burden that eventually led him down the tragic path of suicide several years later. Amena, fortunate to have escaped from this unhappy bond, managed to secure a divorce shortly after the nikah had taken place. Although her legal status had reverted to that of a single woman, it would take longer to heal from the scars left by the traumatic experience.

These early traumas would embed into Amena's character burdens and wisdom far beyond her tender years. At a very young age, she came to understand that when all else is stripped away, the intangible treasures of character – strength, grace, dignity, respect and pride – would always be hers. And so, she learnt to guard them fiercely. In the face of despair, she learnt to wear her dignity like an armour, developing the uncanny ability to navigate life's hardships with unparalleled grace and restraint, conducting herself with tremendous poise even when faced with life's harshest storms.

Her elegance and inner fortitude became her fortress, shielding her from prying eyes and wagging tongues, guarding its secret treasures. It was this quiet strength of character that drew Aziz Ahmadi to her.

By the late 1950s, Aziz had become a nearly inseparable part of the Muchhala household, spending almost all his weekends at the Muchhala mansion. A peculiar connection had blossomed between Aziz and the Muchhala matriarch, their grandmother, characterized by a playful and mischievous camaraderie. He often teased her, and she, in return, would playfully swat him away, responding with the nickname she had chosen for him. '*Jaao, jaao, miyan khaas* (Off you go, my favoured one),' she would retort, followed by a hearty chuckle. The endearing bond between the spirited young man and the wizened old woman was puzzling to the rest of the family, since the old lady didn't hesitate to deliver sharp tongue lashings to the others. But not to her beloved *miyan khaas*.

As Amena's divorce proceedings concluded, Aziz had already established himself in Ahmedabad. Having so far kept his affections for the young woman to himself, he would later admit that many of his visits to the Muchhala mansion were, in part, an attempt to get to know this intriguing woman, sister to his friends, yet so distant, quiet and mysterious. While the Muchhala brothers were gregarious and charming, Amena, fondly referred to as Ama, was a study in contrast. Quiet and reserved, she kept most of her thoughts to herself, piquing Aziz's curiosity.

So, after allowing a respectful period to pass following her divorce, Aziz approached his parents with a request. He wished to marry Ama and hoped his parents would bring a formal proposal to her mother. Aziz's parents were not surprised. Aware of his friendship with the Muchhala boys and holding the family in high regard, they willingly set off from Ahmedabad to Surat.

But there was already another proposal for Amena – from a pilot, also serendipitously named Aziz. So, a confused Ama approached her grandmother for advice. The wizened old lady, despite being bent over double from a spinal condition, peered up at her granddaughter, eyes bright and alert. 'Choose the lawyer,' she said.

And so it was that Amena Muchhala and Aziz Ahmadi were married on 8 December 1960 in a modest ceremony enveloped in much laughter and joy.

The vivacious Aziz and the quiet Ama seemingly polar opposites on the surface, were, in truth, two pieces of a jigsaw puzzle that fit neatly together. Ama's calming presence not only had the power to temper Aziz's fiery temper, but also provided a steady anchor to his impulsive temperament. But, perhaps most importantly, it was her quiet courage that would encourage and support his boldness and determination, enabling him to scale unprecedented heights. Together, they would create an extraordinary partnership where their unique qualities seamlessly intertwined. Their bond would defy conventions and expectations, with Aziz learning to rely on her counsel before taking any decision in his personal life.

It is, therefore, perplexing to comprehend the cause of the hostility that Aziz's parents displayed towards Ama shortly following their wedding. Because of the lack of communication between Aziz and his mother, we cannot conclusively say why the relationship between Shirin Ahmadi and Amena Ahmadi soured so horribly, so quickly. Or, for that matter, the source of the animosity between Zulekha and Ama. From Ama's accounts, we know that the Ahmadis' contempt for the Dai put them at odds with their new daughter-in-law very early on. We also know that there were several cultural differences between the Surti and Amdavadi communities, which played a role in the conflict. Due to the typical formal nature of the Surti lifestyle, Aziz's parents perhaps interpreted Ama's social behaviours and efforts to run the household based on her cultural practices as disrespectful and a personal affront to their ways.

But the matter of the Dai was insurmountable.

In the realm of Islamic practices, the concept of *mahram* by blood is common to all Muslims. These relationships are considered so close that marriage within these categories would be unlawful or *haraam*. Typically, mahram relationships include immediate family members such as fathers, brothers, grandfathers and other close relatives.

But a lesser known and less common idea that runs alongside it connects people through a different route – breastfeeding. While this ancient practice has disappeared in the modern years, it was once a tradition that often shaped familial and social connections. This relatively unconventional concept, known as mahram by milk, binds people as relatives by virtue of breastfeeding. A woman that breastfeeds a child, binds herself and her family to the child and their family in the same way as if the relationship were through blood. This is the bond that bound Aziz's wife's family, the Muchhalas, to the Syedna. Because Amena Muchhala's mother, Fatema Muchhala, had been breastfed by Syedna Taher Saifuddin's wife, she was *mehram-daar* by milk to the Dai – a foster relation that bound the two families.

This is indicative of the closeness between their families and the central role, faith and community played in Amena's life.

But this bond was also forged by steel through tragedy. When Amena Muchhala's father passed away at the age of twenty-six, he left behind a twenty-two-year-old widow and three toddlers. Distraught and desperate, Amena's mother turned to Syedna Taher Saifuddin for guidance. Although the family lived in Surat and Syedna had relocated to Bombay by then, he took the grieving young widow – his *mehram-daar* – and her children under his wing, offered them his protection and helped them rebuild their lives. He offered not just practical advice and economic opportunities, but also helped the family socially and psychologically. Indeed, if there was a father figure in young Amena's life, it was Syedna Taher Saifuddin. Growing up under this influence, the Muchhala siblings developed a loyalty to Syedna and his lineage that they would carry to the ends of their lives.

This bond would endure through generations – the elder son of Syedna Taher Saifuddin, Syedna Mohammad Burhanuddin, who would succeed as Dai in 1965, and the younger, Khuzaima Qutbuddin, who would become his brother's second-in-command and *Mazoon-e-Daawat* – all would hold a place in the family's confidence. As the Dai's trusted second-in-command, the *Mazoon* sits to the right of the Dai and serves as their representative in their absence.

At the time when Amena and Aziz were married in 1960, Aziz's engagement with community matters was, at best, lukewarm. However, Syedna Taher Saifuddin, who held Ama in great affection, embraced Aziz as a de facto son-in-law. A hugely popular leader who was, by all accounts, genuinely loved and respected, Syedna Taher Saifuddin's progressive ideals reflected Aziz's own. Convinced of the transformative power of education, he worked to encourage secular education among the Bohras, distributing scholarships and establishing schools. During his tenure, he set up more than 350 co-educational institutes across India, Africa and the Middle East. One of the schools he set up was located within the premises of the Aligarh Muslim University when he served as the Chancellor of the institution for three terms, a position that Justice Aziz Ahmadi would also go on to hold many years later, for two terms. Additionally, there were schools for girls, reflecting Syedna Taher Saifuddin's advocacy for women's independence. He also popularized several welfare schemes, such as the *Qarz-e-Hasana*, set up to provide interest-free loans to members in need. His teachings were balanced and practical, encouraging Bohras to pursue prosperity while upholding their faith. Perhaps it was these progressive thought patterns of Syedna Taher Saifuddin that challenged Aziz Ahmadi's previously held notions and opened the doors to a world he so far had neither exposure to nor was interested in. Contrary to his father's beliefs, Aziz was beginning to wonder if religion and liberalism were necessarily mutually exclusive. He was surprised to learn that the spiritual head's ongoing projects included many of the ideals he too held dear, primary among them being the commitment to welfare for the less fortunate and the creation of opportunities for community members. He appreciated this genuine commitment towards empowerment and upliftment of the community, especially women. But, above all, he valued the Dai's endorsement of pursuing higher education, even if it meant travelling abroad to expand one's knowledge and seek career opportunities.

And so, he was glad to accept Syedna Taher Saifuddin's invitations to visit him and engage in conversation. Their discussions were not confined to the topic of religion; they spanned the gamut from intricate matters of faith to law, education and academics. Although he did not participate actively in national politics, the Dai kept himself well informed and maintained active communication with the political leaders of his time.

Because the Bohra headquarters had been traditionally situated in

Surat until 1933 before relocating to Bombay, Syedna Taher Saifuddin retained strong connections with the city, visiting frequently and staying for extended periods. This provided Aziz the opportunity to visit him in Surat, just a short train ride away.

This relationship of mutual respect and interest marked the beginning of Aziz's journey as a Bohra on the periphery of the community to an active participant in matters of community life. Yet, throughout his life, Aziz would never become a religious man.

But the rest of the Ahmadis did not share this esteem for the Dai and his family. They held Ama's regard for him in contempt and were also displeased with Aziz's growing closeness to the leader. Unlike his father, the deeply religious Imran Ali Ahmadi, Mushabber Ahmadi was a reformist. His family held a distinct stance – while they were Bohras, their involvement in the intricacies of the Dawoodi Bohra community was limited. They also resisted any involvement of the clergy in their personal matters. This divide ignited a clash of ideals between Aziz's parents and their new daughter-in-law. Ama, a deeply religious lady, well entrenched in community life and with close personal ties to the Dai himself, stood in stark contrast to Shirin and Mushabber's active resistance.

When Ama's daughter was born, and Syedna Taher Saifuddin suggested naming her Tasneem, there was chaos in the Ahmadi household. Zulekha had chosen another name and was furious. Once again, the clash was perceived as a disrespect to the Ahmadis' way of life. Allegations of interference were levelled against Syedna Taher Saifuddin and Ama was forbidden from consulting him on family matters.

But to Ama, this was unendurable. A father figure, it was Syedna Taher Saifuddin who had brokered Ama's divorce, helping free her from a fraudulent union that threatened to destroy her life. It was he who had ensured that her mother was able to live a life of dignity without the protection of a husband. So, to be asked to distance herself from him was simply inconceivable to her.

During these early years, Ama would relinquish many old habits and pleasures to keep the peace within her new family. But she remained steadfast in her determination to preserve her relationship with the Dai and his family, a connection she would hold dear until her last days. Accustomed to consulting Syedna Taher Saifuddin before taking any important decision, travelling to Bombay or Surat at least once in three months to call upon him and share details of her life, Ama refused to forego these familiar and comforting customs. And so, the atmosphere in the family home, where the new couple lived with Aziz's parents, soured rapidly, each day worse than the last.

As Ama dug her heels in and battle lines grew more defined, her in-laws intensified their pressure tactics. Although Ama typically shied away from discussing this traumatic phase of her life, it was in rare moments of candidness later in life that she would reveal some of the painful instances of this time.

At the time, she endured these ordeals in silence, refusing to share them with Aziz. Perhaps she clung to the hope that the situation would improve on its own. Or perhaps she feared their reaction if they discovered she had divulged these matters to Aziz. Either way, Aziz would only learn about these details much later.

Hot on the heels of professional success, the ambitious Aziz had started keeping long hours. As his reputation grew, clients began to seek him out, and he was determined not to lose any opportunity. Evenings, once a time of reprieve and relaxation, now became an extension of his bustling workday, spent in his chambers meeting with clients, delving into case research and studying legal briefs. Family dinners became more and more rare, with Aziz returning home long after the dishes had been cleared away and his daughter put to bed. At home too, after Ama had retired, the serene stillness of the late night hours was interrupted only by the faint rustle of pages and the soft glow of his desk lamp as Aziz continued to read.

The distinction between weekdays and weekends too became blurred in Aziz's pursuit of professional excellence. Perhaps it was this tunnel vision that kept Aziz from fully grasping the extent of suffering endured by his wife. He was only aware of a constant tension in the background of the home, and the continual sharp words that were exchanged between his parents, sister and wife.

When Ama finally poured her heart out to Syedna Taher Saifuddin, he asked her only one question. 'Does Aziz know?' Ama shook her head, eyes welling up. The wise old man placed his wrinkled hand gently upon the hand of his adoptive daughter and said, *'Toh bol, dikri* (Then speak, child).'

And so Ama did, finally standing up for herself. A shocked Aziz was caught in the middle, unsure of how to respond to the allegations, vehemently denied by his mother and sister. Anger and tears filled their home. No longer willing to endure these injustices, Ama was now defiant. Drawing upon the wellsprings of inner strength and fortitude within her, she withdrew into a fortress of resolve, determined to survive.

Aziz was torn – his deep love for his parents and sister could not ultimately condone their treatment of his wife. His own strained relationship with his family only exacerbated the situation, as he did not enjoy the confidence of either his parents or his sister. The young couple longed to move out into a home of their own, but Aziz's resources were limited. The opportunity for escape would only present itself in 1964 when Aziz was offered judgeship of the City Civil Court of Ahmedabad. Even then, the couple would still have to wait several more years until a government accommodation became available and could be allocated to them.

But after the explosive confrontation, overt hostility gradually waned, replaced with a frosty aloofness that further isolated Ama. Shirin Ahmadi, a woman of remarkable strength and resilience herself, was capable of holding a lifelong grudge. Stubbornly egoistic and unwilling to extend an olive branch to her daughter-in-law, she succeeded in pushing away her son as well. The rare moments of tenderness and camaraderie Ama had once shared with her father-in-law also vanished into thin air. It is not surprising then that Tasneem Ahmadi's early childhood memories are marked with persistent arguments, shouting matches and her mother's tears that soaked through the years that she lived in her husband's family home.

This rift would cause Aziz a lifetime of pain and pining. From the letters he wrote to his father once he had moved to Delhi in 1989, we know that he missed his parents desperately, aching to reconnect with them. Every so often, he implored them to make the journey to Delhi. He offered to send them plane tickets several times, always to be stoically declined. He enthusiastically detailed the delightful weather, the grand bungalow that they lived in, and the lush, tree-lined streets of the city. He described the moments they would share, the joy he would derive from their visit – but they never did visit. Shirin Ahmadi would make the journey to her son's home only once – when Aziz was to be sworn in as the Chief Justice of India – a visit she would undertake grudgingly and gracelessly.

The exchange of letters between Aziz and his parents ended abruptly after his father's passing in 1996, pointing to a complete breakdown of relations between himself and his mother, which perhaps existed before this loss as well. Although Aziz routinely addressed his letters to 'My Dearest Daddy and Mummy', the contents spoke to his father alone. While he did enquire about his mother's well-being, his letters did not speak directly to her. Because of this conspicuous lack of communication between mother and son, we do not know Shirin Ahmadi's thoughts or feelings about the loss of her relationship with her son. We do know if her animosity extended to Aziz and Ama's children as well, with Shirin choosing not to maintain relations with them either.

Each time Aziz would speak about inviting his parents to stay, Ama would physically break into a sweat. She never outrightly declined, always offering to set up a room for them should they decide to visit, but when she reached for the handkerchief tucked into the waistband of her ghaghra to dab the perspiration off her neck, one could feel the anxiety radiating from her.

In the end, it was a fracture that inflicted suffering and heartache on all parties involved.

4

From Bar to Bench

As his legal career flourished, Aziz found himself in the thrilling arena of courtroom battles, often locking horns with some of the most prominent members of the City Civil and Sessions Court Bar. In those formative years, he hoped to be able to manage both civil as well as criminal matters. But as his civil caseload burgeoned, he realized he needed to make a choice. The turning point arrived when a frightening incident made the decision for him. One of the cases Ahmadi had argued was a matter involving the defence of a young man accused of stealing cloth bales from mills. It was revealed that the man had discovered a unique modus operandi – to pilfer and store the bales in a railway carriage, safely hidden away until the train set off. Then, as the train approached his village, the accused would swing open the carriage doors, rolling the bales out onto the tracks, to be later collected and stored in a hut belonging to his unsuspecting father-in-law. But the case was complicated as the father-in-law who lived elsewhere and therefore knew nothing about his son-in-law's nefarious activities also became implicated as an accused in the case. As the proceedings unfolded, the young man grew suspicious of Aziz's sympathies towards his father-in-law. Convinced that his lawyer's loyalties were shifting towards safeguarding the unsuspecting father-in-law rather than himself, the young fellow became enraged.

    A man given to rough speech and violent acts, he waited until they had exited the courtroom before approaching Aziz from behind and physically assaulting him. Thankfully, the man's father-in-law too was present. Thinking quickly, he grabbed his son-in-law's arm and prevented the onslaught from escalating into a full-fledged attack that could have caused Aziz serious injury. This incident forced Aziz to question whether he wanted to continue practising criminal law, which often involved dealing with a particular type of clientele and the potential risk of physical harm. Choosing to see this particular case to the end – and the acquittal of both the accused – Aziz decided to eventually shift his practice towards civil law. He referred all his criminal briefs to his trusted friend and colleague, Jayendra Thaker.

Simultaneously, his role as Honorary Government Pleader – a legal practitioner appointed by the government to represent its interests – broadened his legal horizons. It granted him exposure to a diverse range of cases that went well beyond his personal client roster. Very quickly, Aziz became a fixture in the court, arguing cases on a near-daily basis before the eight judges presiding over the City Civil Courts. These engagements brought him in contact with almost every senior member of the Bar. His decision to engage in civil matters turned out to be a strategic one that paid off as it attracted a steady stream of private clients. As was his nature, Aziz dove head first into his work and thoroughly enjoyed every minute of it. He was fast gaining a reputation as a good legal mind in the chambers and a worthy opponent in the courtroom. The judges he argued before had begun to notice him as well. Justice M.P. Thakkar, Aziz's close friend and mentor – and future Chief Justice of the Gujarat High Court – invited him for a cup of tea in his chambers one evening. As the two friends sipped their tea, Justice Thakkar smiled at the young lawyer. Gesturing at his own seat, he remarked, 'I hope to see you occupying this chair very soon.' 'Inshallah, maybe one day,' replied a beaming Aziz. He did not realize that this was going to happen sooner than he had thought.

As Aziz's legal career soared, his days grew longer, stretching into sixteen-hours marathon workdays, each filled with legal triumphs and courtroom battles. His bank account was beginning to mirror his success as well. He now spurned the popular Gujarat Club, which most of his contemporaries frequented for a cheap cup of tea in favour of the more expensive and exclusive Kwality restaurant. A car, a precious, much-used Morris Minor with a faulty gear that needed constant repairs was purchased, only to be used for special occasions and family outings. Lovingly, he checked the car each morning, attempting many of the smaller repairs himself. Due to Aziz's poor directional sense and difficulty in recalling roads, Ama, seated in the passenger seat, showed him the way. He joked that she was his 'guiding light'. Yet, amid the whirlwind of all the excitement, there was one precious commodity he did not notice was slipping away – time. While he could now afford to take Ama to upscale restaurants without worrying about their monthly budget, he rarely had the time for leisurely excursions. His bustling schedule left him with scarcely a moment to spare and his family was beginning to notice.

On an otherwise ordinary day, the sun streamed into Aziz's office, casting long shadows over stacks of legal briefs. He was engrossed in making notes when the unexpected knock of a peon on the door made him jump. It was a simple, matter-of-fact message from his mother. The Chief Justice of the High Court had called the Ahmadi residence, wishing to see Aziz at 5 p.m.

Aziz was caught off guard by the message. As he nodded to the peon, permitting him to leave the room, his mind was a whirlwind of questions, unsure of what to expect when he met Chief Justice J. M. Shelat later that afternoon. He had not interacted with Justice Shelat personally, but he was aware of his tough reputation. His very first thought was that something had gone awry in one of the cases for which he had filed an appearance in the High Court. As a precaution, Aziz had entrusted the monitoring of these cases to a lawyer's clerk, asking to be informed when they came up for hearing. Perhaps one of these matters had appeared on the Hon'ble Chief Justice's board?

Making his way to the High Court, Aziz turned the corridor towards the office of Mr Prabhu, personal secretary to Justice Shelat. His reputation as a 'sealed box' was well-known and he expected no easy answers. 'Mr Prabhu,' began Aziz. 'Could you shed some light on the purpose of this appointment? I received the summons, but its nature remains a mystery to me.' With a knowing smile, Mr Prabhu replied, 'I'm afraid I'm as in the dark as you are, Mr Ahmadi. The Chief Justice has not divulged any details to me.' Realizing that the tight-lipped Prabhu knew more than he was letting on, Aziz began to mentally rehearse the apology he had prepared in case the purpose of the meeting was to berate him for a misstep. 'Shall I let the Chief Justice know that you are here?' enquired Prabhu. Aziz nodded and was asked to be shown into the chamber.

As Aziz entered, the Chief Justice's deep voice resonated, 'Come in, young man,' immediately putting the young advocate at ease. Relieved, Aziz took the seat offered to him. With an air of graciousness, Justice Shelat began, 'I have been hearing commendable reports about your performance at the bar.' Not expecting praise, Aziz was taken aback. 'Your Lordship is very kind,' he mumbled.

The Chief Justice then broached the real purpose of the meeting. 'Don't you think it's time for you to render your services on the bench?' Stunned and momentarily speechless, Aziz stammered, 'My Lord, such a thought never crossed my mind.' At thirty, Aziz was aware that being considered for a position on the bench at such a young age was virtually unheard of. Hesitatingly, he continued, 'Does Your Lordship know my age?' 'Disarmed by the young man's naiveté, Shelat broke into a smile. 'We know more about you than *you* do!'[1]

Aziz requested Justice Shelat for a little time to consider the offer. He promised to keep their conversation confidential but shared that he would like to consult his father and wife. The Chief mischievously responded, 'You may consult your father, but not your wife, for women cannot keep secrets.'[2] Aziz grinned, recognizing the light tone of the judge's voice. Those were times in which it was common and acceptable for men to seek advice and guidance from their male relatives such as fathers on professional matters. But consulting wives was seen as rare and unusual. 'In that case, I will need no time because I know what my father will say. But I need to inform my wife of the restrictions she will have to suffer as a judge's wife,' responded Aziz. Smiling, the Chief said, 'That's a very disarming argument. Consult with your wife then, but tell her to keep it to herself.'

That evening, after dinner, as his parents retired to their room, Aziz gestured to Ama to join him in the bedroom the couple shared with their two-year-old daughter. Seated comfortably on their well-worn couch, Aziz's eyes danced with excitement as he began to share the extraordinary news. It was an offer, a prestigious judgeship, a new chapter in their lives that promised both opportunities and challenges. He was careful to outline not only the perks they would be entitled to, but also the sobering fact that their earnings would reduce significantly.

Ama, listening thoughtfully, turned to glance at their daughter engrossed in her toys on the carpet. With a gentle nod towards the toddler, her eyes returned to Aziz. In a low voice, she said, 'Think about how many nights you have returned home after our daughter has gone to bed this month alone. You have been so busy, you are missing watching her grow. Perhaps this opportunity will give you more time to spend with us.' Scooping little Tasneem into her arms, she continued, 'Take the judgeship, Aziz. I will find a way to manage our finances.' Certainly, she intended to seek Syedna Taher Saifuddin's blessings before Aziz formally accepted the appointment, but for all practical purposes, the decision was already made.

And so, thirty-two-year-old Aziz Ahmadi ascended from the Bar to the Bench on 30 March 1964 at a monthly salary of Rs 1800.

The news of Aziz Ahmadi's appointment to the bench reverberated through the legal circles of Ahmedabad. It was an anomaly, one that had no precedent, for someone of his age to be elevated to the bench so soon in their career, making his case the subject of much surprise and debate. Many of the judges of the City Civil Court, contemporaries of his father, were intrigued and inspired by his appointment. They rushed to congratulate the young man, eager to witness the unfolding of Ahmadi's promising journey. His new colleagues, men his father's age whom he had so far referred to as 'uncle', were now sharing their courtrooms with him.

Aziz himself went through a transformation. No longer the grubby teenager who once paid little heed to his appearance nor the carefree young lawyer, Aziz Mushabber Ahmadi's appearance now befitted his position of a judge. Now he was impeccably turned out in his crisp white shirts and black judge's gowns that were meticulously starched and ironed every day by a peon. Among those captivated by his persona was

Chandrakant Chanalal Rana, a young peon aged 12 years, who swiftly discerned an opportunity to earn a few coins by shouldering Ahmadi's leather-bound briefcase every day. Enamoured by Mr Ahmadi, he would wait for the familiar scooter to round the corner, so that he might escort the court's newest judge to his chamber each morning, and at the day's end, he would accompany him back to the courthouse gates. In recognition of the boy's service, Ahmadi would reward him with four shiny pice coins, a small bronze currency distinguished by a telltale hole at its centre. Now a seventy-eight-year-old man, Rana remains a fixture at the City Civil Court in Ahmedabad, gladly regaling curious enquirers with stories of his days in Ahmadi's chamber seated next to the bench clerk. A spot he coveted for the constant whir of the fan, a welcome relief from the scorching days – a spot he claimed for ten years, the entirety of Ahmadi's tenure.

But not everybody was celebrating Ahmadi's appointment. The legal landscape in Gujarat was ablaze with controversy. Bar Associations throughout the state had united and called for a strike, boycotting Ahmadi's court. The City Civil Court, which was seen as a training ground for grooming future High Court judges, was the epicentre of the agitation. And it was not a peaceful strike. Tensions simmered, often boiling over into violent flare-ups. Caught in the crossfire were Ahmadi's close friends who were still active practitioners at the Bar. Since the striking lawyers were bound by professional ethics from directly targeting a sitting judge, they directed their frustration and anger towards Ahmadi's friends and supporters. Books and files were hurled at them, forcing these young advocates to seek refuge from the unexpected storm directed at their friend.

The crux of the discontent was twofold – Ahmadi's young age and his religion. Many older lawyers understood that their own ambitions towards High Court judgeship were now frustrated by the probability that Ahmadi would leapfrog them in the race for seniority. All the older, more experienced members of the bar, hoping for a judicial career, knew that even if they were appointed, Ahmadi would still be the senior peer, and with a longer tenure than them, whose retirement ages were significantly closer. And because of the length of this tenure, Ahmadi's chances for elevation to a higher court, too, were more likely than for those with fewer years left to serve. Ahmadi's age had magnified the odds of his own ascent and intensified the resistance to his appointment.

But it wasn't just about seniority. With this appointment, Ahmadi had become the only Muslim on the Bench of the City Civil Court at the time – and the youngest-ever appointed. The mere notion of a Muslim judge on his way not only to the Gujarat High Court but potentially all the way to the Supreme Court of India sent ripples through legal corridors, stirring up an unsettling, religiously charged atmosphere. At the time, the Supreme Court had appointed less than a handful of Muslim judges from High Courts across the country – and none yet from Gujarat. Communally charged allegations flew thick and fast. Prominent Bohra figure Akbar Sharafali Sarela,[3] serving as Joint Secretary in the Legal Department of the Government of Gujarat found himself at the centre of swirling rumours absurdly alleging that he was Ahmadi's father-in-law. Another Bohra luminary, Justice N.M. Miabhoy,[4] held the position of High Court judge, sparking rumours that he had somehow orchestrated Ahmadi's appointment.

Both rumours were eventually proved to be false, yet Ahmadi was young and unprepared for the extent of controversy and deluge of animosity that was flung at him. Not yet weathered by the numerous storms that were destined to come his way, Aziz was deeply distressed. Alarmed and shaken, he found himself thrown into the deep end, with no choice but to quickly learn to navigate treacherous waters. The courtroom was no longer just a stage for legal battles; it had become a battleground where personal ambitions and communal anxieties took centre stage. Aziz had to quickly learn to either sink or swim.

In the corridors of power as well, Ahmadi's appointment had become a topic of hot debate with his appointment questioned in the legislative assembly. Concerns about his young age and fitness for the role were voiced – and defended. In the end, his appointment held.

But Justice Shelat had warned him these things would happen.[5] 'There may be some disgruntled elements,' he had said, 'But you need not worry about them. You just do your job; the High Court has broad shoulders to tackle them.'

Notably, the Principal Judge of the City Civil Court was one such disgruntled element. His unhappiness simmered, a quiet resentment born from his belief that he should have been consulted by the High Court before Ahmadi was offered judgeship. Although the matter was solely between him and the High Court, one in which Ahmadi had played no role, he chose to vent his frustrations on the newly appointed judge. And so, Ahmadi was assigned one of the most arduous sessions cases on the Court's docket. That the case fell under the domain of criminal law while Ahmadi had so far established himself primarily in the field of civil law was no coincidence.

It was a sensational case, a high-profile murder of a police head constable during a political agitation. The government, keen to secure a conviction, had engaged not one, but four Special Public Prosecutors – counsel with at least ten years of experience, appointed by the government in cases of public interest – which it had especially handpicked. The number of accused was 22, some of whom were members of the Communist Party of India and highly educated individuals. The legal arena was a battleground, and the government wasn't taking any chances. They enlisted the services of some of the sharpest legal minds in the country, the crème de la crème of the criminal bar. As many as 150 witnesses were examined and cross-examined. With all eyes on the case, and the young judge that was hearing it, Ahmadi was certainly feeling the pressure. The reasons for assigning him this case were also implicitly understood. At a wedding reception of a colleague, Ahmadi overheard a group of lawyers discussing the high-profile case, as one of the guests remarked, 'Who is on trial – the judge or the accused?'

In the courtroom, however, the trial was proceeding smoothly. Once the prosecution had finished its presentation of evidence, the statements of the accused were recorded under Section 313 of the Code of Criminal Procedure. This section allows the court to confront the accused with the prosecution evidence presented against them, thereby explaining any incriminating circumstances appearing against them. With the defence opting not to present any oral evidence, Ahmadi invited the senior Public

Prosecutor to begin his arguments. He did so with gusto, and the defence counsel followed suit with their submissions.

Hearings thus concluded; anticipation ebbed in the courtroom with everyone expecting the judgement to be reserved for the judge to write later. However, Ahmadi was acutely aware that all eyes were on him. He knew why he had been assigned this case, and that he needed to prove his capability in the very beginning. He had also heard the whispers circulating in the corridors of the court – many expected the inexperienced judge to seek assistance from his retired father in drafting the judgement. Determined to lay these speculations to rest once and for all, Ahmadi decided to prove his mettle right there in the courtroom.

He tapped the back of his pencil on the table to catch the stenographer's attention, signalling that he was ready to dictate the judgement right then. Unprepared for this, the sleepy courtroom was suddenly jolted awake, the room filling with an excited buzz. This was going to be no short judgement; the hearings had gone on for several days. Yet, Ahmadi began. Taking two whole days to dictate the judgement, he nevertheless did so in an open courtroom. In the end, he acquitted all the accused, directed scathing critique towards the Investigating Officer and condemned the quality of the investigation. The case went to the High Court on appeal where Ahmadi's judgement was upheld. In an interesting twist, the Principal Judge of the City Civil Court who had since been elevated was on the very Bench of the High Court that confirmed Ahmadi's judgement.

Having thus passed this trial by fire, Ahmadi settled into his new role, tackling civil and criminal cases with equal ease, earning himself the reputation of being an 'all-rounder'. His colleagues, although with decades more experience than him, found themselves occasionally approaching him with curiosity about his legal opinion. One such incident involved an interpretation of the Stamp Act. Because different stamp values are required for different kinds of documents, such as sale deeds, wills or other legal papers, documents that are not properly stamped can be impounded. On this occasion, Ahmadi was asked to accept an unstamped promissory note – a written acknowledgement of a debt to be paid – into evidence by impounding it. There was precedent for such an act, wherein one of the senior judges had accepted such an argument. But Ahmadi disagreed.

The news of his viewpoint caught the attention of the judge who had initially accepted such arguments. During their usual tea break in the library, the judge approached Ahmadi to enquire about his view. Judge Ahmadi explained that for a document to be subject to impounding, it must first be classified as an 'instrument' under the Stamp Act. But at that time, the definition of an instrument did not include a promissory note. Therefore, the question of impounding such a document did not arise. Requesting a copy of the Stamp Act, the judge looked through the relevant portion before confirming Ahmadi's view to be correct. 'I am glad you did not follow my view,' he said, patting the young man appreciatively on the shoulder before returning to his courtroom.

Although Ahmadi had passed his tough initiation where criminal matters were concerned, he would always find these cases the most challenging to preside over. This is because the Indian Penal Code provides a wide range of sentencing options depending on the severity of the offence committed. Punishment for smaller offences can range from a mere slap on the wrist in the form of a simple fine to a brief jail term of a few days, while more serious offences like murder can attract the grim prospect of spending one's entire life incarcerated. And then, at the far end of the spectrum, the gravest of punishments – capital punishment. But in the case of murder, the process of the trial almost always proves more emotionally challenging than the technicality of the sentencing – which is restricted. Ahmadi was faced with this difficult experience very early in his career.

This case, more gruesome and heart-wrenching than most, landed squarely on his desk. It revolved around a young couple, who, like most in the rural setting, lived lives separated by the basic necessity of livelihoods. The wife resided in the family home with her in-laws in their village while the husband lived in the city of Ahmedabad, working at a local bakery. It was a typical story, familiar to the many millions of India's migrant workers and their families. But this particular story would not end well. There had been rumours of an alleged affair between the wife and another man, rumours that soon reached the ears of the husband in Ahmedabad. He embarked on a journey to his village, determined to uncover the truth. Upon arriving at his village, he set out to make enquiries, which confirmed his worst fears. Instead of confronting his wife, he began to coax and cajole her into returning to the city with him, ostensibly so that the two may live together. After a day or two of persistent persuasion, the woman conceded, and the couple set off for the bustling city of Ahmedabad. But the night was to take a horrifying turn. Armed with a serrated bread knife, presumably procured from the bakery where the man worked, he murdered his young wife in the most brutal manner, slicing her neck and completely severing her head from her body.

When the case appeared before Ahmadi, the defence pleaded 'grave and sudden provocation'. But Ahmadi could not agree. He believed that the husband's actions of travelling to the village and spending a few days engaged in persuading his wife to leave the familial home and relocate to Ahmedabad displayed a calculated and premeditated intention. Even as he rejected the plea of 'grave and sudden provocation' and sentenced the man to life imprisonment, Ahmadi's voice faltered momentarily and a chill went down his spine. For it is no trifling responsibility – that of bearing the weight of justice and holding the fate of an individual's life.

Indeed, it is easy to understand why cases like these are particularly agonizing for judges, given that an individual's very life hinges upon their gavel. Ahmadi was no exception to the emotional and ethical challenges of these weighty decisions. In the aftermath of these cases, and later in his life, he would openly share his personal struggles and the emotional toll that came with rendering difficult judgements such as these. In the case of Allauddin Mian vs. State of Bihar, which would come before him in 1989, shortly after he was elevated to the Supreme Court, Justice Ahmadi advocated for restraint in sentencing. In this case involving an unlawful assembly's intent to kill one Baharan Mian but instead leading to the tragic deaths of two infant girls, two of the six accused were initially given the death penalty by the trial court. This decision was upheld by the High Court. However, when the case reached Justice Ahmadi in the Supreme Court, he disagreed. Converting the sentences to life imprisonment, he stressed that the death penalty should only be awarded in the rarest of rare cases. Powerfully, the judgement states, 'When the Court is called upon to choose between the convict's cry "I want to live" and the prosecutor's demand "he deserves to die", it goes without saying that the Court must show a high degree of concern and sensitiveness in the choice of sentence.'[6] This judgement also set sentencing guidelines under Section 235 (2) of the Code of Criminal Procedure. These guidelines lay down the procedural framework for hearing the accused on the matter of sentencing, ensuring the statutory rights of the accused.

In his entire judicial career that spanned over three decades, Justice Ahmadi would hand out the death sentence only once – to General Vaidya's assassins. Trained assassins and militants, Jinda and Sukha had carried out three high-profile political assassinations, the last of which was General Arun Vaidya in 1986. Upon capture, the militants proudly confessed and subsequently received the death penalty in 1992.

But not everything was grim. Family life had begun to flourish like a resilient blossom pushing through the cracks in the pavement. Liberated from the many confinements of living with her in-laws, Ama basked in a happiness she had never known. Although the government-appointed accommodation provided them with a modest flat on the second floor of a building with no elevator, it was her own sanctuary, a place where she could run her household with autonomy and grace. The gated community, housing government servants ranging from City Civil Court judges to secretaries of various ministries, offered her the chance to forge her own friendships. The couple had welcomed another member into their family, a bouncing baby boy they lovingly named Huzefa. Ama's mother, who had longed for her daughter's happiness, began to visit more frequently, her heart uplifted by the positive changes in Ama. Aziz, too, began to participate in family life. After demanding days spent in the courtroom and the library after, he often made a pit stop at the local vegetable vendor on his scooter, choosing fresh ingredients for their evening meal. This routine, far from being a chore, became a cherished ritual – a way to reconnect with the simple pleasures of life amid the complexities of his professional world. Sometimes, when he was in a particularly good mood, he would suggest a spontaneous movie night followed by dinner at a restaurant. Ama and Aziz would patiently wait for their children to fall asleep, and then, leaving them in the care of Ama's mother, would quietly slip out for an evening together. Other times, evenings flowed seamlessly into late-night gatherings and games of bridge, held in their own home or those of close friends. Conversations flowed freely and hearty laughter filled the air, mingling with the delicious aroma of hot, freshly fried *bhajjias* and steaming cups of tea. These delightful gatherings often went on past 2 a.m., creating unbreakable bonds of friendship. As mentioned earlier, these friendships, particularly with Niranjan Bhatt, Jayendra Thaker, Justice D.H. Shukla and Justice M.P. Thakkar would go on to last them a lifetime.

Aziz's troubled relationship with his parents began to improve too, the physical distance providing them all with some much-needed relief. While the couple would continue to maintain cordial relations with Aziz's parents for some time yet, an undeniable distance had begun to take root. For the couple, the currents of change and progress were reshaping the dynamics of their lives as they embraced the new freedom and joys that had almost imperceptibly woven their way into their lives.

Just as the Ahmadis were beginning to feel like all the pieces were finally falling into place, Ahmedabad was suddenly engulfed in violence. The September of 1969 would forever be etched in their memories as a time of unimaginable horror, marking one of the darkest chapters in independent Gujarat's history. It was a period that marked the breakdown of the Gandhian consensus of Hindu-Muslim harmony and the rise of Hindu nationalism as a prominent force in Gujarat. That the violence unfolded during the centurial birth year of Mahatma Gandhi was a painful stab at the heart of his legacy. In the aftermath of the riot, the political landscape of Gujarat would shift. Hindutva would become more prominent, the movement gaining ground. Partisanship and bigotry made a perceptible shift into public life. The ideology began to influence not only social lives but also electoral outcomes. Sadly, present-day Gujarat continues to be defined by this phenomenon.

But the 1969 riot was not a complete anomaly.[7] The communally charged city of Ahmedabad had witnessed twenty-nine communal riots of varying intensity between 1963 and 1968. This riot too, was preceded by several smaller skirmishes and hateful rhetoric. Beginning in Jamalpur where Aziz's parents lived, the riot erupted when a group of Muslims had gathered to celebrate the local Urs festival. Tensions arose when a group of local Sadhus, attempting to bring their cows through the crowded streets to the nearby Jagannath temple, ended up injuring some Muslim women and damaging carts and goods belonging to Muslims. A relatively minor incident ultimately became the catalyst for the horrifying violence that followed.

Ahmedabad was at the vortex of the violence, where the maximum number of casualties took place. The Gandhi ashram – a symbol of non-violence – was attacked, and several places of worship were desecrated. Trains were stopped and passengers killed. Women were raped and their breasts cut off. Children were torn limb to limb. The Justice P. J. Reddy Commission estimates that by the end of the riot, more than 500 people were killed in the city. Although relatively safe in their gated community of Samarpan, the Ahmadis were not immune to the horrors unfolding outside their enclave. Visuals and descriptions of people being slaughtered in the streets, garlanded with burning tyres, filled newspapers and radio broadcasts.

And then, a horrifying piece of news arrived. The streets were rife with rumours of violent mobs advancing towards Kalupur, a neighbourhood where some of Aziz's relatives still resided. It was one of the localities that had been placed under curfew. Among Aziz's relatives was his cousin, Bilkis and her young daughter, trapped in their home as the mobs grew closer. Aziz knew he had to act quickly.

He reached out to a trusted friend, an influential Hindu gentleman with connections, and called in a favour that would eventually save Bilkis and her daughter's lives. He knew he was asking for a lot, but he had no choice. Bilkis and her daughter needed to be rescued and brought to safety in Jamalpur – to Aziz's parents' home. The clock was ticking and the looming threat of the approaching mobs was growing closer.

As time raced on, Bilkis and her daughter endured agonizing hours of paralysing fear and dread. Trapped in their home, they were too scared to step out and look for a rickshaw willing to take them to Jamalpur. The fear of being physically assaulted – or worse – kept them trapped and hidden.

When the rescuers arrived, they were greeted with a scene of raw terror. Braced for the worst, Bilkis stood a short distance from the front door, brows knitted into a fierce line, ready to defend her daughter. Meanwhile, the traumatized child cowered beneath a bed, her innocent world shattered. The rescue mission had succeeded; Bilkis and her daughter were whisked out of Kalupur before the mobs descended and delivered safely to the mohalla in Jamalpur. It was a moment of immense relief; but the scars ran deep, especially for the young girl who would never fully recover from the experience. Throughout her life, she would grapple with the haunting signs and symptoms of PTSD, a reminder of the unspeakable horrors she must have witnessed. The rescue had spared them from a grim fate, but it could not spare them from their memories.

As a Muslim judge, Aziz Ahmadi faced the challenges of perception in establishing his competence in various aspects of the law, including a thorough understanding of Hindu law.[8] One of the cases that came before him involved a complex legal question pertaining to adoption under Hindu law. The authoritative text on Hindu law, *Mulla & Mulla*, presented a perspective that Ahmadi found to be at odds with his own understanding. Undaunted, he delivered his judgement based on his interpretation, which sent ripples of surprise and indignation through the legal community. Many questioned how he, a Muslim judge, could dare to challenge established views of Hindu law?

The advocate who had succeeded in the case took the initiative to share Ahmadi's interpretation with former Chief Justice S.T. Desai[9] who had previously edited an edition of *Mulla & Mulla*. Remarkably, the next edition of the book included a correction to that very point, aligning with Ahmadi's interpretation.

Ahmadi's tenure at the City Civil Court was where his legal skills matured, and he gained invaluable exposure to the diverse aspects of the legal profession. It was only many years later that he would fully understand that the time spent in the trial court was preparing him for the illustrious career that lay ahead. As he would say in an interview several years after retiring, 'It was a virtual training ground for becoming a judge of the High Court.'[10]

One evening, at a function held in the High Court, the new Chief Justice, Justice B.J. Divan, summoned Ahmadi. 'Are you aware,' he asked in a direct tone, 'that a heap of Execution Cases have piled up? What are you going to do about them?' An execution application, also known as a *darkhaast* application, comes into play when a court reaches a final decision on a case and issues a decree, which holds legal enforceability. The winning party proceeds to the execution court to ensure that the decree is carried out. Ahmadi assured him that he would consult with the Principal Judge about this the following day. But when he arrived at the court the next day, he found that the Chief Justice had already taken action, for the darkhaast clerk was prepared with a register containing a comprehensive list of pending cases. Ahmadi was informed that the entire stack had been assigned to him.

Up for the challenge, Ahmadi embarked upon a mission to transform the tangled web of the court's caseload into more manageable chunks. He instructed the clerk to organize the cases into distinct categories. For example, all those falling under Order 21, Rule 30, relating to decrees for payment of money to be placed together in one docket and those falling under Order 21, Rules 54–66, relating to attachment of property under another. And so on. He directed that each group be placed for hearing on a single day. This systematic classification bore results that surpassed Ahmadi's own expectations. Within a few months, 1500 cases were resolved and disposed of. This experience was an eye opener for Ahmadi. As Chief Justice of India, he would go on to apply the same methods to the caseload of the Supreme Court, resulting in a record-breaking low of 18,000 pending cases by the time he demitted office, a legacy that would earn him the affectionate nickname of 'case-cracker' in international circles.

In the bustling Indian courts, one truth is undeniable: judges are overworked and often pushed to their limits, whether presiding over trial courts, sitting in the High Courts or even the lofty Supreme Court. At the time that Ahmadi was on the bench of the City Civil Court, judges assigned sessions cases were expected to go through six cases per month – a daunting task to be sure, but by no means unachievable.

These numbers were carefully monitored and judges who fell short of this benchmark often found themselves on the receiving end of letters from the High Court that demanded explanations. These were considered humiliating and judges spared no effort to avoid such letters. One month, Ahmadi found himself tasked with an ancient, heavy lawsuit that devoured every second of his time. As the days turned into weeks, Ahmadi realized he would be unable to demonstrate any disposals. Nervous about the impending letter, his resourceful bench clerk suggested appending an explanation so as to avoid humiliation. Ahmadi declined to do so, and the dreaded letter never arrived.

Coincidently, the registrar of the High Court was Ahmadi's next-door neighbour and friend. Their camaraderie extended beyond the courtroom, often spilling into the tranquil evenings spent strolling through the lush gardens after a heavy dinner. One such evening, Ahmadi, in his characteristic mischievous way remarked, 'You know, you have let down my bench clerk. No letter has arrived to remind me of my courtroom performance.' The Registrar chuckled, knowing what Ahmadi was alluding to. 'Ah, my friend, we do not dispatch those letters without consideration. We know that judges who consistently exceed their norms usually have good reason for sometimes failing to do so.' A recognition that judges might have numbers to adhere to, but they are not bound by statistics alone; their paramount duty lies in delivering good and fair judgements, considered with meticulous care.

The City Civil Court often found itself assigned with the responsibility of handling motor accident compensation cases. It was a heartbreaking reality that the victims involved in these accidents were often from middle-income backgrounds – individuals who used two-wheelers to take their families for holidays to nearby places. It was especially painful when the breadwinner of such a family met with such a tragic accident. In an instant, children lost their fathers and wives, their beloved husbands. These cases typically pitted a grieving family against the formidable opponent of an insurance company, which most often contested the claims. While the verdicts often involved granting substantial compensation to the widows/dependants, a nagging question weighed heavily on Ahmadi's conscience. Would the compensation be received by the rightful claimant, or would it be siphoned away by opportunistic family members?

In response to the dilemma, he devised a unique formula, one which elicited opposition from claimant lawyers as well as insurance companies. He began directing that the awarded compensation be invested in a long-term fixed deposit. From this financial safeguard, the widow would receive a monthly disbursement, enough to sustain a dignified lifestyle for herself and her children. If the claimant had a genuine need for a lump sum amount, such as for a wedding, they could approach the court to release further funds. This unconventional decision aimed not only to provide financial security but also to ensure that the compensation truly served its intended purpose.

Predictably, those most upset the first time when such an order was passed were the lawyers, who were used to receiving a handsome cut from the overall compensation. They stormed out of the courtroom, convening in the adjacent balcony where they vented their frustrations. In loud voices intending to be overheard, they criticized Ahmadi's judgement and confidently predicted that the High Court would quickly overturn the order, possibly within minutes. Interestingly, the only thing they predicted correctly was the timing, as the High Court promptly dismissed their appeal, upholding Ahmadi's decision. They stated that if the judge believed it was necessary to protect a widow who had never managed such a large sum of money, then it was the right course of action. Many years later, Ahmadi would become Executive Chairman of Lok Adalats. Then, a group of lawyers decided to boycott the Lok Adalats unless these investment orders were abolished and the full amount was paid directly to the claimant. Unfazed, Ahmadi took a firm stand. He directed that if the lawyers were unwilling to participate in Lok Adalats, then so be it. None would be organized in their areas. A tough and astute judge, Ahmadi knew that considering the Lok Adalats' track record of delivering quick and efficient settlements, these threats would eventually fizzle out. And that is precisely what happened in due course.[11] Upon his appointment to the High Court, Ahmadi's judgements would lay down guidelines for Claims Tribunals to follow when disposing of claims applications arising under the Motor Vehicles Act of 1939. As time passed, this approach gained acceptance and was adopted by many tribunals across the country.

This formula was further upheld by a division bench of the Supreme Court comprising Justice Ahmadi and Justice M.P. Singh.[12] This judgement stated, 'We would like to make it absolutely clear that in all cases in which compensation is awarded for injury caused in a motor accident, whether by way of adjudication or agreement between the parties the Court/Tribunal must apply these guidelines.'

Ahmadi had begun to earn a reputation for his boldness. His lack of hesitation when disagreeing with his colleagues and ability to back it up with an instinctively sharp understanding of legal nuances – Ahmadi would maintain these character traits until the very end of his career – earning him bouquets and brickbats in equal measure. The Principal Judge who had initially been unhappy about Ahmadi's elevation would later concede in his memoirs, 'It is a different matter; he has turned out to be a good judge.'

Disagreeing with the views of colleagues was one matter, but Ahmadi did not consider it an inhibition to differ from the binding decisions of the High Courts either.[13] In instances where a High Court's binding judgement clashed with Ahmadi's own perspective, he made it a point to record it as such. In several such cases, he observed, '. . . left to me I would have accepted his line of reasoning, had I not been bound by the contrary view taken by the High Court.' Remarkably, every time he made such a statement, his views were eventually upheld. In appeals, the binding decisions were rectified and in non-binding cases, his viewpoint prevailed - even extending to instances where the case was brought before the Delhi High Court and a full bench of the Madras High Court. Clearly, the countless hours spent in the library researching different points of the law were beginning to pay off.

These experiences helped shape Ahmadi's views on the nature of binding decisions.[14] Later in life, he would maintain that the binding character of these decisions should not exceed 25 years, thereby allowing for periodic re-examination. He was also of the view that glaring errors in judgements should be rectifiable by the High Court, rather than allowing erroneous views to persist.

During his time as a judge in the City Civil Court, Ahmadi was also appointed to the Committee for the appointment of Section Officers – initial-level officers in charge of a section or sub-section in government offices. With three of these vacancies to be filled, the Committee had invited applications. As expected, the Committee soon found it had opened its doors to a tidal wave of eager applicants, each vying for the coveted role. Seated around a wooden table, struggling against the relentless heat of Ahmedabad's sultry summer, the judges convened to meticulously evaluate the candidates. The room's solitary, overworked fan creaked in protest above them, forcing the judges to loosen the bands around their necks as the day wore on. Amongst the distinguished silver-haired legal minds of the bench, Aziz Ahmadi stood as the youngest member – not just in the room but within the entire City Civil Court.

A diligent clerk, bearing the weighty task of managing the candidate list, sat just outside the room, carefully organizing the applicants by number and ushering them into the room to be interviewed. Days bled into each other as multiple rounds of interviews were conducted. At each day's end, the clerk received a list of candidate numbers, signifying which ones were to proceed to the next round. Amid this rigorous process, there emerged one clear winner. Surpassing the others on every parameter, this particular gentleman stood out as the front runner. The unanimous decision of the panel was that one of the vacancies was to be set aside for this deserving gentleman, while they continued to deliberate on the remaining positions.

The following morning, as the Committee reconvened for deliberations, one of the judges requested that the door be closed. The clerk obliged, removing himself from the room to offer the Committee privacy. The judge cleared his throat. 'Ahmadi,' he began. 'I have expressed my reservations to my fellow judges concerning the candidate we had all favoured yesterday.

I fear he cannot be appointed.' Puzzled, Aziz sought clarification. 'Why not?' he asked. 'Has something about him come to light that we were unaware of?' 'Yes.' The reply was hesitant. 'You see, I was only made aware of his name this morning. He is a *dheda*.'

The short, simple statement hit Ahmadi like a punch in the chest. *Dheda* is a commonly used derogatory word in Gujarat referring to lower caste individuals. Flashes of childhood memories raced in front of Ahmadi's eyes – sights no child should ever have to see – of lower caste people being beaten for drinking out of wells that higher castes had claimed, others being forced into humiliating practices like tying broomsticks behind their backs as they walked, banging on old utensils as they passed so others might get out of the way before becoming polluted by their shadows. As his memories came flooding back, Aziz felt a red-hot anger pulsating through his veins. Still a young man, he was unable to control the words that came spilling out.

'Over my dead body!' he thundered, his voice echoing through the room. 'I shall not permit this committee to engage in caste-based discrimination. This candidate has earned the position!'

The room fell into a stunned silence. Nobody moved; the very air appeared to have been shocked into stillness. Ahmadi realized his outburst might have been a bit too fervid. Attempting to regain his composure, he reached for the steel glass that had been placed before him, taking a sip of water.

'I apologize for the tone of my words,' he continued, his voice now measured but firm. 'But I stand by my convictions. I will personally see to it that this candidate is appointed.' He looked around at the perturbed faces in front of him; all at least 15 years older than him, senior not only in age but also in the judiciary. Some of these men were closer to his father's age than his own. 'I understand that you may vote me out, as it appears you hold the majority. And you may do so; but I shall have the meeting documented, recording my dissent and articulating the reasons for this Committee's rejection of this outstanding candidate.'

The room remained in stunned silence, each individual grappling with these unexpected twists and turns. The air in the chamber was viscous and hot, the tension thick enough to cut with a knife. Finally, the eldest judge cleared his throat. 'I suggest we table this discussion for now. We still have two more positions to fill; let us focus on that task first.'

By the end of the day, all three positions were filled. The lower caste candidate was rightfully appointed, the confrontation held behind closed doors never to be spoken of again.

By now Aziz was filled with a burning passion that blazed within him like an unquenchable fire. Fuelled by newfound ambition and a determination that would mark and define the rest of his life, he embarked on a remarkable journey of change. Shedding old habits that no longer served his purpose, he bid farewell to the cheap cigarettes and leisurely tea breaks that once punctuated his days. In their stead appeared an almost obsessive seriousness in his pursuits. He willingly poured himself into his work, dedicating long hours that far exceeded the call of duty. He did not restrict himself to the cases that were assigned to him, but also devoted long hours in the court library, researching the Constitution, laws, their boundaries and intricacies. Countless hours were spent in the chambers of his mentor, Justice M.P. Thakkar, where a free exchange of ideas honed the young judge's understanding of the many nuances of the law. Cut from the same cloth, the two friends bonded over their shared ideas about social justice and the role of the judiciary in safeguarding the rights of the people.

The only remnant of the once-carefree boy was now glimpsed in his love for sports. Weekends were still reserved for cricket – long games played early in the mornings with his good friends, Niranjan Bhatt, Salim Durrani, Jasubhai Patel and Justice M.H. Kadri. Of these, Salim Durrani and Jasubhai Patel would go on to become renowned Indian cricket players, donning the national colours on the international stage. Perhaps Aziz too had once dreamt of a career in cricket. In his later years, when he sat down to watch matches on television, his spirit would come alive. Usually soft spoken, he would suddenly erupt with cheers and applause as if he were back on the field himself. Every now and again, when in a particularly good mood, he would place the television on mute and deliver a spontaneous, animated commentary of the match, much to the delight of the household staff. During commercial breaks, he would demonstrate the correct technique of bowling off-spins, *firkis* as he called them. 'Jasubhai was very good at this,' he would say. But sports were now his only indulgence. In every other way, Aziz Ahmadi was a changed man.

This extraordinary transformation did not go unnoticed, especially by his observant bench clerk, who, upon witnessing Ahmadi's tired, red eyes at the end of a gruelling day, quizzically remarked, '*Saheb, tamne bhi pagaar itluj male chhe.*' Translated, it meant, 'Sir, you receive the same salary as everyone else, (so why do you work so much harder?)' But Aziz Ahmadi was no longer working merely for a pay cheque. He was working to make history.

5

A Fork in the Road

It was this insatiable hunger that was the driving force behind Ahmadi's decision to decline the position of Law Secretary when it came knocking at his door. It was an ordinary day when Justice B.J. Divan, the Chief Justice of the Gujarat High Court approached Ahmadi, expressing his intention of recommending him for the prestigious position of Law Secretary-cum-Legal Remembrancer for the state of Gujarat. In this role, Ahmadi would have been at the helm of the State Legal Department, responsible for advising the State Government on legal matters and offering opinions on legal queries raised by government departments. He would serve as an ex-officio Secretary to the Government, tendering advice on legal points arising under the Constitution, State and Central Acts, and other regulations. The department is also responsible for overseeing legal proceedings pending in courts and tribunals, drafting bills for legislation and appointing counsel.

However, accepting this government position would have meant stepping aside from his role in the judiciary for such time he would occupy the position.

But Ahmadi's ambitions burned bright. His sights were set on a seat in the High Court, the next leap in his career, one he believed was within reach.

In the hierarchy of seniority, Ahmadi stood second only to the Principal Judge. Aware that the Principal Judge had already been passed over for elevation not once but twice before, Ahmadi believed that his own moment might be around the corner. Given this attractive prospect, he felt that transitioning to an ex-cadre post would be counterproductive. So, with the utmost respect, Aziz Ahmadi declined. Twice.

But Justice Divan was not an easy man to refuse. He sought the counsel of former Chief Justice of Gujarat High Court, Justice N.M. Miabhoy, hoping to change Ahmadi's mind about the position. Recognizing Justice Divan's determination, Justice Miabhoy invited Ahmadi for a discussion. Rumoured to possess a gaze so piercing that no witness had ever stood up to it in his courtroom, Miabhoy turned his penetrating light-coloured eyes on Aziz Ahmadi and enquired after the reasons holding the young man back. Candidly and honestly, Ahmadi expressed his ambitions and reservations. Miabhoy nodded in understanding, acknowledging the validity of Ahmadi's perspective. But he also imparted a valuable lesson.[1] 'Young man, there is what we call a "judicial culture" viz., if the head of the judiciary sees the need for your services elsewhere, you must yield and leave it to him to protect your interest,' he said. Those words served as a wake-up call for Ahmadi, jolting him out of the tunnel vision that had consumed him. He suddenly realized the error of his ways – in declining the Chief Justice's offer twice, he had inadvertently undermined the authority of the Chief Justice and his own suitability for the role of Law Secretary.

Embarrassed, he sought an audience with Justice Divan. Humble and sincere, Ahmadi expressed his apologies and wholeheartedly gave his consent for the position. Harbouring no ill will, the distinguished Divan graciously informed Ahmadi that the record would reflect that Ahmadi had accepted the position upon his persuasion.

Fully aware of the immense challenge ahead, the Chief Justice was candid with Ahmadi. Engaging in a straightforward conversation, Divan informed Ahmadi that the department was in a state of disarray, operating at a glacial pace and had gained a reputation of being sluggish and ineffective. At the very onset, Divan frankly informed Ahmadi that he was expected to resuscitate the collapsed department and put it back on the rails.

In response, Ahmadi gave the Chief Justice his solemn assurance and promised to do his very best to uphold the trust placed in him. And so, Mr Ahmadi was appointed Secretary of the Legal Department, Government of Gujarat in 1974.

But the task was not going to be easy.[2] Gujarat had been grappling with political and social unrest due to corruption charges against Chief Minister Chimanbhai Patel and the Nav Nirman movement.[3] Unprecedented in the history of Independent India, the mass agitation in Gujarat continued for a full three months, sparing no town or city. People took to the streets to air their dissatisfaction with the State Government and demand the Chief Minister's resignation. Buses were hijacked, private property was looted and destroyed, colleges and court buildings were vandalized. In response, the government sanctioned tear gassing, *lathi* charges, arrests and prohibitory orders. But the disturbances continued. It is estimated that 100 people died during the unrest and many others suffered injuries due to police firing.

As a result, the government ultimately fell, with Chimanbhai[4] forced to resign amid chants of 'Gujarat mein shor hai, Chiman bhai chor hai (There is uproar in Gujarat, Chiman bhai is a thief).' The Assembly was suspended, and Gujarat was placed under President's Rule. This move replaced the elected State Government with a representative of the President of India.

On his first day, Ahmadi was unaware that as the juniormost Secretary, he was expected to record the minutes of these meetings. Until a recently appointed IAS officer seated next to him nudged him and enquired why he wasn't taking notes. Ahmadi explained that he was not aware that he was to record the meetings. A kind fellow, the IAS officer offered his assistance and Ahmadi began diligently taking notes. Although he didn't fully understand the numerous abbreviations, he decided to simply jot them down and seek explanations later. Referring to his notes, and with the help of the newly appointed IAS officer, the minutes were drafted and subsequently sent to the Chief Secretary for approval.

To Ahmadi's pleasant surprise, the minutes were approved and returned to him by his personal secretary who wore a wide grin. Perplexed at the secretary's joy at such a small matter, Ahmadi enquired as to the reason behind the man's delight. The secretary explained that it had been several months since meeting minutes were approved without significant corrections, except for a minor spelling mistake. He showed Ahmadi a copy of the previous minutes marked with large cross marks as a contrast. 'Isn't this a reason to celebrate?' he remarked.

On another occasion, the Chief Secretary happened to meet one of Ahmadi's colleagues at the City Civil Court and during their conversation, expressed his relief stating, 'Thank God we now have a Law Secretary who follows the discussion.'

These early instances provided a glimpse into the state of the department. Ahmadi realized that Justice Divan was, indeed, right – the department was all but collapsed, in severe need of repair.

Upon assuming his new role, Ahmadi wasted no time. Within a day, he had embarked upon a tour of the various branches within the department. It was an opportunity to assess the situation and devise a strategy for motivating the officers without resorting to undue pressure. A diplomatic man, one of Ahmadi's character traits was a peculiar knack for encouraging people to accomplish tasks efficiently without causing unnecessarily stressful situations.

As he explored the department, he couldn't help but notice the poor condition of the furniture, particularly the bare wooden chairs. Determined to improve the working conditions for the staff, Ahmadi instructed the under-secretary to make a request for cotton cushions to be placed upon the chairs. The file, sent to the Department of Finance was returned, rejected.

Unwilling to accept this, Ahmadi returned the file to the Finance Department with a question regarding their own working conditions. 'I would appreciate the view of the finance department, if they (Finance Department staff) have not been provided such a facility.' This time the file made its way back to the Law Department, with the seal of approval. This seemingly small gesture of arranging for cotton cushions proved to be a shot in the arm of the department. They were just cushions, but the thoughtful act left the staff not only delighted but also instantly boosted their morale.

Because Ahmadi and his fellow secretaries were residents of Ahmedabad, their daily commute to Gandhinagar was in a shared carpool. The journey was an opportunity for them to discuss work and share camaraderie. It was during one of these routine car rides that Ahmadi became privy to a long standing inside joke about the Law Department. Nicknamed the 'dumping ground' among the government circles, the department was considered a convenient repository for files that other departments were reluctant to handle or take decisions on. As he heard this phrase, Ahmadi couldn't help but feel a pang of embarrassment. He decided to take action.

Within a mere fifteen days of taking up the mantle as the Law Secretary, a determined Aziz Ahmadi gathered all his officers for a meeting. The room bore the signs of a typical government office, with wooden furniture and stacks of files haphazardly strewn across the desks. The sun streamed in through the windows as Ahmadi addressed his officers. He began by expressing his concern about the department's inefficiencies, particularly the inordinate delays in providing opinions sought by other government departments. 'I am disturbed by the fact that opinions sought by other departments are being greatly delayed, which makes the opinion redundant,' he said. Ahmadi informed the officers that there were murmurs echoing through the corridors of the Secretariat suggesting that the Law Department was a place to dump files when decisions were being deliberately postponed elsewhere to avoid taking responsibility. This kind of talk, he emphasized, was not only disheartening but also a source of shame for everyone associated with the department. A clear target was set: opinions should be delivered within two months at most, to ensure they remained relevant. As he spoke, Ahmadi noticed some of the officers exchanging knowing looks and smirks with each other. Some of them laughed. It was an open show of disrespect, but Ahmadi chose to ignore them. No doubt these cynical officers had grown accustomed to the revolving door of leadership, with each one's promises no more substantial than soda water fizz. To them, Ahmadi was just another, who would eventually give in to the bureaucracy's entrenched inertia.

But Ahmadi wasn't finished. He singled out the Deputy Secretaries who had joined from the judiciary on deputation. He reminded them of the High Court's growing dissatisfaction with the department's state of affairs. He pressed upon them that the watchful eye of the 'big boss' was upon them all, and it was high time they delivered their best. 'If you have any problems, come to me and I will try my best to help you resolve them,' said Ahmadi, closing the meeting.

He then turned his attention to the department's library, recognizing its potential as a valuable resource for research. Hoping to make it more accessible and useful, he engaged in discussions with the librarian. Together, they created a 'research cell'. When a request for an opinion was received, the research cell was given a one-week deadline to complete the necessary research and deliver the findings to the relevant official.

But most importantly, Ahmadi revamped the ways in which the department handled routine appointment proposals from the High Court. He introduced a new approach called 'level jumping' for these routine files, a system that streamlined the decision-making process. These changes proved to be hugely successful. Increasing the department's efficiency by leaps and bounds, proposals were now being processed within days. Eventually, the administrative machinery became so remarkably quick that it caught the attention of the Administrative Judge at the High Court. On one occasion, the judge informed Ahmadi that although the High Court registry had sent its proposals, it was not prepared for their immediate implementation. Typically, the registry had expected a lengthy processing time. A pleased Ahmadi responded saying that the registry may now send them proposals only when they were ready to implement, for processing would no longer take time.

But by no means was the going easy. In the beginning, Aziz struggled to be accepted; his erstwhile position as a judge placing him at odds with his colleagues from the executive. A few short weeks into his appointment, Ahmadi was invited into a closed-door meeting to discuss a sensitive issue. A few months before, the Gujarat State had suspended Panchayat elections under Section 303A of the Panchayat Act, citing disturbances and exceptional circumstances. This suspension had been challenged in the High Court, and the State had lost the case.

In early 1974, Gujarat had witnessed a wave of disturbances that led to the collapse of the State Government and, as mentioned earlier, subsequently resulted in the dissolution of the Gujarat Assembly and the imposition of President's rule in the state. In response to these extraordinary events, the President of India enacted the Gujarat Panchayats (Amendment) Act 8 of 1974, which officially came into effect on 31 March 1974. One of the key provisions introduced by this amendment was the insertion of Section 303A into the Panchayat Act. Under this newly inserted section, authorities were granted the authority to issue a notification stating that it was not advisable or practical to conduct elections for the reconstitution of taluka and district panchayats.

As this matter wound its way to the High Court, the Panchayat Secretary was tasked with attending all the hearings and reporting back to the Law Department. Upon his reassurance that the case was proceeding well in favour of the government, not much notice was taken. But when the verdict was delivered, it turned out to be far from the outcome they had hoped for.

The High Court of Gujarat declared the notification as invalid because it believed that certain conditions required by Section 303A were not met.[5] The key conditions were the existence of disturbances in the state and the government's satisfaction that it was not suitable to hold elections upon the expiration of the term of the Panchayat. The government had argued that there were indeed disturbances in the state at the time, and therefore this emergency provision in the law was used to postpone the elections. They believed it was necessary. The High Court, however, took a narrower view of the law, insisting that the government could only invoke this provision if all the preparations for the election were already complete, like creating voter lists and defining constituencies. They believed that these preparations were unfinished, and so the government's use of Section 303A was invalid. The court further held that since the essential groundwork required before holding elections had not been completed, it was impossible to definitively conclude the feasibility of conducting these elections. Therefore, the government's imposition of the notification lacked a solid justification.

Taken aback at the judgement, the Secretaries of the concerned departments convened a meeting. During the discussions, the Panchayat Secretary, still smarting from the verdict and his own misreading of the courtroom, made an uncharitable remark. He made an unsubstantiated allegation regarding the motives of the bench that had passed the order. Ahmadi, with his customary low tolerance for loose talk, reacted sharply. Responding to Ahmadi's reaction, the Chief Secretary said sarcastically, 'You must realize that Their Lordships' representative is amongst us,' betraying his own views about the new Law Secretary and his reluctance to accept him.

A few days later, a copy of the judgement was sent to Mr Ahmadi, requesting his opinion on the government's chances of winning the case on appeal. Ahmadi examined the document carefully and opined that they had an excellent case should they choose to appeal to the Supreme Court. He explained that despite the setback from the High Court, their chances of success were more than favourable.

And so, the appeal was filed, with express instructions for Ahmadi to personally supervise the case this time, rather than leaving it in the hands of the Panchayat Secretary again. But many senior lawyers were less optimistic about the chances of success of the appeal than Ahmadi was. A respected counsel, a former Chief Justice, informed the department that they had no case and would be better off withdrawing. Left with little choice, Ahmadi declined to approach any more senior counsel. Instead, he reached out to a lawyer who he knew had a relatively lighter workload at the time. Ahmadi's offer to the counsel was that if he was willing to argue the points as formulated by Ahmadi, he could have the brief.

The lawyer accepted this proposal. Ahmadi then went to work building the case and formulating the points of argument for the counsel to present in court. The matter came up before a division bench of the Supreme Court comprising Justices R.S. Sarkaria and Y.V. Chandrachud. As the petitioner's counsel rose to submit his arguments, Ahmadi watched keenly. He had spent several hours with the counsel, formulating the state's case. Deliberating on these submissions, Justice Chandrachud picked up the sheaf of papers presented to him and examined the Act. He then shared the materials with his fellow judge. Following the counsel's argument, eminent lawyer and state counsel Mr I.M. Nanavati was called upon, who argued six crucial points. As the hearing drew to a close, the presiding judge inquired about the matter of costs, revealing that he had made up his mind in favour of the state. The question of costs relates to the winning party, as they are entitled to be awarded compensation for legal fees and other expenses. Suppressing his excitement, Ahmadi leaned over to the state counsel and advised him not to press for costs, to leave it to the discretion of the bench.

Ultimately, the Supreme Court ruled that 1974 had seen serious disturbances in Gujarat that had led to loss of life and property.[6] The gravity of the situation was severe enough to necessitate the imposition of Article 356 in the state. Even on the date of the notification of the delay of Panchayat elections, the situation remained far from normal. Recognizing 303A as an emergency provision, the court made mention of its inherent capacity to allow the State Government to tide over a difficult situation fraught with dangerous possibilities. The court also took notice of the requirement of a situation 'by reason of' disturbances. The critical phrase implies an immediate and causal connection between the disturbances and the resulting situation. Crucially, the Supreme Court refused to delve into the question of the inexpediency of holding elections. Rather, it focused solely on whether the precondition for exercising this power had been met. 'Once reasonable nexus between satisfaction and facts constituting first requirement is shown then exercise of power under Section 303A not being colourable or motivated by extraneous considerations is not open to judicial review.' The High Court order was set aside, and the judgement was in favour of the State.

During his time as Law Secretary, Mr Ahmadi was entrusted with a unique responsibility of overseeing the administration of two of Gujarat's most revered and prominent temples. As Ahmadi began to examine the accounts of these, he found that the temples were being managed through state funds. But both the temples should have been self-sustaining due to the substantial income generated from devotees.

The first temple, in particular, presented a startling revelation. It was found that the entire income from the temple was being funnelled into the pockets of the *pujari*, the temple priest. Additionally, devotees traditionally offered saris to the deity, each one differing in value, but all considered blessed by the goddess. It was found that in addition to pocketing the entire income received by the temple, the pujari was also exploiting these offerings and selling them at exorbitant prices for personal gain.

When Ahmadi confronted him about the financial impropriety, the impertinent pujari responded saying that since the devotees came to see his *aarti*, the income too was rightfully his. Incensed by the brazen response, Ahmadi took quick and decisive action. He directed that a charity box be placed in the temple, accompanied by a tablet that clearly conveyed that the funds collected would be dedicated solely towards the maintenance of the temple. As expected, the pujari was livid at the curtailment of the income he had become used to. His objections were met with a firm reminder – only the money offered at the deity's feet belonged to him. The remainder was for the upkeep of the temple.

Now, because of the placement of the box, devotees began to place their offerings into the donation box, rather than in the pujari's hand. Powerless, the pujari eventually approached Ahmadi, stating that he was struggling to meet his expenses. With a noticeably changed demeanour, he sought permission to distribute *prasad* from an alternate location where there was no box, hoping that some devotees would offer their donations directly to him. Recognizing the sincerity in his plea, Mr Ahmadi readily granted the request as the donations from the box were more than sufficient to meet the temple's maintenance expenses.

As Ahmadi continued to dig into the temple's affairs, a pattern began to emerge in the visitor's book that caught his attention. A particular deputy secretary's name appeared with remarkable frequency, suggesting unusually frequent visits to the temple premises. Ahmadi grew immediately suspicious and decided to make enquiries. Concerns arose and disturbing rumours began to make their way to Ahmadi. It was whispered that this specific official had been surreptitiously and illicitly acquiring saris from the temple and discreetly selling them in Gandhinagar – some of which were very expensive. Word of these allegations eventually reached Chief

Justice Divan's ears, who reached out to Ahmadi to enquire whether there was any truth to them. After a thorough investigation, Ahmadi confirmed these suspicions and no time was wasted in taking decisive action. A formal departmental inquiry was initiated. The inquiry, conducted fairly and meticulously, eventually led to the dismissal of the deputy secretary from service.

The second prominent temple – the Dwarka Temple – required a different approach. Ahmadi began by issuing an administrative order to the pujaris, directing that 25 per cent of the temple's collections be reclaimed from the pujaris and redirected towards temple repairs. The pujaris decided to challenge this order in the High Court. Ahmadi was prepared for it to be struck down, for his strategy was ultimately a different one. The notice was struck down, and the court directed the Law Department to follow due process by issuing the temple a showcause notice so that both parties could be heard in court. Immediately, the showcause notice was issued, but this time, demanding 50 per cent of the collections. This notice created panic and furore; the pujaris' counsel sought clarification from Mr Ahmadi. Ahmadi calmly explained that they were now bound by the High Court's order, and that all actions would be strictly in accordance with the law. But he also dangled a carrot. He made it clear that if the pujaris were willing to pay 25 per cent by mutual agreement, they could bypass the rigours of legal proceedings as well as possible defeat in which case they would forgo 50 per cent of their income. It was a manoeuvre of the finest diplomatic finesse – the pujaris grudgingly agreed to forfeit 25 per cent of their income towards the upkeep of the temple and legal proceedings became unnecessary.

But Ahmadi's efforts didn't end here. As the administrator of the temples, he was aware that one of them presented a safety concern. On each full moon day, worshippers seeking *darshan* flocked to this temple, converging at the narrow entrance. Many times, these crowds led to dangerous stampedes resulting in several injuries, with some individuals being tragically crushed. Recognizing the urgency of the issue, a decision was made to widen the entry passage at the chowk to ensure the safety of the devotees. The ambitious plan not only included widening the entrance, but also enhancing the surrounding area and renovating the temple premises. It is worth noting that many today might find it surprising that a Muslim official like Ahmadi would invest so much effort towards the beautification and enhancement of a Hindu temple. But for a 'hardcore secularist' like Aziz Ahmadi, such distinctions scarcely crossed his mind.

In the meantime, there was agitation in Delhi. Opposition leader Morarji Desai went on a hunger strike demanding early elections in Gujarat, his home state.[7] At the time, Gujarat had been under President's Rule for a year. The Central Government eventually acquiesced to the demand. But the 1975 Gujarat Assembly Elections threw up a hung house. The Janata Front, consisting of a multi-party coalition, had emerged as the frontrunner but it lacked a clear majority to form a government.[8] Of these parties, the INC(O) had won 56 seats, Bharatiya Jan Sangh won 18, Bharatiya Lok Dal won 2 and the Socialist Party won 1. Babubhai Jasbhai Patel was fielded as the candidate for Chief Minister.[9] This left the Governor of Gujarat in a tricky position, disinclined as he was to ask Babubhai to form the government without enough support to constitute a majority. Attempting to find a way out of the conundrum, Babubhai approached the Governor with a potential solution. He conveyed that Chimanbhai Patel had expressed his willingness to offer external support to back Babubhai's government if it were to take charge in the state. Since his resignation, Chimanbhai had deflected from the Congress and floated a new political party called Kisan Mazdoor Lok Paksha (KMLP) which had secured 12 seats.

This was an unexpected development, since several of the Janata Front's constituents had recently conducted a political campaign against Patel.[10] Seeking counsel on this matter, the Governor called upon the Law Secretary to seek his opinion. After carefully assessing the situation, Ahmadi's recommendation was that any agreement of support should be documented to solidify the basis for inviting Babubhai Patel to lead the government. 'If that is the case, Your Excellency should ask for it in writing and not depend on any oral assurance,' advised Ahmadi.[11] And so, the commitment was provided in writing and Babubhai Patel was consequently invited to form the government in Gujarat.

But peaceful times were elusive. A week after Babubhai Patel formed the government in Gujarat on 18 June 1975, the country stood still in shock and disbelief. The ominous storm of the National Emergency swept across India on the night of 25 June 1975, lasting for almost two years.[12] The trigger for this drastic move was a damning verdict by Justice Jagmohan Lal Sinha of the Allahabad High Court, who had found Mrs Indira Gandhi, the Prime Minister of India, guilty of employing unfair practices during the 1971 Lok Sabha elections. Stunned at the verdict, Mrs Gandhi, represented by the eminent Nani Palkhivala, appealed and the case landed on the desk of Justice Krishna Iyer.[13] Iyer, presiding over the case on the vacation bench, granted a conditional stay on the Allahabad court's order, but with a caveat. Mrs Gandhi was barred from voting as a member of parliament. This decision sparked a tinderbox of protests across the country, demanding her resignation. But Mrs Gandhi refused to step down. Instead, President Fakhruddin Ali Ahmed, acting on the counsel of Mrs Gandhi, invoked Article 352 of the Constitution to declare a National Emergency. This declaration came hand-in-hand with the suspension of fundamental rights under Article 359 of the Constitution, which allows for the suspension of certain Articles; specifically, Article 20, which provides certain protections with respect to conviction for offenses and Article 21, which enshrines the right to life and personal liberty.

The controversial and repressive Maintenance of Internal Security Act (MISA) was enforced, giving the Centre broad powers under which it could make preventive arrests, detain individuals and confiscate properties – powers the government did not hesitate to use.

During these unsettling years of political unrest, a wave of arrests and detentions ensued, making public life heavily restricted. Citizens lived in fear of expressing any criticism of the government, knowing that dissenting voices were swiftly and ruthlessly repressed. Several politicians, journalists and activists found themselves behind bars. Opposition leaders Mr Morarji Desai, Mr Atal Bihari Vajpayee and Mr L.K. Advani were arrested and incarcerated under MISA. The press faced draconian censorship, with journalists being issued 'ground rules' and 'guidelines' under which they were allowed to report. Neither reports on detention nor release from detention were permitted to be printed. These were the 'Black Days' of Indian democracy.

Ahmadi, too, was deeply perturbed by the unfolding events during this period. His principles vehemently opposed any actions that infringed upon the fundamental human rights and democratic freedom of individuals. In his role as Law Secretary, he had a unique vantage point, allowing him to observe closely the wrongful detentions and misuse of MISA. But it was also a difficult time. As Law Secretary, he was acutely aware of the fragile landscape and the tightrope walk required to ensure smooth and cordial functioning between the state and central departments.

As Ahmadi describes it, they were constantly walking on a 'razor's edge'.[14] It took all his diplomatic skills and tact to ensure that a fine rapport was maintained between the two departments. One particular case involved the suggested confiscation of a press for publishing news that displeased the central government. When eminent editor Kuldip Nayar was released from detention, a particular publication having published a news article titled 'Kuldip Nayar released' invited the ire of the central government. At the time, the government had already issued orders to the media preventing them from reporting on both, detentions and releases of detainees. Immediately came the diktat from Delhi. 'Confiscate the press' that had printed the story. Urgently, the home department sought legal advice from the law department on the matter.

The legal department of Gujarat advised against the confiscation; however, the central government appeared adamant. After a few rounds of the file being sent back and forth for review, the Union Joint Secretary made a mistake. He informed the State Home Secretary that the union law department had found their proposal of confiscation legally sound, and that immediate action may follow.

Pouncing on the opportunity that had presented itself, Ahmadi made a recommendation, one he knew they would be unable to follow. He got the state home secretary on the phone and suggested, 'you can inform him (the Union Joint Secretary) that under the concerned law, since both the central government and the state government were concurrently empowered, we suggest to him that since the central law department was of the view that the proposal was sound, let them pass the order and forward the same to the Gujarat government for execution.' But in reality, the union law department had never given their approval to the proposal, which left the Joint Secretary in an impossible predicament. Perhaps he had hoped that upon receiving news of the union government's approval, the state department would follow suit. But Ahmadi's response threatened to expose this manoeuvre. The department couldn't proceed with an order they didn't have, nor instruct the Gujarat government to execute it. Neither could they admit their error. Caught in this inescapable dilemma, they took the only way out: they simply abandoned the project.

And so, the proposal faded away, never to see the light of day again.

One sweltering afternoon around 4 p.m., another file was received from the Home Department. It was a case pertaining to the release of an individual who had been detained. The High Court had already passed an order for his release. Perusing the file quickly, Ahmadi summoned his deputy secretary who arrived in a flurry of urgency. The day was coming to a close and the sun cast long shadows over the bustling streets of Gandhinagar. Ahmadi informed the gentleman that a concise three-line note was all that was required to return the file to the home secretary before the end of the day at 5 p.m.

But at 4.45 p.m., the Deputy Secretary stormed into Mr Ahmadi's office, beads of perspiration forming on his furrowed brow. Fuming, his eyes flashed with frustration as he informed Ahmadi that the Home Department intended to use the Law Department to detain the individual despite the High Court order. He informed Ahmadi that it had been suggested that the Law Department delay the movement of the file, preventing the release of the individual. Ahmadi calmly acknowledged this intention but refused to comply. He quickly signed the note of release and instructed it be delivered to the Home Department before 5 p.m., thereby ensuring the release of the detainee without further delay.

As the day gave way to evening and they embarked on their return journey to Ahmedabad, the car was once again filled with the familiar faces of the Secretaries. As the golden light of the sun gave way to the soothing blue hue of twilight, the home secretary made a light-hearted comment. 'The law department has suddenly adopted a supersonic speed.' Ahmadi laughed. 'No longer a dumping ground,' he said, 'So, you better be on your guard just as I am on mine.' The additional chief secretary interjected saying, 'Mr Ahmadi, this is a great compliment coming from the home secretary. You owe us a chocolate.' Ahmadi readily agreed and the men chuckled as the sun dipped below the horizon, casting a golden glow over the picturesque landscapes of Gujarat.

At home, however, Ahmadi remained alert. The Emergency was in full force, and he knew that despite his position, there would be no immunity offered to him if he or his family were caught on the wrong foot. His son, Huzefa Ahmadi was a curious seven-year-old boy, still trying to make sense of the world around him. Nonplussed by the abstract concept of Emergency, he was more interested in inventing childish games. Having received snippets of information from the radio and older boys in school, he was aware that Indira Gandhi was a controversial figure, deeply disliked. One evening, Huzefa decided to emulate the older boys at school. They had been chanting a catchy and rebellious slogan, 'Indira Gandhi *Murdabad*,' literally meaning 'Indira Gandhi Down'. In his innocence, he thought it was some sort of a game or chant, unaware of its political significance. With mischief in his eyes, Huzefa began to march around the dining table, chanting the slogan he had picked up. His small voice echoed through the room, *'Indira Gandhi Murdabad, Indira Gandhi Murdabad!'* Ahmadi, seated at the table, was startled by his son's sudden and unexpected display. Alarmed, he whipped around urgently and grabbed Huzefa's sleeve to slow him down. 'Sshh, Emergency *chhe*,' he whispered. His son was too young to comprehend the gravity of the situation, but Ahmadi knew that even a child's game within the confines of their home could spell untold troubles. Such was the climate of fear that even Ahmadi, a staunch defender of human rights, appointed by the government, found himself curbing his own fundamental freedom of speech. Two decades later, as a Supreme Court judge, he would uphold another's freedom of speech, stating, 'Speech is God's gift to mankind ... Freedom of speech and expression is thus a natural right, which a human being acquires on birth. It is, therefore, a basic human right.'[15]

Because the enforcement of fundamental rights had been suspended under Article 359 along with the declaration of Emergency, tens of people, many of them journalists and activists, were being imprisoned every day. It is estimated that by the end of the Emergency[16] more than one lakh people had been arrested and placed behind bars. Many of these arrests were conducted in a dubious fashion.[17] District magistrates who held significant administrative authority in their respective districts would simply place their signatures on blank forms, leaving it to the police to fill in the details of the persons to be arrested. Individuals were targeted based on pre-prepared lists and intelligence records. Dissenters, political opposition leaders, activists, journalists – anyone could be next.

Families and well-wishers of the detainees flooded the gates of the High Courts, filing numerous writ petitions seeking the release of their loved ones. Some High Courts delivered judgements in favour of the petitioners, ordering the immediate release of those detained.

But the government, determined to tighten its grip and quash all opposition, took the legal battle to the highest court of the land, the Supreme Court of India. The judiciary, typically the guardian of the fundamental rights of citizens, now found itself facing immense pressure and the fear of upsetting the executive.

A Constitution Bench, composed of five esteemed judges, was constituted to hear the historic ADM Jabalpur vs. Shivkant Shukla case. The question before the bench was whether, under Presidential Orders issued on 27 June 1975, a person detailed under MISA could be prevented from seeking a writ of habeas corpus in a High Court. The bench included Justices A.N. Ray, H.R. Khanna, M.H. Beg, Y.V. Chandrachud and P.N. Bhagwati.

When Justice Khanna asked Attorney General Niren De, 'Supposing some policeman, for reasons of enmity not of state, kills someone, would there be a remedy?' De's response was: 'My Lord, not so long as the Emergency lasts.'[18]

Vehemently opposing this crisis of fundamental freedoms were legal stalwarts such as Soli Sorabjee, Shanti Bhushan and V.N. Tarkunde.

The bench rendered its verdict in April 1976. The decision was divided.[19] The majority upheld the detentions stating that a person's right not to be unlawfully detained (i.e. habeas corpus) can be suspended in the interest of the State.

But there was one lone yet courageous dissenter. In a historic dissenting judgement, Justice Khanna championed the cause of fundamental rights, boldly affirming the detainees' rights in the face of government overreach.

Yet, this principled stand came at great personal cost. Justice Khanna paid for his dissent with the loss of the position of Chief Justice of India, a position that should have rightfully been his. Instead, he was superseded and his junior, Justice Beg, was elevated to the apex position. Justice Khanna immediately resigned, eliciting widespread condemnation of the government among civil society, legal luminaries and intellectuals alike. Khanna's dedication to human rights and civil liberties made his supersession a severe affront to constitutional principles and judicial independence.

Many years later,[20] Justice Bhagwati would apologize for his judgement in ADM Jabalpur, calling it 'an act of weakness'.[21] Forty-two years later, Justice Y.V. Chandrachud's son, Justice D.Y. Chandrachud, would go on to form part of a bench that overturned this judgement, stating he knew his father always believed the judgement to have been wrong.

Justice Ahmadi recalls this judgement as deeply regretful and the era as one of the very few times in the history of Independent India when the judiciary abandoned its duties.[22] Although the judiciary might be considered by some to be the weakest link between the executive, legislature and judiciary, because it is armed with neither the power of the purse nor of the sword, it is nevertheless the only one empowered to protect citizens from the excesses of State and protect their rights.

Holding Justice Khanna in the highest regard, Ahmadi would later describe him as '... an erudite judge, a daring dissenter to sustain people's life and liberty, a gracious defender of the Rule of Law on the Bench whose ambition for promotion to Chief Justiceship gave little purchase over his diamond-hard judicial convictions.'

While Aziz Ahmadi's own journey to the Supreme Court was still many years ahead, the ADM Jabalpur case left a deep mark on him, shaping his own perspectives and convictions.

In the twilight of his life, he would fondly reminisce about the numerous prestigious events he had experienced, including state dinners at the Rashtrapati Bhawan and tea with the Queen of England at the Buckingham Palace. However, he spoke of the invitation to dine at Justice Khanna's residence with genuine delight and respect. Men of similar convictions, Ahmadi held Khanna in the highest regard.

In the meantime, Babubhai Patel's government, having remained in power for less than a year, lost the floor test in the state legislative assembly.[23] Chimanbhai Patel had dissolved his political party, KMLP, and withdrawn support from the Janata Front.

And Gujarat was, once again, placed under President's rule.

During this period of President's rule, two advisors were appointed by the President of India to assist the Governor of Gujarat in governing the state.[24] Ahmadi was assigned to Senior Administrator, Mr H.C. Sarin, a remarkably bright officer, personal friend of Jawaharlal Nehru and trusted confidante of Prime Minister Indira Gandhi who had previously held the position of Defence Secretary of India.[25] Educated at Cambridge University, Sarin was impeccably turned out, well read, soft spoken yet firm. He chaired the weekly secretarial meetings as the principal official in charge of administration and conducted them with exceptional professionalism.

The removal of the right to challenge detention orders in the High Court ushered in a sense of lawlessness paradoxically spearheaded by the government machinery itself. It appeared to have opened the floodgates to what can only be described as a numbers game. Each state was vying to detain as many individuals as possible. Distressed, Ahmadi made every effort to lose this race, with his department detaining far fewer individuals compared to neighbouring states like Maharashtra, which appeared to be winning the game. On one occasion, Mr Sarin jokingly remarked that the State Administrative Officer was miserable as Gujarat's numbers were so much lower than Maharashtra's. Ahmadi responded mischievously saying, 'We do not want too many gentlemen as state guests.' But tensions had never run higher, and the legal department had never been as vigilant as it grappled with this extraordinary challenge.

Mr Ahmadi's role in the law department had become uniquely delicate, especially because Gujarat was again under President's Rule. With the State Home Department receiving directions from the Central Home Ministry, they frequently sought legal guidance from the Law Department, particularly on sensitive matters. It was imperative that the state and central departments maintained cordial terms in such a sensitive environment.

In the meantime, the Congress had used this time wisely to strategically rebuild its support base.[26] Sensing the turning tides, several political leaders had deflected to the behemoth party. By 1976, the Congress Legislature Party had garnered enough support to command a majority in the Assembly and was asked to form the government. Deliberations on possible chief ministerial candidates were ongoing in Delhi.

One morning, amid the ceaseless hum of bureaucratic machinery, Ahmadi's phone rang. It was an unusual phone call from Mr Sarin's office, commanding Ahmadi's urgent presence. Swiftly setting aside the file he was engrossed in, Ahmadi rushed out of the door, informing his personal secretary that he would be gone for the day. Mr Sarin was waiting for Ahmadi at the porch, already seated in a car that was ready and waiting. Ahmadi's curious eyes met Sarin's who smiled and patted the seat next to him. A few minutes into the journey, Sarin leaned in, lowering his voice to a confidential whisper. 'We are going to meet the next Chief Minister-to-be,' he divulged. Upon their arrival at the gentleman's opulent bungalow, the officers were greeted with a lavish spread of tea and snacks, during which several veiled conversations alluding to matters of the state followed.

But doubt had begun to claw its way into Mr Ahmadi's thoughts.[27] It was on the return journey to the Secretariat with the golden sun setting on the horizon that he eventually voiced his concern. Leaning closer to Mr Sarin, Ahmadi said, 'Sir, I doubt if this gentleman can be sworn in (as Chief Minister).' Alarmed, Sarin shot back, 'What are you talking about? Every exercise is complete right up to the Prime Minister's level.' Aziz, now worried, said, 'Sir, give me half an hour to verify my doubt.' Upon reaching the Secretariat, Ahmadi plunged headfirst into the tangle of legal provisions to validate his suspicions. Indeed, he was right. The gentleman was holding an office of profit, thereby legally rendering him ineligible for the position. An anxious Sarin lost no time in contacting Mr Niren De, the formidable Attorney General of India at the time. Mr De responded the same evening, to confirm Ahmadi's suspicions – and to convey a compliment. Mr Ahmadi's astute observation had averted a potential political crisis, sparing Mrs Gandhi, the Prime Minister of India, from an embarrassing predicament. A short time later, in December 1976, Madhavsinh Solanki was appointed as the Chief Minister of Gujarat.

While the identity of the politician who came so close to becoming the Chief Minister of Gujarat remains undisclosed, Ahmadi had made himself an enemy, one who would harbour lifelong resentment and publicly speak against him throughout his career.

Aziz Ahmadi had been Law Secretary for the State of Gujarat for a little less than two years when Justice Divan sent word to him that he was considering his repatriation to his parent cadre, the City Civil Court. Ahmadi did not enquire into the details of the position, but he was informed by the secretary to the Chief Minister that he was being considered for elevation to the High Court. Ahmadi was, of course, delighted at the news and gladly accepted the offer for repatriation. Correctly anticipating the bureaucratic delays that were expected to arise from his transfer from the Secretariat to the High Court, Ahmadi settled down for an eight to ten months-long wait. As Aziz Ahmadi bid farewell to his previous position, the Law Minister commemorated his tenure with heartfelt words. In a poignant send-off speech the minister shared that complaints from the High Court regarding sluggishness had finally been eliminated, and referred to Mr Ahmadi's tenure as a 'golden era,' a recognition that warmed Ahmadi's heart.

But the tussle between the judiciary and executive was far from over. Before Ahmadi's appointment could be confirmed, the central government introduced a new transfer policy for judges. Determined to oust 'difficult' judges who were seen as too independent from their respective High Courts, the government swiftly implemented the policy with the intention of changing the judicial landscape in the country. Consequently, the Gujarat High Court witnessed the departure of its

Chief Justice, the esteemed and courageous Justice Divan, replaced by the equally formidable and respected S. Obul Reddy, former Chief Justice of the Andhra Pradesh High Court. Justice Reddy's reputation as a strict administrator and strong disciplinarian was well known. He had little tolerance for idleness during working hours and would not hesitate to reprimand anyone found nodding off in their chambers. On occasion, he would instruct his private secretary to prepare his car and have the fuel tank filled, often without disclosing his destination. While the car would appear to be heading towards Baroda, it would eventually arrive in Bhavnagar. The purpose of these mysterious trips was to inspect and ensure all courts were operating as scheduled. Under Chief Justice Reddy's leadership, every presiding judge ensured that all courtrooms under their jurisdiction were functioning properly, so as to avoid Reddy's ire.

As the days went by with no news, Ahmadi couldn't help but wonder if Justice Divan had apprised the new Chief Justice of his own upcoming elevation. His question was soon answered in a rather casual yet significant conversation. One day, Justice Reddy casually asked Ahmadi if he knew the Law Minister of the Central Government. Ahmadi responded in the negative, adding, 'but even if I did, I would not speak to him (to extend me any favours).' To this, Justice Reddy responded, 'In that case I will have to shake up the Delhi authorities.' A hint that he intended to take the matter into his own hands and make good on Justice Divan's promise by helping to expedite Ahmadi's promised elevation. It wasn't long before the official orders for Ahmadi's elevation arrived, marking the beginning of a new and momentous chapter in his life. At the time of his elevation, the Gujarat High Court had no Muslim judges, making Ahmadi, once again, the only Muslim judge on the bench – this time, of the High Court. Elevated to the High Court at the rare age of forty-four, he now dared to hope for a seat at the Supreme Court.

What remained was to see if he would make it to Chief Justice. He would.

6

The Citizen's Judge

Amena Ahmadi's life was the very picture of contentment. The large, two-storeyed bungalow near the Law Gardens, Dhulia Court that was allotted to her husband, the 44-year-old newest judge of the High Court, was a far cry from the small flat that the family had been accustomed to squeezing itself into. The sprawling front gardens, a lush oasis of greenery with its dew-kissed grass and the symphony of chirping birds became the family's cherished spot for morning tea. It was where Aziz indulged in leisurely evening strolls, a quiet moment stolen from his ever-growing responsibilities, spent amid the fragrance of blooming roses and marigolds. The smaller back gardens had been turned into thriving kitchen gardens in which Ama had instructed the gardeners to plant a variety of seasonal vegetables. Here, rows of plump red tomatoes, slender eggplant and lush leafy greens thrived under the sun and Ama's watchful gaze. The aroma of earthy soil mixed with the sweet scent of blossoms as she walked around the vegetable beds holding her ghagra a few inches off the ground to prevent it from trailing in the mud. Approaching middle age herself, Ama had put on weight, the new fullness a physical manifestation of the contentment and joy that had taken root within her. She smiled more easily now, her plump, porcelain face telling a tale of happiness. Despite the extra pounds, Ama had managed to gracefully maintain her elegance and poise. No longer required to engage in dull, joyless housework, Ama breathed a sigh of relief and set about delegating these tasks to the staff that had been provided to her. In this, she would prove to be remarkably capable, running the home like clockwork, quickly learning all the norms of propriety and protocol.

On the terrace of the bungalow was a small, sparse room. This room had been claimed by Aziz and converted into a home office. Instead of the conventional table and chair, Aziz had opted for a cosy mattress placed directly on the floor – a *baithak* of sorts – strewn with a mix of cushions and bolsters. It was here, surrounded by towers of heavy hardbound books, dusty court files held together with drawstring and stacks of letters arranged like a fortress around him that Aziz spent long hours engrossed in his cases and the many additional responsibilities he was entrusted with. Here he would remain for most part of the day, dressed in a crisp white kurta-pajama, the front placket held together with small gold buttons, drinking endless cups of sugarless tea, poring over papers and writing on small pieces of paper slowly and deliberately. Cardboard-bound files lay open on either side of him, with notepads and ballpoint pens littered everywhere. In the absence of an air conditioner or cooler, the resourceful staff sprinkled water over the terrace during the summer months to provide him relief from the scorching heat. A large window framed by billowing curtains allowed the warm sunlight to stream in, the molten gold casting a soft glow over him as he sat, legs stretched out and crossed at the ankle, spectacles perched on the bridge of his nose, brow furrowed, with a file on his lap. This was Aziz's private sanctuary, forbidden to anyone but Ama. Even she entered sparingly for this was his sacred legal world, his sanctum. A small bell connected to the kitchen ensured that he was never out of reach of his beloved cups of tea and Surti *chevra* (savoury snack). A pista green telephone rested on the floor, serving as a vital link to his ever-ready stenographer. After dinner, Aziz would return to this baithak, where the files and books would once again come to life. Sometimes, too weary to make the journey to his bedroom, Aziz would fall asleep in his office. Justice Ahmadi had become a busy man indeed. Gone were the days of leisurely strolling through local markets to select the freshest greens and finest cuts of meat for their dinners – the shopping was now handled by the staff. The spontaneous movies and restaurant dinners also became casualties amid Ahmadi's ever-increasing workload. Moreover, the demands of propriety befitting a High Court judge had naturally curtailed these excursions. But the one indulgence the Ahmadis refused to relinquish was the precious evenings spent in the company of friends, where laughter and love provided a welcome respite from their demanding lives. This is where Aziz lit up, infusing the atmosphere with his infectious humour. He delighted in cracking jokes, playfully teasing his friends and their children whom he regarded as his own. His quick wit, mischief and sharp humour infused these evenings with laughter and lively banter.

Yet, with intense focus on his career, there was increasingly less time for family activities. This withdrawal from day-to-day family life occurred slowly at first, but soon solidified into an intrinsic part of his personality. This attribute, having taken root in his forties, would remain a constant until he was well into his seventies.

This new phase of life proved to be a source of delight for both his children. Fifteen-year-old teenager, Tasneem Ahmadi was less concerned about her father's illustrious career and more about the prospect of finally having her own room. A slender girl with thick cascading hair that fell to the small of her back – much like her mother's – she detested her long, tightly woven plaits, admired by everyone else. At the first hint of adulthood, she would rebel and choose a pixie cut, which she sports to this day. Exuberant and spirited, Tasneem and Aziz with their easy laughs and quick tempers, shared a strikingly similar temperament. Huzefa Ahmadi, six years younger and much quieter, took after his mother, content with the large new gardens where he could find solitude. From his father, he had received a love for sports – eventually going on to play table tennis competitively at the national level.

Upon discovering that Justice Thakkar was now their neighbour, Tasneem Ahmadi too made the most of her parents' close friendships. She would often wait eagerly for her father to return from his day at court, knowing that his arrival meant that Justice Thakkar, who lived just three doors down, would have also returned by then. No doubt, Mrs Thakkar, known for keeping a wonderful table, would have laid out a delightful spread of snacks ready for her husband – a temptation too irresistible to overcome. Lured by the promise of delectable treats, Tasneem would embark on the short walk to their bungalow. Soon, it became a routine of sorts, the young teenager spending many evenings at the table of her father's mentor, her lively chatter filling their home with laughter.

This cherished routine was enjoyed and eagerly anticipated by both, Tasneem and the Thakkars alike. In these simple neighbourly gestures, they found the warmth and flavour of their closely knit community, which added a special richness to their lives.

The Thakkars were staunch practitioners of socialism – not only did they donate generously, but they also lived in relative simplicity and austerity. Their home was simply decorated, their lifestyle modest. Special occasions like weddings were celebrated as intimate gatherings devoid of grandeur and unnecessary expenditure. This dedication to simplicity was not merely a political ideology for the Thakkars, but a way of life demonstrated every day in their daily choices.

As a High Court judge, Ahmadi was becoming accustomed to receiving a significant amount of mail, including numerous letters from the general citizenry. One of the tasks his secretary performed was sifting through this daily mail, setting aside those deemed important enough for His Lordship's attention. One evening, Justice Ahmadi was going through his daily ritual. Often, he found the stillness of the night allowing him uninterrupted time to tend to correspondence. As he methodically sliced open envelopes with a silver letter opener, he found that most of the letters were routine matters, legal queries and administrative affairs. But one letter stood out from the rest. Its envelope bore no distinguishing marks and its handwriting was unfamiliar. But the sender was not. The letter bore the distinct seal of the trade union.[1] As he began reading its contents, Ahmadi was shaken, his conscience stirred.[2] The words were a detailed account of the harrowing exploitation of impoverished migrant workers in Gujarat's sugar industry. The letter was no less than a heartfelt plea for help. Reaching out for his notepad, Justice Ahmadi scribbled a rough note. It was a directive to himself, a reminder to take action on this issue. This humble letter, penned by an unnamed hand would lead to one of the seminal cases of Justice Ahmadi's tenure on the Gujarat High Court bench.

Sugarcane harvesting was an incredibly arduous task, one so demanding that even the impoverished Adivasis of Gujarat and those from the Scheduled Castes and Tribes, were reluctant to take it on. Consequently, labourers had to be brought in from Dhule in Maharashtra to work in the sugarcane fields of the South Gujarat sugarcane belt. These labourers were locally referred to as *koytas* – a name derived from the tool they used for harvesting the sugarcane. Paid a pittance, the workers were expected to not only cut the sugarcane, but also clean the shoots, delicately remove the leaves, cut the stalks into appropriately sized sections, skilfully bundle the sugarcane and then manually transport these bundled sugarcane loads to the designated vehicles. Once loaded, the bundles were tied securely with ropes.[3] At the end of the season, the fields were cleaned by the same workers. In exchange for this gruelling labour, these workers were paid a pittance that amounted to roughly Rs. 5–7 per day. Even on these terms, the workers had no idea if the payment they received was fair because the calculation, based on the weight of harvested sugarcane, was undertaken by the company. Because these wages were paid at the end of the season, an advance for millets (jowar) was provided. The workers, therefore, lived on a diet exclusively comprising of jowar rotis and a chutney made of red chillies and salt for the entire season. Without any savings or steady income, the labourers were forced to borrow for sustenance, thus quickly bonding themselves for the next season as well. At the end of the season, they left with a burden of debt, very few savings, if at all, and perhaps a dhoti or a sari and blouse piece each.

Upon receiving a report from the concerned committee that highlighted and verified this information, Justice Ahmadi was satisfied that the case deserved to be heard as a Public Interest Litigation (PIL).[4] He instructed the court registrar to treat the letter he had received as a formal writ petition against all the sugar factories that employed migrant labourers.

The powerful and wealthy sugar industries responded to the court's notice by sending their best lawyers to represent them. Meanwhile, the sugar factories in Maharashtra also realized that an unfavourable ruling by the Gujarat High Court could set a precedent affecting them as well, so they too sent their armies of lawyers. And so, the sugar lobby was ultimately represented by nearly all the leading members of the Gujarat and Maharashtra Bar.

The parties with vested interests in the case were aware that the sugarcane harvesting season was set to end in approximately 15 days. Beyond this deadline, the labourers who were predominantly illiterate, undocumented and living in poverty, would start their journey back to their villages, at which point it would become almost impossible to trace them in order to make additional payments. It was doubtful whether they were even informed about the PIL that was being argued on their behalf in the courts. Given this situation, even a short delay in legal proceedings would serve their purpose of frustrating the judicial exercise. Therefore, the legal counsel representing these parties made every possible effort to drag out and delay the hearings. But the bench had anticipated such manoeuvres. They stymied every attempt at delays and pressed on. Once the hearings were completed, the bench passed an interim order directing that the workers be compensated according to the minimum wage set by the State Government.

Since a team of two workers constituted a koyta, typically an adult male accompanied by a female or a young boy, the wages were fixed accordingly. One koyta would therefore be entitled to receive 1.5 times the full minimum wage. The court directed that the labourers be paid a daily wage of Rs. 29 per koyta; payments that were to be made at the respective factory gates. This was a substantial increase when compared to the meagre Rs. 5–7 per day they had been accustomed to receiving until then.

Predictably, the sugar industry was not happy with the order. Failing to persuade the court to reconsider the daily wage, they shifted their efforts towards convincing the court to permit payments to be made directly in the fields as transporting large numbers of workers to the factories presented a logistical challenge. But the bench did not yield. They were afraid that allowing payments to take place in the fields might result in incomplete payments, given the illiterate and impoverished status of the workers.

But the bench also had another concern.[5] They were worried about the lack of support from the state government, particularly because the then Chief Minister of Gujarat had previously held interests in several of these sugarcane companies. They also did not expect any cooperation from the state government's Labour Department, which raised concerns about the timely execution of the order.[6] Aware that time was of the essence and that any delay would frustrate the entire exercise, the court appointed a group of passionate young activist lawyers to execute the order. The court conveyed to them, 'We are placing in your hands this document to establish the majesty of law.' The bench also issued directives to the judicial bodies located in the same districts as the factories, urging them to provide support to the group engaged in the execution of the court's order. Transport facilities for the labourers were arranged at the cost of the factories.

When the lawyers returned triumphant from their mission, they regaled the bench with their fascinating tale during an informal meeting. They narrated an incident that took place on the final day of their mission as they completed their last stop at a factory located in a thickly forested area. The night was moonless, and the feeble lights of their jeep struggled to pierce the impenetrable darkness of the wilderness. Suddenly, without warning, the driver brought the vehicle to a halt and instructed the young lawyers to disembark. Standing amid the shadowy trees, fear and confusion hung in the air. Some began to pray, fearing the worst. But in an almost comical development, the driver unexpectedly prostrated himself before the group, stating they were doing God's work in helping the very poorest of the poor – a testament to the impact of their mission. Having said his piece, he promptly chauffeured them back to their base.

According to Justice R.A. Mehta, both he and Justice Ahmadi found this case to be greatly rewarding. They had not only succeeded in increasing the wages of the labourers by many times, but also protected them from further exploitation. Yet, they still felt it was not enough, and wished they could have done more.

It was during this time that Ahmadi began thinking about the profound questions about the law – the letter of the law versus the spirit of it, the distinction between delivering judgements versus administering justice. He saw the law as a powerful tool that, when wielded judiciously, could serve as a catalyst for reformative justice. He pondered upon the technicalities of the law and how they may be harnessed to bring about transformative holistic justice. Many years later, he would state at a public gathering, 'We are bound by the letters of the law, yes, but they are not dead letters. We must give life to those letters. I have no interest in engaging in judicial gymnastics, rather it is justice I am interested in.' In those words, Ahmadi captured the essence of his judicial philosophy, which would become more and more evident in his judgements as his career progressed.

This judicial ideology would be demonstrated on many occasions in his career, but particularly on one occasion when he presided over a division bench consisting of himself and his dear friend, Justice D.H. Shukla. The case before them was one that had come up on appeal. It was a murder case involving four brothers, all convicted under Section 302, which stipulates the punishment for murder as either life imprisonment or death penalty. As they began to examine the evidence, Justice Ahmadi leaned in towards his colleague, Justice Shukla, with concern writ large on his face. Referring to his friend by his nickname, he said, 'Bakul bhai, if we impose long sentences on all the brothers, what will become of their wives and children? The children will drop out of school and might turn to lives of crime themselves.'

Bakul bhai turned to look at his friend and colleague, instantly understanding the implications of what had been said. With a shared understanding of the far-reaching consequences of their decision, the two judges began to re-examine the evidence, seeking to find a way to prevent four families from falling into ruin. In their quest for justice that went beyond the immediate context, they determined that one of the brothers had carried a *lathi*, considered a non-lethal weapon, and appeared to have 'no intention to kill'. Reading down the role of this particular individual, the bench granted him a lighter sentence than the others, thereby leaving the families of the convicted brothers with at least one male relative.

Justice Ahmadi had cultivated a unique writing style for his judgements, which would set him apart from his future peers in the Supreme Court. In contrast to the increasingly popular trend of employing complex vocabulary and quoting philosophers, Ahmadi opted for simplicity and clarity in his language. This choice was not arbitrary; his extensive experience in the government sector had taught him a valuable lesson – the primary audience for understanding and implementing his judgements were not historians or intellectuals but government functionaries. Consequently, he crafted his judgements with a deliberate focus on accessibility and practical applicability. Eloquent sentence formation would be reserved for landmark judgements where making a constitutional point was equally important as laying out orders.[7] In his later years, he would dryly remark that one must never fall in love with one's own words.

Justice Ahmadi was gradually being spoken about as a judge with the foresight to consider the ramifications of his decisions – not only within the courtroom but also beyond. And his empathy for the oppressed, marginalized and disadvantaged too was becoming apparent.

So, when a case involving convict labour found its way into his docket, he saw an opportunity to establish a system that would not only be constitutionally sound but also help rehabilitate them and give them a chance at a better life once released from prison.[8] Such an attempt had already been made in Kerala, wherein the High Court had ruled that prisoners were to be compensated for their labour. These earnings were to be divided into thirds. One third was meant for the prisoner's personal needs while in jail, the other was directed to be handed over to the families of the imprisoned individuals and the last portion was to be placed into individual accounts for the prisoners themselves, ensuring that they had a small financial cushion upon their release and were not thrust back into a life of crime. Under this innovative scheme, the prisoners would be fairly compensated for the work they performed while serving their sentences.

Justice Ahmadi had once again received a letter, this time complaining of forced labour and exploitation.[9] Once again, he instructed that the letter be taken up as a PIL. The PIL raised concerns about the labours that convicts were forced to engage in, upon their time in prison. Whether carpentry, plumbing or sewing, these labours were performed free of cost with no remuneration. Upon closer examination, it became evident that these labours amounted to 'forced labour'. Justice Ahmadi, therefore, found it to also be in violation of Article 23, which prohibits forced labour.

Recognizing this as an opportunity for reform, the division bench's aim was to convert the exploitative labour practice into legitimate employment with proper compensation on the lines of the Kerala High Court judgement. Through this visionary approach, prisoners were not merely seen as individuals serving sentences but as members of society deserving a fair chance at redemption and rehabilitation. And so, the Gujarat High Court upheld the principle that prisoners were entitled to compensation at the rate of the minimum wage in similar industries with the same distribution – one-third for personal needs in jail, one-third for the family and the remaining one-third for the prisoner upon release.[10]. This allocation proved to be a lifeline for the imprisoned and their families. It ensured that the burden of imprisonment did not lead to further suffering for innocent family members. The last portion of the wages were a way of breaking the cycle of reoffending and reintegrating them into society as productive members. This financial incentive also motivated prisoners to engage in meaningful labour during their confinement, knowing that their efforts would be rewarded. The bench also directed that the wages be paid after making certain deductions, the monetary equivalent of the food, clothing and other facilities provided to prisoners at State expense. But these deductions became a point of contention when other state High Courts began to rule against it, stating that the obligation to provide food and clothes to the prisoners falls to the State.

The case went into appeal, with the State Government challenging the ruling.[11] It was eventually heard by a full bench of the Gujarat High Court in 1985, which upheld the division bench's judgement, except on the point of deductions. The Full Bench maintained the principle that prisoners were entitled to compensation according to the wages paid to other labourers in similar industries. But such payment cannot be deducted with food and clothing supplied to such prisoners.

These progressive judgements were important as they contributed to the larger goal of rehabilitation and reintegration of convicts into society.

The seeds of a more equitable and humane criminal justice system had been sown.

The significance of PILs in the deliverance of social justice therefore cannot be overstated.[12] The concept was initially conceived by eminent minds like Justice Krishna Iyer and Justice P.N. Bhagwati with the noble intention of delivering justice to those who lacked the means to access the system. Justice Ahmadi, during his tenure, witnessed first-hand the transformative power of PILs in addressing systemic issues, protecting fundamental rights and uplifting marginalized communities. More than once, he took it upon himself to direct the court registrar to treat letters as PILs, recognizing the potential for genuine public interest issues to emerge from unexpected sources. One must acknowledge that PILs have, in many instances, had a positive impact on the quality of governance and provided relief to millions of individuals.

But, by the 2000s, Justice Ahmadi's views on PILs had undergone a shift. He noticed a growing trend where more and more PILs were being filed by individuals looking for personal gains and self-promotion rather than for common good and social justice. To him, this represented a worrisome departure from the original purpose of PILs. He saw this as a waste of time, something that the courts should actively discourage. In his own words, 'As a member of the judiciary, I now feel sorry for the course the public interest litigation has taken, no more to assist the poor and the downtrodden.'

In a speech delivered in 2007, he would voice his concerns about the trend of self-appointed guardians of 'Indian culture' occupying the court's time by bringing PILs related to matters of real or imagined 'offenses'.

'Recently, it has emerged that certain members of the Bar, with a view to gaining publicity, file prosecutions against celebrities. There have, in the last decade or more, emerged self-proclaimed guardians of religion and cultures, who act on their whims, notions and perceptions, and with impunity resort to violence, arson and destruction, secure in the belief that Government in power will not take action. I ask: what does a citizen, who is attacked, do in such circumstances? In order to check such frivolous litigation, I think it would be wise to introduce a rule we had in the

Ahmedabad City Civil Court Rules, which required a litigant seeking an interim order to give an undertaking in the prescribed form to reimburse the opposite side if it is ultimately found that the litigation was frivolous. This would work as a deterrent for busybodies who jump into the fray for cheap publicity.'[13]

In the year 1983, a case relating to the rights of Adivasi people was brought before a bench presided over by Justice Ahmadi and Justice R. A. Mehta.[14] Several writ petitions had been initiated by a marginalized group of Adivasis, specifically identified as Kotwalias and Vansfodias. The Kotwalias represent the most vulnerable segment of the tribal community in the state, whose survival remains precarious.[15]

The petitioners, residing within reserved forested areas, were distressed because the Forest Department officials were preventing them from harvesting bamboo, which they were entitled to do at concessional rates. Further, there were also reports of forest officials raiding the homes of these Adivasis and seizing bamboo chips, which the officials asserted was 'forest produce'. The Forest Department allowed them to remove only twenty bamboos per family per week, an amount grossly insufficient for their needs.

According to the Adivasis, they held certain privileges granted by the State Government, which allowed them to collect forest produce, including a higher amount of bamboo per family from the forest. The bamboo was used to craft items such as *toplas* (threshing trays), *supdas* (baskets) and *palas* (split bamboo mats), which were their primary sources of livelihood. Further, a patent appeal had been filed by a businessman who had purchased these items but was subsequently prevented for removing them from the forest without a pass or permit. This initial writ had been dismissed by Justice P.D. Desai, which prompted the petitioner to file a letters patent appeal – an intra-court appeal which allows a party to appeal to a division bench of the same court against a decision of a single judge.

Since the legal issues raised in these three writ petitions and the appeal were substantially the same, the decision was made to address them collectively in a single judgement.[16] The bench set aside P. D. Desai's ruling and affirmed the rights of the indigenous peoples to collect a specified amount of bamboo for their defined purposes. The judgement also made a distinction between raw bamboo and bamboo products, thereby clarifying that there was no need for a permit when transporting the products out of the forest area.

However, similar cases were heard in other High Courts where divergent views were taken, including the Bombay High Court, which ruled that bamboo products were, in fact, classified as forest produce. This classification is important, because removing forest produce like trees, leaves, flowers and fruits without authorization was punishable by imprisonment and invited a fine under the Indian Forest Act. Eventually, the case went to the Supreme Court which upheld the Gujarat High Court's order. 'We may also state that according to us the view taken by the Gujarat High Court in Fatesang's case is correct, because though bamboo as a whole is forest produce, if a product, commercially new and distinct, known to the business community as totally different, is brought into existence by human labour, such an article and product would cease to be a forest-produce.'[17]

This series of judgements would become important in defining Adivasi Forest and Land rights.

A practical man, Ahmadi's judicial style of delivering judgements was becoming solidified into one that sought to deliver solutions and address real-life problems. He spent long hours by himself in his chambers and his office at home, trying to find ways to ensure that the law was used to serve the people rather than becoming an obstacle to justice.

Justice R.A. Mehta sheds light on this aspect of Justice Ahmadi's judicial philosophy through a specific case. In this case, a group of protesting farmers had been rounded up by the police, arrested under the preventive detention law and were being held in Sabarmati jail. A petition was filed on their behalf and came before Justice Ahmadi. Upon reviewing the case, Ahmadi firmly asserted that the detention had been wrongful. He pointed out that the protest had been peaceful, the farmers were not terrorists, they bore no arms and therefore there was no basis for detaining them under the said law. The claim of public order being disturbed was baseless. He ordered their immediate release. However, there was a practical challenge. The lawyer representing the farmers expressed concerns about how the farmers would return to their village if released. Abjectly poor, they lacked both personal transportation and the financial means to arrange transportation. A stern Ahmadi lowered his glasses, and his piercing gaze bore into the squirming police officers present in the room: As the police brought them to Sabarmati, so shall they take them back, he announced.

But there was more. There was also the opportunity to change jurisprudence.[18] In May 1972, on the bustling NH8 near Vasad, Ahmedabad, an Ambassador car had collided with a bullock cart, instantly killing the bullock cart driver. In the wake of this tragic incident, the brother and nephews of the deceased driver filed a claim before the Motor Accident Claims tribunal. Aggrieved at the award of the Tribunal, which instructed both the owner of the car and the insurer to pay compensation, they decided to take the matter to the High Court. At the time, the legal landscape surrounding motor vehicle accidents was a tangled web of confusion. There existed not one, but two distinct acts that dealt with the thorny issue of compensating the families of those who met unfortunate fates on the road. The crux of this matter lay in the definition of 'dependants' under the Fatal Accidents Act of 1855, which recognized only wives, husbands and children as beneficiaries. This meant that according to this Act, the brother and nephews of the deceased were excluded from receiving any compensation. On the other hand, the Motor Vehicles Act of 1939 spoke of 'legal representatives' rather than 'dependants,' further muddying the waters.

This case was officially categorized as First of a Kind. As the judgement records, 'The point which we are called upon to decide in this First Appeal is not covered by any decision of this court; at least our attention has not been invited to any such decision.'

The Division Bench comprising Justice Ahmadi and Justice J. B. Mehta ruled that 1939 Act was a benevolent Act and a welfare legislation, upholding the right of the legal representatives of the deceased to seek compensation for the loss of their loved one. It was also found that while the 1855 Act only allows for 'proportioned loss,' resulting from the death, the 1939 Act allows for more flexibility. Proportioned loss refers to the monetary amount awarded, designed to be proportionate to the loss suffered. The court's discretion is outlined in the words, 'determining the amount of compensation which appears to it to be just.' Therefore, the concept of 'just compensation' was introduced. This judgement was later upheld by the Supreme Court, which held, 'We feel that the view taken by the Gujarat High Court is in consonance with the principles of justice, equity and good conscience having regard to the conditions of the Indian society. We should remember that in an Indian family – brothers, sisters and brothers' children and sometimes foster children live together and they are dependent upon the bread-winner of the family and if the bread-winner is killed on account of a motor vehicle accident, there is no justification to deny them compensation.'[19]

A few years later, all existing Acts pertaining to motor vehicle accidents were scrapped and replaced with the Motor Vehicles Act 1988.

Rising fast through the ranks, Ahmadi was already on an extremely successful career path, but he was also impatient. As he grew in seniority, he began to undertake a growing number of administrative tasks, shouldering more than his fair share of responsibilities. Eager to learn and hone his skills for the next elevation he hoped would come soon, he refused to turn down any assignment, however seemingly insignificant. His natural aptitude for handling administrative responsibilities, combined with his background as Law Secretary, made him an obvious choice for the Chief Justice to delegate such tasks to.

In the meantime, Justice Thakkar had already been elevated to the Supreme Court in 1983. Closely observing his dear friend's evolving jurisprudential perspectives, Thakkar was growing increasingly convinced of Ahmadi's potential. Men of similar convictions, Thakkar was convinced the apex court needed more judges who were genuinely committed to justice for the people. A sharp, intelligent judge with a keen sense of social justice, Thakkar was convinced Ahmadi would be an asset to the Supreme Court of India.[20] So, with his own tenure coming to an end, Justice Thakkar began to press for Justice Ahmadi's elevation. Thakkar was well respected, well known for his commitment to humanitarian justice and well regarded within government circles. At this time, the Supreme Court had been devoid of a Muslim judge for a full 18 months – the longest in the Court's history. Following Thakkar's retirement, there would be a void in Gujarati representation as well. Ahmadi's nomination, therefore, was timely and fitting. He had already spent twelve years serving on the Gujarat High Court and was ripe for elevation to the apex court.

So it is ironic that when Ahmadi's appointment was proposed behind closed doors, a certain senior member of the Bench is reported to have commented, 'But he is a Muslim. Can we trust him?' Foolishly, the comment was made in the presence of Justice Thakkar, who would not hesitate to express his displeasure with the remark within legal circles and to trusted friends for many years to come. Eyes flashing at the shameless bigotry, Justice Thakkar breathed fire in the meeting. Calling out the bigotry in no uncertain terms, he defended his colleague on the merits of his character and legal acumen, extinguishing any flicker of prejudice that dared to influence Justice Ahmadi's nomination.

In the meantime, the skies were stormy in the Ahmadi household. On the cusp of adulthood, a young and spirited Tasneem Ahmadi was already fielding a barrage of marriage proposals. Although it is not uncommon for girls in the Bohra community to start receiving formal proposals by the age of seventeen, prevailing norms often dictate a more extended period of courtship, with many families choosing to wait until their daughters are well into their twenties before solemnizing nuptials. Long engagements are not only tolerated, but encouraged, especially in families that place a premium on education and career pursuits. Aziz and Ama also had similar plans for their daughter.

But then Tasneem met Murtaza Vahanvaty. A meeting that had been engineered by a well-meaning relative attempting to play matchmaker. Nine years older than her, Murtaza was more than just handsome; he was attentive with a commanding presence. To the eighteen-year-old girl, he appeared charming, eloquent and worldly wise. Young Tasneem was, quite simply, entranced.

Aziz reacted badly. 'She's too young!', he thundered, his voice bouncing off the walls of their home. 'Absolutely not!'

Ama and her mother, Tasneem's grandmother, tried a softer approach. They tried reasoning with the young girl, pleading with her to wait a few years. 'There is no rush, you both will still be here in a few years' time,' they beseeched. 'Then why wait?' shot back Tasneem. The apple had not fallen far from the tree – the girl was as stubborn as her father.

Tension enveloped the household, much to the dismay of Huzefa. At twelve years old, he was too young to comprehend the complexities of the situation, but he hated the constant bickering. He watched his sister and father locked in heated arguments over the smallest things. Mornings were the worst. It had become almost routine for one or the other to storm away from the breakfast table, leaving their bowls of fruit and *khakhras* half-eaten. His mother and grandmother spent long hours consulting each other in the evenings with the door shut, after Aziz had retired to his office and the children to their bedrooms. Ama could see that Tasneem was determined. She had seen it in her daughter's eyes.

One evening, after yet another blowout between Aziz and his headstrong daughter, Ama decided it was time to have a serious conversation with her husband. She caught his eye and silently gestured for him to join her in the bedroom. They entered the room and sat down at the foot of the bed, the familiar spot where every important decision of their lives had been weighed by the couple, together. Ama looked her husband in the eye. 'Aziz, I think we should start making serious enquiries about Murtaza and his family,' she began. Aziz, still agitated from the argument with Tasneem, looked at Ama, eyes flashing. 'So we just let her marry him then?' he retorted, his voice tinged with frustration.

Ama sighed. 'Aziz, she is young and headstrong. We tried waiting to see if this would die out on its own, but it hasn't. We need to face reality now.'

Aziz rubbed his temples, feeling torn. Unwilling to yield without putting up a fight, he lodged a few more protests. 'How will I face the world, Ama? She's still a child – they will think my daughter was a burden to me, and so I married her off so young.'

Ama let him talk, her hand resting on his knee, comforting him. They both hoped the fates would be kind to their daughter.

Before giving his reluctant consent, Aziz decided to have a heartfelt conversation with Tasneem. He asked her to join him in his office upstairs – a rare invitation. Once in the room, father and daughter sat cross legged on the mattress on the floor, facing each other. The father's eyes were thoughtful, the daughter's eager and curious. 'Tasneem, there's something I need you to promise me.' Curiosity piqued, Tasneem leaned in. 'What is that?' Aziz's voice grew serious as he continued. 'I want you to promise me that you will complete your studies and establish a career for yourself. I want you to be independent in every way, *beti*. It is crucial.'

Understanding immediately, Tasneem nodded her head sincerely. 'I will,' she promised. She smiled lovingly at her beloved father; all their heated arguments instantly forgotten. Patting her cheek with affection, Aziz returned to his files, signalling the end of the conversation.

And so, amid much fanfare and celebration, Tasneem Ahmadi married Murtaza Vahanvaty a few months short of her nineteenth birthday. Their wedding was a grand affair, filled with music, laughter and the blessings of elders. Once again, all was well in the Ahmadi household, and young Tasneem started her married life in Mumbai as a happy newlywed.

In the meantime, the union government had decided to try once again to address the protracted deadlock over water sharing among the northern states of Punjab, Haryana and Rajasthan. The tumultuous saga of the Ravi-Beas water dispute has its roots in the Punjab Reorganisation Act of 1966, which restructured undivided Punjab and carved the new state of Haryana out of it. Punjab refused to recognize the Act and Haryana demanded its rightful share of the waters. Over the next two decades, there were several attempts to apportion the waters fairly between the states of Punjab, Haryana and Rajasthan, but each attempt had failed. Then, in 1985, the historic Rajiv-Longowal accord was signed. Brokered between Prime Minister Rajiv Gandhi and Akali leader Harchand Singh Longowal, this accord was significant. Punjab had just emerged from a period under

President's rule, and the accord symbolized a fragile truce between the Central Government and the Shiromani Akali Dal. The accord included, among other things, the establishment of a tribunal that would determine the water shares of the states of Punjab, Haryana and others utilizing the waters of the Ravi-Beas river systems. It was agreed that the award of the tribunal would be binding upon all the states involved.

So, on 2 April 1986, the Eradi Tribunal,[21] led by Supreme Court Justice V. Balakrishna Eradi commenced upon its task of[22] determining how much water the states were actually using, and distributing the surplus fairly. To ensure a comprehensive and fair assessment, the Tribunal was composed of three distinguished members, including Justice Ahmadi from the Gujarat High Court and Justice P. C. Balakrishna Menon from the Kerala High Court. The accord had also set a target date of 15 August 1986 for the completion of the Sutlej Yamuna Link (SYL) canal. This canal would allow Haryana and other downstream states to access the waters that would eventually be allocated to them.[23] But Punjab claimed that the non-riparian state of Haryana could stake no claim over the waters, while Haryana asserted that since it was carved out of an erstwhile riparian state, its water rights remained unchanged.

So, it was agreed that Punjab's farmers would not have to settle for a reduced water supply. The Tribunal, operating at a remarkable pace, was able to submit its report in a record time of just 10 months. Justice Ahmadi recollects the countless trips to Delhi, made nearly every week, to hear oral submissions by leading Senior Counsel such P. P. Rao, Dr Chitale and Kapil Sibal. However, for reasons unknown, the government made the Tribunal's findings public only four months later, in May 1987.[24]

The Tribunal's findings unveiled disparities in the allocation and utilization of waters from the Ravi-Beas river systems.[25] Punjab was found to have been over-utilizing these waters, and consequently, Haryana and Rajasthan were underutilizing their share.

Eventually, the findings of the Tribunal revealed that farmers in the three states were using a total of 9.711 MAF (million acre-feet) of Ravi-Beas waters.[26] Of this, 3.106 MAF were used by Punjab's farmers, 1.620 MAF by Haryana's farmers and 4.985 by Rajasthan. This left approximately 6.6 MAF of surplus waters for further distribution. But the Tribunal recorded a surplus of 8.83 MAF. The discrepancy was accounted for by considering water below the rim stations of the Ravi and Beas, which were the lowest data recording points. Punjab argued that the extra water was unusable as it could not be stored due to the absence of dams and reservoirs along the Pakistan border.

Ultimately, the Tribunal's verdict reshaped the water allocations of two states. Punjab's share was reduced, Haryana's doubled while that of Rajasthan and Delhi remained unchanged. Predictably, the award written by Ahmadi was received reasonably well by Haryana and Rajasthan, but met with tremendous dissatisfaction by Punjab. Refusing to accept the Tribunal's 'binding' award, Punjab launched a political campaign against the implementation of the award.

The Akali Dal wasted no time in recording their vehement resistance. They announced their intention of launching a 'people's movement' in opposition to any decision handed out by the Eradi Tribunal. 'We do not wish other states to be deprived of water, but they can get only what is surplus after Punjab's needs are met,' they stated.

Former Chief Minister Surjit Singh Barnala issued a stern warning, cautioning that the Akali Dal (L), a party he led, was fully prepared to mobilize and rally grassroots support for a robust protest movement against the Eradi award.[27] Manjit Singh Khaira, the General Secretary of Akali Dal (L), went even further, accusing Justice Eradi of attempting to manipulate the accord.

In all this, threats of violence were both implicit and explicit.

The situation reached a boiling point in October 1986, when enraged farmers in Ropar district of Punjab, where the SYL canal originates, forced irrigation workers to abandon the construction work.[28] A few months later, 30 labourers were killed at the canal site. In 1987, Punjab challenged the Tribunal's award, rejecting its findings. Violence in the state was escalating and the situation becoming more volatile by the day. And so, the Tribunal was adjourned sine die. As of the time of writing, the issue remains unresolved.[29]

Disappointed by the outcome of the work done by the Tribunal, Ahmadi returned to Ahmadabad to tackle the backlog of work that had accumulated while he was engaged in Delhi. Apart from the many cases on his docket, Ahmadi had also been entrusted with several important assignments. Over his twelve-year tenure, he served as Chairman of the Advisory Board constituted under the Conservation of Foreign Exchange and Prevention of Smuggling Activities Act (COFEPOSA), Chairman of the Advisory Board constituted under the Prevention of Black Marketing and Maintenance of Supplies of Essential Commodities Act and Chairman of Gujarat State's Third Pay Commission.

Having taken on all these additional responsibilities, Ahmadi was burning the candle at both ends. And these long hours of toil were about to take a toll.

One crisp morning, the sun's golden rays bathed the elegant bungalow as Justice Ahmadi emerged from its porch. As usual, he walked alongside the front porch towards the car waiting to take him to the High Court. But something was wrong today. With each step, his usually confident stride faltered, and he struggled to manage the few short steps from the porch to the car door that was held open by Mohammad, his trusted driver. Arm extended towards the car door, Aziz stumbled and clutched the air as his legs gave way and a sudden vice-like grip clamped down on his stomach. A searing, burning sensation surged through his body and Aziz retched violently, his breakfast splattered over the driveway. But there was something else too. Blood. It poured forth in discerning quantities, staining the pristine driveway crimson.

'*Bai saab!*' Mohammad's panicked cry for Mrs Ahmadi sliced through the morning air as he struggled to keep his beloved *saheb* upright. Within a matter of minutes, the bustling household converged upon a distressed Aziz. Together they guided Aziz to the porch steps where he could sit and catch his breath. Ama's eyes were wide in alarm and panic rippled through the household. The doctor was phoned, and Aziz was advised to rush to the Emergency room. Drenched in sweat by now, his once crisp white shirt spattered with bloodstains, Aziz summoned the last vestiges of his remaining strength, and with the help of Mohammad and the gardener, heaved himself off the porch. Spitting and sputtering as Mohammad frantically turned the ignition key, the waiting car's engine roared to life. Aziz was placed carefully inside with his beloved wife seated beside him, her grip on his hand firm. A staff member occupied the front seat as the vehicle sped towards the hospital, leaving the once-peaceful morning behind in its dust.

It was a perforated peptic ulcer. Fortunately, his relatively young age of fifty-five and swift emergency intervention had spared Justice Ahmadi from more serious consequences, but he was advised substantial lifestyle changes. No more rich, spicy meals, no more late nights burning the midnight oil, only early dinners, and certainly no more endless cups of tea and coffee. Of these, Aziz would grudgingly concede to only two – bland food and early dinners. As for his beloved tea, he would stubbornly continue to drink up to five or six cups a day, even seven when his wife wasn't around. And his penchant for late night reading? That habit, too, persisted, as he spent countless hours immersed in his books and files long after the rest of the world had retired. Openly scoffing at the doctor's recommendation to slow down and reduce his workload, he insisted he was fine.

Neither did Aziz wish to slow down, nor could he afford to. Because, less than a month from then, Rajiv Gandhi's close confidante and Union Law Minister, Mr Shiv Shankar would pay him a visit.

It was the summer holidays. As usual, my brother Adnan and I had been dropped off at my grandparents' home for the vacations. At six years old, I looked forward to these weeks, spent in the indulgent care of my grandparents. Here, we were allowed special indulgences – a spoonful of bitter tea from our *nani ma's* cup in the morning, a sugary treat in the afternoons, no bedtime, and, perhaps most cherished of all, days filled with fascinating stories. The fountain in the middle of the garden, usually non-operational, was turned on when we were visiting, making for many a glorious afternoons spent splashing and paddling about. With no homework and no school, we spent our days roaming the enormous gardens, playing rambunctious games and chewing on peppermint leaves torn from the kitchen garden. Brightly coloured chillies too were plucked, bitten into and hurriedly spat out as we ran to the fountain to cool our burning mouths.

Unlike other grandmothers who cooked and pickled, ours abhorred the kitchen; yet, somehow, she managed to coax delectable *kebabs* and elaborate meals from the household staff, which we devoured hungrily at every opportunity. On Sunday mornings, our great grandmother – *nani ma's* mother – read to us from Gujarati storybooks – tales of imaginary animals and their adventures. Our *mamu* had bought a new motorcycle and could, on occasion, be persuaded to take us for a spin around the compound. Dinners were eaten later here, and because there was no school the next day, we were allowed to eat with the adults. After dinner, as my grandfather rose for his evening walk, I prepared to raise holy hell, insisting on being taken along. Every night, he would lodge a few half-hearted protests before eventually giving in. Carrying me out, he would set me down beside himself on the garden swing, the two of us sitting in silence, enjoying the quiet. Sometimes, there would be a story from his childhood in Surat.

The morning Mr Shiv Shankar visited my grandfather, I was playing on the porch of the bungalow. The small wooden child gate, about the same height as me, had been strategically placed at the top of the porch stairs to prevent unsupervised explorations into the sprawling gardens and tangles of bushes beyond. The older sibling, I knew well the household rules of our Bombay apartment – in the absence of an adult, I was to let no strangers into our home. So, when the unsuspecting Mr Shiv Shankar's car rumbled onto the porch and he descended from it, I clutched the child gate firmly shut, determined not to allow him to cross over.

Surveying the scene, the soft-spoken Mr Shankar sought an adult presence that could resolve the curious impasse he found himself in. Finding none, he embarked on a gentle negotiation, pleading and pacifying, trying to convince me to relinquish my post and let him pass. Indeed, the Law Minister, accustomed to negotiating with seasoned politicians and bureaucrats, had not foreseen that his diplomatic skills would be put to the test by a determined six-year-old. When my grandmother came upon this peculiar standoff bordering on absurdity, I am told she became red in the face from a combination of amusement and embarrassment. Struggling to keep a straight face, she apologized profusely to the minister, hurriedly scooped me up, quickly depositing me into the waiting arms of a staff member and then ushered Mr Shankar inside. When the visit concluded, and the two men finally emerged from the formal drawing room, both their faces were lit up with delighted smiles that stretched from ear to ear. There was a buoyant spring in my grandfather's step as he escorted Mr Shankar out to his car. Our home suddenly came alive with laughter and jubilation to the chorus of *Mubarak*, as our family hugged each other and celebrated joyously. My adventure of the morning was all but forgotten.

Because you see, Shiv Shankar had come on an official yet confidential visit – as an emissary to extract Ahmadi's consent for his proposed elevation to the Supreme Court of India. At fifty six years old, it was now clear that not only would Aziz Mushabber Ahmadi become a Supreme Court Judge, but also, in due course, the Chief Justice of India.

7

Gavel and Grit

When the news of Justice Ahmadi's elevation broke in the corridors of the Gujarat High Court, it stirred up, once again, a roiling mix of reactions and tensions. But Ahmadi was no longer the young man he had been at the time of his appointment to the City Civil Court, alarmed and disquieted by the clamorous opposition to his rise. A seasoned veteran by now, he remained unperturbed by the white noise of swirling protests and angry objections.

This time, the controversy was regarding the judges he had superseded on his way to the apex court, including the Chief Justice of the Gujarat High Court, Justice P.R. Gokulakrishnan. Although there was nothing in the rulebook that prevented the elevation of any High Court judge to the Supreme Court, tradition had long dictated that the senior-most judge be elevated first. At the time, it was also virtually unheard of for the Chief Justice of the same High Court to be bypassed in favour of another, junior judge.

But the troubles did not end there. Rather, they were only beginning.

As is often the norm, an individual's rise through the ranks frequently attracts rivalries and hostilities. In this, Ahmadi's life was no different.

On the day of Ahmadi's official swearing in as Supreme Court judge, a total of five judges took their oaths. Of the distinguished assembly consisting of Justices S.R. Pandian, T.K. Thommen, A.M. Ahmadi, K.N. Saikia and Kuldip Singh, Justice Ahmadi held the third spot in the order of swearing in, and Justice Kuldip Singh, Additional Solicitor General of India at the time, the last. The order of oath taking is crucial as it determines the seniority of judges – a matter that was to cause much heartburn.

Scheduled to be sworn in as a judge of the Supreme Court on the same day as Ahmadi, Justice Singh made no secret of his ambitions – since he and Ahmadi were nearly the same age, he aspired to take the oath before Justice Ahmadi.[1] Justice Kuldip Singh was a bar judge, meaning he had been elevated directly from the Bar, unlike Justice Ahmadi who had steadily climbed the ranks of the judiciary. Justice Singh claimed superiority by virtue of being a bar judge but only over Justice Ahmadi. He made no such claims of seniority over the other three judges who had also ascended through various ranks of the judiciary and were to be sworn in the same day. This matter was of critical importance to Justice Singh because if his claim was accepted and he were to be sworn in ahead of Ahmadi, it would mean a tenure as Chief Justice for him. In this he had the support of then Chief Justice, R.S. Pathak, who also recommended that Singh be sworn in first. But this was not to be. Kuldip Singh's claim was ultimately rejected. One may speculate that the decision to elevate a bar judge over a judicial practitioner who had earned his stripes through years of toil in various lower and high courts might have been considered unfair and met with resistance. It was therefore decided that as a bar judge, Justice Kuldip Singh shall take his oath last. And so, when 14 December 1988 dawned, Justice Ahmadi was sworn in as judge of the Supreme Court before Kuldip Singh, thus forever sealing both their fates. When Singh learnt that Ahmadi had been listed before him, he considered withdrawing.[2] Later, he stated, 'I was perturbed but friends like S.S. Ray persuaded me . . . to join the Court anyway.'

But Singh did not forget.

Apart from Justice Singh, Ahmadi would face significant conflict with two other judges during his tenure as a Supreme Court judge – Justice M.N. Venkatachaliah and Justice J.S. Verma. One was his predecessor and the other, his successor.[3] Over time, Ahmadi realized that Justice Verma too harboured discontent of his own. Because he had been appointed to the Supreme Court a few months after Ahmadi, Verma's own tenure as Chief Justice of India had been substantially shortened.

While further intricacies of the dissonance among the senior-most judges at that time remain undisclosed, what would become clear with the passage of time are the stark ideological differences separating Justice Ahmadi on one hand and Justices Venkatachaliah and Verma on the other.

As Hindutva gained prominence and muscled its way into mainstream politics, prompting the judiciary to intervene, it would become apparent that Justice Ahmadi's strong stance on secularism and staunch opposition to the convergence of state and religion was perhaps not a sentiment shared by Justice Verma who would go on to author the 'Hindutva judgements'.[4] This series of seven judgements delivered between 1995 and 1996 faced heavy criticism for dealing an irreparable blow to secularism, condemning them for permitting the invocation of religion in electoral speeches, defining Hindutva as a 'way of life' and synonymizing it with 'Indianization'.[5] In the most significant of these, R.Y. Prabhoo vs. P.K. Kunte, the Bombay High Court had invalidated Dr R.Y. Prabhoo's (Shiv Sena) election due to corrupt practices under the Representation of People Act of 1951. The Act prohibits candidates from soliciting votes based on religion, race, caste or language, and also prohibits inciting hatred among different segments of society. The controversy stemmed from three speeches by Bal Thackeray during Prabhoo's campaign, deemed inflammatory and divisive by the High Court, as they promoted enmity between different classes on religious grounds and appealed for votes for Dr Prabhoo because of his religion as a Hindu. Although upholding the High Court judgement, Verma's judgement also stated that, 'Ordinarily, Hindutva is understood as a way of life or a state of mind and it is not to be equated with, or understood as religious Hindu fundamentalism.' Further, 'The above opinion indicates that the word 'Hindutva' is used and understood as a synonym of 'Indianization,' i.e., development of uniform culture by obliterating the differences between all the cultures coexisting in the country.'[6] Justice Verma's linking of Hindutva with Hinduism and Indianization provided a tremendous fillip to political forces seeking to intertwine religion with electoral choices. In another one of these cases,

Manohar Joshi vs. Nitin Bhaurao Patil, Verma's judgement held that the candidate's campaign speech containing the statement, 'The first Hindu State will be established in Maharashtra' was not corrupt practice. It stated, 'In our opinion, a mere statement that the first Hindu State will be established in Maharashtra is by itself not an appeal for votes on the ground of his religion but the expression, at best, of such a hope.' Consequently, the High Court judgement that voided Joshi's election was overturned.

The following year, the BJP would go on to include these judgements in their manifesto to showcase the Supreme Court's endorsement of Hindutva.

Twenty-two years later, Verma's daughter would state that her father's judgement had been misread. 'He always had a regret about being misunderstood after 1995 and how for their own purposes, a group of politicians had twisted the spirit of his judgement.'[7]

Legal scholars have found that the court's failure to understand the politics of Hindutva within the ideological framework of the Sangh Parivar, along with crafting a vague definition of Hindutva without considering its connection to real-world circumstances, legitimizes the hateful politics of the Sangh Parivar, a political group that shows little regard for constitutional and democratic values.[8]

Later in life, Justice Ahmadi would desist from elaborating further on his discord with Justice Verma, stating, 'He is no more, so I would not like to say any more about him.'[9]

With Justice Venkatachaliah too, these differences would make themselves apparent. Once retired, Ahmadi would go on to express his disappointment over the *kar seva* that had been sanctioned by Justice Venkatachaliah's bench.[10] On more than one occasion, he asserted that without such permission, the Babri mosque would have been standing today.

As time wore on and Justice Venkatachaliah acceded to the position of Chief Justice of India in 1993, a shift in dynamics became apparent.[11] Ahmadi found himself increasingly at odds with the new Chief Justice, their interactions tinged with an air of discord. One morning, as per usual practice, the judges of the Supreme Court had assembled in the common room attached to the Chief Justice's chambers before dispersing towards their respective courtrooms. As protocol dictated, the Chief Justice seated himself at the head of the table and the two senior-most judges flanked him on either side. But on this day, something strange happened. In an unexpected turn of events, Justice Verma and Justice Kuldip Singh hurriedly took their seats on either side of the Chief Justice, tacitly asserting themselves to be the two senior-most judges. This seemingly harmless move carried a powerful message. Ahmadi, taken aback by this display, cast a sharp look towards Justice Venkatachaliah, awaiting an objection from the Chief. But the Chief Justice remained silent. Although Ahmadi was forced to find a seat elsewhere that morning, he now wondered if there were some who did not wish to see him ascend to the position of Chief Justice.

The rift between the Chief Justice and Chief Justice designate only grew over Venkatachaliah's twenty-month tenure. The strife would become public in 1993 with Venkatachaliah's invocation of a transfer policy for High Court judges, including Chief Justices.

With the verdict in the Second Judges' Case – Supreme Court-Advocates-On-Record Association vs. Union of India (in which Justice Ahmadi had dissented),[12] Chief Justice Venkatachaliah found himself endowed with unprecedented powers and primacy in matters of judicial appointments and transfers.[13] A few days later, he announced the controversial policy of transferring one-third of High Court judges from their parent High Courts, much to the chagrin of many judges.[14] While ostensibly aimed at addressing corruption and removing judges from courts where close relatives were practising, the policy also resulted in the transfer of several other judges to fulfill the one-third quota.

At the time, Justice Ahmadi had just learnt that Venkatachaliah had made a public statement asserting that transfers were necessary to weed out certain judges who had earned a reputation un-befitting of a judge of the High Court and that each High Court should have one-third of its judges from outside the state. Venkatachaliah asserted that these measures were necessary to maintain judicial accountability. But in judicial circles, transfers are often seen as punitive measures, particularly when they involve moving judges from prestigious courts to less prominent ones or result in a loss of seniority.

Since he and Justice Venkatachaliah happened to be in Hyderabad together on this day, Ahmadi thought it wise to express his concerns regarding this move.[15] He laid out his thoughts before the Chief Justice, hoping to convince him to reconsider. In Ahmadi's view, transferring a third of judges from all High Courts would trigger unnecessary heartburn among the judicial community. It would tarnish the reputation of the transferred judges, implying they had not met the expected moral and judicial standards, leaving them with no recourse or remedy to clear their names. Because the Supreme Court has no official investigative mechanism, it would be difficult to test each accusation. Ahmadi emphasized a key point – once a judge was subject to transfer under the existing policy, there would be no avenue for appeal or challenge, bringing with it danger of misuse. It would fall outside the purview of Article 226. Article 226 of the Indian Constitution empowers High Courts to issue writs to any person or authority, including the government, for the enforcement of fundamental rights. But the transfers would be non-justiciable and therefore could not be challenged.[16]

But Venkatachaliah was in no mood to listen. Ahmadi received the impression that he was 'impressed' by the suggestion made by Justice Verma who had also been entrusted with developing a model code of conduct for judges.[17] As the wave of transfers commenced, Ahmadi was astonished to discover that when a difficult judge fell within the net of the transfer policy, he himself was implicated as the source of the recommendation despite his vehement opposition to the policy itself. Several judges approached Ahmadi personally, questioning his role in initiating their transfers. Ahmadi was placed in a difficult predicament.

Despite recognizing the dynamics at play, where Venkatachaliah held the *de jure* position of Chief Justice while Verma operated as the *de facto* Chief Justice, he refused to succumb to bitterness as another might have. Although he was once again walking on a 'razor's edge,' he did so with a smile.[18]

On the professional front, then, this time was one that required mental fortitude and patience.

But this hostility of the Bench did not extend to the Bar. Justice Ahmadi's innate instinct to level the playing field and offer the underdog an opportunity quickly earned him a reputation as one of the more patient judges, especially when young lawyers stumbled through their arguments. He took the time to patiently explain intricate legal nuances, lending them the benefit of his insight. Speaking slowly, deliberately and with clarity, he ensured that junior lawyers experienced no fear while appearing in his court.

His experience as a trial court judge had provided him with a rock-solid foundation in civil and criminal law, which made even the senior-most advocates approach his court with a certain degree of caution. For it was known that many an ill-prepared senior advocate had found themselves tripped up in Ahmadi's court. Well respected for his control over the often noisy and bustling courtroom, Ahmadi did not resort to raising his voice like many others. With a measured, sharp glance in the direction of the offending party and a slight tightening of tone, he would simply say, 'I cannot hear, can I please have a bit of quiet.'

Although he had a sense of humour which he used masterfully to lighten many a tense mood in the courtroom, there was also a steel within him. Justice Ahmadi had little patience for brown nosing, ill-prepared counsel and those trying to take advantage.

So, save for a small group of lawyers who were offended by this occasional toughness, he enjoyed the widespread adoration of the Bar.[19] Many of today's leading legal luminaries who were once young aspiring lawyers appearing in Ahmadi's court fondly describe themselves as beneficiaries of his encouragement and wisdom. His reputation as a citizen's judge, a jurist who sought ways to apply the law in a manner that would serve the common man quickly endeared him to all lawyers, whether senior or junior. His approach was centrist and cautious yet marked by a calculated boldness.

Mr Sudhir Nanavati, a leading member of the Gujarat Bar, provides insights into this characteristic of Justice Ahmadi through a casual conversation they shared while traveling on a flight together. Reflecting on Justice Ahmadi's extensive experience as a judge in lower courts, the High Court and the Supreme Court, Mr Nanavati asked Ahmadi his secret of being not only a good judge, but also a popular one. In response, Justice Ahmadi stated, 'Sudhir, since you are asking me, I'll tell you. To become a good anything, you must first be a good human being. And how do you become a good human being? Whenever somebody is talking to you, put yourself in his place and try to understand where he is coming from. One should be soft while speaking because when you are sitting with the power of the chair, your attitude and aptitude can both change. And to control that you should remain soft. Permit them to speak. You may be firm in your judgement, but you must be soft in your approach.'

It was therefore very early on that Justice Ahmadi became the Darling of the Supreme Court Bar, enjoying the admiration, respect and gratitude of lawyers from all walks of life, eventually earning him a staggering amount of love and goodwill that has endured well past his lifetime.

As Justice Ahmadi took his seat on the Supreme Court bench in 1988, he was acutely aware that this would be a trying time. India was witnessing a turning point, marked by seismic shifts of great proportions. The Mandal Commission report had ignited civil disturbance in the country – cities were engulfed in a firestorm of protests and riots. Hindu nationalism was surging, soon to be catapulted into mainstream national politics. The political landscape too was far from stable – Rajiv Gandhi had been dethroned, with V.P. Singh taking his place. Singh's short tenure as Prime Minister would soon be followed by the even shorter reign of Chandra Shekhar before a semblance of stability was restored under the leadership of P. V. Narasimha Rao. A mere three years after Ahmadi's appointment, the nation would be plunged into shock yet again as another of India's Prime Ministers was assassinated, throwing the country into a state of panic and disarray.

In this turbulent period of political turmoil, Justice Ahmadi would find himself at the epicentre of India's evolving historical and legal landscape faced with some of the most difficult questions that India was grappling with.

One of the early cases that would mark his tenure was the famous Indira Sawhney vs. Union of India case in which the implementation of the Mandal Commission's recommendations for reservations for backward communities was challenged.

Justice Ahmadi's opinion on reservations was, as it would remain till the end, positive. To him, it wasn't just permissible, it was essential. In his view, these policies fell under the ambit of 'affirmative action,' a necessary component of equality. Whether in the context of minority rights or reservations, Ahmadi saw affirmative action not as a component of secularism but of equality. Because, he would explain, when communities have fallen behind over several generations due to historical discriminations, then it is only affirmative action that can help them catch up to the level that is considered the base level for communities that are doing well – and therefore equal.

The struggle to provide affirmative action for backward communities as a remedy for historical discrimination is one as old as Independent India herself. Although successive governments have recognized the necessity of such measures, the hurdles of identification and determination of these backward communities have presented formidable challenges that led to the abandonment of the project itself.[20] One of the first significant attempts, the Kaka Kalelkar Commission Report (1955) was abandoned by the Central Government[21] on the ground that it had not applied any objective tests for identifying the Backward Class. Thus there was a need for a second backward classes commission.[22] In 1961, the union government allowed state governments to select their own criteria to define backward communities, suggesting that economic parameters might prove more useful than caste-based ones. Thereafter, various state governments began drawing up their own lists and implementing reservations in jobs and educational institutions.

But this would change with the introduction of the Janata Party on the national political stage.

The Second Backwards Class Commission or the Mandal Commission as it was popularly known, was constituted in 1979 under the leadership of Prime Minister Morarji Desai.[23] Headed by B.P. Mandal, former Chief

Minister of Bihar and a socialist, this committee determined that caste-based exclusion could not be separated from backwardness, as it was within this social construct that backwardness had its roots.

As stated in the report, '. . . the substitution of caste by economic tests will amount to ignoring the genesis of social backwardness in the Indian society.'[24] The report further explained, 'As the main thrust of the Government's development programmes has always been the removal of mass poverty, this pre-occupation with economic criteria in determining backwardness is quite understandable. But however laudable the objective may be, it is not in consonance with the spirit of Article 340 of the Constitution under which the Commission was set up.'

In this reasoning, the Commission stood on firm ground. By then the Indian judiciary had already clarified the interpretation of Article 15(4), which allows for preferential treatment to be provided to socially and educationally backward groups and Article 340, which empowers the President to establish a commission to investigate the conditions of socially and educationally backward classes in India. They had determined caste to be a class of citizens, recommended that job reservations not exceed 50 per cent of the total and highlighted the necessity to establish objective criteria for identifying Other Backward Classes (OBCs).

The Mandal Commission submitted its report in 1980 wherein it identified 3743 castes as socially and educationally backward. The Commission recommended a 27 per cent reservation in government jobs to uplift the Socially and Educationally Backward Classes (SEBCs).

But, before this recommendation could be implemented, the Janata Party government collapsed. The Janata Dal, a new multi-party merger, would now have to wait till 1989 for the political tides to change once again in its favour. With Janata Dal's V.P. Singh the country's new Prime Minister, the Mandal Commission report was recovered from the dusty corner it had been relegated to and revived.[25] But the new government was facing challenges in staying afloat amid growing indications that V.P. Singh's tenure as Prime Minister was nearing its conclusion. In the end, V. P. Singh would remain Prime Minister for less than a year before being replaced by Chandra Shekhar, prompting him to hurriedly secure his legacy before he was forced to step down.

And so, on 7 August 1990, V.P. Singh informed the Lok Sabha of the government's intent to implement the Mandal Commission Report, followed by the same declaration in the Rajya Sabha on 9 August 1990.[26]

Four days later, on 13 August 1990, V.P. Singh issued an Office Memorandum (OM) that allocated 27 per cent of vacancies in civil posts and services under the Government of India for Socially & Educationally Backward Classes (SEBCs).[27] The OM read: 'In a multiple undulating society like ours, early achievement of the objective of social justice as enshrined in the Constitution is a must. The Mandal Commission was established by the then government with this purpose in view, which submitted its report to the Government of India on 31.12.1980.'

The validity of this OM was contested through writ petitions on the grounds that the procedure used by the Mandal Commission in identifying the SEBCs was flawed.

But V.P. Singh could never have imagined the sheer scale and volume of the outrage that followed this decision. The government watched in stunned horror as students from all corners of the country poured into the streets to voice their dissent. Universities were forced to temporarily shut down as campuses became hotbeds of protest. Violent chaos reigned as buses and trains went up in flames, traffic came to a standstill and the streets witnessed police firings and *lathi* charges.[28] For the first time since Operation Blue Star in 1984, the army had to be deployed to restore peace.

Through the turbulence, V.P. Singh refused to yield.

But when young student leader Rajiv Goswami took the horrifying step of attempting to immolate himself, the protests took an ugly turn. Several other young men and women attempted to do the same, giving the anti-reservation protest a violent colour.

The BJP, having been an ally in Janata Dal's rise to power, found itself under fire from the protestors. As an ally, they found themselves being held equally responsible.[29] When BJP leaders L.K. Advani and Madan Lal Khurana attempted to meet Goswami's parents, they were barred by a group of students, demanding they first denounce the report,[30] which the politicians could not do as the BJP's election manifesto promised its implementation. But it was becoming evident to the BJP leaders that supporting the Mandal Commission report was no longer politically advantageous. The uproar over the Mandal Commission report had divided the Hindu body politic on caste lines, creating groups that were at odds with each other. More importantly, these divisions had fragmented the voter base. It was therefore important for the party to return to Hindutva and consolidate the Hindu vote. And so, in a strategic move, L.K. Advani, then President of the BJP, seized this moment to launch a Ram Rath Yatra (chariot journey).[31] A political and religious procession, this yatra aimed to bolster the agitation by Hindu right wing groups to erect a Ram Temple on the site of the Babri Masjid in Ayodhya. The yatra was meant to serve a two-fold objective: to distance the BJP from V.P. Singh's government and bolster the Hindutva rhetoric. On 25 September 1990, the rath yatra involving hundreds of volunteers from the Hindu nationalist organization, Sangh Parivar, commenced with great fanfare, surrounded by the Hindutva symbols of *trishuls* and saffron flags. On this yatra, Advani was joined by the then junior politician, Narendra Modi.[32] This political manoeuvre would prove to be the biggest mobiliser of Hindutva forces, eventually catapulting the BJP into the forefront of national politics within a few brief years.

In the meantime, the Mandal Commission riots had prompted a challenge in the Supreme Court.[33] In 1990, the Bar Association of the Supreme Court filed a writ appeal challenging the validity of the government's Office Memorandum which sanctioned 27 per cent reservations in vacancies in civil posts and services under the Government of India for SEBCs. The petitioners included heavyweights such as Soli J. Sorabjee, Indra Sawhney, K.K. Venugopal, S. Sukumaran and P.S. Poti.[34] The five-judge bench, constituted to determine the constitutional validity of the Office Memorandum, stayed the operation and directed the matter to a larger, nine-judge bench.

Before the larger bench could hear the case, the political landscape shifted abruptly. The Janata Dal (Socialist) government – a breakaway party from the Janata Dal – led by Prime Minister Chandra Shekhar, collapsed, followed by the tragic assassination of Rajiv Gandhi a few weeks later. Riding a wave of political sympathy, the Congress party surged to victory in the subsequent election of 1991, propelling itself back to the forefront of national politics under the leadership of P.V. Narasimha Rao.[35] Prompted by the upcoming hearing in the Supreme Court, the new government decided to implement the Mandal Commission report recommendations in 1991. They included the introduction of an economic criterion to prioritize the economically disadvantaged sections within the proposed 27 per cent reservation for the SEBCs. Going a step further, they also decided to grant a further 10 per cent reservation to economically challenged sections of the population who did not fall under any of the disadvantaged groups and therefore was unable to benefit from the schemes.

The nine-judge bench that had been constituted to hear the case comprised Justices M.H. Kania, M.N. Venkatachaliah, S.R. Pandian, A.M. Ahmadi, K. Singh, P.B. Sawant, R.M. Sahai, B.J. Reddy and T.K. Thommen.[36] A notice was issued to the government, seeking an explanation for the criteria used to implement the 27 per cent reservation.[37] At the onset, it was clarified that the question before the court was not the validity of the Mandal Commission report, but, rather, the validity of V. P. Singh's Office Memorandum.

The case revolved around key issues that questioned whether Article 16(4), which empowers the state to make reservations for backward groups, is an exception to Article 16(1), which promises equality of opportunity to all citizens. Further questions regarding the basis of reservations, whether on caste or economic criteria should be considered. It also deliberated on the limits of exceeding 50 per cent of government posts or appointments within an organizational structure.

Argued by legal notables like Nani Palkhivala, K.K. Venugopal, P.P. Rao and Indira Sawhney amongst others, the petitioners were well represented.[38] The respondents, too, were represented by counsel of equal calibre, with K. Parasaran and Additional Solicitor General Altaf Ahmed presenting arguments.[39] The petitioners argued that caste-based reservations indirectly served to promote the caste system, which contradicted the principle of secularism and infringed upon Article 16(2), which promises that no citizen shall be discriminated against based upon caste, sex, creed, etc.[40] Nani Palkhivala stated that it would 'cleave the nation'.

Another concern was voiced that reservations would lead to a shift from meritocracy to mediocrity, with sub-standard candidates replacing those based on merit.[41] Counsel for the state extended counter arguments stating that denying these disadvantaged groups reservations by accepting the petitioner's argument would deny SEBCs their rightful benefit under Article 16(4), which is considered a fundamental right. Article 16(4) was designed to ensure equal opportunities in public employment and provide adequate representation to the marginalized sections of society. It was highlighted that although the report aimed to reserve 52 per cent of Central Government posts for OBCs, but due to legal limitations, it recommended a 27 per cent reservation, despite the OBC population being nearly double that figure.

The nine-judge bench delivered what would become a landmark judgement in the legal history of reservations in India.[42] The majority of the bench in a 6:3 ratio ruled that backward classes could be identified on the basis of economic factors as well as the caste system, thereby not limiting it to one criterion. Importantly, it was clarified that Article 16(4), which allows the state to provide special assistance to disadvantaged groups, did not exempt Article 16(1), which guarantees equal job opportunities to all citizens in government offices. Rather, it was designed to address specific sections of society, allowing reservation under Article 16(1) for groups other than those mentioned in Article 16(4). The court also clarified that the creamy layer – a term that refers to affluent or privileged members within these groups – should be excluded from these benefits, reservations should not exceed 50 per cent of positions and there should be no reservations for promotions.

The judgement stated, 'Article 46 contains a very significant directive to the State. It says: Promotion of educational and economic interests of Scheduled Castes, Scheduled Tribes and other weaker sections. The State shall promote with special care the educational and economic interests of the weaker sections of the people, and, in particular, of the Scheduled Castes and the Scheduled Tribes, and shall protect them from social injustice and all forms of exploitation. It is evident that 'the weaker sections of the people' do include the 'backward class of citizens' contemplated by Article 16(4).'

And so, the bench held the memorandum to be constitutionally valid.

But there were also three dissenting opinions on the bench.[43] Justices Kuldip Singh, T. K. Thommen, and R. M. Sahai. In their opinion, inadequate representation should be the sole criterion for determining backwardness under Article 16(4). Justice Kuldip Singh opined that poverty was the leading cause of backwardness and therefore economic criteria should be the determining factor for backwardness. Justice Pandian disagreed with the majority opinion of sub-classifying OBCs based on social backwardness and having separate quotas for them.

This was not all. The consideration of the question of whether Article 16(4) should apply to reservations in promotions was met with vehement opposition by K. Parasaran, counsel for the state, particularly as the question was not part of the original memorandum, and therefore not an issue before the court.[44] To this, Justice Ahmadi having sustained this preliminary objection, did not associate himself with the bench's deliberations on the subject.

Additionally, the court mandated the establishment of a body, either in the form of a commission or tribunal, to address complaints related to the incorrect inclusion or exclusion of groups in the lists of OBCs, which led to the National Commission for Backward Classes Act of 1993.

But the matter did not end with the verdict. Many states would go on to violate the 50 per cent cap on reservations, others would flout the exclusion of the 'creamy layer' rule to avoid upsetting influential groups and yet others would promise to include additional societal groups, such as Muslims. In the end, all political parties would manipulate reservations to their own political advantage.

Then there were other rights - those which all citizens are entitled to, regardless of caste, religion, or region. Fundamental rights such as life and liberty, bestowed upon all by the Constitution and protected by the judiciary. And within these broader rights, there is another important fundamental right – the right to freedom of speech and expression. Justice Ahmadi's thoughts on this are well demonstrated by his words, 'The Creator, call him by any name, gave the humankind the mind and the pen to be able to think rationally and to express their thoughts freely so that they may prompt others to think. That is why all modern Constitutions make freedom of speech and expression a fundamental right and so does our Constitution in Article 19(1)(a).'[45]

This was noted in LIC Insurance Corporation of India vs. Prof Manubhai D. Shah, a case that comprised two appeals, both emphasizing the plaintiff's right to freedom of expression.

And both the appeals revolved around incidents that criticized the government machinery.[46]

In the first appeal, the LIC Corporation's magazine had issued a response to an academic paper that criticized its policies, citing the premiums to be unnecessarily high. This response was in the form of a counter-article published in the national daily *The Hindu*, challenging the conclusions drawn by the respondent in his study paper. In turn, the author of the paper crafted a rejoinder, which was also published in the same newspaper.

Thereafter, LIC published its member's article – the critique of the academic study – in its own magazine but refused to publish the author's rejoinder, on the grounds that their internal magazine was not available to the general public, and therefore, the content was under LIC's discretion. But it was also true that the magazine was available to the public on subscription, and it invited articles from the general public.

In the second instance, a documentary film titled *Beyond Genocide* on the Bhopal Gas Tragedy, a catastrophic event involving a leak of hazardous gases and the culpability of Union Carbide for the ensuing fatalities, had won a national award. During the ceremony of the award presentation, the Central Minister for Information & Broadcasting had announced that the award-winning short films would be broadcast on the state-controlled Doordarshan channel. However, Doordarshan later declined to air the film.

Given that both LIC and Doordarshan were entities under government control, it was considered that fundamental rights were enforceable against them.[47] Separate writ petitions were filed before High Courts, and the appeals from both cases were consolidated to address a common question of law.

It was argued that in both cases, the matter was in the discretion of the relevant bodies. Since the LIC's publication was an internal one, the exercise of discretion was claimed to be within their purview. Similarly, for Doordarshan, given that not all award-winning films were necessarily broadcast, the same argument was applied.

But the petitioners alleged that the discretion was, in reality, a matter of the State suppressing dissent. And therefore, a violation of their fundamental rights.

The court found evidences in favour of the petitioners. Placing a greater burden on publications using public money to recognize these freedoms, it expanded the interpretation of freedom of expression, stating that it not only grants citizens the right to express their views, but also includes the right to defend them.[48] The judgement, authored by Justice Ahmadi stated, 'The LIC's refusal to publish the rejoinder in its magazine financed from public funds is an attitude, which can be described as both unfair and unreasonable; unfair because fairness demanded that both viewpoints were placed before the readers, however limited be their number, to enable them to draw their own conclusions, and unreasonable because there was no logic or proper justification for refusing publication. A monopolistic state instrumentality that survives on public funds cannot act in an arbitrary manner on the specious plea that the magazine is an in-house one and it is a matter of its exclusive privilege to print or refuse to print the rejoinder.'

The High Court's view was upheld and LIC was not only directed to print the rejoinder but also accompany it with an apology and explanation for the delay.

In the case of *Beyond Genocide*, the court stated that when the State rejects certain content, it must present legally valid reasons for doing so.

Arguments like the content presenting only one side of the debate were considered inconsistent with the principle of the freedom to express one's perspective on an event. ' . . . The petitioners, therefore, concede that the film faithfully brings out the events that took place at Bhopal on that fateful night. Therefore, the respondent cannot be accused of having distorted the events subsequent to the disaster. How then can it be alleged that it is not fair and balanced or lacks in moderation and restraint?'

Further, it stated, '[sic] To bring out the inadequacy of the State effort or the indifference of the officer, etc., cannot amount to an attack on any political party its the criticism is genuine and objective and made in good faith. If the norm for appraisal was the same as applied by the censors while granting the 'U' Certificate, it is difficult to understand how Doordarshan could refuse to exhibit it . . . It is even today of relevance and the press has been writing about it periodically . . . Doordarshan being a State-controlled agency funded by public funds could not have denied access to the screen to the respondent except on valid grounds.'

And so, both the appeals were dismissed. This judgement established a precedent that several future cases would eventually rely upon when tackling the complex questions of freedoms of speech and expression.

A rather intriguing skill that Justice Ahmadi had managed to master early on in his career was the art of compartmentalization. Each evening, as he took his place at the dining table, he made a conscious effort to clear his mind of the day's proceedings and fully engage in light-hearted family conversations. He would slip into playfulness with his grandchildren, teasing them and participating effortlessly in their made-up games. And when it was time to return to work after the table had been cleared away, he did so seamlessly and with equal ease. Family dinners were a time that, no matter the circumstance, were light, engaging and filled with animated chatter. It was almost impossible to fathom that just minutes before joining the table, Justice Ahmadi had been grappling with questions that had the potential to end an individual's life or charter the course of history. Not once did he disclose the nature of his work or the deliberations occurring either in the courtroom or his own mind.

His family routinely gleaned more about his work from newspapers than from Ahmadi himself. Colleagues and observers marvelled at this ability. However, for Justice Ahmadi, this skill was not just a matter of intrigue, it was a survival skill. He explained this to his curious law clerk on one occasion. 'If you keep thinking about work when you are not working, there is a danger you might let something slip. And I have never let anything slip or spoken to anyone – even Amena – about what I am thinking regarding a judgement. Accidently also I shouldn't reveal what I'm grappling with.' Admitting that it took a lot of years of practice, training and frustration before he was able to master the skill, he credited it to his long years as a trial court judge. 'It was tough for me as a young person, but now it is a part of my ethos. I have to be careful that I shouldn't think about it – so that it doesn't inadvertently come out. It is a responsibility to ensure that what is confidential remains so.'

With confidentiality, there was also the challenge of withstanding the watchful eye of an unforgiving public gaze. The media's scrutiny, marked by sensationalism and unforgiving criticism, was entirely unpredictable. Facing affections and disaffections that oscillate wildly, making the same person a subject of admiration one day and animosity the next, judges face the challenging task of maintaining objectivity even in the face of unpopularity. It requires immense strength of character and conviction to remain true to one's course and not become swayed by the capricious tides of public perception.

Every action, expression and statement is observed minutely, scrutinized and dissected for public consumption. One day there are brickbats, the very next day, bouquets. Ahmadi had recognized this character of the press early on in his career, and so, maintained his equilibrium with relative ease.

These challenges are unique to decision makers that work in the public eye. In Justice Ahmadi's own words, ' . . . unlike the members of the bureaucracy, who mostly work in their chambers, the judges work in the full gaze of the public, the media, the lawyers and the staff-members who watch their performance and form impressions. There is always the pressure that they are being watched. The entire process of adjudication is transparent. Their decisions are reasoned. Their judgments criticised in the press and even on TV.'[49]

And yet, in the quiet corridors of justice, he had achieved this remarkable feat – the mastery of isolating the cacophony of media scrutiny from the essence of his convictions. Despite his commitment to staying well-informed by thoroughly reading every national daily from cover to cover, once the newspapers were laid aside, his mind was cleared like a slate wiped clean. The skill of compartmentalization that helped him maintain confidentially also played a fundamental role in preserving clarity and independence of thought. Unfazed by the unpredictable tides of public opinion, his judgements were dispensed without concern for the narratives that newspapers might weave the next day. His ability to shield his judicial decisions from the ebbs and flows of media influence revealed a profound resilience. Behind the measured words of his judgements lay the weight of a mind unburdened by external pressures, a testament to his immense mental fortitude. This was important, given the essential nature of judicial independence. In Ahmadi's words, 'Judicial Independence is not a privilege enjoyed by judges; it is a privilege of, and protection for the people.'[50]

While the professional and personal pressures that judges go through are relatively well documented, there is limited understanding of the mental strains they endure. And for Justice Ahmadi, these were only going to get worse, because, although he didn't know it yet, his personal life was on the brink of a major upheaval.

Twenty-seven-year-old Tasneem Ahmadi was in a dilemma. Taking a deep breath, she picked up the phone and dialled her parents' home. An unfamiliar voice answered – a new staff member, she guessed. She asked to speak with her mother, Amena Ahmadi. After what felt like an eternity, her mother's soft voice on the phone, '*Haan*, Tasneem *dikra?*' In that moment the floodgates opened, releasing a torrent of emotions, some coherent, some incoherent. But the message was clear – Tasneem had decided to end her marriage.

Amena Ahmadi was in shock. Slowly, she returned the phone to its cradle, but her daughter's voice wouldn't stop ringing in her head. The revelation that things had taken a turn for the worse a full seven years earlier coinciding with the birth of her granddaughter in 1982 gnawed at her thoughts. How had she missed the signs? Chaotic thoughts churning within her, she picked up the phone and dialled Justice Ahmadi's office intercom number.

Half an hour later, the distressed parents, seated at the familiar foot of their bed, exchanged worried glances. That evening, a call was made to Tasneem Ahmadi. An anxious Ama and Huzefa huddled around the phone receiver, straining to catch every word as Justice Ahmadi, his tone suddenly softening, asked his daughter if she was sure she wanted to end her marriage. She was.

And so it was armed with nothing but the clothes on her back, two small children and a pair of her favourite *jootis* tucked in her armpit that Tasneem Ahmadi fled from Bombay to Delhi.

The next few years would include negotiations and promises, but Tasneem remained firm. She and her children were safe – and that was enough.

At first, my five-year-old brother and seven-year-old self assumed that we were on yet another vacation at our grandparents' home – this time in Lutyens Delhi, known for its wide, tree-lined streets and majestic bungalows. Excited at the prospect of a new city and a new house, we knew nothing of the difficulties and challenges that had preceded our arrival. Instantly captivated by the sprawling gardens that beckoned us to explore on our bicycles and the old gnarly trees laden with fruits that invited us to clamber upon them, we proceeded to make the most of the visit, greedily plucking the sweet mulberries and sour raw mangoes off the trees and taking shameless advantage of the tolerant staff who revelled in our playful energy and indulged our every whim. Because it took a small army to run and maintain the enormous bungalow and its vast grounds, the staff quarters were almost a settlement in and of itself. Located behind the back gardens and separated by a rickety gate were rows of small accommodations occupied by the staff and their families, a kitchen garden for their own use, tended to carefully by the gardeners, and even livestock. A cow and a buffalo ensured that the milk was always fresh and creamy, the handful of hens provided the staff and their families with fresh eggs. The offices located on the right side of the bungalow, where my grandfather's secretaries worked seemed boring to us at first, but we quickly changed our minds when we discovered the presence of a single desktop computer, loaded with pre-installed games – a rare find in 1989. Very quickly, we figured out that if we timed our visits correctly on days when their workload was light, the three secretaries were too gentle to refuse us access to their computer.

A few weeks in, and we had already given this new bungalow our official stamp of approval. The sprawling gardens and fruit trees were the clinching factor, and we were pleased, thinking our summer holidays would now be spent here. Not only was this bungalow three times the size of the last one, we also had our own room here. The long corridors were perfect for running about and the many smaller rooms made games like hide-and-seek even more exciting. The large verandas opening into massive lawns were perfect for the antics of two noisy children. It was only when we were informed that we would be attending school in Delhi that realization dawned upon us. Far from being dismayed, we were delighted at the prospect of living with our loving, indulgent grandparents in a home with huge gardens to play in. I cannot say we suffered from any challenges of adaptation or adjustment.

At the time, we were oblivious to the fact that the course of our lives had been reshaped and redirected. Our mother was working hard, determined to build a legal career for herself, and our grandfather had assumed the responsibility of supporting an additional three people on a judge's salary. Family finances were stretched thin, leaving little room for extravagances. Family dynamics had changed as well, with profound implications. Our father figure was now our grandfather. We would grow to rely on his counsel before taking any decisions in our adult life. We would observe him closely as he navigated the often-stormy waters of his career and matters of national importance, learning the difficult lessons of integrity, courage and dignity under fire. Our *nani ma* would raise and nurture us, reinforcing these lessons. She would provide solace and support to both us and our mother.

But we would not realize the enormity of these changes until much later. For now, climbing trees and running about in the lawns was enough.

As time passed and we settled into our new home almost effortlessly, the only pesky annoyance that surfaced time and again was the security detail that we now needed. Each member of the family was assigned a security officer responsible for ensuring our constant protection. These sentinels, known as Personal Security Officers (PSOs), were a source of constant exasperation. Suddenly, our anonymity had become a casualty of our new life. Now, we were never alone. In the mornings, as my brother Adnan and I were bundled into the car for school, like clockwork, two beefy men materialized in the driveway. They slid into the front seat of the white Ambassador, their presence as unwelcome as the morning sun to reluctant school goers. Initially, they had wished to station themselves outside our classrooms through the day. But even they had their limits, and we breathed a sigh of relief when our school principals intervened. After some negotiations, a compromise was reached – the PSOs would be permitted to position themselves at the school gates, as long as they agreed to wait outside until the end of the school day.

Now, whether it was a casual evening stroll beneath the dusky sky, or an afternoon spent at a friend's home, these well-trained, discreet men were always a few steps behind. They blended into the background, keeping a respectful distance, their poker faces revealing nothing. They had become, to our dismay, an integral part of our lives, causing us much childish embarrassment.

Yet, this was a minor inconvenience. For the most part life was grand, although occasionally perplexing when we grappled with our grandfather's public identity. We were only just beginning to suspect that he was an important man.

Even so, it would still take me some time to truly understand why my grandfather could no longer do the simple things other families did, like go to the cinemas or restaurants, or why his movements had to be planned days in advance, requiring elaborate security arrangements. While the rest of us occasionally took our evening walks on the broad leafy streets of Krishna Menon Marg, albeit under the watchful eyes of our PSOs, my grandfather was compelled to take his within the compound of our bungalow. I know now that, aside from the financial aspect, it was these sorts of 'sacrifices' that Aziz Ahmadi had spoken to his young wife thirty years ago, before accepting judgeship of the City Civil Court.

Our grandmother had slipped into her new role with remarkable ease, almost as if it were a second skin. As the matriarch of the enormous household, she conducted its affairs with the precision of a seasoned orchestra conductor, arranging each task and responsibility with effortless grace, ensuring that every aspect of our daily lives flowed harmoniously. Whether it involved managing the diverse schedules of six family members each day or organizing flawless, elaborate dinners for VIPs in the impressive stately dining room with all the necessary protocols, she made it all look deceptively effortless. This quiet and meticulous oversight was the glue that held our household together, making it a place of order, warmth and hospitality.

One of the few things she struggled with in those initial years was the Hindi language. Having so far had no need to speak the language, both my grandparents spoke an endearing version of Hindi that contained several Gujarati words and phrases. The staff, amused by this comic blend of languages, nevertheless adapted quickly. The second challenge was the pervasive sense of loneliness. Because Supreme Court judges are bound by a far more stringent sense of propriety and security than their counterparts in High Courts, Ama found forming meaningful connections to be uniquely challenging. The camaraderie that she had enjoyed with her friends and neighbours in Ahmedabad and Surat was now elusive. Still, this was alleviated to a large extent with the arrival of her beloved daughter and grandchildren.

Although she and Justice Ahmadi shared a rare partnership, Justice Ahmadi remained the undisputed patriarch of the family. Every major decision in the lives of his children and grandchildren would only go through with his approval. Yet, if he was to be persuaded to change his mind, it could only be engineered through the gentle hands of Ama. With her quiet demeanour, her usual stance was of deference, preferring the role of quiet influence. But on occasion, she would feel strongly enough about something to voice her dissent, demonstrated by a purposeful clearing of the throat. A gentle gesture; repeated if not acknowledged. But on the rarest of occasions, when she inserted herself into a family drama, clearing her throat in her deliberate manner and commencing with a deliberate, 'Aziz . . .' we knew that although Justice Ahmadi might protest in the beginning, he would eventually yield to her quiet strength. Quickly we learnt to route special requests through our grandmother, realizing they had a greater chance for *nana jaan's* approval that way.

Justice Ahmadi was beginning to look noticeably different. His once-jet black hair now had a salt and pepper shade around the ears. He had put on weight, giving him a robustness that suited him well. His lean frame had softened slightly, his waistline expanded with a new, soft roundness around the belly. The chest hair that peeked out of the collar of the white kurta pyjamas he wore at home had shifted from black to shimmering silver. His taut jawline looked slacker, a slight hint of a double chin when he peered down at his files.

But the most striking change was the air of seriousness and gravity that now enveloped him. Looking more and more distinguished as the days passed, he wore the weight of his new responsibilities well. It was as if they had infused him with an even greater sense of purpose. Busier than ever before, he no longer had the time for long tales and frequent leisurely walks. And yet, he had never looked more content, more assured and more certain. He was on the cusp of the very pinnacle of his life, and it was evident in every aspect of his being. With not the slightest shred of nervousness or hesitation, he was simply . . . ready.

The transition from judge to legal statesman was complete.

But every now and then, the playful *nana jaan* of earlier years could be persuaded to emerge. There was the occasional game of table tennis, played on the large dining table with a makeshift net that could sometimes entice him, the sound of the ping pong ball ricocheting off the wooden table, a temptation too sweet to resist. Or a friendly game of cricket between the Bar and the Bench that he allowed himself the indulgence of. On rare occasions, he could be tempted into a game of *kola daam* (a traditional version of ludo) – but only after the 9 p.m. news telecast at the end of the day. Sometimes, however, these evenings were quieter, with deep conversations that were held during post-dinner walks in the gardens among the scent of *raat ki raani* and jasmine flowers. It was in these moments that I truly discovered my grandfather, his depth of character, mischievous wit and contagious zest for life.

On occasion, I witnessed him dictating letters to one of his three secretaries. Effortlessly speaking from memory, he dictated pages upon pages of information, addressing each aspect he wished to include with astonishing clarity before moving on to the next. With his legs crossed at the ankle and arms casually spread out on the armchair, Justice Ahmadi spoke slowly and deliberately as the secretary, hunched over a notebook, furiously scribbled notes in shorthand. The room buzzed with focused energy as the pen scratched across the paper, capturing every uttered word. Amid his intense concentration, a short pause usually meant a reconsideration of the sentence structure he had just dictated. 'Change that last word,' he would instruct, seamlessly continuing without any break in concentration or interruption in the train of thought. One can only imagine the intense focus and mastery of the mind required to dictate hundreds of pages of judgements.

His wicked sense of humour, too, remained unscathed by the passage of time. On one occasion, as he sat in the barber's chair, his hairdresser helpfully suggested that Ahmadi dye his greying sideburns black. With mischief in his eyes, Aziz turned to the well-meaning man and said in Gujarati, 'My dear man, it has taken me 60 years to turn these white, you want me to undo all that in one minute?' This sense of humour, especially demonstrated in tough times, would remain with him until his last breath. In the twilight of his life, when a health scare forced him into a brief hospitalization, he turned to his doctor in his characteristic fashion and demanded impatiently to be discharged and sent home. Upon learning that yet another day in the hospital was needed to run additional tests, he fixed the doctor with his stern, piercing gaze and quipped, 'Now you are reminding me of a lawyer, always seeking adjournments.'

A storm of unrest had been brewing in North India for many years, one which would, over the course of several years, become marked by bloodshed and high-profile assassinations. Eventually, and many years later, these events of the 1980s would finally culminate in a case that was destined for Justice Ahmadi's courtroom in 1992. It would become the only judgement of his career in which the typically restrained Justice Ahmadi handed out the death sentence.

At the heart of all these events was the growing fervour for Khalistan, an independent Sikh state within the borders of Punjab – a movement that had been ongoing for several years. The Golden Temple in Amritsar, a site holier than any other for the Sikh community, was used as an operational hub for these factions, serving as a stronghold for their activities. Faced with the escalating situation and growing popularity of separatist elements, Prime Minister Indira Gandhi made a fateful choice that would eventually end her own life. In 1984, she ordered Operation Blue Star, a military operation aimed at regaining control of the temple complex from the militants. The four-day-long clash between the Indian Armed Forces and the militants at a time when large numbers of civilians were trapped in the temple resulted in tremendous loss of life. The world watched in horror as the death toll grew, and Sikhs across the world responded with outrage. The Operation may have been successful in wresting control of the site, but it came at a heavy cost. The decision to use military force on a sacred site was not a wise one, the ramifications of which would prove to be tragic. A mere four months after the deeply contentious move, Indira Gandhi was assassinated by her Sikh bodyguards, sparking nationwide riots. But the Sikh factions, still boiling with rage, were not finished. Two years later, in 1986, General A.S. Vaidya was assassinated by two Sikh youths.

General Vaidya was, at the time of the operation, Chief of Army Staff and therefore responsible for much of the coordination that went into Operation Blue Star. On 10 August 1986 in Pune, while the retired General and his wife were in their Maruti car, two motorcycles pulled up beside them. Before their bodyguard could even turn to look, a black-jacketed individual pulled a revolver out of his boot and pumped a whole magazine of bullets into the car before speeding off. But the first bullet itself was enough – the General was dead and his wife badly injured.[51]

General Vaidya's assassins, Jinda and Sukha, were captured the same day and subsequently tried for murder. Shockingly, this was not their first assassination. The two men had previously assassinated Lalit Maken[52] and Geetanjali, son-in-law and daughter of then future President of India Shankar Dayal Sharma as well as Congress leader Arjan Dass.[53] Dass had been murdered for his alleged involvement in the 1984 anti-Sikh riots.[54] Maken, too, faced a similar fate for the same alleged reason, and his wife Geetanjali, sadly, got caught in the crossfire and became collateral damage. Upon capture, the two men boldly admitted that they had, indeed, assassinated General Vaidya. Further, they informed the trial court that they were proud of their act and unafraid of death. The trial court viewed the case as 'rarest of rare' and awarded both men the highest form of punishment – the death sentence. Appealing to the Supreme Court, the case was then brought before a bench which consisted of Justice Ahmadi and Justice K. Ramaswamy. This bench also upheld the sentence of the Designated Court. But the fervour around their cause had catapulted Jinda and Sukha into the spotlight – they had morphed into legends within certain segments of the Sikh community, their act elevating them to a demi-god status. As the execution loomed, attempts were made to stall its implementation.[55] In September 1992, the President of the Akali Dal, Simranjit Singh Mann filed a petition seeking a stay on the execution orders of Sukha and Jinda.[56] Mann demanded to be allowed to enter the courtroom with his sword, but he was denied entry by court security. Justice Ahmadi maintained that if the security arrangements didn't allow it, then the judges would not interfere. He pointed out that should Mann wish to hear the court proceedings, he must 'abide by the discipline of the court'.

Two days before the scheduled execution, fifteen Sikh leaders and their followers assembled in the Supreme court, seeking an audience with the Chief Justice, Justice M.H. Kania.[57] Their letter to the Supreme Court stated that the accused, 'in the eye of every Sikh, are heroes and living martyrs and it is the bounden duty of all Sikhs all over the world to save their lives.' This attempt was made despite their plea being turned down just the previous month.

But there was one more petition pending.[58] The petitioner, an undertrial who had spent the past six years in Tihar jail for an attempt on the life of Rajiv Gandhi, had approached the court as the 'next friend' of Jinda and Sukha. The petition had been filed under Article 32 of the Constitution questioning the legality and validity of their conviction as sentenced by the Designated Court as well as the Supreme Court. Appearing on behalf of the Union of India was the Additional Solicitor General.

Viewing this as a diversionary tactic, Justice Ahmadi took a bold and unusual step. Determined not to be arm-twisted into delaying the execution, he decided to hold a late night hearing at his residence. Calling upon his brother judge, Justice K. Ramaswamy, the bench was constituted, and the proceedings unfolded into the wee hours of the morning.

As the night wore on, security presence swelled around Krishna Menon Marg. The usually quiet street flanked by ancient gnarly trees was bursting at the seams with police and security personnel. The bungalow was sealed off, a virtual fortress with barricades positioned at every entrance and every exit. The street was closed off, and traffic was re-diverted to parallel streets. As the clock ticked, the two judges deliberated upon the maintainability of the petition before pronouncing their judgement. It was found that the petitioner had no locus standi to move the court as he did not do so on behalf of the convicts.[59] In fact, the convicted had issued oral and written instructions that their friends and family should refrain from seeking mercy for them, making it clear that this petition was not filed at their behest. Further, the argument that the two convicts were mentally impaired due to their 'obsession' that the person responsible for desecrating the Harminder Sahib should not be allowed to live, thus constituting a legal disability, was also deemed untenable. The judgement clarified that any disability that permits a third party to initiate legal proceedings must be one that the law recognizes. The judgement stated, 'Such a submission, urged the learned Additional Solicitor General, is fraught with grave consequences and would, we agree, shake the very foundation of the rule of law on which a civilised society is based if the aggrieved person is allowed to take the law in his own hands and later plead disability on the ground that his action emanated from an acute obsession that his victim had by his action forfeited the right to live and deserved to be punished with death. Such a submission cannot be countenanced.'

In the pitch blackness of the night, the original verdict was upheld.[60] The next morning, on 9 October 1992, General Vaidya's assassins were hanged until death.

During this time, a subtler implication began to emerge from the shadows. One of Justice Ahmadi's most trusted secretaries happened to be a Sikh gentleman. As the case was placed before Ahmadi in the Supreme Court, and then again in the wake of the late night hearing, whispers of concern were voiced. There had already been two high profile assassinations at the hands of Sikh individuals, and it was feared that Justice Ahmadi might be the next target in this grim sequence – chosen for his verdict that upheld the death sentence for Jinda and Sukha.

So, to ensure Justice Ahmadi's safety, it was thought best to eliminate any potential connection that could attract danger. And so, the Chief of Security approached Justice Ahmadi with a proposition. He suggested that Ahmadi dismiss his Sikh secretary, offering to replace him with another, equally capable gentleman of a different religion. Bristling at the suggestion that an employee be dismissed based on their religious background, this struck at the very core of his principles. Justice Ahmadi refused outright. Over the course of the next few weeks, the Chief of Security continued to apply pressure on Ahmadi, hoping to change his mind. But Ahmadi was unmoved.

A true secularist, Justice Ahmadi was also a member of a minority community himself, and as such, he was no stranger to the experiences that come with bearing a minority identity. He too belonged to a community that is vilified for the acts of a select few. He too had been the subject of many a whisper that questioned his motives because of his religion. He knew all too well the humiliation of being singled out, of being forced to prove one's loyalty to the nation when others are not. And so, in a resolute stand against any form of prejudice, Justice Ahmadi rejected the proposal outright. The Sikh secretary remained faithfully and steadfastly at Justice Ahmadi's side until the day he retired and even beyond.

But the potential dangers persisted.

Years later, during an official trip to Nanded, Justice Ahmadi would receive an invitation to visit Gurudwara Huzoor Sahib.⁶¹ In response, he politely reminded his well-meaning host of this judgement, hinting towards a potential threat to his life if he were to accept their kind invitation. The invitation was immediately retracted, and his colleagues went on the excursion without him.

It was in the 1990s that the hate mail started pouring in. The more controversial cases that Justice Ahmadi ruled on, the bigger the stacks of hate mail grew. In the beginning, his diligent secretaries took it upon themselves to discreetly dispose of these offensive letters. They dismissed them as the rants of disgruntled individuals unworthy of His Lordship's attention. However, when he got wind of this practice, Justice Ahmadi directed that the letters be sent to him. And so, at the foot of his bed, where a makeshift baithak was created for him to sit on the floor and read as he preferred to do, there was now a new addition. A pile of letters, each brimming with a cocktail of indignation and hostility. It was in this private sanctum that he confronted the unfiltered sentiments of those who were displeased with his judgements.

One afternoon, soon after Huzefa Ahmadi was married in 1994, Justice Ahmadi's new daughter-in-law happened to be in the room when Ahmadi opened one of these letters. Observing her face filled with curiosity as he peered over the bifocals perched precariously over the bridge of his nose, he handed the letter to her. Recoiling at the vicious language and contents, she asked her father-in-law, 'Why do you read these?' 'It's important, *beta*,' he responded, 'We must understand the minds of the people we serve. We must not become so detached that we lose sight of their perspectives.'

And so, Justice Ahmadi continued to read the letters filled with hate just as he did the congratulatory ones.

But the climate of hate was not confined to his home. The waves of hatred that threatened to blow through the nation were only just stirring. The year was 1992, which stands out as a watershed moment that forever changed the country's socio-political landscape. With the ascent of the BJP in mainstream politics after years of Congress monopoly, the Hindutva movement was gaining newfound momentum. Hindu nationalist rhetoric, which had so far been mostly ignored by the educated elite as a far-fetched improbability, was beginning to appear more regularly in mainstream media. Drawing room conversations began to frequently include worried allusions to 'fringe elements' destroying the peace of the nation. Speeches by L.K. Advani and others targeting secularists and advocating for a Hindu *rashtra* were first dismissed as laughably outrageous, but later became alarming and difficult to discount.

Extremist groups armed with weapons, hateful rhetoric and a divisive agenda were becoming not only more vocal in their ideals, but also more visible on the streets, intimidating and terrorizing local populations. Although their rhetoric and actions were met with widespread condemnation from secular Indians – including several BJP politicians who chose to maintain a safe distance – the unchecked rise of these groups in the political sphere led to the emergence of a new chapter in India's history, one that would have profound implications for the country's future. L.K. Advani's contentious rath yatra had concluded in a blaze of political glory, and the hardline Hindutva gaze was now fixed firmly on the next target. The Babri Masjid.

8

The Ayodhya Matter

A word which many had never heard before was now coming up every single day. *Kar seva*.

The television in Justice Ahmadi's bedroom, the only one equipped with cable, stayed locked on the news channel from morning to night. His three secretaries burned the midnight oil, and Ahmadi himself spent all day in his private office located just off the main bungalow. He only emerged at dinnertime, which was eaten in the family room in silence while the adults intently watched the 9 p.m. news on Doordarshan. The news hour would inadvertently be followed by passionate discussions between the adults regarding the contents of the news telecast. Soon after dinner, Justice Ahmadi returned to work. The rest of the family turned in for the night.

The TV's constant murmur, the secretaries rushing to and from the offices with pens and notepads in hand, the focussed huddle around the dinner table and Justice Ahmadi's continued absence from family life – all were pieces of a vivid puzzle that defined those days.

But it was clear that there was trouble between Hindus and Muslims. Dinnertime conversations in the Ahmadi household often contained worried allusions to the future of the Indian Muslim, the position of the Supreme Court after its 'blunder,' the demolition of the Masjid and, sometimes, how many people had died.

The cause of all this distress were the events of 6 December 1992, which witnessed the brazen impunity with which a large group of Hindu extremists and their supporters violated the Supreme Court's status quo order and illegally decimated the Babri Mosque in Ayodhya.[1] The audacity of this act was astonishing as the demolition took place under the benign gaze of officials, politicians and police personnel, all of whom were either unable or unwilling to stop the destruction. The aftermath of this event swept through the country but was felt most acutely in Mumbai, where the city was plunged into a cycle of bloody riots and bomb blasts. These riots blazed across all of India killing approximately 2000 people,[2] mostly Muslims. In response, Bangladesh and Pakistan saw retaliatory violence against local Hindus and the destruction of several temples.

The stage for this carnage, however, had inadvertently been set by the Supreme Court of India.

In 1992, the VHP and other Hindu organizations received permission from the Supreme Court to conduct a 'symbolic kar seva,' which was essentially authorization for a group of *kar sevaks* (religious volunteers) to assemble at the site of the mosque and perform Hindu religious rituals. But this was not the first time the Court had heard a petition for a kar seva at the contentious site. Earlier the same year, the Supreme Court had permitted another such kar seva in July 1992, only to witness a flagrant violation of the status quo order by the groups of people who had congregated at the site. The act of violation included the illegal construction of a platform at the site of the mosque, which was declared as the foundation of the Ram Temple that would one day replace the Babri Mosque. Wary of the possibility of another such transgression and contempt of the Court, the bench demanded an assurance from the State Government this time. Before granting permission for the kar seva, the Supreme Court Bench comprising Justices Venkatachaliah and G.N. Ray mandated that the Uttar Pradesh State Government, which was under BJP rule, provide a formal undertaking stating that if permission for the kar seva was granted, the sanctity of the status quo order would be upheld and not infringed upon again.

In response to this, Kalyan Singh, the Chief Minister of Uttar Pradesh furnished an affidavit assuring the Court of the competence of the state's law and order machinery and stating that negotiations with the kar sevaks had been fruitful. However, it also stated that while they were confident of the ability of the law and order department to handle any situation, they would not, under any circumstance, fire upon the kar sevaks.

The peculiar framing of the statement coupled with the historical contempt of the court order, created consternation in the courtroom with opposing counsel O. P. Sharma articulating his doubts about the intentions of the Uttar Pradesh government. Sharma's astute observation as recorded in the court order of 28 November 1992 stated, 'Shri Sharma said that once a large mass of humanity is allowed to congregate on the spot, the State Government on its own self-confessed inability or disinclination to use force against the devotees would achieve indirectly what it was forbidden to do directly. Shri Sharma asserts that the previous experience of what happened between 6 and 26 July 1992, should put the court on guard and examine whether the State Government is adopting a stratagem to enable the collection of a large mass of people who ultimately will be allowed to, and formally blamed for taking the law into their own hands and pleading its own helplessness.'[3] Later proved to be astoundingly accurate, this cautioning was, at the time, disregarded by the Court. Adding to the gravity of the situation, Attorney General Milon Banerji raised urgent concerns on 27 November 1992, alerting the Court about vital intel provided by the Intelligence Bureau, which pointed to an imminent threat to the mosque. Urging the bench to act in protection of the mosque, the Attorney General informed the court that the situation in Ayodhya was rapidly deteriorating with the arrival of large numbers of men. Responding to the concern, Justice Venkatachaliah is reported to have stated, 'Preparation is not an offence. Only on our fullest satisfaction before us that the State Government has failed in its duty will we pass any orders. The locus penitentium is still not crossed by them. We will see when they do.'[4]

And so, despite these warnings recorded in the courtroom, Justice Venkatchaliah decided to grant permission for a symbolic kar seva just a few days before he was to be sworn in as Chief Justice of India.

The foundation was laid for a clash of ideologies and a test of the Court's authority.

And so it came to be that on 6 December 1992, in what was clear and blatant contempt of the court order, a mass of youths who were insofar described as 'peaceful kar sevaks' turned into a raging mob of vandals who rapidly breached police cordons, clambered atop the mosque and proceeded to desecrate and destroy the three signature domes.

The event was, by all accounts, a shameful act of illegal vandalism and in grave contempt of the Supreme Court.[5] As a consequence of no limits being set on the numbers of people permitted to participate, the morning of 6 December saw a wave of humanity, numbering nearly 1.5 lakh self-proclaimed kar sevaks, thronging to the mosque. Almost all of BJP's top leaders were present in Ayodhya at the time, as well as local leaders of Hindutva organizations such as the Vishwa Hindu Parishad (VHP) and Bajrang Dal. As the town pulsated with growing hysteria, armed men eventually broke into the mosque, breaching the security cordons, easily overpowering the scanty number of police personnel deployed and scaling the outside walls. Slithering over the masjid armed with hammers, ropes and pickaxes, these young men who had been inducted into the movement over the past several years by fringe elements of the VHP, Bajrang Dal and other Hindu extremist groups triumphantly waved about saffron flags and trishuls in a show of victory. Inciting and divisive chants of '*Jis Hindu ka khoon na khaule, woh khoon nahin pani hai* [The Hindu whose blood doesn't boil, doesn't have blood in his veins but water].' '*Jai Shri Ram, mandir yahin banayenge* [We will build the Ram temple right here]' pierced through the cold December air, further whipping the crowd into a frenzy. It was to this rhythm of hate that the Babri Masjid was ravaged, and its domes fractured. As the mosque began to crumble under the assault of the swarming gangs of Hindu extremist foot soldiers, delighted chants of '*Ek dhakka aur do, Babri Masjid tod do* [Give one more shove, bring the masjid down]' accompanied the final thunderous heave before a saffron flag was planted firmly atop the small mosque accompanied by jubilant kar sevaks who pranced around on top of the sacred mosque for the news cameras. And so it was that the ancient mosque, which had quietly and sturdily withstood the elements for almost half a millennium, finally succumbed to the assault by a well-trained infantry. The onslaught, which had started at 11 a.m. on 6 December 1992, was neatly concluded by 5 p.m., well before teatime. By 6 p.m., the site was quiet again, except this time enveloped in a thick red cloud of dust and debris with pieces of dome and centuries of history lying in ruins around it.

But the kar sevaks weren't finished. Going on a rampage over the town of Ayodhya, they demolished homes and shops, attacked local Muslims and destroyed 23 smaller mosques.[6] Significantly, one of the homes they destroyed belonged to Mohammad Hashim Ansari, one of the original litigants of the Babri Masjid case.[7]

Furious at the impunity and brazenness of the contempt, Justice Venkatachaliah held a special hearing at his residence on the same day, despite it being a Sunday. K.K. Venugopal, counsel for the Uttar Pradesh government, is said to have immediately withdrawn from the case saying, 'My head hangs in shame.'[8]

At home, we watched these scenes on television in horror. My grandparents sat close together at the foot of the bed as they always did, the rest of us scattered around the room. We watched L.K. Advani and Uma Bharati hug each other in joy as the domes fell, and then our grandparents' ashen faces. Justice Ahmadi records this moment as being a deeply regrettable error by the apex court. Disappointment was writ large across his face. Dressed in his usual white kurta pajama, he turned the TV off and got up from the bed with a sigh. Barefoot and with his hands clasped behind his back, he started pacing up and down his large, carpeted bedroom, as was his way when he was uneasy. With sorrow, he said, 'Remember my words, India will never be the same again.'

But even he had not anticipated the full extent of the assault and the subsequent loss of lives that followed. As the events unfolded over the next few days, he remained publicly silent. Restrained by propriety while in office, he refrained from criticism of the bench and its ruling. However, once retired, he was free to speak about the role that the Supreme Court played in the demolition on several occasions.[9] Speaking at a seminar in

2010, he pointed out that Milon Banerji had repeatedly warned the Court of the impending dangers to the mosque, but to no avail. 'Instead, the court passed an order allowing a symbolic kar seva. Had that order not been passed, the mosque would have been standing today,' he said.

Predictably, the public backlash was tremendous. Emotions were running high and endless criticism and condemnation were levelled at the Supreme Court for permitting the kar seva despite the numerous warnings recorded in the courtroom. Deeply uncomfortable questions were raised by the media, whose indignation over the demolition was fierce. 'Nation's Shame' bellowed the headline on the cover page of the *India Today* magazine.[10] 'The Republic Besmirched' was splashed on the front page of *The Times of India*.[11] Chief Minister Kalyan Singh resigned, and Uttar Pradesh was finally brought under President's rule, although sadly too late to salvage the mosque.

Twelve days after the nightmarish incident, the apex court responded by issuing notices to Kalyan Singh and six senior officers for breach of the undertaking submitted to the Court.[12] But the Court found itself on a back foot when the accused filed their counter affidavits, which posed embarrassing questions that turned the spotlight back onto the Court's own role in the event. After all, Kalyan Singh had plainly stated that they would not use force on the kar sevaks under any circumstances, so how could they be faulted for the uncontrolled crowds that breached the security cordons? Questions were also raised regarding the wide publicization of the permission for the kar seva granted by the Court and its consequence of attracting larger numbers of Hindus on the day.

Besides, the harsh glare of the media was unrelenting. Why were the warnings of Milon Banerji and O.P. Sharma disregarded when considering the petition for the kar seva? Why did the Court not act at the time of the first violation of the status quo order six months ago? Did their inaction not encourage the kar sevaks to breach the court order once again? Why did the Court grant permission despite Kalyan Singh's blunt refusal to fire upon the kar sevaks if they were to lose control over the crowds? Why did the Court allow an unlimited number of people to congregate at the site, with no cap placed on the number of kar sevaks permitted? These were all tricky questions, which the Court was ill-equipped to answer.

Ironically, the Supreme Court order had become the BJP's legal shield.

Perhaps this was the reason no action was taken against the Uttar Pradesh government for all twenty months of Venkatachaliah's tenure. In the end, Kalyan Singh faced no punishment except for a token one-day imprisonment on a lesser charge of a smaller contempt committed by him five months before the demolition, on the very last day of Justice Venkatachaliah's tenure as Chief Justice of India.[13] Calling it a 'farce' in his personal writings, Justice Ahmadi recounts the sentence that was handed out. The sentence condemned Kalyan Singh to a token imprisonment for the remainder of the day at a time when the Court was to be adjourned in a mere hour or two, thereby signalling the end of the day. Witnessing this empty gesture, Ahmadi was once again disappointed by the Court's unwillingness to take a tough stand and punish the guilty. In later years, once retired and released from the bounds of propriety, Ahmadi would openly and publicly attribute these missteps of the apex Court to the erosion of secularism in India.

The failure to take contempt action against Singh for breach of undertaking has been noted as not only a damaging blow to the sanctity of the Supreme Court, but also as the setting of a dangerous precedent, one which the Supreme Court has been observed to maintain till date in its consistent failure to punish those responsible for the events of the fateful day in Ayodhya – this pattern of inaction too, Justice Ahmadi would publicly condemn once retired.

The Congress party would pay a heavy price for their error in judgement. Declining to impose President's rule in Ayodhya under Article 356 ahead of the kar seva, as well as failing to intervene and block the demolition on the day itself, would serve as the final nail in their coffin. Evidently, Advani's proclamation in a public speech held less than a week before the kar seva assuring the crowd that the kar seva would be held with 'bricks and shovels'[14] – a statement he would later deny making – was not considered alarming enough for the Centre to take pre-emptive action. Further, when he received news of the kar sevaks having breached the police cordons, Prime Minister P. V. Narasimha Rao appeared to have got cold feet and failed to invoke Article 356, which would permit the Centre to override the state administration in order to restore law and order. It is ironic that the Congress party, repeatedly criticized for its indiscriminate use of Article 356, chose not to employ it on this critical occasion.

Narasimha Rao faced tremendous public and political criticism for his failure to act. Perhaps he truly felt as betrayed as his statement suggests, 'The Constitution is the mother of the central and the state governments. The state government's act on December 6 is like the child stabbing the mother.'[15] But Rao's professed astonishment and insistence that the government could not have foreseen the calamity were debunked by the revelations in the memoirs of then Union Home Secretary, Madhav Godbole who had resigned in protest against the Babri demolition.[16]

Initially promising to rebuild the mosque, Rao eventually capitulated to the Hindutva rhetoric of 'righting historic wrongs'. The Congress party responded by disowning Rao, isolating him and leaving him politically untethered. But the damage was done. Rao's political career and the Congress party's fate lay in ruins right beside the fractured domes of the Babri Mosque, from where neither would recover.

Atal Bihari Vajpayee, a top leader of the BJP at the time, maintained a safe distance from the fiasco that was the Babri Masjid demolition. Known for his political shrewdness, aversion to lumpen violence and reluctance to associate with the leaders of Bajrang Dal and other Hindutva groups, he chose not to be present at Ayodhya on 6 December 1992. Displaying horror at the turn of events, he stated, 'This is the worst miscalculation my party has made.'[17] However, it is also true that a mere two days after the demolition, he commented on the BJP's chances of winning the upcoming election to have improved significantly. Veteran journalist and editor Kuldip Nayar recounted that when he met A.B. Vajpayee the day after the demolition to implore that BJP make amends, Vajpayee responded, 'Let the temple come up.'[18]

To quote one of Justice Ahmadi's favourite sayings, it was an example of 'contempt in open court, apology in chambers.'

The Rao government, which had initially promised to rebuild the mosque, had suddenly fallen suspiciously quiet, suggesting a tacit acceptance of the wrongdoing by the Hindutva machinery. Publicly, however, Inquiry Commissions were formed and assurances to hold the culprits accountable were given, but with little consequence.

As the storms of communal violence, fuelled by the demolition of the mosque, swept through the country, the Indian political landscape grew increasingly turbulent and polarized. The Union government found itself grasping for ways to restore order and regain control.[19] In a desperate bid to control the rioters and salvage its secular image, the central government imposed a ban on the Hindu extremist organizations RSS, VHP and Bajrang Dal under the UAPA law. A few days later, on 15 December 1992, the BJP-led state governments of Rajasthan, Madhya Pradesh and Himachal Pradesh were dissolved under Article 356 and placed under President's rule. In fact, a total of four state governments were dismissed as a consequence of the demolition, including, as mentioned before, the Uttar Pradesh government, which had been dismissed earlier upon the resignation of Kalyan Singh. But the BJP was riding a wave of growing influence and power and was unwilling to accept these dismissals. And so, the three state governments of Rajasthan, Madhya Pradesh and Himachal Pradesh moved the Supreme Court, questioning the validity of imposing President's rule and dissolving the respective legislative assemblies of these states. Only Uttar Pradesh chose not to challenge the dissolution in Court.

In a political climate where the dismissal of state governments had become a common tool to settle political scores, S.R. Bommai vs. Union of India would emerge as a seminal case in 1994. For the very first time, the contours of Article 356 would be conclusively defined.

The President's Proclamation regarding President's rule in Rajasthan was based on the Governor's report sent to the Prime Minister.[20] The report did not mince words, stating that the Rajasthan government had played an 'obvious role' in the Ayodhya incident. The report also raised red flags about the Bharatiya Janata Party's influence over the banned organizations of RSS, VHP and Bajrang Dal and pointed out that the ban was not being effectively enforced in the state. One minister had resigned from office, and along with him, 22 MLAs and 15,500 BJP workers from the state had participated in the Ayodhya kar seva, which had led to the demolition of the Babri Mosque. These participants had received enthusiastic send-offs and welcomes from influential figures in the BJP. The law and order situation in the state had severely deteriorated for over a week after the demolition, marked by anti-minority activities. In this charged atmosphere, the Governor arrived at the conclusion that the Administration could no longer function effectively, impartially or in accordance with the rule of law. The situation had reached a point where the state government's functioning was no longer in alignment with the provisions of the Constitution.

In Madhya Pradesh, the President's Proclamation was a result of three alarming reports sent by the Governor to the President. These reports painted a grim picture of the deteriorating law and order situation in the state. The Governor also referred to a statement by the then Chief Minister of Madhya Pradesh, Shri Sunder Lal Patwa, in which he had openly expressed his disapproval of the ban on the RSS and VHP. Patwa, a man with staunch affiliations to the RSS, referred to the ban as a 'heinous law' and declared 13 December as a black day in protest. This vocal opposition by no less than the Chief Minister raised questions about the state government's commitment to enforcing the central government's directive. Adding to the mounting apprehension was the suspicion that the RSS was concocting a fresh strategy. There were indications that leaders of the banned organizations might attempt to evade legal consequences and seek refuge under the protective wing of the state administration. These signals left the Governor with deep reservations about the state's intentions. And so, the Governor recommended the issuance of the Proclamation.

Himachal Pradesh presented a case less severe than Madhya Pradesh, but with striking parallels. The Governor's report dated 5 December 1992 revealed that the Chief Minister and his Cabinet were believed to have fuelled the Ayodhya controversy by encouraging kar sevaks from the state to actively participate in the kar seva at Ayodhya – the event which ultimately resulted in the demolition of the Babri Masjid. Further, some

Aziz Mushabber Ahmadi – recently graduated, 1953

Aziz Ahmadi in his chambers – a young lawyer at the Gujarat Bar, 1958

Aziz and Amena Ahmadi at the Ahmadi family home on their wedding day, 1960

The Muchhala family with Aziz Ahmadi, 1962. Standing, left to right – Taher Muchhala, Yusuf Muchhala (brothers of Amena) and Aziz Ahmadi. Seated, left to right – Ayman Muchhala (wife of Taher), Hani Muchhala (wife of Yusuf), Amena Ahmadi and Fatema Muchhala (mother of Amena, Taher and Yusuf)

Aziz Ahmadi being awarded a cricket trophy by Justice B. J. Divan at the City Civil Court, Ahmedabad

The Ahmadis – seated are Aziz's parents, Mushabber and Shirin Ahmadi. Standing, from left to right are Amena Ahmadi, Tasneem Ahmadi, Huzefa Ahmadi and Aziz Ahmadi

Justice Ahmadi being sworn in by President Shankar Dayal Sharma as Chief Justice of India at Rashtrapati Bhavan on 25 October 1994

Justice Ahmadi's swearing-in ceremony. From left to right – Law Minister H.R. Bhardwaj, outgoing CJI Justice Venkatachaliah, Prime Minister of India P.V. Narasimha Rao, President Shankar Dayal Sharma and Chief Justice A.M. Ahmadi.

Chief Justice Ahmadi sharing a light moment with Prime Minister P.V. Narasimha Rao and Law Minister H.R. Bhardwaj. In the background are Finance Minister Dr Manmohan Singh and Railway Minister C.K. Jaffer Sharief.

At a reception held at Rashtrapati Bhavan: From left to right – Prime Minister Narasimha Rao, former Prime Minister Chandra Shekhar, former Prime Minister V.P. Singh, Labour Minister P. A. Sangma, Chief Justice A. M. Ahmadi, Leader of the Opposition Atal Bihari Vajpayee, Vice President of India K. R. Narayanan.

Supreme Court Judges, 1994 – CJI Ahmadi seated at the centre

Mrs and Justice Ahmadi welcoming Mrs and Vice President K.R. Narayanan to Huzefa Ahmadi's wedding reception, 1994

Justice Ahmadi receiving future Prime Minister Dr Manmohan Singh at Huzefa Ahmadi's wedding reception, 1994

Amena and Aziz Ahmadi on an official trip abroad during Justice Ahmadi's tenure in the Supreme Court

Chief Justice of India, A.M. Ahmadi in his office, 1995

Justice Ahmadi sharing a joke with Mother Teresa in Kolkata

At a reception held at the Rashtrapati Bhavan. Left to Right – Vice President K.R. Narayanan, President Shankar Dayal Sharma, Justice Verma and Justice Ahmadi, 1997

With President A.P.J. Abdul Kalam at the Bhopal Memorial Hospital, 2002

Chief Justice Ahmadi in conversation with Prime Minister Atal Bihari Vajpayee

Justice Ahmadi welcoming Vice President M. Hamid Ansari to Insiyah Vahanvaty's wedding reception, 2009

Justice Ahmadi with His Holiness, the 14th Dalai Lama, in Delhi

The Family. Left to right – Adnan Vahanvaty, Justice Ahmadi, Shaurya Roy, Mrs Amena Ahmadi, Tasneem Ahmadi, Insiyah Vahanvaty, Insia Ahmadi, Aliasghar Ahmadi, Huzefa Ahmadi, 2009

Justice Ahmadi with Insiyah Vahanvaty in Pune, on a visit to meet his mother for the final time in 2022. This photograph, taken seven months before Justice Ahmadi's passing, is one of the last images of him.

Justice Ahmadi receiving a ring from Syedna Khuzaima Qutbuddin as a token of esteem and affection. This photograph was taken shortly after Syedna Qutbuddin's proclamation and claim to the position of Dai in 2014.

ministers had sought permission from party leaders to participate as well. Others openly criticized the ban orders. The Governor further disclosed that although Chief Minister Shanta Kumar had expressed his intention to implement the ban orders on the Hindu extremist groups; he and several of his cabinet members maintained strong ties to the RSS. The Governor felt these deep-rooted associations would prevent the state administration from carrying out these directives in an impartial and effective manner.

It is worth noting that Madhya Pradesh, Himachal Pradesh and Rajasthan were all led by BJP governments at the time.

As a result, the three state governments were dissolved, and the states brought under President's Rule under Article 356.

In the meanwhile, a seemingly unconnected story of political intrigue had made its way to the Supreme Court after six long years of legal battles and a series of appeals.

In 1985, the Janata Party, holding a majority in the Karnataka State Legislature, had established a government with Ramakrishna Hegde as Chief Minister.[21] However, Hedge's reign was short lived due to allegations that ultimately forced him to step down. In his stead, S.R. Bommai was appointed in 1988.

Shortly after, in September 1988, a merger between the Janata Party and Lok Dal gave rise to Janata Dal. This merger led to the expansion of the ministry by adding thirteen new members to the cabinet.

However, the political landscape quickly shifted when K.R. Molakery, a legislator from Janata Dal, defected from the party.[22] He presented a letter to Governor Pendekanti Venkatasubbaiah, accompanied by nineteen letters purportedly signed by legislators who were withdrawing their support from the ministry. Consequently, in April 1989, the Governor sent a report to the President, indicating internal dissension and defection within the ruling party. He argued that due to the withdrawal of support by these legislators, Chief Minister Bommai no longer commanded a majority in the Assembly.[23] He believed it was constitutionally inappropriate for the state to be governed by an executive consisting of a council of ministers that lacked majority support in the state assembly. As a result, he recommended to the President that Article 356(1) should be invoked.

However, a startling turn of events unfolded the next day when seven of the nineteen legislators who had allegedly signed the withdrawal letters sent a complaint to the Governor.[24] They claimed their signatures were obtained under misrepresentation and reaffirmed their support for the ministry. To prove the Assembly's confidence in his ministry, the Chief Minister and his Law Minister met with the Governor the same day and offered to undergo a floor test to prove their majority, even if it meant advancing the scheduled Assembly session. But they were not allowed this opportunity.

Instead, on the very same day, 20 April 1989, the Governor sent a fresh report to the President, informing him of the seven retractions. However, he expressed his belief that the retractions had been procured by coercive means and that horse trading was underway. He reiterated that the Chief Minister had lost the majority's confidence in the House and repeated his earlier request for action under Article 356(1). In response to these reports, the central government, led by Prime Minister Rajiv Gandhi, dismissed Bommai's government without affording Bommai the chance to demonstrate his majority. As a result, President's rule was imposed in Karnataka.

Unwilling to accept this dismissal, Bommai wasted no time in filing a writ petition challenging the validity of the Proclamation on 26 April 1989. However, a special bench comprising three judges in the Karnataka High Court dismissed the writ petition. And so Bommai decided to move the Supreme Court.

But the dismissal of the Karnataka government in 1989 was part of a larger pattern. At the time, it had become commonplace for a hostile central government to wield Article 356 as a political weapon in order to remove opposition-led state governments and bring the state under the centre's control.[25] During this same period, northeast India saw two swift, successive dissolutions. In 1988, the Government of Nagaland was dissolved on the grounds of alleged horse-trading and links between legislators and insurgents, and in 1991, Meghalaya's Legislative Assembly was dissolved on grounds of unconstitutional governance.

Until 1991, President's rule had been applied a total of 95 times. What had been envisaged as a dead letter had become a freely invoked provision.[26]

By the time Bommai's case was ready to be heard by the Supreme Court in 1994, the petitions against the dismissals of the Rajasthan, Madhya Pradesh and Haryana governments in the aftermath of the demolition of the Babri Masjid had also been filed.

And so, the Supreme Court braced itself for a wave of legal challenges and a landmark legal battle.

A nine-judge Constitution Bench consisting of Justices A.M. Ahmadi, Kuldip Singh, P.B. Sawant, K. Ramaswamy, S.C. Agrawal, Yogeshwar Dayal, B.P. Jeevan Reddy, S.R. Pandian and J.S. Verma decided to hear all the petitions together, since they all raised similar fundamental questions. With legal stalwarts like Soli Sorabjee, Milon Banerji, Ram Jethmalani, Shanti Bhushan, K. Parasaran and T.R. Andhyarujina appearing, the stage was set for a historic case that would go on to significantly impact the relationship between state governments and the central authority.

The bench deliberated on three key questions. One, can the President's Proclamation under Article 356 be subjected to judicial review? Two, if yes, then to what extent? And lastly, the interpretation of the phrase in Article 356(1), 'A situation has arisen in which the Government of the State cannot be carried on in accordance with the provisions of the Constitution.'[27]

The verdict marked a significant turning point in Indian constitutional jurisprudence, with a series of crucial determinations. Characterizing Article 356 as an 'awesome' power, the bench established the authority of the judiciary to scrutinize the President's decisions under Article 356 of the Constitution, thus rendering presidential actions justiciable.

The bench unanimously concurred that Article 356 was not beyond the scope of constitutional courts and was, indeed, subject to judicial review. The judgement also stated that the President's authority to dismiss a State Government is not absolute. It emphasized that the Legislative Assembly should not be dissolved until the Parliament approves the Proclamation (of President's rule) in both houses. The Court stated, 'The dissolution of Legislative Assembly is not a matter of course. It should be resorted to only where it is found necessary for achieving the purposes of the Proclamation.'[28]

If the Proclamation was found to be invalid, even if approved by both houses, the Court can reinstate the dismissed government, or, when applicable, issue an interim injunction to prevent the holding of fresh elections until the final challenge to the Proclamation is resolved. The judgement categorically stated a floor test to be the primary indicator of the majority enjoyed by the government in power, and not the opinion of the governor who is typically appointed by the central government.

Justice Ahmadi authored a 37-page separate judgement in which he clarified:

> Merely because a different political party is elected to power at the centre, even if with a thumping majority, is no ground to hold that "a situation has arisen in which the Government of the State cannot be carried on in accordance with the provisions of this Constitution", which is the requirement for the exercise of power under Article 356(1) of the Constitution. It is a matter of common knowledge that people vote for different political parties at the centre and in the States and, therefore, if a political party with an ideology different from the ideology of the political party in power in any State comes to power in the Centre, the Central Government would not be justified in exercising power under Article 356(1) unless it is shown that the ideology of the political party in power in the State is inconsistent with the constitutional philosophy ...

On the basis of these deliberations, the Court held that the dismissals of the state governments of Karnataka, Nagaland and Meghalaya were unconstitutional. However, since fresh elections had already taken place in these states, the status quo was accepted.

But the Court also explored the question of secularism as a constitutional provision, and its place in the spate of dismissals of governments after the demolition of the Babri Mosque. It was highlighted that secularism is a fundamental part of the Constitution's basic structure and that religion should have no place in matters of the state.

> No political party can simultaneously be a religious party. Politics and religion cannot be mixed.[29] Secularism is a part of the basic structure of the Constitution. The acts of a State Government, which are calculated to subsevert [sic] or sabotage secularism as enshrined in our Constitution, can lawfully be deemed to give rise to a situation in which the Government of the State cannot be carried on in accordance with the provisions of the Constitution.[30]

And so, while the dismissals of the governments of Karnataka, Nagaland and Meghalaya were struck down as unconstitutional, those of Rajasthan, Madhya Pradesh and Himachal Pradesh were upheld. The Court held that the evidence provided gave sufficient reason to believe that secularism was jeopardized, and therefore, the dismissal of these state governments was justifiable.

This judgement is important not only as a landmark ruling on President's rule and Article 356 but also on the definition of secularism as mandated by the Constitution, demanding a definite delinking of religion from politics. It went on to state:

> To it (the State), all are equal and all are entitled to be treated equally. How is this equal treatment possible, if the State were to prefer or promote a particular religion, race or caste, which necessarily means a less favourable treatment of all other religions, races and castes. How are the Constitutional promises of social justice, liberty of belief, faith or worship and equality of status and of opportunity to be attained unless the State eschews the religion, faith or belief of a person from its consideration altogether while dealing with him, his rights, his duties and his entitlements? Secularism is thus more than a passive attitude of religious tolerance. It is a positive concept of equal treatment of all religions.[31]

Six of the nine judges authored separate judgements, each touching upon various facets of the case, most notably, secularism and the necessity for the separation between religion and state. Justice Ramaswamy emphasized that the State must enforce secularism through laws and executive orders. He explained that when political parties create programmes or principles based on religion, they are allowing religion to influence political governance, which goes against the Constitution. According to him, the Court should intervene and correct any political party that promote ideas that go against secularism.

Quoting Mahatma Gandhi to emphasize the importance of the separation of Church and State, Justice Ahmadi wrote, 'I swear by my religion. I will die for it. But it is my personal affair. The State has nothing to do with it. The State will look after your secular welfare, health, communication, foreign relations, currency and so on, but not my religion. That is everybody's personal concern.'[32]

It is notable that only two judges on the bench, Justices Verma and Dayal, expressed no opinion on secularism.[33]

Mr Ram Jethmalani argued that Section 123(3) of the Representation of People Act of 1951 did not ban appeals to religion in general but only appeals to the religion of the candidate and soliciting votes in the name of that particular religion.[34] He contended that it did not forbid candidates from seeking votes based on a religion they didn't belong to. But the Court did not agree. It pointed out that when Subsections (3) and (3A) of Section 123 are read together, it becomes clear that seeking votes in the name of any religion is prohibited.

The S.R. Bommai vs. Union of India judgement stands as a milestone, celebrated not only for its resolute support of Indian federalism but also for its strong critique of the intrusion of religion into politics and its defence of Indian secularism.[35] This ruling helped end the arbitrary dismissal of opposition-led state governments by hostile central governments. The verdict significantly limited the misuse of this constitutional provision and defined the contours of Article 356, which allow for the union government's dismissal of state governments. The judgement also made a compelling call for robust measures to address political parties and state governments that breach the constitutional principles that forbid the fusion of religion and politics.

One of the earliest impacts of the judgement was seen in 1999, when the Vajpayee government was forced to reinstate the Rabri Devi government in Bihar when it became clear that the central government would suffer a defeat in the Upper House over the matter.[36]

Although the country had received some much-needed relief from religiously loaded politics, it would be short lived.[37] This strong stand towards secularism would quickly become diluted by the Supreme Court in Ismail Faruqui vs. Union of India – only a few months later.

A few weeks after the illegal demolition of the mosque, the then President of India, Shankar Dayal Sharma made a Presidential Reference to the Supreme Court under Article 143(1) of the Indian Constitution, seeking the Court's opinion on whether a Hindu structure existed at the site of the Babri Masjid before it was built.[38] Meanwhile, the Centre passed an Act, which allowed it to acquire approximately 67 acres of land in and around the Babri Mosque. This was the Acquisition of Certain Area at Ayodhya Act which was subsequently challenged by Ismail Faruqui and brought to the Supreme Court in 1993. The bench comprising Chief Justice M.N. Venkatachaliah, Justice A.M. Ahmadi, Justice G.N. Ray, Justice S.P. Bharucha and Justice J.S. Verma declined to answer the Presidential Reference.[39] The majority of the judges, Justices Venkatachaliah, Verma and Ray dismissed it as 'superfluous and unnecessary'.

The minority opinion by Justices Ahmadi and Bharucha also declined to answer the Reference, stating that the Supreme Court bench had no possible way of knowing whether a Ram temple existed on the site before the Babri Masjid was built there. Also, the words 'Hindu religious structure' and 'Ram Temple' had become somewhat synonymous, further clouding the issue. Ahmadi explained this in further detail in an interview several years later:

> The dispute, it will be remembered, was that a Rama temple had stood on the disputed site and it was demolished to make place for the disputed structure (Babri Masjid); the question posed, however, is:

Was there "a Hindu temple or any Hindu religious structure" on the disputed site? Secondly, the salient fact as to whether the temple, if any, was demolished to make place for the disputed structure is not to be gone into . . . In other words, we were being asked to give an opinion on whether there existed a temple or a Hindu religious structure, not whether a Rama temple existed. However, the cause of the dispute was that a Rama temple had been demolished to build the Babri Masjid in 1528 AD. It was akin to shifting the goalpost, so to speak.[40]

In a rather scathing paragraph, the minority opinion pointed out that it was clear that the government did not intend to bind itself by the judicial decision.[41] 'It leaves us in no doubt that even in the circumstance that this Court opines that no Hindu temple or Hindu religious structure existed on the disputed site before the disputed structure was built thereon, there is no certainty that the mosque will be rebuilt.'[42]

In doing so, the Court sent a resounding message to Prime Minister Rao; it also highlighted that the Reference sought to 'favour one religious community and disfavour another.'[43]

Simultaneously addressed in conjunction with the Presidential Reference was the matter of Ismail Faruqui vs. Union of India – a challenge to the Acquisition of Certain Area at Ayodhya Act – an attempt by the Central Government to gain control of administration and maintenance of the Ram Janma Bhumi-Babri Masjid structure along with its premises. The attention of the entire nation was riveted on the proceedings of this high profile case, for by now it had become abundantly clear that this decision would define the fate of not only the Babri Masjid but also the secular character of India.

But although the bench would ultimately rule in favour of the Centre, declaring the Acquisition of Certain Area at Ayodhya Act valid, this judgement was not unanimous. The minority of the bench that dissented from the majority opinion consisted of Justice Ahmadi and Justice Bharucha, who both considered the Act to be unsecular and constitutionally unfit.[44] The bench struck down one of the clauses that sought to end all legal proceedings related to the dispute.

The Ayodhya Matter

Under intense pressure to succumb to the majority on the bench, Justice Ahmadi put pen to paper many decades later, revealing for the first time details about that period.[45] Judicial deliberations on the Reference having concluded, a meeting of the bench was called to discuss the matter of Ismail Faruqui vs. Union of India. As he walked into the room, Ahmadi noticed that while Justices Venkatachaliah, Ray and Verma were present at the meeting, strangely, Justice Bharucha was not. The judges present began the meeting with the perfunctory opening remarks, and then produced a draft judgment that had evidently been prepared in advance, asking Justice Ahmadi to peruse and endorse it. Ahmadi raised a primary objection that Justice Bharucha was not present at this meeting, and it was improper to conduct these discussions in his absence. To this he was told, 'Once we four agree, he too will agree.' Uncomfortable with this reasoning, Ahmadi nevertheless agreed to look at the draft. Having read through the draft, however, he found that in validating the Acquisition of Certain Area at Ayodhya Act, the bench would be tacitly sanctifying the acts of trespass and destruction that had taken place – all offences under the Indian Penal Code. Not least because there was no mention of any adverse consequences for the parties who had allowed or participated in the demolition, nor any orders of status quo against both communities offering prayers at the site. Of course, he was unwilling to do this. Recognizing the meeting for what it was, Ahmadi told the Chief that he would sign their draft if they amended it to include the allocation of a small piece large enough for a *moulvy* (Islamic priest) to spread his mat and offer *namaaz* on the land parcel, thereby maintaining the right of the Muslims to offer prayers there too – especially since the effect of the Act would include retaining the idols where they had been placed and requiring the *pujas* to continue in the manner that they had been done since the demolition, indefinitely. Recoiling at the suggestion, the Chief Justice and his two colleagues refused outright. At this point Justice Ahmadi expressed his inability to continue further discussions on the topic and left. It is through Justice Ahmadi's own personal writings that we now have insight into the precise details and considerations of the bench during this profoundly significant case.

Walking away from the meeting, Justice Ahmadi appeared outwardly calm, but was seething inside. Once inside the official white Ambassador car, he drew the little lace curtains across the car windows for privacy. Face flushed with fury, he wrenched his bands off. He was sure he had left the three judges frustrated and bitter. The next day, he spoke with Justice Bharucha, and they agreed to record their dissent as neither one of them could agree with the majority view.

Poised to take over as the next Chief, Ahmadi knew that there is many a slip between the cup and the lip. He knew he was stepping into the bullring – defying the Chief Justice and the executive on this high profile matter with such high stakes could mean risking it all, his career, his shot at the Supreme Court's top spot. The pinnacle of success was within grasp, but dissent at this stage could lead to supersession by a junior judge as retaliation. There was precedent for such things – it had happened before in the history of the Indian judiciary. He also knew that the nature of his relationship with the Chief Justice of India was an open secret within the courtroom corridors as well as in government circles.

But, in the depths of his being, he realized the truth. This wasn't a choice; it was a litmus test. In a test of integrity and ideals, there really was no option.

We know of the extent of the pressure he was under at this time not only through Justice Ahmadi's private writings and conversations with him, but also through the memories of his children and grandchildren. One that sticks out is a particular phone call that was received one evening when the family was in the middle of dinner. The secretary in the office at the time called on the phone in the family room, which also doubled up as an informal dining room where the family would gather to spend time together on most evenings. Answering the intercom, Justice Ahmadi asked for the call to be transferred to his bedroom – a clear indication that the contents of the call were expected to be confidential. Leaving his mound of *khichdi* and mutton curry half eaten on the plate, he left the room to attend to the phone call. Continuing with our meal, we thought nothing of this somewhat common occurrence, until a few minutes later we heard the booming voice of Aziz Ahmadi thunder from all the way down the bottom of the corridor, 'I don't care about becoming Chief Justice, I won't do it!' Like a sharp slap, the room fell into stillness as we exchanged uneasy glances and waited for him to return to the dining table. That night he did not.

Because he never revealed who was at the other end of that phone call, all we could do was speculate.

As ever, Justice Ahmadi, when upset, would retire to his haven, his work. Some days, he would emerge only for meals, eating quickly and retreating again to his baithak on the bedroom floor to prepare for the next day before finally turning in for the night, hours after everyone else had. A man who required no more than five, sometimes four hours of sleep each night, he did most of his thinking when the world was dark and quiet. Pacing on the carpeted floor, he fought the numbness in his legs from hours on the floor. In the morning, a stack of carefully drafted notes in his tiny, angular handwriting was ready for his secretaries to type out. Positioned across from the secretary in his office, he'd unleash a torrent of dictation. Scribbling furiously in shorthand, the secretary transcribed his judgements, the marathon sessions stretching for hours on end, broken only by the cups of black tea fuelling them both.

When I approached Justice Bharucha shortly after Justice Ahmadi's demise for more clarity on the machinations of the time, he stated that there was much that had taken place, but he did not wish to elaborate on the 'persuasions' that were attempted before he and Justice Ahmadi took the decision to disagree with the majority on the bench and write their dissenting opinion. Instead, he encourages the public to read the minority judgement to understand why the two judges found the majority view unacceptable.

Finding the Act to be unsecular and unconstitutional, the opinion authored by Justice Bharucha had noted,

> ... no account is taken of the fact that the structure thereon has been destroyed in a most reprehensible act (sic) ... No account is taken of the fact that there is a dispute in respect of the site on which puja is to be performed... the disputed structure was being used as a mosque; and that the Muslim community has a claim to offer namaz thereon ...'[46] 'the perpetrators of the deed struck not only against a place of

worship but at the principles of secularism, democracy and the rule of law...'[47] 'When ... adherents of the religion of the majority of Indian citizens make a claim upon and assail the place of worship of another religion and, by dint of numbers, create conditions that are conducive to public disorder, it is the Constitutional obligation of the State to protect that place of worship and to preserve public order, using for the purpose such means and forces of law and order as are required. It is impermissible under the provisions of the Constitution for the State to acquire that place of worship to preserve public order... To condone the acquisition of a place of worship in such circumstances is to efface the principle of secularism from the Constitution'

The dissenting opinion also expanded on the secular character of the state.

Secularism is thus more than a passive attitude of religious tolerance. It is a positive concept of equal treatment of all religions. This attitude is described by some as one of neutrality towards religion or as one of benevolent neutrality... What is material is that it is a constitutional goal and a basic feature of the Constitution... Any step inconsistent with this constitutional policy is in plain words, unconstitutional.[48]

Poignantly, it also stated, 'Ayodhya is a storm that will pass. The dignity and honour of the Supreme Court cannot be compromised because of it.'[49]

The passage of the Act also dealt a blow to the legal argument that Muslims had a right to the site due to adverse possession over the years. Adverse possession is a legal principle allowing one to claim ownership of land or property through open and continuous use as that of a true owner, for a stipulated period of time. Due to Babri's long-standing presence, and the land's consistent use by the Muslim community, this argument was a viable legal recourse. But now, with the passage of the Ayodhya Act, this argument was no longer available to the Muslim community, despite the mosque (and the land it stood upon) having been in their possession for several centuries. Justice Ahmadi later explained this as another reason why the dissenting opinion was necessary. 'This is bound to happen as we are a very old civilization. Layers upon layers of human construction stretching across centuries took place. That is why there are limits to how far back in the past you can go to claim ownership rights. The argument of adverse possession doesn't just apply to historical monuments. For instance, if your property is in the possession of someone else and you have kept quiet for 12 years, then you lose your right. The other person acquires it by adverse possession.'[50]

The seismic aftershocks of these events would continue to send tremors across the political landscape of India for many years to come. A different course of events might have salvaged communal harmony, a casualty of the incident. The episode also ushered in a new style of politics in India – a muscular defiant approach that did not believe in restraint and diplomacy, rather one that was battle ready and at ease with conflict. It blew the lid off communal and casteist sentiments that, so far, were only uttered in close huddles and in whispers. Hate speech became a common aspect of public discourse, and majoritarian sentiment was legitimized. Perhaps it also served to expose the brittle nature of India's secularism, which often consisted of tokenism and symbolic efforts towards inclusion of minority communities.

The complexity surrounding these matters would deepen over the next few years with the emergence of the Hindutva Judgements, which reopened the door to allow the invocation of religion in political speeches, once again muddying the waters and blurring the lines between religion and politics. As time wore on, this view would increasingly show its damaging consequences.

Shortly after Justice Ahmadi retired in 1997, and Vajpayee had once again ascended to the position of Prime Minister, he phoned Justice Ahmadi at his residence, requesting his help to calm the waters between the Hindu and Muslim communities over the matter of the mosque and the dispute over the land it had stood upon.[51] 'The Muslim community has great regard for you and will listen to you,' he said. Justice Ahmadi responded, 'I am not aware if they will listen, but I would be happy to try, provided you have a formula to offer.' Vajpayee asked Ahmadi to speak to the community and ascertain the position of the Indian Muslim for the moment. However, Ahmadi was reluctant to approach the Muslim community without the express assurance of a fair resolution and a political olive branch. He said to the Prime Minister, 'I cannot tell them that I am approaching them to know their general reaction, as whatever little confidence they have in me would be lost. I would not like to venture into this without a political formula. Think it over, consult your colleagues and party-men and come up with a 'balanced' formula for me to work on, and if I find the formula sellable, I will take it up.'

Justice Ahmadi did not hear from the Prime Minister again.

Some years after retiring, in a speech delivered in 1999, Justice Ahmadi would speak out condemning the government's failure to punish the guilty by burying the findings of the Inquiry Commission that had been set up after the Mumbai riots, pointing the needle of suspicion at the authorities and their suspect motivations.[52]

'We have seen the fate of (earlier) riot commissions, the latest being the Justice Srikrishna Commission who inquired into the post-Babri Masjid demolition riots in Bombay. We all know the dilatory tactics adopted by the State Government, its administrative and police wings, to keep the damning verdict in wraps and how unabashedly it was rejected calling the courageous judge names.'

In allowing the kar seva and legitimizing the subsequent Ayodhya Act, the Supreme Court had inadvertently laid the foundation for the 2019 verdict, which resulted in the complete ousting of the masjid from the site where it had stood for 400 years.

But hindsight is always 20/20 and it is quite possible that the judges might not have realized the possible repercussions of allowing the kar seva. It would not be right to infer that any of these developments were deliberately facilitated by lenient judgements or that any of the judges intended harm. While it is true that the judiciary cannot always foresee public reaction, nor is it responsible for the maintenance of law and order in the country, however, in these instances, the Supreme Court fell short of maintaining the principle of secularism as enshrined in the Constitution. This is why Justice Bharucha and Justice Ahmadi's dissenting opinion also gains relevance. Executive acts have often been found to be politically motivated and not always constitutionally sound – acts that only the judiciary is empowered to strike down. Although the majority on the bench did ultimately uphold the Act, the dissenting opinion is historically significant because it not only turns the spotlight onto the difficult questions of secularism and the role of the judiciary in safeguarding it, but also the fundamentality of independence of the judiciary from the executive.

In the words of another courageous dissenter in history, Justice H.R. Khanna, '... A dissent is an appeal to the brooding spirit of the law, to the intelligence of a future day, when a later decision may possibly correct the error into which the dissenting Judge believes the court to have been betrayed.'[53]

And in Justice Ahmadi's career on the bench, this would not be his only dissent.

9

Triumphs and Trials

Justice Ahmadi had found himself thrust into yet another significant matter, this time, one of constitutional interpretation. This new legal battleground, equally momentous, would continue to fuel debates and discontent within the legal fraternity long after the gavel had fallen in the courtroom. It was a case that would, until this day, continue to cause much distress and heartburn within the legal community. And once again, Ahmadi would find himself writing a dissenting judgement.

The methods and processes behind the selection of judges to the Indian judiciary has been a long-standing source of intense debate and discussion that has raged over decades. At the heart of this matter lies the question of the extent of authority wielded by the Chief Justice of India and the procedures by which recommendations for judicial appointments are made.

Over the years, these processes have undergone several changes, which have taken place through judicial interpretation rather than legislative amendments. These interpretations were formalized through the milestone cases of the First Judges Case 1981, the Second Judges Case 1993, the Third Judges Case 1998 and the Fourth Judges Case 2015.

The Indian Constitution details the procedure for the selection and transfer of judges, stating that Judges of the Supreme Court are to be appointed by the 'hand and seal' of the President of India in consultation with the Chief Justice of India and other relevant judges from both the

Supreme Court and High Courts – a process that remained uncontroversial until 1973.[1] But when Justice A.N. Ray superseded three judges involved in the Kesavananda Bharti case to become the Chief Justice of India, this appointment process quickly became a subject of fierce debate.[2]

And so, Justice Ray's supersession, which was widely seen as a punitive measure against the other judges for their unfavourable judgements against the government, followed by transfer orders against 'inconvenient' judges, marked the beginning of a prolonged power struggle between the executive and the judiciary.

In 1981, then, in response to writ petitions filed against a circular by the Union government that was seen as executive interference in the appointment and transfer of judges, the Supreme Court heard S.P. Gupta v Union of India and Ors, or what would come to be known as the First Judges Case.[3] The seven-judge bench, in a majority verdict of 4:3, held that the word 'consultation' in Article 124(2) and in Article 217(1) of the Constitution did not mean 'concurrence,'[4] and if there was a disagreement regarding the appointment of a judge, the final word would lie with the Union Government and not the Chief Justice of India.[5]

The Supreme Court emphasized that the Chief Justice was merely a constitutional consultee, which affirmed the practice of the time. It was in this verdict that the idea of a collegium system was first introduced.

Initiated as a review of the First Judges Case, the Supreme Court Advocates on Record Association vs. Union of India (1993), commonly known as The Second Judges Case, was heard by a nine-judge bench comprising Justices S.R. Pandian, A.M. Ahmadi, Kuldip Singh, J.S. Verma, M.M. Punchhi, Yogeshwar Dayal, G.N. Ray, Dr A.S. Anand and S.P. Bharucha. Of these nine, five would go on to become future Chief Justices of India. But, again, the verdict was not unanimous. In a majority ruling with seven judges in favour and two in opposition, the S.P. Gupta judgement or the First Judges Case was partly overruled. The verdict introduced a substantial alteration in the method of selection of Supreme Court judges, despite the absence of legislative amendments.

The majority opinion, delivered by Justice J.S. Verma, who would go on to become the Chief Justice of India five years later, interpreted the word 'consultation' to mean 'concurrence,' thereby transferring the power of appointments onto itself, the judiciary. In practice, this gave the Chief Justice a position of primacy, while diminishing the role of the executive branch to almost a mere formality. Further, it directed that the Chief Justice of India, in collaboration with two senior judges, should provide recommendations for new appointees, which the executive, in the normal course of things, should accept. Thus was born the collegium system.

Unsurprisingly, this imperious method would prove to be deeply problematic, sparking scathing criticism from legal luminaries in India and abroad. Many have highlighted the problems of the collegium system; others have criticized the verdict for blurring the lines of constitutional provisions. This interpretation of the Constitution would go on to create several issues and prompt pushback, not only within judicial circles but also the executive.

The two dissenting voices on the bench, Justice Ahmadi and Justice Punchhi, articulated some of these problems. Justice Ahmadi's dissent was rooted in deep concern regarding the possible misinterpretation of the Constitution, which is evident from the excerpt of his dissenting opinion below:

> A word of caution before we proceed further. The Constitution is what the Judges say it is. That is because the power to interpret the Constitution vests in the Judges. A heavy responsibility lies on the Judges when they are called upon to interpret the Constitution, the responsibility is all the more heavier when the provisions to be construed relate to the powers of the judiciary. It is essential that complete objectivity is maintained while interpreting the Constitutional provisions relating to the power of the judiciary vis-a-vis the executive in the matter of appointments to the superior judiciary to avoid any feeling amongst the other constitutional functionaries that there has been usurpation of power through the process of interpretation ...[6]

It further states that the majority judgement was an overreach, as such a verdict could only be possible through an amendment in the Constitution, which, in its current form, does not allow for this manner of judicial appointments. Ahmadi further pointed out that the manner in which the Constitution was framed was intentional, providing a middle path for the executive and judiciary to work together.

> The method of selecting a judge for the Supreme Court and the High Court is outlined in Articles 124(2) and 217(1) of the Constitution. While in the United States, the United Kingdom, Australia and Canada appointments to the superior judiciary are exclusively by the executive, our Constitution has charted a middle course by providing for 'prior consultation' with the judiciary before the President, i.e. the executive, makes the appointment to the Supreme Court or the High Courts. Therefore, however convincing it may sound to the ideal of judicial independence that the views of the Chief Justice of India must have primacy as his views expressed after consulting his two seniormost colleagues would he [sic] symbolic of the views of the entire judiciary, the submission cannot be accepted unless the Constitution is amended. As the constitutional provisions presently stand, the submission based on this line of reasoning is unacceptable [sic].[7]

Justice Ahmadi was also troubled by the daggers drawn between the judiciary and executive. He pointed out that in the history of India, there had been only seven instances in which the judiciary and executive failed to reach an agreement on a particular appointment. Such a limited number of disputes hardly constituted a crisis significant enough to justify a sweeping overhaul of the system.

> The executive and the judiciary are not adversaries, they are not supposed to work at cross purposes, then what is so surprising if in a vast majority of cases barring seven they have reached an agreement on the selection of the candidates for appointment? And what is the justification in believing in the absence of statistical information, that in all these cases it was the executive which yielded to the view of the Chief Justice of India? Could it not be that in some cases the executive

was able to convince the Chief Justice of India to its point of view and in some others the Chief Justice of India was able to persuade of the executive to his point of view? If the attitude of the executive has been to arrive at a consensus to minimise differences of opinion, it is in fact a healthy attitude which need not be read as yielding to the primacy concept.[8]

Justice Punchhi, the second dissenter on the bench, revealed the adhoc manner in which the bench had deliberated on the question that lay before it, and the lack of consultation among the judges themselves.

This nine-Judge Bench sat from April 7, 1993, to hear this momentous matter concluding its hearing on May 11, 1993, close to the onset of the summer vacation. I entertained the belief that we all, after July 12.1993 [sic], on the re-opening of the Court, if not earlier, would sit together and hold some meaningful meetings, having a free and frank discussion on each and every topic which had engaged our attention, striving for a unanimous decision in this historic matter concerning mainly the institution of the Chief Justice of India, relatable to this Court. I was indeed overtaken when I received the draft opinion dated June 14, 1993 authored by my learned, brother J. S. Verma, J. for himself and on behalf of my learned brethren Yogeshwar Dayal, G.N. Ray, Dr. A.S. Anand and S.P. Bharucha, JJ [sic]. The fait accompli appeared a stark reality; the majority opinion an accomplishment. The hopes I entertained of a free and frank discussion vanished. But then came the opinion dated August 24, 1993 of my learned brother Ahmadi, J. like a pebble of hope hewn out of a mountain of despair, followed by the opinions of my learned brethren Kuldip Singh and Pandian, JJ [sic], dated September 7, 1993 and September 9, 1993 respectively. No meaningful meeting thereafter was possible as the views by that time seemed to have been polarized. So now the firm opinions of the eight brethren, as communicated are known to me. Loaded with these opinions I set out to express my own, more as a duty to the venture embarked upon, for I owe it immeasurably, for being party to the referral.[9]

Justice Puncchi agreed with Justice Ahmadi on several aspects, including what was seen as a 'rewriting of the Constitution,' and the interpreted role of the Chief Justice of India.

> I am in dis-agreement [sic], though regretfully but respectfully, with the views of the majority in virtually re-writing the Constitution to assign a role to the Chief Justice of India, in the whole conspectus of the Constitution, as symbolic in character and to his being a mere spokesman representing the supposed vies of entire judiciary. I also disagree [sic], likewise, in the creation of and vesting of powers assumed, in the hands of the oligarcy [sic] representing the judiciary as a whole created by adding words to the Constitution by interpretative exercise so to silence the singular voice of the Chief Justice of India of ever. I also disagree to the denial of judicial review on the subject on the supposition that it would be the judiciary's act, as that is against the basic structure of the Constitution.[10]

One might wonder why Ahmadi did not align with the majority view, given his upcoming term as Chief Justice of India, during which he could have enjoyed unrestricted powers and primacy over all judicial appointments and transfers. But to Justice Ahmadi, the sanctity of the judiciary and Constitution of India were far more important than individual power. Indeed, he did not care for it, preferring to keep a distance from such appetites. In his words, 'Of course there are those who like judges to believe they alone are the true oracles of the law and are the only bulwarks against abuse of power by other organs. Judges should guard against such flattery as it may tarnish the image of the judge and the judiciary.'[11]

This perspective is evident in his dissenting opinion, which cautions against misinterpreting the Constitution and the possible repercussions of such overreach. Ahmadi warned that if the judiciary were perceived as compromising its duty of accurately interpreting the Constitution and if judges were seen as having departed from their sworn duty, it would result in an even greater clamping down on the independence of the judiciary.

To put it differently where the language of the Constitution is plain and the words used are no [sic] ambiguous, care should be taken to avoid giving an impression that fancied ambiguities have been conjured with a view to making it possible to place a convenient construction on the provisions. If the words are plain and unambiguous effect must be given to them, for that is the constituent body's intent, whether you like it or not, and any seeming attempt to depart therefrom under the guise of interpretation of imaginary ambiguities would cast a serious doubt on the credibility and impartiality of the judiciary . . .[12]

The minority opinions of Justices Ahmadi and Punchhi cautioned against absolute powers being conferred upon the Chief Justice of India such that it diminished the roles of other important figures in the process. They were apprehensive that such a concentration of power might not only undermine the principle of separation of powers, a fundamental aspect of the Constitution, but also lead to problems like bias, conflicts of interest and subjective decision-making within the judiciary. The two judges were not alone in their views. Several jurists and respected members of the legal community have since pointed out that it is uncommon practice in large democracies for such large institutions to select their own members. Critics have raised concerns about the collegium system, which they argue lacks transparency and is susceptible to nepotism.

Interestingly, Verma himself would later express his dissatisfaction with the collegium system and its functioning, saying, 'My 1993 judgment which holds the field, was very much misunderstood and misused. It was in that context that I said the working of the judgment now for some time is raising serious questions, which cannot be called unreasonable. Therefore, some kind of rethink is required.'[13]

As mentioned earlier, it was at this time that Justice Venkatachaliah initiated a policy to transfer one-third of High Court judges from their parent High Courts, a directive that would create much resentment amongst High Court judges and further deepen the discord between him and his successor, Justice Ahmadi.

As Ahmadi would explain in a speech delivered in 2000 in Toronto,

'On the question of appointment and transfer of High Court judges, I am afraid the policy of transferring one third of the judges from their parent High Court to any other High Court has not proved to be beneficial to the system. It has diluted the status of the High Court judges.'[14]

'Internationally too, the majority judgement in the Second Judges Case received scathing criticism. Lord Cooke, of Thorndon, one of New Zealand's most influential jurists criticized the judgement so strongly that he said the decision dealt a significant blow to the principle of judicial independence, not only in India but also internationally.[15] H.M. Seervai, a renowned expert on Constitutional Law, wrote, 'Never has a majority judgment of the [Supreme Court] reached a lower level of judicial incompetence.'[16]

In 1998, Chief Justice Punchhi submitted his recommendations of judges for elevation to the President.[17] According to the Second Judges Case, these appointments were mandatory for the President, except in case of disagreement between the judges. As a delaying tactic, the President made a Reference to the Supreme Court on the consultation process between the Chief Justice of India and his colleagues. By the time a decision was arrived at, all three judges involved in making these recommendations, Justices Punchhi, Agrawal and Ray, had retired, thus reducing the whole process to an eyewash. As Fali Nariman pointed out, this move was intended 'simply to avoid a possibly ugly situation from developing.'

The Third Judges Case, which was initiated through the Presidential Reference, would see no dissenters on the bench and go on to change little from the verdict of the Second Judges Case, besides expanding the strength of the Collegium to five.[18] It would also re-emphasize that in the event of a disagreement within the Collegium, the Chief Justice should not recommend a name that a majority of his contemporaries were against. The Court held that in such cases, the President shall decline to make such an appointment, further muddying the waters and bringing into question the 'primacy' of the Chief Justice of India.

The tangle that had been thus created prompted international condemnation. Sir Robin Cooke commented, 'The Second Judges Case was built on sand, and the Third Judges Case is built of sand.' Cooke would continue to be vocal about his thoughts on this judgement.[19] A few months later, when Justice Ahmadi and Justice Verma were on a delegation to the UK, Cooke leaned over to Justice Ahmadi to curiously ask if his 'colleague who thinks Consultation means Concurrence' was also present, revealing his own thoughts on the interpretation.[20]

Meanwhile, the Executive was not content to lie quietly and allow the judiciary an interpretation that excluded it from the process completely.[21] And so, it passed the National Judicial Appointment Commission Act of 2014 along with a constitutional amendment, which allowed the Commission to make recommendations instead. The Commission was to comprise the Chief Justice of India, two senior-most judges of the Supreme Court, the Union Minister for Law and Justice and two eminent persons nominated by a committee comprising the Prime Minister, the Chief Justice of India and the Leader of the Opposition. One of the two nominated members must belong to the Scheduled Castes, the Scheduled Tribes, OBC, minorities or women.[22] This composition aimed to curtail the powers the judiciary had awarded itself, returning some authority to the Executive. This move, too, had been foreshadowed by Ahmadi in his judgement:

> For, if people and Parliament come to think that the judicial power is to be confined by nothing other than the judge's sense of what is right (off as Selden put it by the length of the Chancellor's foot[23]), confidence in the judicial system it becoming replaced by fear of it becoming uncertain and arbitrary in its application [sic]. Society will then be ready for Parliament to cut the power of the judges. Their power to do justice will become more restricted by law than it need be, or is today.

The actions of the Executive led to a flurry of legal challenges, leading very quickly to the Fourth Judges Case, which struck down both, the constitutional amendment as well as the NJAC, citing impediment to the independence of the judiciary, which is a basic structure of the Constitution.

The hotly contested collegium system, then, remains one that continues to attract criticism for its lack of transparency, accountability and objectivity.

From former Chief Justice of India Ranjan Gogoi's autobiography, we know that the collegium system simply doesn't work.[24] He describes in detail the internal disputes and various conflicts and distresses caused by the lack of confidence and cooperation between Collegium judges and the Chief Justice of India. As articulated by him, 'There is a danger to control the judiciary from a group of people holding cards of judicial independence.'[25]

What, then, is a plausible way forward? It may be of value to once again return to the Constitution and place faith in the document's wisdom and the wisdom of the giants who gave it to us, as Justice Ahmadi had done. There is an argument to be made for preserving the fundamental principles of the Constitution as they were intended, for tinkering with them might come at a price too heavy to bear – the compromise of the independence and integrity of our judiciary.

As Justice Ahmadi said, 'It must be remembered that it is the Constitution that is Supreme, and no one organ that it creates.'[26]

While Justice Ahmadi was busy shaping constitutional jurisprudence, his two children were only just embarking on their own professional journeys. Both of them had chosen careers in the law, young and eager to build their practices. In the very beginning, a family meeting was held between the adults to establish procedures and practices that would ensure no fingers could be pointed at either Justice Ahmadi or their children. A collective decision was arrived at. Both Tasneem and Huzefa, recognizing the sensitivity of the moment, agreed on a voluntary, self-imposed restriction – to refrain from practising law in the Supreme Court entirely, for as long as their father held the position of a judge. This decision was not made lightly; it came with profound implications for their careers and professional growth. Yet, it was a sacrifice they were willing to make for the sake of their father's legacy and the sanctity of the Supreme Court – an ideal they all held dear.

In Justice Ahmadi's view, this was the right thing for them to do. He writes,

> Legally there was no restriction on their practice (in the same court) but morally it seems awkward and creates a wrong impression in the minds of the litigants. People's trust in the institution of judiciary is necessary for a healthy judicial system based on the Rule of Law. I personally believe that the judges should not allow their children to practice in the courts where they are posted. It gives people an opportunity to tarnish their image. After their retirement, their sons and daughters can certainly practice in those courts. This system would be better to strengthen the institution of judiciary.[27]

A stringent protocol was established in the offices of Justice Ahmadi. Every brief that was offered to either Tasneem or Huzefa would require a check with Justice Ahmadi's secretaries to ensure there were no possible conflict of interest. If a potential client had another (even if unrelated) case before Justice Ahmadi in the Supreme Court, it was an automatic disqualification. This protocol would remain in place for many years, even after Ahmadi's retirement when he immersed himself in arbitrations. It was instituted to ensure that neither Tasneem nor Huzefa inadvertently accepted briefs from clients involved in arbitrations before Justice Ahmadi. These precautions, as it turns out, were not unwarranted. During Ahmadi's tenure in the Supreme Court, both his children would encounter numerous attempts to influence them or persuade them to take up a case that would serve to embarrass their father. The vigilance against such dubious characters was, therefore, necessary.

Despite these stringent protocols and restrictions, the young and unassuming Tasneem and Huzefa found themselves being ruthlessly attacked. At the threshold of their careers and still naïve, they had not anticipated being turned into unwitting targets in a larger game, a means to reach their father.

A bewildered young Tasneem and Huzefa were, suddenly and without warning, catapulted into the unforgiving spotlight of media attention. Allegations swirled, claiming that Ahmadi was misusing his position, wielding his influence to advance his children's careers and that alleged conflicts of interest were rife. The press did not hold back on amplifying these accusations, rarely bothering to verify any of them, and the Bar Association went as far as to go on strike on one occasion. Another group of lawyers attempted to pass a resolution that sought to bar the practice of daughters of sitting judges who lived with their fathers. Sons, inexplicably, were exempt. At the time, there was no sitting judge apart from Ahmadi who had a daughter living with him and practising law in Delhi – but several had sons.

Instead of celebrating their budding professional journeys, the siblings found themselves thrust into the headlines for all the wrong reasons. The rumour mill was in full swing, spewing sensational and bizarre news. Among the curious items circulated was one that alleged Justice Ahmadi's two sons had somehow managed to secure petrol pumps in Delhi. The fact that Ahmadi did not have two sons to begin with became almost inconsequential amid the frenzied attacks.

Absurd and unsubstantiated, these escalating attacks on the two young lawyers – and Ahmadi himself – pointed to a deliberate smear campaign aimed at tarnishing Justice Ahmadi's impeccable reputation, with the intention of derailing his eminent appointment as Chief Justice of India.

While the family chose not to dignify any of these attacks with public responses, private moments revealed the strain everybody was under. Ahmadi's short temper was flaring up more often than usual and Ama was scouring the newspapers with trepidation every morning, hoping not to stumble upon another unfounded, vicious accusation against her husband and children. As a father, Justice Ahmadi was naturally worried about the detrimental impact of these attacks on the careers of his children. But as a legal statesman and person of impeccable reputation, it was the assault on his integrity that cut the deepest.

As a result, both Tasneem and Huzefa's legal practices took longer to take off than they should have. The need for extreme caution in accepting cases acted as a significant obstacle to their professional growth. While newspapers gleefully printed news of their imaginary high profile clients and unheard-of fees, in truth, the siblings were both erring on the side of caution, rejecting more cases than they were accepting. It was only after some years, following their father's retirement that the tides began to turn. Slowly but surely, their practices began to flourish and they both evolved into successful advocates in their own right. But in those initial years, both Ahmadi's children bore the brunt of the targeting that they and their father were subjected to.

There were other restrictions too. Required to conduct themselves in a manner that befitted the children of the future Chief Justice of India, the two siblings refrained from several typical youthful activities that their peers took for granted. There were no parties or social gatherings held at home, nor fraternizing with lawyers, especially those practising in the Supreme Court. Barring a handful of family friends, those friends who happened to be practising lawyers were prohibited from visiting them at home.

It would not be an exaggeration to say that if there was a price that was paid for Justice Ahmadi's ascension to the highest position of the judiciary, it was borne not only by him, but equally by his family.

Festivals were a time of increased vigilance. At the end of every Diwali and Eid, the Ahmadi residence was flooded with an avalanche of flowers, sweets and gifts. But these were not accepted carelessly. Throughout the festive day, all received gifts – including boxes of sweets and dry fruits – underwent a meticulous inspection under Amena's eagle eye, immediately after the guests had departed. On numerous occasions, an excessively extravagant gift would quickly but discreetly be handed over to a waiting staff member with urgent instructions to rush after the guest and politely – but insistently – return it before they left the premises. The returned gifts ranged from ostentatious items like jewellery to more subtle ones like luxury handbags. All were uncompromisingly returned. This stringent protocol was especially observed during Huzefa Ahmadi's wedding. The exhausted newlyweds would stay up long after the guests had departed, carefully unboxing and inspecting each gift under the watchful scrutiny of

Ama, ensuring the family's commitment to propriety was upheld without any exceptions.

These precautionary measures were established to avoid any perception of undue influence or impropriety that might compromise the reputation and integrity of the future Chief Justice and his family.

As the senior-most judge of the Supreme Court with an upcoming term as Chief Justice, as well as Executive Chairman of Lok Adalats, Ahmadi had begun to keep a close eye on the performance of various High Courts and their case disposals. Like his mentor Justice Thakkar who was the driving force behind the very first Lok Adalat organized in Una, Gujarat in 1982, Ahmadi too firmly believed in the importance of alternate dispute resolution forums. Unlike traditional courts, Lok Adalats do not charge court fees and operate with flexible procedural norms, contributing significantly to reducing court backlog. Establishing these forums is the prerogative of legal authorities at various levels, including State, District and High Courts. They are temporary courts that sit for a single day or a limited number of days and are headed by serving or retired judicial officers. The decision of a Lok Adalat is deemed to be a decree of the civil court.

Justice Ahmadi noticed that in Andhra Pradesh, a backlog of 98,000 land acquisition cases had piled up.[28] Taking action, he assembled a team including a retired judge from the same court to address this extraordinary backlog. Two truckloads of paperwork were received, and Ahmadi worked closely with the team for two years while the paperwork was sorted and categorized. Eventually a pattern emerged. These were mass cases, all to do with land acquisition as a consequence of the acquisitions made for the Srisailam Dam, and therefore required a systematic approach. The Srisailam project had displaced 100,000 people who had been removed from their homes and relocated 10–15 kilometres away via tractors, lorries and bullock carts. Further, to deter villagers from returning if the water levels decreased, the irrigation canals in the villages were also destroyed.[29]

'It was an unpleasant, heart-rending and [a] thankless job,' remembers K. Krishnamoorthy, an executive engineer in charge of the evacuation.

Recognizing the need for a fair and transparent pricing mechanism, Ahmadi and his team conducted a thorough evaluation, arriving at a total figure of Rs. 257 crore to settle the cases. Armed with this information, Justice Ahmadi then approached the Chief Minister of the state.

Caught off guard, the Chief Minister suggested the formation of a committee with key officials, including the Finance Secretary and Revenue Secretary. But Ahmadi was not willing to wait. He informed the Chief Minister that he was going to Kareem Nagar to settle the first lot of 30,000 cases and suggested that an initial amount of Rs. 87 crore be released for these settlements, with the remaining amount to be later settled in two instalments. Alarmed, the Chief Minister tried to deter Ahmadi from going to Kareem Nagar, a known Naxalite-prone area. Brushing off the safety concerns, Ahmadi informed the Chief Minister that he was not looking for additional safety measures from the State, but remained determined to resolve the cases.

Simultaneously, the Finance Minister interjected saying they did not have sufficient funds for Justice Ahmadi's requirements. Slightly annoyed by the minister's seeming apathy and lack of initiative in resolving the matter, Ahmadi responded sharply. 'If you do not know where your money is lying, I can tell you where it is. [sic]'

In the end, a Lok Adalat was held, in which 98,000 cases were disposed of in one day; an astonishing feat indeed. In a separate occurrence, the district of Tharwad in Karnataka too earned the appreciation of the litigant public.[30] Here, during a Lok Adalat and its preliminary sessions held between 25/9/93 and 24/12/93, a notable accomplishment was achieved. A remarkable 1564 Motor Accident Compensation Claims were effectively settled through a Lok Adalat, leading to a substantial compensation amount of Rs. 3,15,29,786.

Through his years as a High Court and Supreme Court judge, Ahmadi would put his weight behind these dispute resolution mechanisms, working with state advisory boards and conducting Lok Adalats to reduce case pendency and ensure quick disposal of cases. Under his guidance, Lok Adalats offered the economically disadvantaged a direct and impactful form of support by resolving specific categories of cases.[31] This initiative, which waived court and counsel expenses, particularly benefited individuals from the Scheduled Castes and Tribes, ex-army personnel and those facing economic challenges.

As Executive Chairman of Committee for Implementating Legal Aid Schemes (CILAS), Justice Ahmadi was equally committed to Legal Aid, an initiative he had championed since his days in the Gujarat High Court. The Right to Legal Aid, rooted in Article 39A of the Constitution mandates the State to provide free legal assistance. Eligible individuals include members of marginalized communities, victims of various disasters and those in custody or juvenile homes. Legal aid is accessible from lower courts to the Supreme Court, with Legal Services Authorities established at various levels. The realization of these schemes was important to ensure that justice was not denied on the grounds of lack of convenience, discrimination or disability.

During this time, Justice Ahmadi participated in the Indo-British Forum Exchanges three times – twice as a Supreme Court judge in the capacity of Executive Chairman of CILAS, and once as Chief Justice and Patron-in-Chief for Legal Aid Schemes in India.[32] It was during his first visit that he successfully formalized a reciprocal arrangement to extend Legal Aid services in the United Kingdom, should the need arise. This happened sooner than he had expected. In an unexpected development, a young Indian woman found herself facing the nightmare of an arranged marriage gone awry. Her journey to England, in anticipation of a new life with her husband, had turned into a horrific situation when she discovered that he was already living with another woman.

Trapped in a foreign country and devastated by her husband's deceit, she confronted him, only to be threatened with eviction if she didn't succumb to his oppressive demands. Helpless and financially dependent on him, she began preparations for her escape. Through a newspaper advertisement, she found a job and started building her savings.

Through her new colleagues, she learnt of the Legal Aid scheme and the recently established reciprocal arrangement between India and the United Kingdom.

Hopeful, she wrote to the Legal Aid office in India, seeking justice. Initially, the application was filed by the office and was to go through routine procedures. But when the resilient girl filed a second application, it was put before Justice Ahmadi. The distressing case stirred his conscience. Disturbed by the injustice, he issued a simple directive. 'Prepare for the girl's defence.'

As a first step, Justice Ahmadi directed the Joint Registrar to make contact with the distressed girl. Simultaneously, he extended his outreach to the Legal Aid authorities in the UK as well as his friend and High Commissioner, Dr L.M. Singhvi, seeking the cooperation of the local authorities in extending cross-border legal aid.

The formulation of the case compelled the erring husband to return to India where his passport was confiscated for the duration of the case. Unwilling to reconcile, the young lady stood her ground requesting to be set free of the man who had betrayed her. A settlement was brokered, necessitating the estranged husband to financially support her while she re-established her life in India, thereby liberating the young wife from a life of humiliation.

Filled with gratitude, the young lady offered to pay for her defence, an offer which was politely declined by the Legal Aid team. Despite the cross-border nature of the case, the proceedings were carried out as discreetly as possible in order to protect the woman's privacy.

Justice Ahmadi would hold the United Kingdom judiciary and legal fraternity in the highest regard until the end of his life, a sentiment that was reciprocated in full by his peers in England and Wales, in particular, Baron Harry Woolf who would go on to become Lord Chief Justice of England and Wales in 2000.

When he ascended to the highest echelons of the judiciary in his own country, Baron Woolf would write a personal note to Justice Ahmadi stating that in his upcoming role, he too aimed to model himself on Justice Ahmadi.

On another occasion, when the Right Honourable Lord Woolf, as he then was, had a request from the Director of Andhra Pradesh Judicial Academy to write a foreword for their publication titled *Thoughts and*

Reflections of Shri Justice A.M. Ahmadi, the learned law lord stated in his animated style as under:

> It gives me great pleasure to associate myself with the honour which is being done to Chief Justice of India A.M. Ahmadi. The Chief Justice is a Judge who is internationally admired. This is particularly true of this country where he is extremely well known because of his leadership in relation to the Indo-British Forum meets. India has produced many distinguished judges in the past but Chief Justice Ahmadi is among the most distinguished. He has all the qualities required of his high office. He is intelligent, courteous and understanding but firm. He commands the respect and admiration of the judiciary throughout the common law world.

These experiences, combined with the many years spent in the High Court and City Civil Court deliberating on and grappling with the issue of case pendency would eventually pave the way for the extraordinary accomplishments he would achieve as the Chief Justice of India.

In the meantime, the legal community was becoming increasingly distressed and uneasy over the calibre of legal professionals in India. Fresh graduates seemed alarmingly ill-equipped to step into courtrooms, their grasp of the law noticeably poor. A concerning number of students were obviously products of low-quality institutions, which had earned a reputation of being diploma mills where degrees were awarded with little regard for the quality of education. Many were known for handing out degrees under coercion and threats of violence.

There was a distinct sentiment within the legal and judicial communities that India's legal education system was in crisis, which was evident from the noticeable deterioration in the skill levels of advocates at the Bar. This raised significant concerns about the future of legal practice in India and the need for urgent reforms in legal education.

Justice Ahmadi's own views were concurrent with the larger observation. He shared the view that the legal education system in India was in decline, and urgently demanded a comprehensive overhaul, along with significant reforms. In a lecture titled 'Repairing the Cracks in Legal Education',[33] he painted a bleak picture of the dismal state of legal education in India.

> ... the creamy layer of the students prefer to choose other disciplines like medicine, engineering, electronics, etc., and drift to law as a last resort when they do not secure admission in the disciplines of their choice. The presence of a large number of such "drifters" can hardly generate an atmosphere conducive to a centre of learning. Their casual approach would only dampen the enthusiasm of other students as well as the teachers, causing environmental degradation. Added to that is the fact that at certain examination centres there is no supervision for fear of violence and the examination results are extremely liberal. As one Principal of a law college put it: "It is difficult to fail." What then is the scenario? Ill-equipped law colleges; a large body of students being "drifters" to the law course on their failing to secure admission to the disciplines of their choice; training personnel lacking in competence and knowledge; access to knowledge being limited on account of want of proper libraries; absence of proper filtering with extra-liberal examination results, etc., etc. etc. What a dismal picture! Is it then surprising that the product of such institutions is hardly possessed of either the skill or knowledge to practise in courts of law?

Former Chief Justice of India, Justice Kania, responded to Ahmadi's lecture saying he had been far too restrained in his description. In truth, the edifice was collapsing.[34]

It was in response to this crisis of legal education that The Conference of Chief Justices established the High Powered Ahmadi Committee on Legal Education under Justice Ahmadi's chairmanship in 1994.

The Committee comprising Justices A.M. Ahmadi, B.N. Kirpal and M. Jagannadha Rao embarked on its mission by actively engaging with the High Courts of India, seeking the valuable insights of their Chief

Justices.³⁵ The consensus among the majority of these Chief Justices was the view that given the decline in student standards and advocacy skills, it was essential for the Bar Council of India to reintroduce a training programme for law graduates. The Committee recommended modern teaching methods like the case and problem methods, with emphasis on practical training. It proposed amending exam marking systems to focus more on problem-solving skills and suggested a mandatory internship followed by a Bar Council examination for aspiring lawyers.

The Committee's thoughts on the improvement of the legal education system included the establishment of institutions similar to the National Law School, Bangalore, in each state. These institutions would offer a five-year programme, with the initial three years covering traditional legal subjects. Students could exit with a basic law degree if they didn't wish to practice law or pursue a judicial career.³⁶

Following the recommendations of the Ahmadi Committee in 1994, the Bar Council of India, which is the regulatory body for legal education and function, decided to act on the findings of the Committee.³⁷ But many Indian universities and law colleges faced challenges of infrastructure and necessary expertise to effectively deliver these clinical courses. And so, while these reforms became a part of the curriculum, the practical implementation lagged behind the intent. These reforms would go on to become further improved when clinical courses were officially integrated into the Bar Council of India's Legal Education Rules in 2008. This added more details and guidelines for how the courses should be conducted.

It is not an exaggeration to say that the efforts of this Committee have helped shape and define legal education as we know it today. The five-year law course, which has since become standardized, is a direct outcome of the work carried out by the Ahmadi Committee. So is the establishment of National Law Colleges in different states. As of today, India has twenty-six National Law Universities, located in different states.

But Justice Ahmadi was not content simply with educational reforms.³⁸ His experience had taught him that no problem, nor solution exists in a vacuum; its impacts are often felt elsewhere. So he turned his attention to the fiscal position of the Bar Council of India and the Bar Councils of the states. These bodies rely heavily on enrolment fees from new lawyers, creating incentives for lax examination standards. The more students pass and enter the legal profession, the greater their revenue. This situation had led to the proliferation of substandard law schools churning out underprepared lawyers who would eventually be enrolled by the state Bar Councils.

And so, it was that Justice Ahmadi persuaded the central government to grant Rs 10 lakh to the Bar Council of India, to offset the negative impact their efforts to improve the education standards were having on their income, thereby reducing the reliance of the Bar Council on enrolment fees from students.

Following his retirement, Ahmadi remained vocal about the need to address this matter. He continued to emphasize the importance of eliminating low-quality schools that were churning out large numbers of ill-prepared advocates and restricting the entry of their students into the profession if one truly hoped to see meaningful effects of educational reforms.

But this was not all. The National Judicial Academy, which had been in the pipeline for some years, was eventually brought to fruition by Justice Ahmadi.[39] Envisaged as an academy for the training of judges, Ahmadi saw this as an extension of his commitment towards education and uplifting the quality of legal professionals in India. Having taken up the task, he travelled extensively to Bhopal, where the government had offered a large, 62-acre piece of land towards the campus of the Academy. Once satisfied, he returned to Delhi and immediately the Governing Body of the Academy decided to accept the offer of the Government of Madhya Pradesh. This Academy would go on to conduct numerous training programmes and legal education for judges, judicial officers and ministers of the court. It would also engage in training and capacity building programmes with international institutes and authorities.[40]

In October 1993, a flurry of disturbing reports began to emerge from the heart of Kashmir. The reports suggested that a group of militants in Kashmir had seized control of the Hazratbal shrine, holding people within the sacred site hostages. Although the number of militants was unknown, they were presumed to be armed and therefore dangerous. The Indian Army had responded to the threat by dispatching two army battalions and sealing access to the shrine.

After several days had passed, it became evident that those confined inside were deprived of basic necessities such as food, water and proper sanitation facilities, forcing them to relieve themselves within the premises of the shrine itself. In response to this dire situation, Wajahat Habibullah, the Divisional Commissioner of Kashmir and government-appointed chief negotiator, arranged to send food supplies into the shrine. But the Army was fiercely opposed to this approach and after Habibullah's first attempt, they did not allow further supplies of food into the shrine. They believed these efforts might inadvertently provide sustenance to the militants as well as endanger those carrying the food into the shrine.

Wajahat Habibullah maintains a slightly different version of the siege. The alleged militants, he explains, were a part of the local population itself, seen as 'freedom fighters'.[41] As such, they had the sympathies of the local population and saw the Indian Army as their adversaries. This was not helped by the Army's aggressive stance towards them, nor by their refusal to allow food and medical supplies into the shrine. The widely held belief surrounding the siege suggested that it was a deliberate effort by the State to reinforce its authority, aiming to take command of a holy shrine and location known to be a stronghold of the Jammu and Kashmir Liberation Front (JKLF) – a political organization that advocates for the independence of Jammu and Kashmir from both India and Pakistan.

Further, in his negotiations with the militants, Habibullah learnt that their motivations were simple – to protect the *Moi-e-Muqqadas*, which is housed in Hazratbal.[42] Believed to be a hair of the Prophet Muhammad, this is a most revered relic. They feared the Indian Army wished to desecrate it and were willing to guard it with their lives. The militants also claimed that the so-called hostages were not forcibly confined and were free to leave if they so wished.

Mr Habibullah confirmed this fact at the time of writing, explaining that the locals did indeed choose to stay within the premises voluntarily. They believed that as long as there were civilians inside, the Indian Army would not use force that might desecrate the precious relic.

In the meantime, the local population remained resentful of military presence in the area. Appeals to allow 'the boys' – the militants – to leave unmolested were rejected. The Valley was under curfew, and the Kashmiris were demanding the siege be lifted. On 22 October 1993, fifty-one people protesting against the siege would be shot dead by the BSF in the infamous Bijbehara massacre.[43]

In this intense standoff between the chief negotiator and the military, a deadlock emerged, creating an impasse. As the discord persisted, the only viable recourse was to appeal to the Supreme Court to intervene.

This troubling matter arrived before a bench of the Supreme Court that was presided over by Justice Ahmadi. The hugely sensitive case was of critical importance, leaving no room for error. Watched closely by the media both nationally and internationally, a misstep by any of the judges would no doubt be amplified and used as fodder for various agendas.[44] The case was, therefore, heard in a closed-door hearing. As the judges took their seats on the bench, the Additional Solicitor General, Mr Altaf Ahmed, mentioned the matter. He briefed the judges, detailing how a group of militants had infiltrated the mosque and taken over 150 people hostage, threatening to shoot anyone who might try to enter.

As the bench heard the case, the apparent sensitivity of the situation became more and more clear. The judges were also aware that the case had attracted the attention of international human rights organizations who were closely following the events as they unfolded. Justice Ahmadi voiced his concern for the civilians who were believed to be hostages and the fact that they had been devoid of food for days. Directing a question to Mr Ahmad, he asked, 'Do you have a scale map of the mosque?'[45] Ahmad was taken aback. He had not expected to be asked for a map. Ahmadi said, 'Surely someone must have come to brief you?' At that point, a gentleman rose from his seat and introduced himself as an officer of the Jammu and Kashmir government. He produced the map Ahmadi wished to peruse. By then it was time for lunch, and the bench rose. Retiring to his chambers for lunch, Ahmadi pored over the map, trying to find a resolution that would address the urgent needs of those trapped without compromising any lives. Hunched over a table, he traced his finger over the blueprint, familiarizing himself with the apertures of the dome and the alleged position of the militants, drawing imaginary lines from the militants' position to the outside of the mosque. After a few minutes, he requested his brother judge's attention. He believed he had identified a spot the militants did not have a direct line of sight to, and therefore would not be able to shoot at.

Returning to the courtroom, the bench directed that food and water be served at this particular point, rather than inside the mosque, and that there be no restriction on who consumed the food. It was pointed out that the state could not deny anyone their constitutional right to life and therefore, meals must be served to all those inside the shrine.[46] The bench further specified the kind of food that was to be served – it need not be luxurious, but it must be nourishing and fit for human consumption.[47] The court recognized the need to preserve all lives, without discrimination.

Wajahat Habibullah recalls that this order was met with mixed reactions. While the Indian Army was disgruntled and dissatisfied, international media and human rights institutions commended it, calling it one of the finest orders.

A few days later, the militants were persuaded to surrender in exchange for lenient treatment by the authorities. There were no fatalities in the shrine.

At home, the Government of India was ecstatic at the outcome. Prime Minister P.V. Narasimha Rao had been sitting at the edge of his seat for the duration of the siege, fearing international uproar. In the aftermath of Operation Blue Star and the more recent Babri Mosque demolition, India had faced tremendous backlash in global media coverage questioning its dedication to secularism and human rights. It was, therefore, imperative that neither the shrine nor human life suffer any harm. The Court's definitive order earned India international acclaim, prompting President

Shankar Dayal Sharma to reach out to Justice Ahmadi and inform him that 'the country was filled with pride.' He said, 'You have shown the world the sensitivity of our Supreme Court towards human rights. Even the alleged militants were not deprived of food and water.'[48]

As Justice Ahmadi's tenure as Chief Justice of India grew closer, one of the very last judgements that he delivered as puisne judge of the Supreme Court was one that would go on to protect the rights of undertrials and address excesses by the police force.

This case was Supreme Court Legal Aid Committee Representing Undertrial Prisoners vs. Union of India.[49] Under the Narcotic Drugs and Psychotropic Substances Act, all offences were to be tried exclusively by Special Courts. But a combination of factors, including the lack of these special courts in many states and the stringent bail conditions, meant that the rapidly swelling number of undertrials languishing in jails was growing at an alarming rate, without visible recourse.

There was also the worrying trend of certain state police forces wrongly capturing innocent individuals under this Act in order to reach their quotas and create an illusion of efficiency.[50] As detailed in a media report, the Uttar Pradesh police had been found to be employing deceitful tactics, including the planting of five grams of narcotics on unsuspecting individuals such as rickshaw drivers, subsequently arresting them under the Narcotics Act. A shocking 60 per cent of undertrials in the Uttar Pradesh jails were found to have been charged under this Act. Further, since the burden of proving innocence lies with the accused in these cases, it meant they were, in effect, imprisoned indefinitely. As of 1996, the country had an estimated 1.63 lakh undertrials, making up 72.32 per cent of the total prison population. Disturbingly, many among them had already spent more time behind bars than they would have had to, even if convicted.

Invoking the fundamental right of these undertrials to a speedy trial, the Supreme Court Legal Aid Committee filed a PIL in 1993 seeking the quashing of the prosecutions and freeing the accused.[51]

Initially, the petition aimed to specifically address the case of foreigners who had spent two years or more in Indian jails. But the Court pointed out that such a distinction between foreigners and Indian citizens was impermissible under the Constitution. Consequently, the amended petition sought the release of all undertrials fifty-one had been imprisoned for more than two years, regardless of their nationality.

The Court found that the refusal of bail coupled with a delay in trials is unfair and in violation of the spirit of Articles 14, 19 and 21 of the Constitution. But it also acknowledged that the offences under the Act were grave and therefore freeing the accused without trial was not possible.

The judgement authored by Justice Ahmadi was a careful consideration of the plight of the imprisoned along with the constraints of the bench. For offenses carrying a punishment of five years or less and a fine, the undertrial would be released on bail if they had spent half the punishment duration in jail, accompanied by 50 per cent of the prescribed bail amount and two sureties. Those under trial were required to present themselves at the police station monthly. For offenses with a punishment exceeding five years and a fine, bail was to be granted after half the punishment duration was served, with a bail amount not less than Rs. 50,000 and fortnightly police station visits. In cases with a minimum imprisonment of ten years and a fine of at least one lakh rupees, release on bail was made contingent on spending at least five years in jail, with a bail of one lakh rupees and weekly police station visits. Offenses falling under Sections 31 and 31A of the Act were deemed ineligible for bail due to their severity involving repeat offenders and more serious crimes and prescribing harsh punishments.

10

The Chief's Chair

The day 25 October 1994 brought forward a humid, sun-drenched morning. The excitement in the air was electric. The family's once-private space was transformed, with mattresses strewn across the floor to accommodate the incoming tide of guests. The largest room in the bungalow now accommodated several ladies – relatives and friends who were already awake and bustling about just as the children were being shaken awake. Some were calling out to the others, looking for safety pins to secure their saris or a hand with a bracelet clasp, while others who had woken up early were already at the breakfast table. The room was bustling with activity. The gentlemen who had been accommodated in the study where the children normally did their homework were beginning to stir from their sleep. Some held steaming cups of tea in their hands, a morning ritual impossible to forego.

'Hurry up, get into the shower quickly,' Tasneem instructed her children. 'Everyone has to get ready on time, so don't dawdle.' An hour and a half later, the family was on its way, bundled in a gleaming white Ambassador. Mrs and Justice Ahmadi were in a car by themselves, and the rest of the relatives would follow in the convoy of vehicles that had been readied for the day. As the line of cars turned away from Krishna Menon Marg towards the Rashtrapati Bhavan, the usually bustling roads were eerily empty. Traffic had been diverted and the roads had been barricaded by police and security personnel for VIP movement. Because today was the day India was to receive her 26th Chief Justice. The journey towards the official residence of the President of India was like a regal procession through the silent, empty streets, each moment stamped with the grandeur and honour of the day.

The imposing and resplendent corridors of the Rashtrapati Bhavan are awe-inspiring to even the most blasé eye. Lofty ceilings that seem to touch the sky, hallways that glitter with a dazzling display of grandiosity and the gleaming marble floors all spell regality and stateliness. Enormous chandeliers drench the rooms in a rich golden light, casting an air of magnificence over everything. As Justice Ahmadi's family and relatives took their seats, some of the faces in the front row were visible. Prime Minister P.V. Narasimha Rao, retiring Chief Justice Venkatachaliah and President Shankar Dayal Sharma's wife, Vimlaji had all just arrived. So had Mrs and Justice Ahmadi who were being greeted by the dignitaries in attendance.

Once seated, the proceedings began to unfold. As the first notes of the national anthem began to play, the attendees rose in unison, the anthem filling the room with a shared moment of solemnity and respect. The room remained in respectful silence as Dr Shankar Dayal Sharma, the President of India, entered to the powerful sound of a bugle, assumed his place at the dais and initiated the ceremony. A few minutes later, Justice Ahmadi rose from his seat and strode deliberately across the room towards the dais, his gown flowing behind him. The oath he was about to swear were the same words that had echoed through these corridors of power twenty-five times in the history of Independent India, but only twice before by a Muslim.[1] It was a journey that held within its few short strides, a culmination of a lifetime of hope, determination and countless hours of blood, sweat and sacrifice; all made worth it in this magnificent moment. And then, the moment was here. With a clear and powerful voice, he began. 'I, Aziz Mushabber Ahmadi . . .'

And so, Chief Justice Aziz Mushabber Ahmadi assumed the mantle of the highest judicial authority. But even more remarkable was the distinction of having become the first – and only – Chief Justice of India in history to have risen from the very lowest rank of the Indian judiciary to the very topmost. This incredible journey served as a powerful testament to the foundational principles of meritocracy and equal opportunity. As such, this historic day turned the nation's gaze upon him, seeing in him not just a legal luminary but a symbol of diversity, progression and the potential for upward mobility within the judicial system.

But that wasn't all. At sixty-two years and a few months old, Justice Ahmadi had a long tenure of over two years ahead of him. Because longer tenures allow Chief Justices the unique opportunity to implement far-reaching legal and institutional reforms, they allow for the potential to leave a lasting impact on the Indian judicial system. This length of tenure was a rare opportunity that not many Chief Justices are fortunate enough to have. It meant that Chief Justice Ahmadi had the opportunity to make substantial contributions to the legal landscape of the country – an opportunity he intended to make the most of.

Hitting the ground running, the new Chief Justice began his tenure with the one issue that had niggled at him his entire career. Tackling the long-standing problem of case pendency. Drawing from his experiences and success in reducing case pendency in the City Civil Court, he decided to apply the same methods now, determined to demonstrate the soundness of the slogan he had coined, 'Don't get scared by numbers.'[2] Ideally, he would have preferred to tackle the issue of arrears from the grassroots level, starting with the trial courts, but he realized that leading by example would be a better approach to achieve both, visibility and credibility.[3]

Eventually he decided on a two-pronged approach, tackling the issue simultaneously at both, the trial court and the Supreme Court levels. To confront the problem of backlog of cases at the trial court level, he formed a team comprising lawyers practising at various courts. This team was tasked with conducting a detailed investigation into ground-level issues. Notably, Mr Niranjan Bhatt, Justice Ahmadi's dear friend and seasoned lawyer with a wealth of experience in trial courts, was requested to contribute his expertise to the team. This team would go on to work closely with the Indo-US team constituted by Justice Ahmadi, which would eventually lead to the incorporation of Section 89 in the Civil Code Procedure. As the team delved into the intricacies of the functioning of trial courts and

High Courts, Chief Justice Ahmadi embarked upon addressing the matter at the Supreme Court level.

Embracing technology, Ahmadi initiated reforms that consisted of a uniform classification system, computerization in filing, listing and allocation processes within the Supreme Court registry.[4] He applied the time-tested method of categorization and allocated these categorized groups of cases to particular benches, maintaining the composition of the bench until the group of cases was entirely disposed of.[5] In order to prevent regular court proceedings from being disrupted, a group of district judges worked through the summer vacations, examining each case manually, categorizing and entering them into a newly developed computerization system. Three tracks were created – normal, medium and fast tracks. It was found that because the cases within each category were similar, it only took the benches a little time to dispose of the first few cases before gaining momentum and moving swiftly through the remainder of cases within the same group. Another advantage of this method was that it turned the benches into 'specialist benches,' allowing them to tackle similar cases quickly.[6] Simultaneously, judgements were digitized and made available in floppies and disks for easy access, which helped not only the bench and the Bar but also other functionaries, including academics and journalists.

This method of efficient docket management proved to be hugely successful. So successful, in fact, that one of the Supreme Court judges, in a moment of mischievous humour, quipped to Justice Ahmadi, 'Chief Justice, when can we expect retrenchment?'[7]

But no reform takes place without some resistance. When Ahmadi insisted on establishing a computer filing system to streamline dockets and their movement through the system, the court registry, preferring their old ways, opposed the initiative, refusing to give up their typewriters. Eventually, in an almost comical move, these typewriters were physically removed from their desks, compelling the staff to embrace the transition.

When Justice Ahmadi assumed the role of Chief Justice, he had inherited a caseload of approximately 1,20,000 cases.[8] By September 1996, this number had been reduced to 28,000.[9] And by the time he retired in

March 1997, the number stood at 18,000. This, despite the average number of cases being filed every year standing at a staggering 30,000.

It was this resounding success that prompted the replication of this method throughout the country.[10] It was to this end that an 'Indo-US' team was constituted, consisting of lawyers, judges and scholars from both countries. Because this time Justice Ahmadi hoped to make a lasting change that would revolutionize the way cases were dealt with in the Indian judiciary. In pursuit of a long-term solution,[11] Justice Ahmadi had reached out to his friend, Judge Clifford Wallace from the Ninth Circuit Court of Appeals in California as well as Justices of the US Supreme Court Justices Ruth Bader Ginsburg and Antonin Scalia.[12] Ahmadi requested Wallace to recommend an organization or institute that could help undertake the exercise of examining the Indian legal system and suggest ways to tackle the long-standing issue of case pendency.[13] Judge Wallace, in turn, contacted Dr Stephen Mayo, an expert associated with the Institute for the Study and Development of Legal Systems (ISDLS). Mr Mayo agreed to constitute a Legal Study Group that would examine the issue as well as agreed to fund the project.[14] The endeavour also received support from Mr Frank Wisner, the US Ambassador to India, who believed that a collaborative effort involving legal professionals from both India and the United States could prove highly beneficial. Mr Mayo was to lead the American group and also aid the Indian team.

This Indo-US national legal exchange programme involved every High Court in India appointing a dedicated study team to work alongside delegates from ISDLS.[15] These teams collected extensive data and information from their respective states, analysed the information and, finally, formulated concrete recommendations to tackle institutional backlogs. These recommendations were then presented as a proposal for the introduction of amendments related to case management within the Civil Procedure Code with a focus on the Indian context.

The study revealed some interesting findings. It was found that the Indian legal system was plagued by significant structural issues that demanded innovative solutions. Firstly, there was a need for reform of court administration at every phase of the litigation process. The administrative bodies were failing to keep tabs on the status, nature and speed of civil litigation, leading to duplication of work and prolonging of unresolved disputes. Secondly, judicial management of the legal process was found to be undisciplined, resulting in delays, repetition and fragmentation in cases. Further, legal professionals often overlooked procedural requirements in the early stages of cases, causing further delays. Lastly, it was recommended that alternatives to formal adversarial litigation by a variety of conciliatory processes conducted outside the courtroom be explored. It was found that a lack of available means for peaceful collaborative dispute resolution was forcing more cases into the formal legal process.

The team led by Justice Saikia presented three copies of their report – one for the Supreme Court library, the second for the government and the third was in Ahmadi's possession.[16] But after Justice Ahmadi's retirement, the report was relegated to a dusty corner, with no attempt made by his successors to implement it.

After he retired, Justice Ahmadi's copy too was collected on the pretext of having it printed and filed but was never to be seen again. Nor were the other two copies. Tenacious as he was, Mr Niranjan refused to be defeated by these suspicious disappearances. He later tried to implement the recommendations of the team at the City Civil Court level. Additionally, he set up a non-charitable trust called the Institute for Arbitration Mediation Legal Education and Development (AMLEAD) to train mediators.[17] Both initiatives yielded promising results.

Soon after the Indo-US team presented its report, the Indian Parliament acknowledged the need for incorporating mediation as an alternative to traditional court-based processes and the Civil Procedure Code was amended, resulting in the incorporation of Section 89 in the CPC, which includes mediation as an alternative dispute resolution method.[18] This particular section was introduced by the CPC (Amendment) Act in 1999 and officially came into effect in July 2002 – a development that has been credited to Justice Ahmadi and his efforts to promote ADR mechanisms aimed at reducing case pendency in India.[19]

However, this amendment initially faced a legal challenge from a group of lawyers. In response, the Malimath Committee and the 129th Law

Commission were constituted to further explore the matter.[20] Subsequently, in the case of Salem Advocates Bar Association vs. Union of India, the Hon'ble Supreme Court ruled that courts were required to refer cases to alternative dispute resolution forums if they found it suitable.

Since then, ADR mechanisms have received significant impetus from the Supreme Court as well as various legislations, making it an important part of Justice Ahmadi's legacy.[21] In 2009, at the Annual Symposium of the BYU Law International Centre of Law and Religion Studies, Judge Wallace publicly credited the establishment of mediation in India to Justice Ahmadi.

These efforts were noticed internationally. The New York University took an interest in the exercise and published this work in the *Journal of International Law and Politics*, Volume 30, during the Fall of 1997 and Winter of 1998.[22] This article, authored by Justice Ahmadi, Abhishek M. Singhvi, Hiram E. Chandosh and Stephen A. Mayo, is a significant contribution to the discourse on reforms in the civil justice system. It brought Justice Ahmadi great satisfaction to witness the validation of his strong conviction that tackling case pendency was not an insurmountable task.

His peer, Sir Harry Woolf, humorously nicknamed Justice Ahmadi the 'case cracker' for his hugely successful efforts in reducing the backlog of cases in the Indian Supreme Court.

In the years following his retirement as well, Justice Ahmadi would continue to advocate for the merits of mediation, encouraging the courts to embrace it as an opportunity to achieve results that traditional judgements could not do.[23] He observed that court rulings, while legally binding, often left one party aggrieved or dissatisfied. In contrast, mediation held the promise of discovering a middle ground where both parties could find satisfaction and resolution.[24] In his words, 'Dialogue, even if it fails to find a solution, certainly promotes better agreed understanding and appreciation of each other's points of view and softens the conflict.' Looking back, he would recount his efforts to persuade Justice Venkatachaliah to consider mediation to resolve the dispute over the Babri mosque in Ayodhya, thereby keeping the conflict out of the courtroom. It was a suggestion stemming from a profound understanding of the potential consequences of generations being poisoned by feelings of bad blood and the infiltration of sectarian sentiment amongst the Indian people. At the time, however, Justice Venkatachaliah, considering the issue too emotionally charged, had preferred the traditional route of courtroom litigation.

One can't help but wonder about the outcome if mediation between the warring parties over the Ram Janmabhoomi issue had been successful in nipping the prolonged legal battle in the bud, circumventing the decades of acrimony that followed.

Speaking at the annual general meeting of the Association of All India Retired Judges of Supreme Court and High Courts of India after his retirement, in 2005, Justice Ahmadi stated, 'Judicial Reforms is a dire necessity and not a luxury; even if it does not have a measurable impact on economic development, it certainly will expedite the disposal of cases and will save considerable time, effort, energy and cost to both the litigant and the State. It will certainly impact society. I say this from experience. It is worth the effort.'[25]

It would have given Justice Ahmadi tremendous satisfaction to know that twenty-six years after his retirement, the Mediation Act[26] was passed in both houses of the Parliament in 2023, receiving Presidential assent on 14 September 2023.

As a Chief Justice who had received an unusually long term, he was acutely aware of the critical role he played in shaping the image of the Supreme Court, both on the national and international stage. Each evening, the Supreme Court librarian sent a stack of newspaper clippings to his home so that the Chief could glance through them and stay informed about public discourse surrounding the judiciary. Beyond the courtroom, he accepted invitations to international and domestic tours, lecture invitations, conferences and seminars, fostering a global understanding of the Indian legal system and elevating the Supreme Court's visibility and influence to levels it had seldom enjoyed in previous times.

To this end, Mrs and Justice Ahmadi had begun to travel extensively. Every few weeks, they found themselves in another city or another country, with Justice Ahmadi attending judicial functions, conferences or leading delegations and Amena accompanying him. There were also felicitations; six Indian universities had bestowed upon him an honorary degree of Doctor of Laws (Honoris Causa). In 1995, he was honoured with membership in the American Inn of Laws, and the following year, he was felicitated as Honorary Master and Bencher of the Middle Temple Inn of the Honourable Society of Middle Temple in London. The University of Leicester conferred upon him the esteemed degree of Doctor of Laws (Honoris Causa).

But there was another outcome of these extensive travels, one that significantly shaped Justice Ahmadi's ambitious implementation of judicial reforms in India. During these trips overseas, he took a proactive approach to examining the practices and methodologies employed by other countries within their judicial frameworks. The knowledge he gained from foreign courts and systems was not merely to satisfy his intellectual curiosity but was intended to adapt and implement international best practices to the Indian legal context. Indeed, it was thanks to these visits that he was able to initiate crucial endeavours like the Indo-US national legal exchange programme. While these trips primarily helped to generate visibility about Indian judicial initiatives and build exchange programmes, they also served the purpose of bringing home lessons, experiences and strategies that would enhance the efficiency and address the challenges within the Indian judicial system.

It was during one such visit to Washington DC in 1995 that Justice Ahmadi had the opportunity to explore the inner workings of the US Supreme Court, where he encountered the concept of law clerks.[27] These judicial assistants are assigned to judges, entrusted with various responsibilities including conducting legal research, analysing case law, assisting in drafting documents, citing sources accurately, and proofreading materials. By performing these tasks, law clerks not only ease the workload of the judge but also acquire invaluable knowledge about the functioning of the courtroom and the legal system as a whole. Intrigued, Ahmadi delved into the details, seeking to understand the benefits and value they brought to the judicial process. Convinced of the merits of institutionalizing such a process, he decided to try and implement it. So, a few days later while attending the convocation ceremony at the National Law School in Bangalore, he leaned over to the Director and posed a question. 'Would your students be interested in working at the Supreme Court?' The Director expressed that many students would have eagerly seized such an opportunity, but the cream of the batch had already secured positions in prestigious law firms or won scholarships for foreign studies. However, there was one student, Arun Thiruvengadam, who had not yet made a binding commitment and was both willing and eager.

Although there were no legal or ethical obstacles barring Justice Ahmadi from immediately appointing Arun as his law clerk, he was determined to follow established protocol. His reasons for doing so stemmed from a combination of integrity and a strategic vision that extended beyond the appointment of a judicial clerk for himself. His goal was to ultimately institutionalize a programme that would endure long after his tenure as Chief Justice had ended, becoming a part of the judicial landscape.

Armed with this vision, Arun was sent to meet the other two senior-most judges, Justices J.S. Verma and Kuldip Singh. It was clearly conveyed that the initiation of the clerkship programme would only proceed if the majority of the three senior-most judges were in agreement. As mentioned earlier, it was an open secret that the three senior-most judges found themselves at odds over a range of issues, but Justice Ahmadi was not prepared to push the programme unilaterally only to see it discontinued as soon as he demitted office.

Arun's appointment with Justice Verma was brief, with the meeting lasting mere minutes before the potential appointee was dismissed. But Justice Kuldip Singh's response left him surprised. Perhaps touched by the young man's nervousness, Singh received him kindly and ultimately approved his appointment. And so, an idea sparked in Washington gave the Indian Supreme Court its judicial clerkship programme, which is now perhaps the most prestigious in the country.

Justice Ahmadi's life now revolved around two primary domains: the hallowed halls of the Supreme Court and the sanctuary of his bedroom, where books and files were piled waist-high on the floor by the foot of his bed. His personal study, attached to the bedroom was a labyrinth of legal tomes, case records and reference materials where the sounds of furious turning of pages, scratching of pens and rustling of papers served as implicit warning signs not to interrupt.

Rarely emerging for anything other than meals, the nightly news broadcast and his evening walks, Justice Ahmadi was completely immersed in his work. However, even the most dedicated individuals are disrupted by life's unexpected turns. It was during a still, peaceful afternoon in Delhi when Aziz Ahmadi received the phone call that would momentarily pull his focus away from his work. The news was not good.

Mushabber Ahmadi was critically ill. A previous fall from a bus had left him with a broken femur, an unwelcome companion in the form of a steel plate and the memory of two agonizing surgeries, ultimately compelling the senior Ahmadi to navigate life with the help of a walking stick. Yet, even in his frailty, Mushabber Ahmadi remained a paragon of willpower. It was a trait that appeared to be a genetic inheritance passed down through the generations, received in undiluted and resolute form by his son, Aziz. This time, however, age had caught up with the elder Ahmadi. Past the milestone of ninety years, he was now much frailer.

As Aziz sat beside his father at the edge of the white hospital bed in Ahmedabad, his hand gently cradled the wrinkled hand of his father. Mushabber, unable to speak, gestured for a piece of paper and a pen. Scanning the room for a notepad, Aziz found nothing except the doctor's prescription. With a hand that shook but a spirit that remained unbroken, Mushabber Ahmadi inscribed his declaration on the prescription. 'Take me home, I am not dying, I will still live.'

And so, Mushabber Imran Ali Ahmadi was taken home, where he lived for another few years, finally passing away in 1996 at the age of ninety-five.

Over the years, Aziz's relationship with his parents had weathered its fair share of challenges. But we know from their letters to each other that father and son had shared a deep bond. Within the lines of their weekly correspondence, hidden behind routine words and mundane accounts lay the true depth of their love and care for each other.

Although his father was unable to attend Aziz's swearing-in ceremony as the Chief Justice of India due to his failing health, Aziz took comfort in the knowledge that his stoic father remained mentally sharp and cognizant of his son's success, recognizing that Aziz had ascended to the highest echelons of the judiciary. Not a man of many words, the father's pride in the son remained an unacknowledged sentiment throughout his lifetime.

It would be many decades later that the family would learn of this love and pride, discovered within private writings and diaries among Mushabber's belongings. Every news clipping that had mentioned Aziz over the years was carefully cut out and stacked together in a yellowing pile, bound together with a crusty rubber band. Every elevation, appointment and important case his son had presided over was transcribed in a small diary, in meticulous handwriting that bore a striking resemblance to Aziz's own. It was in these hidden records that a father who struggled to articulate his feelings towards his son finally found a voice.

Aziz's relationship – and communication – with his mother, on the other hand, had all but broken down. Unable to refuse his invitation to attend his swearing-in ceremony, she had reluctantly made the trip to Delhi. But this visit only served to widen the chasm between mother and son, destroying any chance of reconciliation. During this visit, Shirin Ahmadi ventured into the kitchen one evening. Unfamiliar with the dynamics of her new surroundings, she attempted to help herself to some food from the fridge, much as she did in her own home. Ama, who was instructing the kitchen staff on what to cook for dinner that night, happened to be present. She suggested that her mother-in-law need not trouble herself with warming the food herself; a staff member would be more than willing to assist.

The refrigerator door was slammed shut; the final thread of a strained relationship snapped. Shirin accused her daughter-in-law of forbidding her from helping herself to food from the fridge. 'My own son's home and I can't even open the fridge!' She stormed out, swearing she would never set foot in Aziz's home again – a promise she would keep until the end of her life. A minor misunderstanding had irrevocably severed an already strained relationship.

When Mushabber Ahmadi's time eventually came to an end, Aziz received the news thousands of miles away, at an International Conference on Human Rights in Helsinki where he was poised to deliver the keynote address. With a sinking heart, he cancelled his speech and rushed back for his father's funeral and to comfort his mother. But even in this tragic moment, there was to be no reconciliation between mother and son. At the time, he had no way of knowing that although his mother would live to the astonishing age of 109, he would see her only twice more after this occasion.

As Justice Ahmadi grappled with personal loss, India's political leaders found themselves battling a strange adversary – the country's 10th Chief Election Commissioner (CEC). This discord had begun a few years earlier, when Tirunellai Narayanaiyer Seshan had been appointed CEC in 1990, quickly earning himself a reputation of being the toughest CEC India had seen. When T.N. Seshan assumed the role of CEC, the Election Commission of India (ECI) was structured as a single-member institution, where the CEC held ultimate authority, bestowing upon him unparalleled influence. Article 324 of the Constitution empowers the Election Commission with powers for the 'superintendence, direction, and control . . . of the conduct, of all elections to Parliament.'[28] As far as poll watchdogs go, the ECI is considered the most powerful election monitoring body in the world, given the autonomy and influence it enjoys.[29]

However, despite the immense powers vested in the EC, Seshan's predecessors had been relatively passive, content to do little more than the bare minimum required for the conducting of elections. The code of conduct was rarely adhered to, and there were minimal restrictions on campaign methods.

But T.N. Seshan's appointment in 1990 changed all this. India's new CEC understood that the EC was more than just a bureaucratic entity; it was a statutory body drawing its legitimacy directly from the Constitution. And so, realizing the scope of Article 324 of the Constitution and protected by the autonomy and authority of the institution, the CEC set to work, institutionalizing sweeping reforms. From the very beginning, he was undeterred by the collective displeasure of various political leaders that he faced.

Seshan was a force of nature, working at a whirlwind pace and with astonishing efficiency. A seasoned bureaucrat with a reputation for being tough and incorruptible, he embarked on a mission to clean up the electoral process. He enforced the model code of conduct rigorously, a comprehensive set of rules and regulations to be adhered to before and during the election process. These guidelines came into effect as soon as election dates were announced. He did not hesitate to impose severe penalties on those who violated it, causing tremendous frustration among corrupt politicians.

Booth capturing, bogus voting, vote buying, loudspeakers during campaigns and election graffiti consisting of political slogans were all quickly axed.[30] Contesting candidates were compelled to submit records of expenses and adhere to spending limits. Liquor sales were banned before elections, and the EC maintained zero tolerance for caste-based or religion-based campaigning that stoked hatred.[31] Corrupt officials were swiftly suspended and adequate police deployment during elections ensured reductions in booth capturing and election-related violence. Voter ID cards were made mandatory, and violations were ruthlessly punished, including the cancellation of elections in some instances.

In an environment where political parties had become used to elections and campaigns being conducted with little oversight and almost no regulation, Seshan became a nightmare for all, whether in power or in the opposition. It soon became said that politicians feared 'only God or Seshan,' indicating not only Seshan's unbridled powers but also his fearlessness in applying them. His reputation for being incorruptible left little scope to influence him. Almost overnight, state and central elections began to exhibit an unmistakable discipline and a certain level of austerity that was unprecedented. Campaigns and elections became an astonishingly clean affair. It would not be an exaggeration to say that Seshan had reformed the election process in India for the better.

But, in the process, he had become deeply disliked within political circles. His abrasive comments like, 'I eat politicians for breakfast'[32] did not win him any fans in political circles. Seshan was fast gaining a reputation for being egoistic and arrogant.[33] Many were beginning to think of him as a megalomaniac dictator who often overstepped his institutional mandate.

By 1992, an attempt to impeach him for cancelling elections in Bihar and Punjab had already been carried out.[34] In 1993, fresh demands for impeachment of the CEC began to crystallize in the Lok Sabha.[35] Former Prime Minister Chandra Shekhar, who had appointed Seshan, referred to him as a 'mini-Fuhrer' and stated that, 'This (Seshan's threat to postpone by-elections if his conditions were not fulfilled) is not acceptable to Parliament and he should be got rid of.'

In 1994, Seshan made headlines by publicly condemning Welfare Minister Sitaram Kesri and Food Minister Kalpnath Rai for their attempts to influence voters.[36] He went a step further and demanded that the Prime Minister remove these ministers from their positions. This caused a flurry within political circles with many accusing the CEC of exceeding his jurisdiction by offering the government such unsolicited advice.

Seshan had also made enemies within the BJP by entertaining Congress' Arjun Singh's petition to derecognize the BJP and freeze the party symbol for violating secular principles.[37] The contention was that the BJP's use of the lotus symbol alongside images of Lord Ram and the proposed Ram Mandir during the Rath Yatra imbued the symbol with religious significance, contradicting secular principles. Seshan had agreed to hear the petition. Intervening in the matter, the Supreme Court had stated that Seshan could not 'change the law through executive orders,' preventing him from taking action.

Seshan's feuds with the politicians of the time were becoming increasingly bitter, descending into a quagmire of acrimony and hostility. His demeanour grew even more abrasive, egoistic and arrogant. With a keen understanding of the media and its power to influence, he did not shy away from making controversial statements, attacking almost every institution of the country. His remarks were often in poor taste and, on more than one occasion, directed towards the judiciary. His arbitrary and unsubstantiated allegations of corruption within the judiciary compelled the usually restrained Supreme Court to direct him to 'keep his mouth shut.'[38] Seshan's inflammatory comments and unfounded allegations eventually strained his relationship with virtually every institution he attacked during his tenure, causing further discord and controversy. Throwing caution to the winds, T.N. Seshan had begun to believe he was invincible.

It is no wonder, then, that politicians across parties wanted Seshan gone. But constitutionally, the process of removal of a CEC is as cumbersome as that of a judge. And Seshan knew this.

It was perhaps for this reason that the Congress government led by P.V. Narasimha Rao initiated processes for the conversion of the Election Commission from a single-member body to a multi-member one for the second time in the history of Independent India.[39] This had been attempted only once before, in 1989, a fleeting affair lasting only three months with the President eventually rescinding the notification that allowed for the alteration of the structure of the Election Commission.

Indeed, the rescinding of the notification had faced a legal challenge from one of the newly appointed Election Commissioners, S.S. Dhanoa. But the Court's ruling had firmly supported the retention of the EC as a single-member body. The Court held that it had found no compelling need for additional Election Commissioners and maintained that they should not be accorded the same status as Chief Election Commissioner – thus setting a precedent that Seshan would rely on when his own time came.

But the storms of discontent were brewing, and change was imminent. In 1993, when in a swift and sudden decision the government issued an ordinance with the President's approval titled 'The Chief Election Commissioner and other Election Commissioners (Condition of Service) Amendment Ordinance, 1993,'[40] none were as outraged as the CEC himself, who had been left in the dark, blindsided by a decision about which he had been neither consulted nor informed. The ordinance which sought to amend 'The Chief Election Commissioner and other Commissioners (Condition of Service) Act of 1991' addressed several aspects, of which the most profound was the expansion of the single-member body to make room for two Election Commissioners in addition to the Chief Election Commissioner. The two new additions to the institution, Mr M.S. Gill and Mr G.V.G. Krishnamurthy found themselves thrust into their new positions with remarkable swiftness. Because the move was so sudden, the two appointees were only informed about their new roles a few hours before the announcement was made. To T.N. Seshan, an immensely powerful man, this constitutional shift was seen as a calculated move aimed specifically at clipping his wings and cutting him down to size.

But Seshan wasn't one to go down without a fight. He argued that the government's intention behind issuing such an ordinance was mala fide and that the real motive behind this constitutional amendment was to curtail his powers and prevent him from taking action against alleged violations of the election code of conduct by the ruling party. He asserted that it was an assault on the authority and autonomy of the Election Commission and the integrity of the CEC.

And so T.N. Seshan approached the Supreme Court of India.[41] The petitioners' main contentions revolved around two critical issues. One, whether the appointment of the additional Election Commissioners was consistent with the provisions of the Constitution; and two, the constitutional validity of the ordinance and by extension, the Act that resulted from it, as well as the subsequent orders associated with the change.

Seshan alleged that his unbending insistence on compliance with the Model Code of Conduct had irritated and embarrassed the ruling party as a few by-elections were postponed due to the government's failure to deploy sufficient staff and police force.[42] The ruling party had lost the elections in Tripura due to the CEC's action against erring officials, which ultimately led to the postponement of the elections. He also alleged that the ruling party's attempts to influence him were unsuccessful as he refused to meet their emissaries. Further, the CEC had declined requests to postpone elections for four state assemblies, including those made by the Prime Minister, further frustrating the ruling party.

As a result, the ruling party decided to misuse the power of the President under Article 324(1) and amend the law. The CEC further alleged that the appointed Election Commissioners had been chosen to enable the ruling party to secure favourable orders.

The respondents denied all these allegations, stating that various committees and bodies had previously recommended the formation of a multi-member Election Commission and that this reform had been in the pipeline for a long time. The Joint Committee of both Houses of Parliament had submitted a report in 1972 supporting the proposal. The Tarkunde Committee had advocated the same in 1974 and the Committee on Electoral Reforms appointed by the Janata Dal government had done so in 1990. Several members of Parliament representing different political affiliations had raised similar demands at various points in time. Most recently, a meeting of the Advocates General of various states held in 1993 saw a similar demand being raised.

In the beginning, it appeared that Seshan just might win the case. An interim order was passed, which stated, 'Until further orders, to ensure smooth and effective working of the Commission and also to avoid confusion both in the administration as well as the electoral process, we direct that the Chief Election Commissioner shall remain in complete overall control of the Commission's work. He may ascertain the views of other Commissioners or such of them, if he chooses, on the issues that may come up before the Commission from time-to-time. However, he will not be bound by their views. It is also made clear that the Chief Election Commissioner alone will be entitled to issue instructions to the Commission's staff as well as to the outside agencies.'[43]

This interim order, rather than pacifying Seshan's temperament, seemed to inflate his ego even further, making him even more overbearing and dismissive of his new colleagues. Instead of fostering a spirit of cooperation, he actively sidelined them, setting the stage for many an ugly spat, which would play out in full view of the public, gleefully reported by the media, causing much discord and heartburn amongst the newly appointed Election Commissioners.

Once again, the Election Commission was Seshan and Seshan was the Election Commission. The individual had become the institution.

But Seshan was in for a rude shock. Presiding over the five-member Constitution Bench that was to hear his case was Chief Justice Ahmadi, whose aversion to the idea of absolute power was well established.

A firm believer in the supremacy of the institution over the individual, Ahmadi's commitment to upholding institutional integrity and the principles of democracy would play a crucial role in the legal showdown between Seshan and the Government. These principles had already been tested in a prior case. In the Second Judges Case, Ahmadi's dissent effectively sought to curtail the Chief Justice's powers – a position he knew he would soon assume – cautioning against the perils of placing vast discretionary powers in the hands of an individual. A champion of democratic principles, then, the Chief Justice was not one to bestow unchecked authority upon any one individual.

And so, the Constitution Bench comprising Justices A.M. Ahmadi, J.S. Verma, N.P. Singh, S.P. Bharucha and M.K. Mukherjee observed:

> It would be wrong to project the individual and eclipse the Election Commission. Nobody can be above the institution which he is supposed to serve. He is merely the creature of the institution, he can exist only if the institution exists. To project the individual as mightier than the institution would be a grave mistake. Therefore, even if the Election Commission is a single-member body, the CEC is merely a functionary of that body; to put it differently, the alter ego of the Commission, and no more.[44]

The Court also rejected the CEC's claim that the ECs had been appointed specifically so that the ruling party might obtain favourable orders. 'It is wrong to think that the two ECs were pliable persons who were being appointed with the sole object of eroding the independence of the CEC.'

The judgement authored by Justice Ahmadi clarified the interpretation of Clause 2 of Article 324, which clearly states that the Election Commission is to comprise the CEC and any additional number of ECs that the President might choose to appoint. Further, the Article mentions that when it is a multi-member body, the CEC is to act as Chairman of the Election Commission. The court, therefore, rejected the claim that a multi-member body would be unworkable or inconsistent with the Constitution.

It also determined that the government could not be charged with having malicious intentions as the deliberations on expanding the Commission had been in progress for many years.

Further, the Court refused to grant the CEC powers to overrule the other ECs, emphasizing that the ECs should enjoy the same status as the CEC, and disputes must be settled by way of majority, in keeping with democratic principles.

> 'If the CEC is considered to be a superior in the sense that his word is final, he would render the ECs non-functional or ornamental. Such an intention is difficult to cull out from Article 324 nor can we attribute it to the Constitution-makers. We must reject the argument that the ECs' function is only to tender advise to the CEC.' It further stated, 'the submission proceeds on the basis that the other two ECs will join hands to render the CEC non-functional, a premise which is not warranted. It betrays the CEC's lack of confidence in himself to carry his colleagues with him. In every multi-member commission it is the quality of leadership of the person heading the body that matters.'

The Bench also dealt with a request from Seshan that the Chief Election Commissioner be ranked alongside Supreme Court judges in the Warrant of Precedence.[45] This request, made by Seshan to Home Secretary Godbole and to the Prime Minister, sought to move the CEC from the 11th position to the 9th in terms of precedence. While hearings were underway, it was found that this had already been done without waiting for the judgement, placing the CEC, the Comptroller and Auditor General of India at No.9A. The Court made a clear distinction between a statutory body and a constitutional body, stressing that the government 'should not confer such equivalence nor interfere with the Warrant of Precedence, if it is likely to affect the position of High Court and Supreme Court Judges, however pressing the demand may be, without first seeking the views of the Chief Justice of India. We may add that Mr. G. Ramaswamy, learned counsel for the CEC, frankly conceded that the CEC could not legitimately claim to be equated with Supreme Court Judges. We do hope that the Government will take note of this and do the needful.'[46]

The judgement also rapped Seshan on the knuckles for his unbecoming conduct.

> We may incidentally mention that the decisions taken by the CEC from time-to-time postponing elections at the last moment, of which he has made mention in his petition, have evoked mixed reactions. This we say because the CEC uses them to lay the foundation for his contention that the entire exercise was mala fide. Some of his other decisions were so unsustainable that he could not support them when tested in Court. His public utterances at times were so abrasive that this Court had to caution him to exercise restraint on more occasions than one. This gave the impression that he was keen to project his own image. That he has very often been in the newspapers and magazines and on television cannot be denied. In [sic] this backdrop, if the Government thought that a multi-member body was desirable, the Government certainly was not wrong and its action cannot be described as mala fide. Subsequent events would suggest that the Government was wholly justified in creating a multi-member Commission. The CEC has been seen in a commercial on television and in newspaper advertisements. The CEC has addressed the Press and is reported to have said that he would utilise the balance of his tenure to form a political party to fight corruption and the like [*Sunday Times* (Bombay) dated 25 June 1995 page 28] [sic]. Serious doubts may arise regarding his decisions if it is suspected that he has political ambitions, in the absence of any provision, such as Article 319 of the Constitution. The CEC is, it would appear, totally oblivious to sense of decorum and discretion that his high office requires even if the cause is laudable.[47]

Ultimately, the Court found T.N. Seshan's petition to be wholly without merit. And so, much to Seshan's disappointment, the Ordinance was upheld in entirety, forcing him to share the stage equally with two additional Election Commissioners.

Meanwhile, there was another political drama playing out in South India, one that would be impacted greatly by the Court's dismissal of T.N. Seshan's petition.

In a politically sensitive case that would eventually be brought to the apex court by political heavyweights and arch-enemies Dr Subramanium Swamy and Mrs J. Jayalalitha, the matter of bias within the Election Commission was addressed.

Mr Seshan's long-standing friend and ally, Subramaniam Swamy was seeking to disqualify his arch-enemy and political nemesis J. Jayalalitha from the position of Chief Minister of Tamil Nadu on grounds of holding a subsisting contractual obligation with the State Government.

In 1991, All India Anna Dravida Munnetra Kazhagam (AIADMK) leader, J. Jayalalitha had been elected to the Legislative Assembly of Tamil Nadu and then became the Chief Minister of the state.[48] However, in 1992, Subramaniam Swamy lodged a petition with the state governor invoking Article 192 of the Indian Constitution, which pertains to decisions on questions regarding the disqualification of members of a House of the Legislature of a State. He drew attention to Jayalalitha's involvement with a firm, Messrs Jaya Publications, which had engaged in a contractual agreement with the state government. Consequently, she stood disqualified from holding such a position.

Dr Swamy first approached the State Governor with these concerns, requesting they be forwarded to the Election Commission for examination. But the governor failed to do so. Frustrated, Swamy filed a writ petition against the Governor for his failure to forward his petition to the EC. In 1993, while the writ was still pending, the Governor finally sent the matter to the EC for its opinion.

In the meantime, Jayalalitha filed two writ petitions in the Madras High Court, both of which were heard by a single judge. The first one was against T.N. Seshan, forbidding him from handling the matter alleging bias in favour of Swamy. This petition was granted because there was enough evidence to suggest possible bias. The Court felt it was fair to prohibit Seshan from expressing an opinion. In response, an appeal invoking the Doctrine of Necessity was presented. The Doctrine of Necessity is an exception to the principle of Natural Justice, which prohibits judging one's own cause due to bias. However, the doctrine of necessity allows for this when no other competent person is available or when essential for decision-making. This is because sometimes there's no choice but to let the designated person who may be biased decide, otherwise the case won't move forward at all. But in this case, the Bench determined that there was no compulsion for this as Article 324 already provided for the possibility of appointing an additional EC as an alternative avenue to handle the matter. It must be remembered that at this time, the EC was still a single-member body, under the sole authority of the CEC, T.N. Seshan.

The second writ petition aimed to declare that Dr Swamy's petition for the CM's disqualification lacked substance. The Court dismissed this petition saying that this was exclusively under the Governor's jurisdiction, while also stating that the CM had not incurred the alleged disqualification. So while the second petition was technically dismissed, it was, in practicality, allowed.

Dr Swamy challenged this judgement and so the matter was heard by a Division Bench of the Madras High Court, which decided that the single judge should have left the decision about disqualification to the EC since it was within their domain. They also acknowledged that Jayalalitha's apprehension of bias against Seshan was reasonable.

Amid these proceedings, the government issued the Ordinance that transformed the EC from a single-member body to a multi-member one. This meant that the Doctrine of Necessity was rejected as the EC was now a multi-member body and therefore able to rule on the matter without the involvement of the CEC.

The division bench issued a writ of prohibition against Seshan, forbidding him from handling the case. They suggested the case be handed to one or both of the other ECs.

Unhappy with the verdict, Seshan appealed to the Supreme Court. The court was now tasked with deciding whether Seshan should be permitted to participate in the decision of this particular case.

The judgement authored by Justice Ahmadi emphasized that according to Article 192(2), the Governor must 'take a decision in accordance with the opinion of the Election Commission.' The final decision should align with the EC's opinion.

The friendship between Seshan and Swamy was known to be a close one, dating back to the 1960s during their time at Harvard University, where Swamy was a Professor of Economics and Seshan was pursuing a master's degree in public administration.[49] They both shared a deep interest in Indian politics and public policy, bonding over similarities in their backgrounds.

In addition, Swamy's wife was also the lawyer representing Seshan in a case where potential damages amounted to one crore rupees.[50]

The Supreme Court accepted Jayalalitha's apprehension of bias acknowledging that her fears were well founded and deliberated on the necessity of Seshan's presence in the matter. Under Article 32, the CEC's role as Chairman is vital. Seshan had expressed his willingness to recuse himself from the proceedings if he was constitutionally permitted to do so now that the EC was a multi-member body. The Court, too, believed it prudent for the CEC to abstain from expressing his opinion to avoid bias.

The judgement authored by Justice Ahmadi therefore directed that the two Election Commissioners adjudicate on the matter of Jayalalitha's disqualification, while the Chief Election Commissioner was directed to act as Chairman but refrain from expressing his opinion. Seshan was instructed to intervene and break the deadlock only if the two Election Commissioners were unable to agree on a decision, thereby invoking the Doctrine of Necessity. The judgement noted, 'If the choice is between allowing a biased person to act or to stifle the action altogether, the choice must fall in favour of the former as it is the only way to promote decision-making.'

But the battle between the two political adversaries did not end with this. In a dramatic turn of events in 1995, Jayalalitha's government issued an arrest warrant against Swamy on the allegation of making casteist comments. He had referred to LTTE's Prabhakaran as an international 'pariah,' a Tamil-origin term, which is seen as derogatory to Dalits. Immediately, an arrest warrant was issued, and attempts made to detain Swamy at the Madras airport.[51] Forced to disguise himself, Swamy changed his clothes and dyed his hair to escape the police. Eventually, he managed to escape to Bombay, from where he boarded a flight to Delhi to approach the Supreme Court.[52] Here, Justice Ahmadi's bench issued orders that allowed Swamy to be served a warrant only in Madras, whereupon he was to be released upon furnishing a bond of Rs 100. Further, the State was directed to provide Swamy with Z-category security to ensure his safe passage to the Court so that he may present his case.

During his tenure as Chief Justice of India, Justice Ahmadi repeatedly faced allegations of favouring the appointment of numerous Muslim judges to High Courts and the Supreme Court. Unperturbed, he said, 'Such an allegation every Muslim Chief Justice, I suppose, has to face.'[53] But such allegations can only be made by those who do not understand the appointment process. Chief Justices do not unilaterally determine the elevation of judges to the High Court; the recommendations originate from the Chief Justice of the respective High Court. He writes, 'If the High Court has recommended a Muslim amongst the names forwarded, should the CJI shoot down the appointment merely because he belongs to a certain religion? It would be gross injustice.' Further, when Ahmadi ascended to the position of CJI, the collegium system had already been institutionalized, limiting the CJI's role in the appointment of judges. From his writings, we know that Justice Ahmadi felt disappointment in witnessing prejudice even in the highest offices of the country, which fuelled talk of this nature.

One of the lesser known yet significant cases that Justice Ahmadi presided over during his term as Chief Justice of India was one that played an important role in shaping the criteria for conferring National Awards – the Bharat Ratna and Padma awards.[54] It was contended that the awards were being used as titles and also being given too freely, often to undeserving persons. Efforts had previously been made to abolish the decorations. 'The Conferment of Decoration on Persons (Abolition) Bill, 1969' was introduced in Parliament but ultimately defeated.

The two petitions, which once again gave rise to the issue, were filed in the High Courts of Madhya Pradesh and Kerala, respectively. Because Article 18 had abolished titles, the use of these awards as prefixes and suffixes was challenged as a 'back door' channel to reintroduce titles. It was also suggested that the political dispensation of the time had been handing these decorations out too freely, and not always to persons of merit.

A Constitution Bench comprising Justices Ahmadi, Kuldip Singh, B.P. Jeevan Reddy, N.P. Singh, and S. Saghir Ahmed ruled that the awards themselves didn't violate Article 18, yet the excessive numbers were diluting their significance. To uphold the highest standards of merit, the bench proposed the formation of a national committee at the Prime Minister's discretion, in consultation with the President and comprising individuals such as the Speaker of Lok Sabha, the Chief Justice of India or their nominee and the Leader of the Opposition in the Lok Sabha. Similar committees at the state level, formed by the Chief Minister in consultation with the Governor would recommend candidates, with the National Committee having the final decision. Awards could only be conferred upon the National Committee's recommendation, requiring approval from both the Prime Minister and the President. To preserve their prestige and dignity, the number of awards per year was capped at fifty. This ruling is to be credited for preserving the exclusivity, reputation and high standards of these prestigious honours.

During his term as Chief Justice of India, Ahmadi's staunch opposition to any actions that encroached upon the fundamental freedoms of speech and expression was evident through a number of cases.[55] In 1995, the highly controversial film Bandit Queen was released with an 'A' certificate from the censor board. The movie portrayed the distressing narrative of Phoolan Devi, a low caste woman who endured repeated rape and abuse at the hands of several men, including the ruthless Babu Gujjar and the gang of dacoits he commanded, ultimately transforming into one of India's most feared bandits. However, this cinematic portrayal sparked a legal challenge. Because the rapist in the film was named Babu Gujjar, the Gujjar community felt it portrayed them in poor light. A writ petition was filed in the Delhi High Court seeking the cancellation of the film's certificate on the grounds that it portrayed moral depravity within the Gujjar community, affecting their reputation. The High Court halted the screening of the film.

However, the Supreme Court would not agree. The Bench comprising Chief Justice Ahmadi, Justice Bharucha and Justice Kirpal would hold that 'A film that illustrates the consequences of a social evil necessarily must show that social evil. The guidelines must be interpreted in that light. No film that extols the social evil or encourages it is permissible, but a film that carries the message that the social evil is evil cannot be made impermissible on the ground that it depicts the social evil.' Regarding the explicit scenes of nudity in the film, the judgement stated,

> It is not a pretty story. There are no syrupy songs or pirouetting round trees. It is the serious and sad story of a worm turning: a village born female. becoming a dreaded dacoit [sic]. An innocent who turns into a vicious criminal because lust and brutality have affected her psyche so ... Rape is crude and its crudity is what the rapist's bouncing bare posterior is meant to illustrate. Rape and sex are not being glorified in the film. Quite the contrary. It shows what a terrible, and terrifying, effect rape and lust can have upon the victim. It focuses on the trauma and emotional turmoil of the victim to evoke sympathy for her and disgust for the rapist. It is in this light that the individual scenes have to be viewed.

And so, the High Court order was set aside, and Bandit Queen's certification restored.

Equally unwavering was Justice Ahmadi's commitment to the rights of life and liberty. In his words, 'Life and liberty are great values and when violated by state officials or other political heavyweights, the court must have the strength, courage and determination to intervene. Judges must never forget that in a democracy it is the rule of law that governs the State, and they, as judges, are the inherent defenders of the rule of law.'[56] In Chakma and Hajong vs. State of Arunachal Pradesh, he did not hesitate to rap the State Government of Arunachal Pradesh on the knuckles for its failure to protect these rights, stating that, 'Every person is entitled to equality before the law and equal protection of the laws. So also, no person can be deprived of his life or personal liberty except according to procedure established by law ... No State Government worth the name can tolerate such threats by one group of persons to another group of persons; it is duty bound to protect the threatened group from such assaults and if it fails to do so, it will fail to perform its Constitutional as well as statutory obligations.'[57]

The PIL, filed by the National Human Rights Commission (NHRC), sought to protect the rights of the Chakma/Hajong tribals who were being persecuted and threatened by the All Arunachal Pradesh Students Union (AAPSU) in Arunachal Pradesh. The tribals who had been displaced from Bangladesh due to the construction of the Kaptai Hydel Power Project and were forced to seek refuge in India in 1964 had initially settled in the states of Assam. Later, they were moved to areas within the state of Arunachal Pradesh. This is where they had been living for more than three decades, forming strong social, religious and economic ties. The NHRC had indicated that state officers were working with the AAPSU to expel the Chakmas and Hajongs from the state of Arunachal Pradesh to a neighbouring state that was unwilling to accept them. There were reports of human rights violations and economic blockades, which adversely affected the supply of rations, medical and essential facilities, leading to deaths within the refugee population.

In addition to these hardships, the struggle for citizenship had been a long, tedious one with no clear end in sight. Individual applications for citizenship were scuttled at the deputy collector level with the central government pleading inability to process applications it had not received.

In his judgement, Justice Ahmadi noted that the state had failed in protecting the Chakmas and Hajongs and safeguarding their rights guaranteed by Article 21 of the Constitution. The state was therefore directed to fulfil its obligation in protecting the rights of this population, dealing with those issuing threats and violence towards them appropriately, engaging the services of paramilitary forces if required. It was also directed that applications for citizenship under Section 5 of the Act be recorded and forwarded by the Collector or DC to the central government for consideration. During the pendency of such applications, no Chakma or Hajong should face eviction or termination from employment on the pretext of not being recognized as Indian citizens.

A forward-looking judgement, it sought to bring relief to a community long persecuted at the hands of the state, local populations and the bureaucracy. Sadly, however, the present-day reality is that successive state governments have refused to implement this order, and the Chakmas and Hajongs continue to be faced with persecution and hostility.[58] They continue to struggle for citizenship in the face of the looming threat of becoming both homeless and stateless.

A lesser-known facet of Justice Ahmadi's legacy has been his role as a progressive champion of women's rights. His aversion towards misogyny was well known to friends and family alike. On the bench too, he was troubled by the lack of gender sensitivity in justice provided to women, especially victims of sexual violence.

This was noticed on several occasions, including in the case of State of Maharashtra vs. Madhukar Narayan Mardikar. On 13 November 1965, Police Inspector Shri M.N. Mardikar, from Bhiwandi Town Police Station (Thana District), visited the house of a local woman – Banubi, the victim – demanding to have sexual intercourse with her. Subsequently, the Inspector was dismissed from service by the Inspector General of Police. However, the division bench of the High Court quashed the removal order, referring to Banubi's self-admitted intimacy with another person. Stating that 'since Banubi is an unchaste woman it would be extremely unsafe to allow the fortune and career of a Government Official to be put in jeopardy upon the uncorroborated version of such a woman.' Nearly three decades later, in 1991, an SLP arrived before a division bench at the Supreme Court.

The wording of Justice Ahmadi's judgement reveals his thoughts on such matters. Setting the High Court order aside, he wrote,

> Even a woman of easy virtue is entitled to privacy and no one can invade her privacy as and when he likes.[59] So also it is not open to any and every person to violate her person as and when he wishes. She is entitled to protect her person if there is an attempt to violate it against her wish. She is equally entitled to the protection of law. Therefore, merely because she is a woman of easy virtue, her evidence cannot be thrown overboard...The High Court was completely wrong in concluding that her evidence was not corroborated in material particulars by independent evidence.

Coming down on the High Court, the judgement stated, 'We are afraid that the High Court embarked upon a reappreciation of the evidence as if it were silting [sic] in appeal against the decision of the departmental authorities.' It was found that Banubi's evidence stood the test of scrutiny and the officer was, once again, removed from service.

When Sakshi, a feminist NGO based in New Delhi that focuses on sexual violence and women's rights, approached Chief Justice Ahmadi to help reform the way the judiciary is trained to respond to victims of sexual violence, they discovered in him a supportive ally.[60] It had been contended that while the law was not at fault, the insensitive attitudes of male judges was problematic. Having faced rejections from several other judges who were wary of associating themselves with an NGO, Sakshi was finally able to make a breakthrough when Chief Justice Ahmadi's endorsement served to cut through the scepticism and give impetus to their work, encouraging the judiciary to participate.

In January 1997, Sakshi organized a workshop titled 'Regional Perspectives on Gender Equality' in collaboration with the National Judicial Academy, which Justice Ahmadi himself had helped set up a few years before. The assembly brought together eminent judges, lawyers and NGO representatives from India, Nepal, Sri Lanka, Pakistan, Bangladesh, Fiji, Canada and Australia, emphasizing the need for gender equality in the legal domain.

Speaking at the plenary session of this conference, Justice Ahmadi pointed out that 'wittingly or unwittingly we all carry biases within us and reflect them in the quality of justice that we make available for women.'[61] Recognizing this as an opportunity to address the sensitive nature of cases of violence against women, Ahmadi sought a holistic approach. In an experimental initiative, he appointed several women judges at the additional sessions judge level and assigned women public prosecutors to these cases in the hope that the victims would be more forthcoming in the quality of the evidence they provided. He hoped that this would encourage the victims to stay strong and withstand familial and societal pressures to abandon their cases, ultimately improving their chances of receiving justice.

It was under the aegis of Justice Ahmadi that Sakshi was able to establish the Asia Pacific Advisory Forum on Judicial Education on Equality Issues, a robust judge-NGO platform recognized as the best practice programme by UNIFEM.

A few months later, Sakshi's work would culminate in the Vishakha guidelines, the foundational judge-made law on the Prevention of Sexual Harassment at Workplace instituted by the Supreme Court in 1997. Since then, these guidelines have served as the benchmark for addressing cases of sexual harassment against women, providing a comprehensive framework for legal proceedings in such matters.

Justice Ahmadi's commitment towards women's rights remained steadfast until his last days. Encouraging the participation of women of all ages and walks of life in his own offices during his tenure and after retirement, he spoke about the importance of encouraging women to enter the workforce.

As he would state in a speech delivered in 2006, 'I have always lamented the fact that we have kept almost 50 per cent of our human resource, I mean the women folk, virtually out of effective participation in state affairs ... Please bear in mind that without educating the women folk you are denying to yourself empowerment.'[62]

A mere six days before retiring as Chief Justice of India, Justice Ahmadi delivered the very last landmark judgement of his career. The long-standing question pertaining to the jurisdiction of the High Courts in matters dealt with by Tribunals had finally culminated in L. Chandra Kumar vs. Union of India. This judgement would pave the way for the establishment of a dedicated adjudicatory system – a practice that has become routine in the present day.

In accordance with the authority granted by Article 323A of the Constitution, the Parliament had passed the Administrative Tribunals Act of 1985 (Act 13 of 1985).[63] Under this Article, the Parliament is empowered to create specialized Administrative Tribunals authorized to handle and resolve cases concerning the recruitment and conditions of service of public servants working for the union or any state. Individuals employed by corporations controlled by the Government of India also fall within the jurisdiction of these tribunals. The Act's Statement of Objects and Reasons explicitly states that it aligns with the provisions of Article 323A of the Constitution and was enacted because there was a substantial backlog of service-related cases in various courts. The establishment of these Administrative Tribunals, dedicated to addressing service matters, was expected to alleviate the caseload of these courts. This move aimed not only to free up the courts to handle other cases more efficiently but also to provide individuals covered by the Administrative Tribunals with prompt resolutions for their grievances.

As per the Act's provisions, the Central Administrative Tribunal, consisting of five Benches, was established on 1 November 1985. However, even before the Tribunal became operational, numerous legal challenges had been initiated through writ petitions in various High Courts and various High Courts and the Supreme Court. These challenges primarily questioned the constitutional validity of Article 323A of the Constitution and the provisions of Act. The core issue raised was the exclusion of the Supreme Court's power of judicial review under Article 32 of the Constitution and the High Courts' power of judicial review under Article 226/227 of the Constitution.

It was in response to these legal challenges that the Supreme Court issued an interim order on 31 October 1985, in the case of S.P. Sampath Kumar v. Union of India. This order instructed that specific measures be carried out to ensure the tribunals function along principles that are constitutionally sound. As per an undertaking given to the Court by the Attorney General at an interim stage, an amending Act known as Act 19 of 1986 was enacted to implement the changes described in the interim order.

By the time the final hearing of the Sampath Kumar case arrived, it was observed that the changes had already been incorporated into the Act and therefore the initial grounds for legal challenge, including the challenge to the constitutional validity of Article 323A, were no longer relevant. Therefore, the focus shifted to evaluating the constitutional validity of provisions within the Act. The Court ruled that even though judicial review is an essential element of the constitution, transferring this authority to an alternative institution once it is removed from the jurisdiction of the High Court is not violative of the basic structure. However, this alternative institutional mechanism must serve as an efficient and genuine replacement for the High Court.

Building on this principle of effective alternative institutional mechanisms, the Court proceeded to analyse the provisions of the Act to determine their constitutional validity. The Court ultimately concluded that, at that point in time, the Act did not meet the criteria of an effective substitute for the High Courts. As a remedy, the Court proposed several amendments to the provisions that governed the structure and content of the Tribunal. These suggested amendments were later enacted into law through an amending Act (Act 51 of 1987) after the conclusion of the case. Since then, the Act has remained unchanged.

But the Bench had not clearly addressed whether the tribunals established under the Act had the authority to invalidate statutory provisions or rules on constitutional grounds. This omission left many questions unanswered and different benches took different views in the cases that followed. Therefore, it was found that a 'fresh look' by a larger bench was necessary to revisit the matters decided in the Sampath Kumar case.

And so, in 1997, a Constitution Bench comprising Justices A.M. Ahmadi, M.M. Punchhi, K. Ramaswamy, S.P. Bharucha, S. Saghir Ahmad, K. Venkataswami and K.T. Thomas was constituted to hear L. Chandra Kumar vs. Union of India.

The bench clarified the role of tribunals in matters of judicial review. It emphasized that while tribunals can exercise judicial review in cases where the constitutional validity of statutory provisions is questioned, this power is supplementary rather than a complete substitution for the High Courts and the Supreme Court. The judgement stated, 'If the power under Article 32 of the Constitution, which has been described as the 'heart' and 'soul' of the Constitution, can be additionally conferred upon 'any other court', there is no reason why the same situation cannot subsist in respect of the jurisdiction conferred upon the High Courts under Article 226 of the Constitution. So long as the jurisdiction of the High Courts under

Articles 226/227 and that of this Court under Article 32 is retained, there is no reason why the power to test the validity of legislations against the provisions of the Constitution cannot be conferred upon Administrative Tribunals created under the Act or upon Tribunals created under Article 323B of the Constitution.'

Advocating caution in the functioning of tribunals in relation to the jurisdiction of High Courts, Justice Ahmadi's judgement rejected the suggestion of the Malimath Committee that advocated the complete abolishment of tribunals.

> In the years that have passed since the Report of the Malimath Committee was delivered, the pendency in the High Courts has substantially increased and we are of the view that its recommendation is not suited to our present context. That the various Tribunals have not performed up to expectations is a self-evident and widely acknowledged truth. However, to draw an inference that their unsatisfactory performance points to their being founded on a fundamentally unsound principle would not be correct. The reasons for which the Tribunals were constituted still persist; indeed, those reasons have become even more pronounced in our times.[64]

The Court held that decisions taken by the tribunals are subject to review by a division bench of the respective High Courts. The judgement also suggested measures to improve the functioning of tribunals.

Until a fully independent agency is established to oversee these tribunals, the Court recommended that they be placed under a single Nodal Ministry capable of supervising their operations. Furthermore, when issues arise concerning the interpretation of a statutory provision or rule in relation to the Constitution, the Chairman or the relevant Member must refer the matter to a bench comprising at least two Members, with one being a Judicial Member.

It was ordered that Tribunals retain their role as the first instance courts in their respective areas of law. This meant that litigants could not directly approach the High Courts, even when challenging the constitutionality of statutory legislations.

This judgement has been widely celebrated for protecting the independence of the judiciary and emphasising separation of powers between the judiciary and executive by articulating that while Administrative Tribunals could adjudicate specific matters, the ultimate power of judicial review by the higher judiciary is an essential feature of the Constitution that cannot be abrogated.

It is said that 'A great judgment is one that restores the constitutional values of a polity from the waywardness into which it may have fallen, while a landmark judgment is one which opens up new directions in our constitutional thinking and, in the process, adds new dimensions to what are regarded as established constitutional principles.[65] If 'great' restores the centrality of constitutional values, 'landmark' revitalises them.'

As Justice Ahmadi approached the end of his tenure, it was evident that his legacy encompassed both in equal and robust measure. During his years in the Supreme Court, he authored 232 judgments and was a part of 811 benches. His views and decisions were not only corrective, bringing wayward constitutional values back into focus, but also innovative, contributing to the evolution of constitutional thought in India. In the end, Justice Ahmadi had managed to safeguard both, constitutional values and his own conscience. And in the process, shaped the trajectory of Indian jurisprudence.

When Justice Ahmadi finally demitted office, he did so with only one regret. A reform that he believed had the potential to change the judicial system, but which he did not have the time to implement. As he would wistfully say '...if only I had just 6 more months...' His visionary idea was of the transformation of the judicial services into an elite establishment, much like the Indian Administrative Services (IAS). He envisioned the creation of an All India Judicial Service (AIJS) where judges, including city civil judges and sub-judges, would be recruited from all corners of the country. This innovative reform would have gone a long way in addressing the burden of excessive caseloads in states where there was a challenge in attracting high-quality talent. Through this reform, states struggling to find highly skilled individuals could have benefitted greatly from other regions that contained competent candidates eager and willing to adapt to the local language and culture. Drawing parallels with the IAS, where officers move to different states and immerse themselves in new languages and cultures, he envisioned establishing a national talent reservoir to form this elite judicial service. But time had run short.

With the delivery of the judgement in L. Chandra Kumar vs. Union of India, Aziz Mushabber Ahmadi knew he had come to the end of his tenure. It was a moment of exquisite paradox, a blend of nervous anticipation and exhilarating freedom. But he was not afraid of change, in fact, his agile mind thrived on it.

One morning, in a rare candid moment, he made an offhand comment in the presence of his law clerk, Arun Thiruvengadam. 'You know, Arun, it has been so long that I have driven a car. I am quite looking forward to that.' The exciting thought stayed in his mind, so much so that by the time afternoon rolled in, the yearning could no longer be contained. The driver was instructed to bring the car around to the porch. Easing himself into the driver's seat with an air of childlike excitement, Justice Ahmadi turned the key. Word of this spontaneous adventure spread through 5 Krishna Menon Marg, and soon the driveway was swarming with a curious assembly of staff, domestic help, family members and peons. A nervous Huzefa mumbled, 'Dad, be careful, don't hit a flowerpot.' Grasping the steering wheel firmly in his hands, Aziz felt the familiar low rumble of the engine under his control after more than two decades. A brief spin around the compound of the bungalow confirmed that Aziz Ahmadi indeed remembered how to drive. The moment was a blend of nostalgia and anticipation – a yearning for the comfort of the familiar and the thrill of embracing the unknown.

As Justice Ahmadi's illustrious judicial career came to a close, another awaited its beginning in the wings. Liberated from the constraints that his high office had demanded, Ahmadi was now free to offer his time and expertise to the matters that he held close to his heart – human rights, minority rights and education. Additionally, he would be appointed Chairman of the Bhopal Memorial Hospital Trust – a pro bono assignment he would accept with open arms. In his own words, 'I told myself that having spent over 33 years as a Judge this was a task I knew

I must undertake. I have done many difficult tasks but none to match this one and perhaps it was God's command that I get involved. I knew that God will certainly help me in serving humanity that had suffered so greatly.'[66]

As he retired, Justice Ahmadi's name was firmly etched alongside those rare judges who refused to bend to the will of the Executive or succumb to external pressures.

Filled with boundless optimism about the future, Justice Ahmadi was determined not to 'retire,' anticipating his life to continue to be filled with meaningful endeavours. And so it began.

But like every phase in his life, this too would not be free of turbulence. A case he had adjudicated just a few months before his retirement was to resurface fourteen years later, requiring from him an extraordinary display of mental fortitude and dignity under fire. But to understand this we must journey back to 1984 – and the catastrophic events of the Bhopal gas disaster.

11

The Bhopal Gas Case: Courage Under Fire

In the vast tapestry of history, there exists a chapter so dark and unsettling that it continues to cast a haunting shadow not only over India but also the world at large. Etching itself into collective memory as one of the most horrific industrial disasters of all time, the Bhopal Gas Tragedy was no ordinary calamity. A combination of human suffering, corporate negligence and unimaginable despair, the ensuing legal battle played out on the international stage under the watchful gaze of the entire world. Nearly 600 kilometres away, in the city of Ahmedabad, on a seemingly unconnected path walked Justice Ahmadi. Still donning the robes of a High Court Judge then, he had no inkling that in less than ten years, his career was destined to intersect so profoundly with the catastrophe and would require from him unprecedented levels of mental fortitude and dignity under fire.

But all this remained in the distant future, many years away from unfolding.

On the night of 2 December 1984, a sinister event was about to take place at the Union Carbide India Limited (UCIL) pesticide plant located in Bhopal. The stillness of the night was pierced by a hissing sound, the deadly sound of toxic gas leaking from the plant. Before the plant technicians could raise the alarm, a poisonous cloud of Methyl Isocyanate (MIC) gas was released into the air. As the gas swirled into the darkness, it spread quickly throughout the densely populated neighbourhoods surrounding the plant, causing immediate and catastrophic consequences. Unsuspecting residents were roused from their sleep itchy eyed and in inexplicable discomfort. It started with coughing fits and burning eyes, quickly escalating into a desperate struggle for breath. Then, as realization dawned, panic spread. Those who were able to move tried to flee, running through the streets that were once quiet, now filled with terrified, screaming people. Tragically, the act of running only led them to inhale larger quantities of the lethal gas before collapsing. The air became a toxic haze, and the sleepy night was suddenly filled with the sounds of people coughing, gasping for breath and pleading for help.

As dawn broke, revealing the aftermath of the night's horror, Bhopal lay paralysed, stilled by shock.

Thousands of people were dead within the first few days, and the death toll continued to rise in the following weeks and months due to the effects of the exposure. Many would develop symptoms later; some would be chronic and others would plague generations to come. Birth defects and genetic abnormalities would emerge as a consequence of exposure to the toxic gas.

The local police swung into action immediately, arresting five junior employees of UCIL.

On the morning of 7 December, Chairman of Union Carbide Corporation, Warren M. Anderson, accompanied by Chairman of UCIL Keshub Mahindra and Managing Director of UCIL Vijay Gokhala, arrived in Bhopal to assess the extent of the damage. Anderson's expectations of cordiality and cooperation from the authorities were evident by his air of casual detachment as he strolled into the airport, gas mask in hand. But his nonchalance was to be short-lived. Before he could step foot outside the airport, he was apprehended by the authorities.

All three big fish were arrested – Warren Anderson, Keshub Mahindra and Vijay Gokhle.[1] An FIR was filed and a total of nine employees were charged under Section 304A[2] for causing death by negligence and rash acts, which attracted a maximum punishment of two years. Simultaneously, the case was transferred to the CBI who elevated the charges to Section 304 (II) – If act is done with the knowledge that it is likely to cause death, but without any intention to cause death, etc. – a charge that attracted a punishment of ten years.³

Meanwhile, the three men were taken to the Union Carbide guesthouse, an establishment that stood apart from the affected areas and placed in separate rooms. A nervous Anderson spoke to Moti Singh, the then-collector of Bhopal who had escorted him from the airport. 'What should I do?' he asked. Moti Singh did not respond, removing himself from the room. But the authorities had been careless. A phone, still connected, had been left in Anderson's room. Seizing the opportunity, a phone call was made. A few hours later, instructions were received to release Anderson. Moti Singh recalls, 'No one was willing to stand surety for Anderson. So, the police got a junior employee of the plant to stand surety for Anderson's bail. We stopped him from going to the affected areas and put him on the state plane which took him to New Delhi. It wasn't our decision. We were following the government's orders.'⁴ The Superintendent of Police at the time would break his silence thirty years later to disclose that, 'We arrested him on the basis of a written order but released him on an oral order.' He also revealed that the oral order came 'from higher-ups'.

And so, the three were released on bail and Anderson granted safe passage back to the United States of America. He would never return to face trial for his role in the Bhopal gas tragedy. We would hear no more of the machinations that took place until many years later when Sushma Swaraj, a BJP leader, would make an astonishing allegation.⁵ In 2015, she claimed that the then Prime Minister Rajiv Gandhi had made a secret deal with Ronald Reagan – a quid pro of sorts. Warren Anderson's immunity from prosecution or extradition for his role in the Bhopal gas disaster in exchange for a Presidential pardon for the son of a close associate of the Gandhis who was facing serious charges of fraud and arson in the USA. Unproven though the allegation may be, it is unlikely that Anderson would have been able to leave safely on a state aircraft without state complicity.

In the meantime, the legal journey that would go on for well over thirty years was yet to begin.

While he did follow the developments with great interest, recognizing the historical significance of this legal saga, Justice Ahmadi saw himself as a spectator rather than an actor. As the Gujarat High Court's corridors buzzed with routine proceedings, Justice Ahmadi's connection to the distant legal drama was confined to news updates and discussions. The case was unfolding thousands of miles away in the United States of America, a world apart from his judicial jurisdiction, making his own involvement in it a distant improbability. But fate had its own plans.

At this time, the legal proceedings were unfolding under the purview of Judge Keenan in New York.[6] It was in the year 1985 that the Indian Parliament passed the Bhopal Gas Leak Disaster (Processing of Claims) Act. Under this Act the Union of India as *parens patriae* stepped in and took over the litigation on behalf of the victims, thereby conferring upon itself the exclusive right to represent their interests and concerns. This meant that the State was acting as a guardian on behalf of the victims, thereby relieving them of the burden of legal action. But it also meant that the victims were prohibited from filing individual claims. The case was heard in the District Court of the Southern District of New York, specifically addressing the issue of compensation for the damage inflicted upon the victims. To this end, the Union of India filed a claim for USD 3.3 billion against the corporate behemoth Union Carbide.

But the company being sued, UCC (parent company of UCIL), attempted to thwart the progress of the lawsuit by asserting that the US court was not the appropriate forum for the case.[7] Their preference was for the legal battle to unfold in an Indian court where the compensation claim was expected to be much lower. Realizing this, the Union of India opposed this request, citing concerns over potential delays, lack of proper procedures and difficulties in enforcing judgements. The Indian authorities viewed UCC's objection as a strategic manoeuvre, a form of 'forum shopping' aimed at selecting a jurisdiction more favourable to its interests. This high stakes tug-of-war, a first in India's history, was being watched keenly over the world.

Eventually, Judge Keenan accepted the plea of forum *non conveniens*, a provision that allows for the transfer of a case to a more convenient forum to enable the trial to proceed smoothly.[8] He stated that retaining the litigation before [the New York Court] would be 'yet another example of imperialism which would deprive the Indian judiciary of this opportunity to stand tall before the world,' thereby sending the litigation back to India, to the court of the district judge, Bhopal.[9] He stated that since all the victims and evidence were in India, it was impractical to hold proceedings in the United States of America.

The rejection of India's claim in the USA and the subsequent shift in jurisdiction dealt a body blow to the hopes of a larger compensation amount for the victims. This was because the assets of Union Carbide India Limited (UCIL) in India, against which any settlement amount would be recovered, were notably less valuable compared to those held in the United States. And so, the once-optimistic aspirations for a recovery worth billions of dollars were shattered. As the harsh reality set in, it became clear that the initial claim of USD 3.3 billion would no longer be tenable.

Now on Indian soil, with drastically changed circumstances, the case journeyed through a labyrinth of appeals, several courts tracing its path through the various tiers of India's judicial system before finally arriving at the hallowed doors of the Supreme Court.

After meticulous consideration of the case's nuances, the negotiations that had transpired and the prevailing circumstances, the Supreme Court Bench presided over by Chief Justice R.S. Pathak found it fit to engineer an all-encompassing settlement.[10] UCC was directed to pay $470 million to the Union of India towards settlement of all claims by 31 March 1988. All civil cases linked to the disaster were transferred to the Court for settlement and all criminal charges were dismissed. Prioritizing swift relief for the gas victims, the court settled on $470 million as compensation after weighing UCC's offer of $426 million against the Indian government's minimum requirement of $500 million.

Barely had the gavel landed in the courtroom, when the nation erupted in collective outrage. The scale of the tragedy, measured not just in lives but also in the unspeakable suffering endured, had seemingly been reduced to a mere number, a number that fell woefully short of the expectations that had been pegged at the original demand of USD 3.3 billion. In contrast, the sum of $470 million was a deep disappointment. The media roared with public outrage, indignant headlines thundering from the pages of newspapers and magazines. NGOs and other stakeholders joined the chorus.

But this amount was still approximately four times the value of UCC's assets in India.

And then there was another related case that had been pending since 1985.[11] The Bhopal Gas Leak Disaster (Processing of Claims) Act had attracted much consternation and debate among the general public. Why should the government be allowed to represent the victims, thereby preventing them from filing individual claims? Would the government, who had nothing to gain, fight the case with the same dedication that a suffering victim would? Many doubted this, and thus, the Act found itself facing a legal challenge in the Supreme Court. The hugely high profile case of Charan Lal Sahu Etc. Etc. vs. Union of India And Ors sought to contest the constitutional validity of the Act, and the Government of India's decision to act as *parens patriae*. But in 1989, the Supreme Court upheld the validity of the Act, determining that the State had appropriately assumed the exclusive right to represent and act on the behalf of the victims as the majority of them were impoverished and illiterate and therefore may be unable to approach the courts themselves. But the Court did clarify that the Act only addressed civil liability, not criminal.

In this instance, the judgement was authored by Justice Mukherjee. Justice Ahmadi and Justice R. Ranganathan delivered a separate but concurring opinion. In this opinion the two judges emphasized the need for the Central Government to impose certain safeguards before allowing transnational companies to operate in the country, ensuring liability and jurisdictional issues can be adequately addressed. Highlighting the challenges faced by victims of disasters like Bhopal, the judges advocated for international consensus or unilateral legislation to ensure corporations are held accountable globally and victims can seek redress across borders. They also included a call for the development of an international code to deal with such calamities.

Justice Ahmadi's involvement in the multifaceted Bhopal case and its many legal intricacies was just beginning.

The year was 1991, and Justice Ahmadi had already spent three years in the courtrooms of the Supreme Court when', the weighty case files of Union Carbide Corporation of India vs. Union of India were laid at his desk.[12] A Constitution Bench headed by Chief Justice S. Mukharji had been constituted to hear a review petition regarding the settlement awarded to the victims of the Bhopal gas tragedy, as well as the contentious quashing of criminal charges. But before a judgement could be pronounced, a shocking piece of news broke. Justice Mukharji had passed away suddenly. By then, the bench had heard the matter for eighteen days.

A fresh bench, composed of Justices M.N. Venkatachaliah, R. Misra, A.M. Ahmadi, N.D. Ojha and K.N. Singh tookover the reins of the case.[13] Appearing for the various parties were legal bigwigs Attorney General Soli Sorabjee, F. S. Nariman, Shanti Bhushan, Indira Jaising and Prashant Bhushan.[14] This new bench found that the compensation amount was reasonable and fair. It also highlighted that if the settlement were to be overturned, UCC would be entitled to reclaim the amount it had already paid, with interest. Further, the judgement decreed that any shortfalls in funding for rehabilitation should be supplemented by the Union and State governments. On this point alone, Justice Ahmadi dissented from the majority viewpoint of his brother judges.

'For reasons which I will presently state I am unable to comprehend how the Union of India can be directed to suffer the burden of the shortfall, if any, without finding the Union of India liable in damages on any count . . . I do not think that the Union of India can be saddled with the liability to make good the deficit, if any, particularly when it is not found to be a tort-feaser.'[15] (A tortfeaser is understood as an individual or entity accused of committing a wrongful act.)

The dissenting judgement further stated, '[I]t is impermissible in law to impose the burden of making good the shortfall on the Union of India and thereby saddle the Indian taxpayer with the tortfeasor's liability, if at all. If I had come to the conclusion that the settlement fund was inadequate, I would have done the only logical thing by reviewing the settlement and would have left the parties to work out a fresh settlement or go to trial in the pending suit.'

However, all the judges agreed that Union Carbide's criminal case must move forward, thus overturning the quashing of criminal charges. They ruled that the Court did not have the authority to grant immunity from criminal prosecution and penalties. This was because it was seen as a task reserved for the legislature, and offering immunity to specific individuals might lead to unequal treatment. Additionally, they emphasised that individuals have the right to be governed by the principles of the legal system rather than the exercise of discretion.

The bench expressed its regret in the manner in which the settlement had been arrived at, without consultation with the victims or obtaining their consent. Recognizing the long-term repercussions of the MIC gas exposure, which could lead to delayed health issues and genetic abnormalities, the Court demanded the establishment of a hospital for present and future needs of the victims. The hospital was to be a well-equipped one with a capacity for 500 beds, with provision for maintenance for a period of eight years. The estimated cost for this hospital, which was expected to be around Rs 50 crore, was to be borne by UCIL and UCC while the land was to be donated by the state of Madhya Pradesh. But the Court didn't stop there. It also directed that a medical group insurance cover from the General Insurance Corporation of India or the Life Insurance Corporation of India be obtained for compensation to this contingent class of possible prospective victims.

Amid these legal proceedings, a separate saga was unfolding on the geopolitical stage. The Indian government, under intense pressure from its citizenry, sought to extradite Anderson from the United States, officially declaring him an absconder. The goal was to bring him within the jurisdiction of the Indian judicial machinery where he would face the criminal charges levelled against him. But this was not to be.[16] Eventually, Anderson would die of natural causes in 2014 without ever seeing the inside of an Indian courtroom.

In the meantime, criminal proceedings against Union Carbide were revived. In the absence of Anderson, nine other accused, including Keshub Mahindra, were charged with culpable homicide not amounting to murder under Section 304 (II) of the IPC.

A few months before he was due to retire as Chief Justice of India, another docket arrived on Justice Ahmadi's desk. This was the famous Keshub Mahindra vs. State of Madhya Pradesh case, which would go on to represent perhaps the most controversial judgement of Justice Ahmadi's career. The accused, Keshub Mahindra, who was the Chairman of UCIL at the time of the Bhopal gas leak, had moved the Court challenging the criminal charges against him.

The original FIR filed by the Bhopal police initially contained criminal charges under Section 304A against the accused.[17] Later, these charges were heightened to a more serious offence under Section 304(II), which indicates culpable homicide not amounting to murder. This elevation of charges brought with it the potential for a more severe punishment, including imprisonment for ten years. This charge was upheld by a Sessions judge in Bhopal.

However, when the case arrived at the Supreme Court, a bench consisting of Justice Ahmadi and Justice S.B. Majumdar amended these charges. The bench examined the definition of culpable homicide as it appears in the IPC; 'whoever causes death by doing an act with the intention of causing death, or with the intention of causing such bodily injury as is likely to cause death, or with the knowledge that he is likely by such act to cause death, commits the offence of culpable homicide.' In the context of this case, it meant that the prosecution would need to provide evidence showing that the accused either intended to cause death or knew their actions could lead to death. On 13 September 1996, the bench ruled that given the lack of evidence, the original charges under Section 304A would be reinstated. Under this section, punishment may extend to a maximum sentence of two years.

The public's response was a volcano of discontent and fury. To say they were not happy with the judgement would be an understatement. Amid the uproar, there lurked a primal thirst for avengement, an unyielding call for a pound of flesh. Voices were raised, demanding not just justice, but vengeance and retribution. While the judges were unrelentingly vilified for denying them this satisfaction, there was, interestingly, very little debate on the legal nuances of the charges.

Culpable homicide is a complex charge that often struggles to hold up under close scrutiny because of the inherent difficulty in proving intent, or a 'guilty mind'. In this case, demonstrating that a particular 'act' was carried out with the intention to cause death was unlikely to withstand legal scrutiny as well. The 'knowledge' of the act being likely to cause death would also be untenable without the determination of the 'act' itself. Because one cannot successfully argue that the mere knowledge of danger is enough to attract a homicide charge without any positive act that causes the harm. The IPC makes separate provisions for negligence and homicide on this very point, otherwise the same charge would well stand for both cases.

Ironically, the reduction of charges actually ensured that a more tenable legal stance be taken. Without this adjustment, the accused might well have evaded any legal consequences altogether. This hinges on a crucial principle: once the charges of culpable homicide are found to be unsubstantiated in Court, it is untenable to introduce another charge. The two charges, negligence and homicide, are inherently contradictory; asserting one negates the other. So, if evidence were presented for the charge of culpable homicide and it failed to find substantiation in Court, as would likely have been the case, a modification in charges would not have been a permissible legal recourse.

Simply put, without this amendment in charges, the accused would have likely walked free. But perhaps there was an assumption that public outcry and demands would suffice to shape the outcome of the case.

At home, this was not an easy time. At the receiving end of vicious brickbats and dreadful accusations, the days had once again become tense. News broadcasts devoted a significant portion of airtime to amplify the criticisms and grievances voiced by different groups. Justice Ahmadi was no stranger to the ebb and flow of the media's tides, nor to public criticism. But he was not immune. After one particularly caustic news broadcast, he allowed himself a rare moment to vent in the confines of his home. 'What is the expectation? That judges should operate beyond the boundaries of the law?' he remarked; his short outburst hanging briefly in the air before he swiftly resumed his stoic demeanour.

As Ahmadi would later go on to explain in several interviews, the Indian criminal law simply does not provide for cases such as these. 'There is no concept of vicarious liability,' he explained in an interview to the *Times of India* in 2010.[18] 'If my driver is driving (my car) and meets with a fatal accident, I don't become liable to be prosecuted under section 304 (II).' Meaning, one cannot be held responsible for the act or omission or another (usually an employee). The general rule is that criminal liability is personal, not vicarious, other than where a person has aided, abetted, counselled or procured the act of another.

On several occasions, Ahmadi has publicly pointed out the absence of provisions in the law to deal with disasters such as Bhopal Gas Tragedy and suggested that appropriate amendments be explored proactively. Unfortunately, that is yet to happen.

Even more curious is that despite the discontent resonating from various quarters, it would take a staggering fourteen years for a curative petition to finally be submitted.'

In 1998, the Supreme Court approached a newly retired Justice Ahmadi, seeking his help in the setting up and running of the super speciality hospital. He was offered Chairmanship of the Bhopal Memorial Hospital Trust (BMHT) and requested to take up the task. It was a demanding task, one that would require many years of his life, and it was pro bono.

Yet, Ahmadi gladly accepted, embracing the opportunity to give back to society. As he put it, the offer was a '. . . God-sent opportunity to do social service after almost 33 years of judicial service. I also knew that God will certainly help me in serving humanity that had suffered so greatly.'[19] Throwing his heart and soul into the building and then running of the hospital, he worked tirelessly towards the project for a full twelve years. Setting an almost-impossible deadline of one year for the hospital to become operational, Justice Ahmadi's sole aspiration was to provide those who had suffered with some relief without any further delay. With a handpicked team of enthusiastic and skilled medical experts, staff and management, all fuelled by the common goal of relieving some of the hardship the victims had already suffered, work commenced. Indeed, the hospital stood ready and operational by 1 July 2000, to the astonishment of many.[20]

For Justice Ahmadi, the Bhopal Memorial Hospital was a true labour of love. Driven by a desire to make a meaningful impact on the lives of the gas victims, he sought no monetary compensation for his tireless endeavours. Adamant in ensuring that the hospital's funds remained untouched, he personally covered the expenses of his many trips to Bhopal whenever required.[21] For more than a decade, the hospital operated under the stewardship of Justice Ahmadi, establishing itself as a top-notch super speciality facility in India. Mr Aziz Siddiqui, working trustee of the Bhopal Memorial Trust who was also a gas victim himself, shared several astonishing revelations. He revealed that not only did Justice Ahmadi personally fund his monthly visits to Bhopal, but he also refused to drink a single cup of tea on the premises, unwilling to give the impression of having become too familiar.

But, as the age-old adage warns, no good deed goes unpunished. Ahmadi received yet another deluge of criticism for his decision to accept the position of Chairman of the Bhopal Memorial Hospital Trust. Allegations of conflicts of interest began to circulate, the lack of evidence not overly concerning to those levelling them. Sadly, the unfounded accusations not only questioned his propriety but also overshadowed his commitment to public service.

It was in 2010 that the CBI filed a curative petition seeking to challenge the 1996 judgement and reinstate charges under Section 304 (II) of the IPC.[22] The petition argued the previous bench had failed to properly consider the evidence presented,[23] igniting a newly energized interest in the case. At the heart of this unexpected tempest, the Ahmadi family found themselves grappling with the visceral displays of public outrage that had now made its way to their doorstep.

Although Justice Ahmadi was long retired and had nothing to do with this curative petition, a fresh tsunami of hate and hostility was piled onto him. The peaceful neighbourhood where the most notable excitement typically came from spotting a wandering *nilgai* or fox from the neighbouring forested areas had turned into a battleground. Day after day, groups of fervent protestors and demonstrators gathered. Unflattering posters were waved angrily, emblazoned with aggressive messages of condemnation. Angry slogans of disappointment with the legal outcome of fourteen years ago filled the air. Justice Ahmadi had, once again, become a target.

For a fleeting moment, it seemed that the protestors' anger might escalate into something more menacing as they edged uncomfortably close to the main gate of the bungalow. Justice Ahmadi's government-appointed Personal Security Officer positioned himself at the forefront, urging the protestors to retreat. The society guards joined him, standing firm between the home and the demonstrators.

And protestors weren't the only presence; there was sometimes a media van or two, too. Reporters, clamouring to get a byte or an interview waited patiently outside. For the most part. Sometimes they managed to slip inside and had to be asked to come back with an appointment.

Through this, Ama spent her days keeping a keen eye on the unfolding scenes outside, while concealing the extent of her stress at home. Silent, with jaw clenched and lips pressed thin in a taught line, she observed the angry men and women outside and their posters carrying hostile messages held high from the first-floor window. She wasn't troubled by the prospect of them breaching the gates; her worry was centred on her husband and the dignity they had diligently preserved all their lives.

This was not an easy time. Ama had only recently beaten uterine cancer, undergoing gruelling surgery and radiation, the effects of which she would battle throughout her life. Aziz too, had suffered a mild but sudden stroke in 2009. Although not immediately serious, it had placed him on lifelong medication, and he had been advised to relinquish some of his responsibilities. Family concerns revolved less around the public display of hate outside the front door, and more around how this challenging time would be impacting them at their age.

But through all this, Ahmadi kept his cool and remained calm. He granted interviews to several press outlets, some of whom misquoted him and distorted his viewpoints. Yet, Justice Ahmadi did not react. Politely refusing to engage with the more hostile journalists, he ensured that dignity was always maintained.

Eventually, the curative petition was, once again, rejected. Consequently, the altered charges were upheld, effectively validating Justice Ahmadi's 1996 verdict.

As age advanced, the weight of professional obligations gradually became a heavier burden for Ahmadi to bear.[24] Despite his appeals to the Supreme Court to be relieved of his duty as Chairman of the Bhopal Memorial Hospital Trust on three separate occasions, he was repeatedly persuaded to continue. But his health after the stroke had forced him to slow down. No longer a young man, the burden of unfounded accusations too began to weigh heavy on his shoulders.

And so, Justice Ahmadi's active involvement with the BMHT drew to a close.[25] When Ahmadi handed over charge of the hospital, it was discovered that the facility, which had an original corpus fund of Rs 470 crore, was transferred to the union government only Rs 110 crore less than the original amount.[26] This astonishing fact turned the tables, silencing critics and earning him appreciation from the Supreme Court.

The subsequent deterioration of the hospital and quality of its services under the charge of the union government caused Justice Ahmadi considerable pain. As he said in an interview in 2020, 'It was given to the government after which the deterioration took place. I feel sorry about it (the current state of affairs at BMHRC).'[27]

A few days after the protesters had been cleared away and the news channels had moved on to something else, the family convened for dinner as usual. The television was turned off, the family silently savouring this rare private time together, away from the cacophony of news broadcasts and protests that had dominated the past few weeks. Tasneem and Huzefa were both successful, well-established advocates by this time and had been following the events closely. In the middle of the meal, Huzefa paused, his expression pensive. His gaze turned to his father. 'Dad, have the harsh accusations of the press ever hurt you? Their words have been so vicious.' Taking a moment to frame his answer, Justice Ahmadi looked into his son's eyes and responded, 'My conscience is clear, so why should

I be hurt? The press is fickle, *dikra* – we must always be guided by the truth alone.'

There can be no truer encapsulation of the lessons Justice Ahmadi passed onto his children and grandchildren. The constant reminder that amid the chaos, one's own moral compass is the only North Star worth looking to.

12

Beyond the Bench

The months preceding Justice Ahmadi's retirement had unfolded as a whirlwind of activity, a period where the family found themselves immersed in preparations for the impending transition. These weren't easy preparations – they involved, for the first time, arranging a home. What had always been a matter of official business was now distinctly personal. In this, Tasneem had taken the reins. She spent countless long days and nights identifying a piece of land the family could afford, negotiating with banks for loans, poring over architectural drawings and coaxing labour to work overtime so that the home may be ready in time.

For the first time, the Ahmadis would live in a home of their own.

And so, when the day came to bid adieu to the streets of Lutyens Delhi and embrace the warmth of their new home on the outskirts of Delhi, a bittersweet excitement welled up within everyone.

It was the end of an incredible era, but with it came the promise of fresh adventures and joys. For Justice Ahmadi, the challenges of the inevitable arbitrations and international assignments stood before him like untrodden paths. In contrast, Amena looked forward to the prospect of not being bound by the rigid constraints of etiquette at every turn. Although the thought gave her relief at the time, in truth, propriety had ingrained itself into her personality by then, and she would continue to conduct herself accordingly. As for Tasneem and Huzefa, who had so far refrained from practising in the Supreme Court to avoid the perception of influence, they were now eager to end their self-imposed bans. For my brother Adnan and me, the first whispers of adulthood beckoned, carrying with them the promise of new experiences and opportunities.

Initially looking forward to a brief hiatus to explore other interests such as Sufi music and *shayari* (Urdu poetry), Justice Ahmadi had hoped to enjoy a welcome period of rest before restarting his professional life. But, as it turned out, he was not a man made for rest. After the first few days spent exploring the new surroundings and immersing himself in his library, he began to grow restless, snapping irritably at the staff and family alike. The stillness that initially held promise became a source of discomfort, urging him to return to professional engagement once more. And the universe was in alignment. In a matter of mere weeks, the floodgates opened with requests for high-profile domestic and international arbitrations pouring in, quickly making Ahmadi one of the most highly sought-after arbitrators of his time. In addition, he was called upon by world agencies to lend his skills and insight to the international community, quickly filling up his small leather-bound diary with commitments once again. Simultaneously, as mentioned earlier, he had been appointed as the Chairman of the Bhopal Memorial Hospital Trust and was working towards the swift operationalization of the hospital. If that weren't enough, he was invited to scores of international conferences and wrote several papers on a variety of subjects ranging from human rights, equality, gender justice and preservation of the environment to legal education, legal aid, arbitration-mediation and judicial reforms.

Rather than an ebbing, it was a grand resurgence of his professional life; ironically, my retired grandfather was now busier than ever, swept up in a whirlwind of activity at a pace that surpassed even the busiest days of his life as a judge. Now, he was rarely in Delhi for more than two weeks at a stretch.

It was a few months into his retirement that Justice Ahmadi received four successive calls from prestigious international bodies – the International Commission of Jurists (ICJ), the United Nations Security Council, the World Bank and the International Bar Association (IBA). These calls weren't mere invitations; they were requests for him to undertake urgent diplomatic and fact-finding missions into countries facing critical challenges.

The first of these came in 1998, with a request for his service and expertise to evaluate the collapsed judicial system in Liberia.

In response to the request from Chief Justice Gloria M. Scott of the Republic of Liberia, the ICJ sent a mission to evaluate the requirements of the judiciary, provide observations on administering justice effectively and contribute insights on revitalizing and re-establishing the rule of law in Liberia.[1] Led by Justice Ahmadi, the mission included prominent members such as Mr Sam Okudzeto, President of the Ghana Bar Association, Mr Raymond C. Sock, Legal Practitioner and former Solicitor-General and Legal Secretary of The Gambia, and Ms Tokunbo Ige, Legal Officer for Africa at the ICJ.[2]

Liberia, still reeling from a history of bloody military coups and a recent seven-year-long civil war, was grappling with the challenging task of establishing a functional judicial system.[3] The country's precarious situation was further aggravated by the election of Charles Ghankey Taylor as President, an unpopular choice that resulted in the eruption of the second civil war.[4] As Justice Ahmadi stepped onto Liberian soil, he knew was stepping into a war-torn nation where street shootouts were commonplace. The team was lodged in a sparse building with each room lit by a single, dim, low-wattage bulb. Strict instructions were issued – the light was to be kept turned off as much as possible, to be flicked on only when absolutely necessary, for as short a time as possible. Despite their curiosity, the delegates were instructed to stay away from the single window, with strict warnings not to look out of it or even pass by it for fear of being shot by a stray bullet. The streets outside echoed with the sounds of gunfire, a grim reminder of the turmoil that ensued just a few steps away.

In his writings, Justice Ahmadi categorized this as the most dangerous mission he had been entrusted with.

In the course of their investigations, Justice Ahmadi's team discovered that the civil war had destroyed many of the democratic institutions of the country and reduced the judiciary to a toothless tiger.[5] Judges were appointed – and dismissed – at the pleasure of the warring factions. The court and law school libraries had been burnt, looted and destroyed, leaving the judges with no reference materials, court precedents or research materials. In an economy where a bag of rice cost $25, a Circuit Court judge's salary was $17, forcing judges to engage in other businesses as well as corrupt practices. They were given few perks and no security, leading to an acute shortage of judicial personnel. Court infrastructure was a testament to the ravages of the civil war. As per the team's report, 'When we visited the Kakata Circuit Court in Margibi County we were ushered to the top floor of an incomplete two-storey structure used as the court room. There were no windows, doors or even railings on the stairs leading to the second floor. The corrugated iron roof, with no ceiling, was dotted with so many holes that we were informed court sessions are inevitably suspended when it rains.'

Confronted with Liberia's post-war challenges, the team stressed the crucial need for an independent judiciary as the cornerstone of democracy and human rights. Recommendations included improving material resources, training judges and establishing processes for their appointment. They proposed seeking support from institutions like the American Bar Association and the Library of Congress for refurbishing critical materials. Additionally, they called for the establishment of a Judicial Service Commission to oversee judicial appointments and advocated for financial autonomy to empower the judiciary in disbursing funds without executive interference.

Upon his return, Justice Ahmadi did not speak about what he had witnessed to anyone. He had chosen to keep the true extent of the dangers he had faced during this mission a secret. He writes, 'Never told my family members how risky the trip was – not yet.'

A few months after his return from Liberia, one late evening Justice Ahmadi received a phone call from his good acquaintance, Mary Robinson. Former President of Ireland, she was then the United Nations High Commissioner for Human Rights and was hoping to enlist Ahmadi's skills towards another sensitive and dangerous mission.

East Timor's struggle for self-determination dated back to 1975 when the Portuguese colony of East Timor was annexed by Indonesia leading to a long history of resistance.[6] In the 1990s, resistance groups had formed and the nation was gripped in violence, with armed militia groups operating with the blessing of the Indonesian authorities. In 1991, Indonesian forces fired into a crowd at a cemetery, tragically killing a large number of people and putting the spotlight of international attention back on the atrocities taking place in East Timor.

In January 1999, President Habibie made an offer of independence or autonomy to the people of East Timor, which was followed by an agreement between Indonesia, Portugal and the United Nations. A consultation process was established for the East Timorese to either accept or reject the offer. The vote revealed that an overwhelming majority of East Timorese had chosen Independence, with 78 per cent rejecting the offer of autonomy within Indonesia. The announcement of these results prompted another wave of violence.

The Commission on Human Rights passed a resolution condemning these widespread human rights violations in East Timor, including violence and forced displacement. It also reported collusion between militias and the Indonesian armed forces. An International Commission of Inquiry was called for with a mandate of investigating violations of international humanitarian law since January 1999 and providing recommendations.

The report was to be shared with the Secretary General for recommendations and presented to the Security Council, General Assembly and the Commission on Human Rights.

As she obtained Justice Ahmadi's consent to serve on the International Inquiry Commission, Mary Robinson warned him of the dangerous conditions that he would be facing in the country that was gripped with violence.[7] She also revealed that two UN personnel had been killed there recently. Justice Ahmadi's response, characteristic of his temperament, was, 'Too late – I am not going to back out.'

The other esteemed members of the team included, as chairperson, Sonia Picado, a member of the Costa Rican Legislative Assembly and

Vice-chairperson of the Board of Directors of the Inter-American Institute of Human Rights.[8] Judith Sefi Attah was a former Minister of Women's Affairs and Social Development of Nigeria. Mari Kapi was the Deputy Chief Justice of Papua New Guinea and Sabine Leutheusser-Schnarrenberger was a member of the German Bundestag (Parliament) and former Federal Minister of Justice.

After a series of meetings in Geneva and Darwin, the team was flown to East Timor, where they spent one week, from 25 November to 3 December 1999. As the small military aircraft carrying the members of the Commission of Inquiry touched upon the East Timor soil, everyone on board looked around in curiosity.[9] A haunting scene greeted them. The town stood almost deserted. Surveying the area, Justice Ahmadi observed partially burnt and abandoned residential buildings. The window frames bore the dark scars of fire, and the corrugated roofs were black from smoke. Many roof sheets were missing. Later, it was discovered that the local population had retreated into the forests, carrying these sheets with them to construct temporary shelters.

Accommodations for the team were makeshift – there were no beds or mattresses. That first evening, Justice Ahmadi recalls emptying his suitcase and spreading his clothes on the floor to create a padded surface and somehow pass the night. The following morning, Sonia Picado's voice rang out from the neighbouring room, 'How are things at your end?' Without missing a beat, Justice Ahmadi shot back, 'My shower has undergone capital punishment and is dangling from the neck.' Picado burst into a loud roar of laughter. It was under these conditions that the team began the physically and mentally taxing task of interviewing more than 170 men, women and children for their testimonies, all of which consisted of stories of unspeakable violence and cruelty.

The mission revealed several sobering findings. It was found that systemic and widespread terror and violence had been inflicted upon the people of East Timor to alter the outcome of the popular consultation and prevent people from exercising their political choice.[10] Much of this violence was carried out by militia groups engaged by Indonesian authorities. About 60–80 per cent of all public and private property was destroyed in a planned manner – including schools and hospitals – leading to mass-scale displacement of people. Thousands of people were forcibly moved to West Timor.

The Commission's report recommended certain immediate steps that included the rapid return of displaced persons and immediate disarming of militia. It also recommended the establishment of an international investigation and prosecution body as well as an international human rights tribunal for accountability and justice.

In the meantime, Zimbabwe's legal and judicial arena too was in chaos.[11] Several lawyers and judges had expressed concerns about the government pressuring independent judges to resign and replacing them with those favouring the ruling party, thereby 'packing the bench.' In 2000, allegations of the Zimbabwean government having consistently and unfairly pressured judges were rife, resulting in the early retirement or departure of many respected and independent judges. The government had publicly questioned the independence of both white and black judges, alleging a racial divide. However, evidence showed that resignations had come from judges of both races, all individuals known for their independence and fearlessness.

Chief Justice Anthony Gubbay had invited the wrath of President Mugbae for his judgements upholding freedom of the press and the opposition to Mugabe.[12] Faced with government pressure and mounting threats to his life, Gubbay had recently become compelled to resign.

It was against this backdrop that the IBA constituted a fact-finding mission in 2001. The delegation consisted of former Chief Justice of India, Justice Ahmadi; Eastern Caribbean Supreme Court Judge, Justice Byron; the then Co-Chair of the IBA's Human Rights Institute, Lord Goldsmith QC; Former Counsel to Nelson Mandela, George Bizos SC; Judge Andre Davis US; and Ashwin Trikamjee, IBA Human Rights Institute Council Member.

Justice Ahmadi recounts the first night spent in Zimbabwe. Despite being accommodated in the city's reputedly finest hotel, he had a peculiar experience.[13] As he lay in bed, he was awakened by an unsettling, creepy sensation of something crawling on him. When he turned on the light, he was startled to see the room – including the bed he lay on – teeming with small bats that had crept in through a slit above the air conditioner. The hotel staff, in their efforts to clear the unwelcome guests, found the creatures not only in the room but also clinging to Ahmadi's clothes, shoes, and floor. Despite the bizarre circumstance, he had to make the best of the situation, for the next morning he was to meet Chief Justice Gubbay.

When asked why he had resigned, the courageous Gubbay responded, 'To protect my judges.' Deeply appreciative of many decisions taken by the Indian courts, Gubbay's appreciation prompted Ahmadi to send him a compiled volume of Supreme Court decisions spanning from Independence until 1997 upon his return to India – a gift for the Zimbabwean court library.

Justice Ahmadi had been entrusted with the responsibility of interrogating President Robert Mugabe.[14] Recollecting this intense session, Justice Ahmadi noted President Mugabe's resilience, withstanding the probing questions for a duration spanning two to three hours. But when faced with a loaded question and pressurized to the point of discomfort, he began shaking his leg agitatedly, signalling his unwillingness to go further. It was a sign for Ahmadi to back off and allow the President a moment to regain his composure before resuming questioning.' Through the questioning, President Mugabe staunchly reiterated his primary grievance, emphasizing that white populations had occupied lands belonging to the black population without paying fair compensation. However, Peter Goldsmith stated that the British Government had paid compensation but stopped due to distribution issues. Goldsmith revealed that Mugabe had utilized the funds for other purposes, leading to discontinuation. Throughout the questioning, Mugabe remained adamant about farmers' rights on the lands they till. When questioned about 'packing the bench,' Mugabe denied the allegation and assured the delegation that no such attempt would be made.

The report submitted by the delegation stated that 'The events of the past 12 months have put the rule of law in Zimbabwe in the gravest peril' as a direct result of the disregard with which President Mugabe had treated the judiciary and the government's failure to protect its judges.[15]

The report condemned the pressures that had finally forced Chief Justice Gubbay to resign as well as the government's failure to take action against the war veterans who had stormed the courts chanting 'Kill the judges'.

The report was met with opposition from Zimbabwean authorities, who claimed that it would contribute to 'a new wave of international condemnation' of the country – a contention that was subsequently dismissed by the IBA.[16]

A year later, the IBA would discover that the Zimbabwean government had failed to honour the assurances provided to the delegation in 2001, which pertained to safeguarding judges and adhering to court rulings. Additionally, the government neglected to implement any of the recommendations put forth by the delegation and did not fulfil its constitutional obligation to protect members of the legal profession and judiciary.

Justice Ahmadi had also undertaken a mission for judicial reforms to Bangladesh at the behest of the World Bank, but since this report is not in the public domain, not much is known about the operation.

At home, there was growing concern that the National Human Rights Commission, headed by Justice Venkatachaliah at the time, was unable to function in a meaningful way due to many limitations, particularly in its ability to effectively address issues such as the immunity of the armed forces from prosecution according to Indian law.[17] Acknowledging the necessity for an impartial and thorough scrutiny of the Act, the Commission enlisted the expertise of Justice A.M. Ahmadi to head a distinguished Advisory Committee assigned with conducting a meticulous examination of the Protection of Human Rights Act 1993 and propose amendments to it with the objective of improving the effectiveness of the NHRC.

The unfortunate incident of Bijbehara, Jammu and Kashmir, in which the BSF had opened fire upon a peaceful group protesting the siege on Hazratbal, resulting in 51 civilian deaths, coupled with the complications brought about by TADA became a litmus test for both the Commission's operations and the effectiveness of the Act.[18] The Ahmadi Committee was therefore constituted in response to scepticism regarding the Commission's ability to operate independently and with integrity under the existing Act. Doubts were raised about whether the Protection of Human Rights Act of 1993, which outlined the Commission's statute, was sufficient to ensure genuine efforts to promote and safeguard human rights in the country.

Soon after its appointment, the Ahmadi Committee noted that there were significant design flaws in the Act and that the Commission required greater autonomy to function properly.'

The J&K government had expressed reservations concerning the NHRC's ability to investigate human rights violations.[19] In response, the Committee proposed amending the Act to include matters relating to international covenants. This was an attempt to reassure victims of human rights violations in Kashmir of a fair examination.[20] It is important to note that the very inception of the NHRC in 1993 was India's reaction to extensive criticisms and global condemnation regarding the violations of human rights by security forces in Jammu and Kashmir and other insurgency-torn regions.

Additionally, the Act originally exempted all armed forces including BSF, Assam Rifles and other paramilitary forces from scrutiny by the NHRC, inviting significant international criticism.[21] The Committee stressed the importance of granting the NHRC the power to inquire into human rights violations by the armed forces and suggested defining armed forces as the army, navy and air force, bringing the remaining forces under the purview of the NHRC.

'There were several other recommendations too, including' providing greater financial and administrative autonomy to the NHRC. But most of these recommendations would not see fruition.

Despite several requests from the NHRC to implement the Ahmadi Committee recommendations, they were largely ignored with the new Act only serving to cripple the NHRC by further tightening government control over its functioning.

As stated by a retired High Court judge, 'Whichever government is in office, human rights are always a casualty.'[22]

In addition to these assignments, Justice Ahmadi seized the opportunity to champion a cause that had always resonated deeply with him – the cause of education. To his mind, education was not simply the route to a career of choice, but rather, the pathway to free thinking and eventually empowerment of individuals as well as communities. He would speak publicly about the need for disadvantaged individuals and communities to invest in educating their youth, especially women, for true upliftment. It was perhaps due to these passionate views and his vocal advocacy for maintaining academic independence and freedom from political involvement that he was approached to help resolve the issue of the Vice-Chancellorship of Jamia Millia Islamia University.

One evening in 1997, President Shankar Dayal Sharma invited Justice Ahmadi for a cup of tea. During the meeting, he presented a delicate challenge. The selection of the Vice-Chancellor for Jamia Millia Islamia is typically made through a committee, which President Sharma had constituted under the chairmanship of Governor Akhlaqur Rahman Kidwai, former Rajya Sabha member and Governor of Bihar, West Bengal and Haryana. However, upon submission of the report to the HRD, the Committee's report had leaked, causing controversy and leaving the President with no option but to constitute a fresh committee. He expressed that he wished Justice Ahmadi to chair this committee. In response, Ahmadi stated, 'Your Excellency, Mr Kidwai has been my friend since long and I would not like to hurt Mr Kidwai. But if he has no objection I will take it up.' Immediately, a phone call was made and it was ascertained that Mr Kidwai had no objection to Justice Ahmadi chairing the new committee.

The three-member committee, shrouded in secrecy, convened for a meeting at Justice Ahmadi's residence without any prior intimation to anyone else. Much to the astonishment of the Committee, a joint secretary from the HRD arrived at Justice Ahmadi's residence, asserting that he had been dispatched to brief the Committee on procedural aspects. When pressed about how he knew the date and time of the meeting, he remained silent. When asked to leave, he was reluctant to do so. Suspicions arose that the leak might have indeed been an inside job. The HRD representative was eventually compelled to leave, and the Committee agreed on three names for the position of Vice Chancellor. Concerned about the circumstances, Justice Ahmadi decided that as the Committee had been convened by the President of India and not a ministry, he would personally deliver the Committee's recommendations to Dr Sharma. As they met to review the recommendations outlined in the report, President Sharma sought Justice Ahmadi's personal insights on the most suitable candidate. During this discussion, Ahmadi also apprised the President of the HRD joint secretary's instruction to forward the report to the ministry for processing. In response, President Sharma remarked, 'That is where politics enters; I therefore want to put an end to it here and now.' So saying, it was agreed that the University was in need of a firm disciplinarian, and so the decision to appoint General Zaki was taken. A distinguished former general officer of the Indian Army, Zaki had earned several awards for gallantry and would go on to receive the Padma Shri in 2001.

Shortly after, in 2003, Justice Ahmadi was asked to assume the distinguished role of Chancellor at Aligarh Muslim University, a position that he held for two consecutive terms. During his tenure, Ahmadi went beyond the ceremonial duties associated with the role of Chancellor. A fervent advocate for the transformative power of education, he lent his voice to the cause on various public platforms.

But there was a legal matter too. Coinciding with his term as head of the University was the raging debate surrounding the minority status of the institution – a matter of great angst within the Muslim academic community. The debate, nuanced and complex, reflected the broader challenges faced by educational institutions in grappling with issues of identity, representation and community aspirations.

During his own tenure as Chief Justice of India, Justice Ahmadi had taken the proactive step of convening a special eleven-judge bench to re-examine the interpretation of minorities' educational rights under Article 30 of the Constitution, hoping to resolve the issue before his retirement.[23] Judiciously, he had kept himself off this bench. Recognizing the significance of the matter, Tahir Mehmood who was Chairman of India's National Commission for Minorities at the time advocated for the body's formal involvement in the case as *amicus curiae*. However, delays from the government's end resulted in the case remaining unresolved until Ahmadi demitted office. This was indeed unfortunate, as the issue became hopelessly tangled in later years.

The history of Aligarh Muslim University is more than a century old.[24] In 1877, Sir Syed Ahmed Khan, a 19th-century Muslim reformer, established the Muhammadan Anglo-Oriental College (MAO College) in Aligarh, aiming to promote modern British education among Muslims while preserving Islamic values. The Aligarh Muslim University Act of 1920 (AMU Act) merged the MAO College and another Muslim University Association into one institution known as the Aligarh Muslim University (AMU). The University's governing body, known as the Court of the University, was required to comprise exclusively individuals belonging to the Islamic faith. But subsequent amendments in 1951 and 1965 altered its structure.[25] Financial challenges faced by the AMU in later years led the Government of India to take over its maintenance, transforming it from an aided to a maintained institution. The 1951 amendment eliminated compulsory religious education for Muslim students and removed the provision enforcing only Muslim representation in the Court. In April 1965 when violence erupted during an AMU Court meeting, leading to the humiliation and injury of Vice-Chancellor Ali Yavar Jung, the Education Minister, M.C. Chagla pushed through an amendment, known as the AMU (Amendment) Act of 1965, granting extensive control to the Central Government. This amendment effectively placed executive and administrative control in the hands of the Visitor, typically the Union Minister of Education, and sidelined the University Court. The 1965 Act raised questions about the AMU's status as a minority institution under Article 30 of the Constitution, which grants minorities the right to establish and administer educational institutions of their choice.

In response, Muslim organizations appealed to the Supreme Court, arguing that the 1965 Act violated the AMU's constitutional protection as a minority institution. The pivotal S. Azeez Basha case in 1967 challenged these amendments, asserting violations of educational, religious and cultural rights. However, the Supreme Court upheld the changes, stating that AMU wasn't solely established or administered by the Muslim minority.

But then in 1981, the AMU Act was amended once again to redefine the University as an institution 'established by the Muslims of India'. Government representatives in Parliament hinted at restoring AMU's 'minority character' without explicitly committing to it. This implied a legislative basis for considering AMU as protected under Article 30(1), satisfying both parties without a firm assertion. But when the University reserved 50 per cent of medical seats for Muslim candidates in 2005, its minority status once again became contentious. Legal battles ensued claiming that the educational institution was a secular one, with the University contending that S. Azeez Basha was nullified by the 1981 amendment, and therefore it was permitted to make provisions for the benefit of Muslim students.

But the Allahabad High Court rejected the University's claim. In 2006 the Supreme Court, stayed the reservation policy and later referred its constitutionality to a larger bench.

Since then, the issue has remained contentious, prompting a reconsideration of the S. Azeez Basha decision by a seven-judge bench in 2019. In October 2023, a bench led by CJI D.Y. Chandrachud convened to re-examine the matter, delving into the intricate history and legal nuances surrounding the Aligarh Muslim University's governance. At the time of writing, the matter is still undecided.

Justice Ahmadi's views on this were, however, unambiguous. 'I have no doubt in my mind that the character of AMU is that of minority institution. But unfortunately over a period of time some judges in the Supreme Court and in the High Court gave their own interpretation.'[26] He also believed that the Azeez Basha judgement was flawed and not in keeping with the principles of natural justice. 'Now if you look at the Azeez Basha case it was deciding on the character of the university and the university was not made the party in that. The basic tenet of law that natural justice has to be done and for the purpose of deciding the character of the university, it was important that you have the university before you as a party to defend its character. The larger bench hearing should be fixed as early as possible.'

In a speech made in the capacity of the Chancellor of the University, he stated:

> Every dark cloud has a silver lining, and so does this, because it gives the University an opportunity to question the correctness of the decision in Azeez Basha. It is a thorn which will pinch again and again. Because of the view taken by the Division Bench on the competence of Parliament to amend the 1920 Act in view of the Entry 63 in List 1, there is no alternative but to challenge the decision in the Apex Court. As I said, there are flaws in the judgements of the learned Single Judge as well as the Division Bench, and I do hope a larger bench of the Apex Court will correct them.

In this speech, Justice Ahmadi makes reference to the seventh schedule of the Indian Constitution, which outlines the division of powers between the union and states through three lists: Union List, State List, and Concurrent List. The Union List (List 1) empowers Parliament to legislate on specific subjects, while the State List (List 2) delineates areas under state legislatures' authority. Entry 63 of List 1 includes Aligarh Muslim University, Benares Hindu University (BHU) and Delhi University and refers to them as institutions of national importance. Because these universities were established through an Act and fall under Entry 65 of the Union List, any changes to their administration will have to be codified in the statute through the Parliament. Any new legislation or changes in existing laws regarding these two universities would have to be enacted by the Central Parliament.[27]

Justice Ahmadi has termed the view of the Allahabad High Court as 'grossly erroneous,' stating that he was sure the central government would make every effort to have it reversed, '... otherwise it will be forced to go in for a constitutional amendment as it would also reflect on the Parliament's power to amend the Acts concerning the other two universities, the BHU and the University of Delhi.[28]

In his personal writings, Justice Ahmadi also makes mention of attempted interference in the affairs of the Aligarh Muslim University by the Ministry of Human Resource Development. During his first term as Chancellor, he was compelled to remind the ministry that the University was regulated by the Central University Statute and therefore their interference in the admission process was unwarranted. A similar situation arose when the ministry invoked the UGC and attempted to interfere in the financial management of the University – another attempt that was blocked by Ahmadi. In these writings, Justice Ahmadi expresses the hope that those at the helm of the University will be able to stand strong and resist attempts at political meddling, which have the potential to dilute the University's autonomy.

For a brief moment, it appeared that Ahmadi might be pulled back into public life – as rumours of him being considered for the position of Vice-President began to circulate. In the year 2000, former Prime Minister Deve Gowda reached out to former Chairman of India's National Commission for Minorities, Tahir Mehmood, requesting a recommendation for a suitable candidate who could stand as the joint opposition candidate for the impending Vice-President of India election.[29] Mehmood, in turn, approached Justice Ahmadi in strict confidentiality, securing his consent before presenting his name for consideration. In principle, Ahmadi had agreed to this proposition, demonstrating a willingness to serve in this capacity. Despite the confidential nature of the matter, news of this potential development quickly became public knowledge. The media caught wind of the discussions, resulting in a flurry of articles and reports on the subject. However, perhaps due to the political climate of the time, the government eventually decided not to proceed with the proposal.

Although a staunch advocate of minority rights, especially for Muslims and oppressed caste Hindus, Justice Ahmadi had no patience for those attempting to take advantage of his own Muslim identity. One of his legal assistants recounts a revealing incident that took place during an arbitration that Ahmadi was presiding over. The day had begun with one party grappling, seemingly drowning in poorly formulated arguments. Justice Ahmadi, ever meticulous, took a deep dive into the arguments, deftly uncovering loopholes and weaknesses. Yet, despite his insights, the struggling lawyer only became more nervous, tripping himself up.

The next day, the party surprised everyone by replacing their lawyer with a heavyweight – a renowned Muslim legal expert who was known to have good relations with Justice Ahmadi. It was also known that the new counsel's proficiency lay in other areas of the law unrelated to the specific matter at hand in the arbitration. His legal assistant watched as Ahmadi's face became black as thunder as he proceeded to rigorously dissect the counsel's arguments, objecting to the framing and the choice of questions. Visibly displeased, his stern demeanour reflected his deep disapproval of the attempted manipulation on religious lines. As the senior counsel became increasingly flustered, Justice Ahmadi did not yield, and the tension and awkwardness in the room mounted. It was an uncharacteristic departure from his usual kindness and patience towards an arguing counsel.

It was only later in the evening, in the reflective quiet of the post-arbitration drive, that his assistant plucked up the courage to broach the subject with Justice Ahmadi. They delicately inquired if something had happened to upset 'Chief'. Calmly, Ahmadi responded, 'This is not (name of the counsel's) area of expertise. I don't know why they have brought him in. If they think putting a Muslim lawyer before me will change the way things are going, we will have to set them straight.' The remark laid bare the offence he took at the insinuation that his fairness and integrity could be manipulated based on religious grounds.

The next day opened with a welcome surprise. The Muslim lawyer, whose presence had seemed more about identity than expertise, was replaced by yet another practitioner, demonstrating the message Ahmadi had sent out had been understood. The party attributed the change to the senior lawyer's summons to the Supreme Court for an unrelated case.

There were personal and religious milestones too. In 2007, at the invitation of the Saudi government, Justice Ahmadi embarked upon the pilgrimage of Hajj. But despite these displays of personal religious practice, Justice Ahmadi remained steadfast in his commitment to the principle of separating personal faith from the affairs of the State. While his pilgrimage was a personal and spiritual undertaking, he consistently emphasized the importance of maintaining a clear distinction between matters of personal religious conviction and the impartiality required in the legal and public domain. He would continue to speak publicly about the harms caused by the intermingling of the two domains. This commitment was not just a personal virtue but a guiding principle he believed should be upheld universally to ensure the integrity of legal and public institutions.

So when known Rashtriya Swayamsevak Sangh (RSS) member, Narendra Modi was elected to the position of Chief Minister of Ahmadi's own state, Gujarat, Justice Ahmadi was filled with a sense of foreboding. Having lived in Ahmedabad for more than 50 years, he knew the character of the state well. Gujarat was a constantly simmering cauldron of communalism that could explode at the slightest provocation. In Justice Ahmadi's eyes, the state desperately needed leadership that would unite its people, yet it seemed to have received the opposite. But still, in the beginning, Ahmadi harboured a cautious hope. Eternally optimistic about the system and its inherent strengths, he also believed that everybody deserved a fair chance and the benefit of the doubt.

But hope was shattered less than six months into Modi's first term as Chief Minister, with the devastating Gujarat riots claiming the lives of 2000 Muslims.[30] The carnage, persisting for three whole days with minimal intervention from law enforcement agencies, is one of the bloodiest communal riots in independent India's history.[31] Some international scholars have termed it a pogrom, a term usually used for organized, state-sponsored violence against a particular group of people.[32] Others have referred to it as 'ethnic cleansing' because of the targeted and systematic nature of the violence.

The catalyst for this horror was the train carriage that was set on fire in Godhra.[33] The train, carrying Hindu pilgrims on their way back to Gujarat from Ayodhya, made a stop in the town of Godhra, which has a history of religious tensions. The pilgrims, reported to have been chanting religious slogans, became embroiled in a conflict with Muslim residents at the railway station.

Tragically, within minutes, a fire erupted in Coach S-6 of the train, setting off a spasm of violence that would engulf cities, towns and villages across Gujarat. In a hugely controversial and provocative move, the

Gujarat government decided to place the charred remains of the fifty-nine victims of the fire on public display in Ahmedabad, inciting passions and fanning public rage. The next day, rivers of blood would flow through the streets of Gujarat.

Incensed by the gruesome sight of the dead bodies and blaming Muslims for the pilgrims' deaths, mobs of enraged Hindus went on a rampage that engulfed the entire state, unleashing a horrific wave of violence that persisted for over two harrowing months. While the rest of the country recoiled in shock and disbelief, news broadcasts seared the airwaves with horrific images – chilling accounts of pregnant women being impaled on swords, innocent children set ablaze, girls and women brutally raped and men ruthlessly dismembered.[34] The unbridled slaughter of the Muslim community in Gujarat surged diabolically, with the police responding to panicked Muslims begging for intervention with an indifferent 'We have no orders to save you.' Several reports suggest the police actively participated in the massacre.

Nobody was spared, not even the most influential. Ehsan Jafri, a former Member of Parliament from the Indian National Congress party, opened his home to a crowd of terrified Muslims seeking refuge, only to be dragged out in the open, hacked to pieces and set alight in full view of those he was attempting to protect.[35] Despite desperate pleas and panicked calls made to the most powerful circles including Mr Modi himself,[36] no help arrived, and Mr Jafri, along with 2000 others, lost his life.[37] High Court judge, Justice M.H. Kadri was forced to evacuate his home and Justice Akbar Divecha's home was burnt down. Muslim police officials were attacked as well.

In our home in Delhi, an eerie blanket of silence and disbelief hung thickly in the air. Surely this could not really be happening! Uncharacteristically shaken, Justice Ahmadi – perhaps for the first time in his life – abandoned his office for three whole days, remaining transfixed before the television in a state of utter shock and despair.

When the reports of the first violence began trickling in, he started impatiently flipping from one news channel to another in desperate hope for some signs of order – news of the first arrests, the swift response of the police or the firm hand of the Central Government. There was none.

By the end of the first day of unmitigated bloodshed, Ahmedabad, the largest city in the state, bore witness to a disturbing reality: not a single arrest had been made. Throughout the day, our home phone had been ringing off the hook with pleas for help from friends and relatives – both, Hindu and Muslim – trapped in the violence-stricken Ahmedabad. Each call carried desperate appeals for Justice Ahmadi to use his influence and authority to intervene and alleviate the suffering or at least, help them escape the city. It was a role he had played many times before, offering the community guidance and support.

As the clock struck 10.30 p.m., an ominous sense of foreboding had settled in.[38] With mounting suspicion that state intervention to quell the bloody massacre might not take place at all, Ahmadi reached for his telephone and instructed his office to connect him to the President of India, Mr K.R. Narayanan. In a voice fraught with urgency, he appealed to the head of the country to intervene by urgently deploying the armed forces to rein in the escalating violence. Justice Ahmadi voiced his deepest fears on the phone. '. . . else we might be in for a holocaust.' Assuring him that the government was aligned with his thoughts, the Central Government did eventually intervene the very next day by dispatching the army to stem the tide of violence. But a cruel twist awaited. The troops were denied entry into the city of Ahmedabad, asked instead to remain *tehnaat* (posted) outside while the violence continued unchecked within. Witnessing the disheartening turn of events, Aziz Ahmadi remained glued to the television, speaking to nobody. The phone was still ringing, but for the first time in his life, Justice Ahmadi felt helpless.

It remains a haunting memory, the sole instance when the depths of my grandfather's despair were so dark that there was not even a glimmer of his characteristic optimism.

As news of state complicity trickled in, at first mere whispers that soon became a deafening chorus, Justice Ahmadi's pain and disappointment turned into a growing disquiet. His beloved state of Gujarat where he had invested more than half his life was being torn limb from limb, his most precious and cherished ideal of secularism being sacrificed at the altar of religious fanaticism. Ahmedabad had been reduced to a city consumed by bloodthirst, echoing with anguished cries. He would not remain quiet.

Chief Minister Narendra Modi responded with an astonishing lack of remorse, stating his only regret to be an inadequate management of the media.[39]

Despite deafening calls for the dismissal of Narendra Modi in the aftermath of the riots, Prime Minister Atal Bihari Vajpayee chose not to take action against the Chief Minister of Gujarat, choosing instead, a light rebuke in which he urged Mr Modi to follow 'Rajdharma'.[40] Despite this apparent condemnation, Vajpayee would refer to Hindus as 'our people,' and Muslims as 'aliens' in a speech a few weeks later.[41] Further, the BJP's call for early elections that were initially set for 2003 to be held in 2002 set the stage for Mr Modi's campaign, which he chose to centre around Hindutva and sectarian politics – a strategy that won him another term as Chief Minister of the state with the Bharatiya Janata Party doing exceptionally well in the areas that were worst hit by violence.[42] Pravin Togadia, International General Secretary of the World Hindu Council, jubilantly summed up the victory saying, 'Gujarat is the graveyard of secular politics,'[43] further promising to bring this graveyard to the capital city of Delhi.

The following weeks and months brought forth much skullduggery.

Investigations into alleged state complicity become murky. Whistle-blowers were murdered, and accusations against the Chief Minister were rife, with officials claiming they had been instructed to stand by and allow Hindus to 'vent their anger'.[44] A UK government enquiry report revealed that the carnage had been premeditated, planned well in advance to 'purge Muslims' by the Vishwa Hindu Parishad, a hardline Hindutva organization. It also stated, 'A conservative estimate based on information from reliable human rights contacts puts the number of deaths at 2000 ... The killing was accompanied in many areas by widespread and systemic rape of Muslim women, sometimes by police.'[45] Other reports described the highly coordinated attacks, conducted by attackers dressed in saffron robes and khakhi shorts, armed with a variety of weapons and government issued lists of Muslim-owned homes and businesses. While the Muslim-owned structures were burnt to the ground, neighbouring Hindu-owned ones remained unscathed.

The brutal riots attracted worldwide condemnation, prompting the United States of America to go so far as to slap Modi with a visa ban. Simultaneously, Great Britain enacted a diplomatic boycott against him. Although the UK would lift this boycott ten years later in 2012, it wasn't until 2014 that the USA re-engaged with him as he emerged as a Prime Ministerial candidate.

Ten years later, Mr Modi would receive a 'clean chit' from the SIT appointed by the Supreme Court, exonerating him of any responsibility in the riots, paving the way for his meteoric rise to the position of Prime Minister of India.

Over the years that followed the bloody carnage of 2002, Justice Ahmadi would speak without inhibition about this devastating event.

Fearlessly calling out those in power on public platforms, Justice Ahmadi stated:

> The Chief Minister talked of having controlled the riots within 72 hours, as if it was so timed, but the Frankenstein once let loose could not be bottled for over two months.[46] What was witnessed in Gujarat was nothing short of a genocide. The rabid statements made by some hardcore Hindutva militants amounting to penal offences under our laws have gone unpunished, they feel emboldened, secure in the belief that no action will be taken against them by the government in the State or at the Centre. Gujarat has shown the most ugly face of cultural and religious conflict where the spirit of tolerance breaks down and hatred turns human beings into monsters (*Rakshasha*). The incident at Godhra was highly condemnable but what followed was worse, an unpardonable systematically organised pogrom. [sic]
>
> It is unfortunate that no less a person than the Prime Minister of the country should speak in different voices on such a sensitive issue. If he said he felt ashamed at the events in Gujarat while at a refugee camp in Ahmedabad, he advised Mr Mody [sic] that he should know his Raj Dharma, he took a somersault while addressing a pre-election rally at Goa where he blamed Muslims as a class and spoke of Dharma Raj and now again in his speech on 31' July, 2002 he has changed and

spoken of the need for religious harmony and unity. Will the Prime Minister clarify by which of his Statements the nation should take a surmise. And his No.2 man unabashedly states in Parliament that Modi has been the best C.M. in 50 years . . .

. . . The Sangh Parivar elements including members of the BJP often speak of Sardar Vallabhbhai Patel in laudatory terms. He was undoubtedly a great leader whose contribution in unifying India will always be remembered. The Nation will always remain grateful to him for this service. I was, therefore, pained to read in the press that some Hindutva elements raised Mr Modi to his pedestal - what an insult to that great leader, a comparison of the tall with a pigmy. Did the role of Modi in any manner bear comparison with that of Sardar Patel? The only contribution of Mr Modi is the Gujarat carnage; how then is he being compared with Sardar Patel?

Over the years, Justice Ahmadi became increasingly vocal about the need to administer swift and just punishments to the perpetrators of the Gujarat carnage – if at all India's secular fabric was to be rescued from the blow of the riots. Sadly, this did not happen.

The systematic attacks on innocent citizens, with a view to ethnic cleansing or marginalisation of vulnerable groups, need to be condemned in strongest possible terms.[47] The activities of certain forces cause grave concern to the concept of the rule of law. Unless these are put down with a strong hand this disease will spread threatening the very fabric of democracy. Granted that courts decide only when there are actual cases, prompt action on the part of the judiciary would serve as a strong deterrent and would help control such behaviour in future. It is important to realize that a brooding sense of injustice in the minds of the victim groups can stir up emotions for revenge. Prompt action by courts can calm such blood-boiling. If the victim group(s) can be heard and can reasonably hope to get justice from courts particularly when the other two democratic agencies have failed them, there would hardly be any motivation for revenge. Judiciary is the last hope; it must act impartially and fairly; it must also be so perceived; it must be just and must also be seen to be just; prompt action on Its [sic] part to act firmly, fairly and with a sense of urgency for doing justice to the victims alone will enhance judicial credibility. If judges are perceived to be guardians of one group or clique, rather than be seen as dependable stewards of the legal order, the victim group(s) will despair and lose faith in the system.

He pressed further:

'Courts should not hesitate to use their power to do justice to the victims of violence and thereby strike at the very roots of mischief-mongers. If we do not act now, our eventually [sic] democracy will be eroded and eventually lost. I say this because if you were to cast your glance all over the globe you will not find a single country where genuine democracy has survived with a theocratic form of governance.'

Despite his pain at the injustices faced by Muslims, he advocated restraint, urging the community not to resort to violence
'. . . what is important is to achieve is [sic] social harmony and peace, not to humiliate the majority through revengeful violence but to make it understand that the type of Hindutva it is practicing is injurious to the unity and integrity of the country . . . Violence is immoral because it thrives on hatred and not love which is the message of all leading religions, including Islam.'[48]

Yet, Ahmadi remained deeply troubled by the systemic discrimination and marginalization faced by the Muslim community and felt compelled to raise his voice. He did not hesitate to point out that minority rights have been recognized as essential internationally. And that the Indian Muslim had chosen to remain in India at the time of Partition trusting in the promises of 'equality, non-discrimination, religious and cultural freedom and fair play,' all of which the state was obligated to uphold.

Fearlessly questioning the authorities on several occasions, he urged them to recognize and address the plight of the marginalized. He pointed out that the Muslim community had long been deprived of its right to equality of opportunity – a denial that not only hindered individual progress but also thwarted the community's potential to contribute meaningfully to the nation's growth and development. It was in these contexts that he persistently advocated for minority rights.[49] Addressing Prime Minister Manmohan Singh at an event in 2005, he said:

> Unfortunately, of all the minorities, the Muslim minority has, over these 58 years of independence, remained marginalised in all walks of life. Periodic riots have ruined them economically. They have been victims of both, direct and indirect discrimination. The benefits of state schemes have not reached them. A special effort is needed to bring them into the mainstream of society, but unfortunately whenever some step beneficial to them is sought to be taken, members of the opposition parties raise the scare of pseudo-secularism, appeasement or Common Civil Code to deter the party in power from taking such action. What were they doing when they were in power? I think these scarecrows need to be shooed away . . . The battle against bigotry, religious fanaticism and the like can and must be fought through the teachings of Mahatma Gandhi i.e., non-violence and sadbhavana. Let the likes of Togadia call the Mahatma a 'kayar,' for he knows not what courage has to be mustered to own mistakes of the past and seek forgiveness for the wrongs done to the families of the victims.

Speaking at another event, he stated:

> There is a widespread perception and feeling among Muslims – which is shared and echoed by fair-minded non-Muslims as well – that Muslims often face overt and covert discrimination in private and public sectors, in recruitment and promotion in the police and paramilitary forces and in the administrative services, and in matters of getting loans, financial assistance and subsidies from government agencies. In my view, the marginalised groups should be perceived, not as passive, parasitical

recipients of a largesse, but as active participants entitled to equality of opportunity which has unfortunately been denied to them. Can any country afford to marginalise a sizeable section of its population and deny them the opportunity to contribute to national growth? A country's development and prosperity depends on its commitment and ability to offer equitable treatment to every section of its population; it must, therefore, frustrate every effort by those who seek to marginalise a section or group on grounds of religion. The failure of our secular state lies not in the appeasement of Muslims but in our failure over five decades to provide them with even a modicum of their rightful place in nation building.[50]

Justice Ahmadi was a man who believed in action. While he did not hesitate to frequently hold the government accountable for their duties of protecting minorities from violence and discrimination, he also emphasized the community's inherent duty to itself, a responsibility that should not be overlooked or underestimated. He encouraged the Muslim community to embrace secular education, a scientific temperament and a fearless attitude. In his vision, true upliftment would arrive from a combination of external powers meeting their duties and internal commitments towards empowerment.

Directly addressing the Muslim community, he said, 'Empowerment is a demanding maid, it will need considerable industry and commitment and then and only then will we reach our *manzil*. Do not resign to your fate but demand your rights, struggle for what is due to you; I am confident success lies ahead. What the Constitution grants you is your right, it is not charity.'[51]

Equally, he strongly urged the Muslim community to wait no longer to take the reins of their own destiny – through education.

We Muslims believe that Qur'an was revealed by the Almighty to our beloved Prophet (pbuh). Then we must also accept the fact that Allah could foresee how science will mould the society in the years to come. We must attribute to Allah the vision to see the future developments and mould the way of life for his *ummah* in changing circumstances. That is the reason why he gave the human-kind the power to think rationally. Think, use your thinking power, rationalise your thoughts and take the decision which you consider best. Do not mortgage your decision-making power – Allah will help you reach the right decision.

It is high time that we stop living in the past and start living in the present and work for a brighter future. We have to mould our own destiny – '*mustaqbil*,' no one else can do it for you. The only sure way is through education using the constitutional right of free and compulsory education promised by the proposed Article 21A in Part III, viz., Chapter on Fundamental Rights. Let us stop blaming others for our miseries, let us introspect and correct our mistakes, and march on. Not to provide education to our children is a serious crime since you are destroying their destiny and leaving them to suffer the same plight as you presently are suffering.[52]

Anyone who knew my grandfather even peripherally, knew his great commitment to secularism and his oft-repeated saying, 'For most of us, religion is an accident of birth.' Several times I have heard him tell the story of President Zakir Husain who was met with a delighted journalist extolling the great day that secular India was witnessing in the appointment of its first Muslim President. President Husain's response, while dampening for the poor man's excitement, revealed his true statesmanship.[53] As the journalist congratulated him, Dr Husain enquired, 'How is my becoming the President of India a victory for secularism?' The journalist replied: 'Sir, when a Muslim becomes the President of India for the first time, it is a victory for secularism.' Dr Husain responded, 'I think your concept of secularism must change drastically.' The journalist though taken aback, ventured to ask, 'Why is that, Sir?' To which Dr Saheb replied, 'Secularism is achieved only when you do not know my religion.'

And this would soon be demonstrated in Justice Ahmadi's personal life.

The year was 2009 and my attempts to build a career in journalism had taken me to the vibrant metropolis of Mumbai. Amidst the pulsating energy and rhythmic hustle and bustle of the city, my grandfather and I found a renewed opportunity to spend time in each other's company. For as a highly sought-after arbitrator, my grandfather now found himself spending up to two weeks each month in Mumbai, engaged in professional commitments. During his visits, we established a tradition of spending many an evening together, meeting at his favourite restaurant in his hotel on Marine Drive. As the sun dipped below the horizon casting the ocean in a fiery gold, we settled into his usual table. My grandfather, with his very particular tastes, would order a curated selection of off-menu dishes, customized exactly to his liking – a familiar routine among the chefs and waitstaff.

Here, we shared everyday stories, thoughts and observations. In those precious moments, there was an almost imperceptible shift in his personality that I did not fully grasp until years later. His questions now delved into the nuances of my daily life, revealing a newfound curiosity that went beyond mere information gathering. It was more than a familial interest; it was a genuine engagement in the day-to-day challenges of my life as I navigated the complexities of living alone for the first time. It was a subtle transition – my grandfather, no longer distracted and half-listening to chatter at the table, had discovered a renewed involvement in family life that would endure until the end of his days. The stoic *nana jaan* of my formative years was gradually softening around the edges, expressing his affection more openly. What used to be a simple pat on the cheek had evolved into warm embraces and hugs. The more awkward my anecdotes of stumbling through domestic chores in a new city without my doting grandmother's help, the more tickled he was. It was at this time that I was becoming interested in politics and world events. Sometimes he would ask me a provocative question like, 'Are you going to write anything about what Bal Thackeray said yesterday?' igniting long, impassioned and idealistic tirades from me, that he listened to with interest and also a glint of amusement. At the end of these, a gentle nudge with a twinkle in the eye. 'There is still time, become a lawyer.'

We passionately debated matters of the law as well. On one occasion, in the aftermath of a brutal gangrape in Delhi that had left a shocked India grappling with its ideas of justice, resulting in a public outcry demanding capital punishment for rapists, I found my grandfather remained firmly opposed to such measures. Young and impassioned, I questioned his reluctance seeking to understand his perspective on the matter. With the quiet wisdom of a seasoned jurist, he responded, 'Capital punishment is unlikely to stop the rapes, but it might increase the number of victims killed afterwards, to prevent the rapists from being identified.' It was a brief snapshot into the intricate interplay of morality and justice that had defined his career, and the difficult decisions judges must navigate. It was a lesson too; in restraint and the importance of analysing choices from all possible perspectives before forming a stance.

I had begun to rely heavily on his sound, practical advice, not only as my de facto father, but also as a confidant.

And so, when the time came to speak to my family about my decision to get married, I strategically awaited my grandfather's next visit. This time, instead of the restaurant, I suggested a different venue – his hotel suite. Sensing my desire for a more private conversation, he immediately understood and readily agreed.

As we settled down, he looked me straight in the eye, his own eyes filled with curiosity. Although I knew well my grandfather's commitment to liberal and secular values, I would be the first one in my immediate family to propose an interfaith marriage. And so, with some trepidation, I cleared my throat and began.

As I spoke, my grandfather lowered his glasses further down the bridge of his nose, listening intently. Peering at me from the top of his spectacle frames, as was his way when the conversation was an important or intense one, he waited for me to finish. When I revealed that the person I wanted to marry was not a Bohra, or even a Muslim, but in fact, a Hindu, he interrupted me mid-sentence and brushed my concerns away, saying, 'You know I don't care about that. All that matters is the boy's character.

Not his religion. Ask him to come home on the weekend to meet me.' Leaning forward, his expression open and reassuring, he continued, 'I make no promises right now, but if I find the boy to be all right, you will have no objection.'

After all, '. . . it is not enough to show tolerance and respect for each other's culture, more is required – they should be able to enjoy each other's culture.'[54]

It was during these years, well after retiring as Chief Justice, that he finally rekindled his lifelong love for *shayari*. In the evenings, when the burdens of workload were light, he spent many an evening poring over books of translations and the works of Iqbal, Ghalib and Khusrau. His secretary, a devout Hindu man who, by virtue of being raised in Uttar Pradesh, spoke fluent Urdu became an unexpected ally in this poetic journey. Their shared passion for the beauty of the language and the fine nuances of its poetry created an unexpected bond as the secretary assisted my grandfather with particular translations and linguistic interpretations. Later, and upon their request, my grandfather accepted a position on the Board of the Ghalib Institute.

As time flowed, my grandfather developed a fondness for sharing the tales that had shaped his life. Enlisting my husband Shaurya Roy, the newest addition to our family, as an eager and willing audience, he spent many a long evening unfolding the rich length and breadth of his life's experiences. Regaling him with lively narratives of the twists and turns of his life where he had skilfully navigated unpredictable currents, he recounted instances where he had to 'swim against the tide' armed with little more than the strength of conviction and spirit. Pausing for effect, he would finish with a flourish, '*Muddae laakh bura chahe to kya hota hai, wahi hota hai jo manzoor e khuda hota hai* (No matter how much the complainant wishes ill, only that will happen which is in accordance with the will of God).' Interspersing his stories with dramatic pauses, cleverly peppered with *shers*, gave him great pleasure and there would be a satisfied, throaty chortle following the recitation. On occasions when responding to a family member's request for advice, he would offer practical counsel, followed by another one of his favourite shers, *'Khudi ko kar buland itna ki har taqdeer se pehle khuda bande se khud poochhe, bata, teri raza kya hai.* (Raise yourself to such heights that, before decreeing your fate, even God asks you, What is your will?)'

There were light-hearted stories too, of diplomatic faux pas, personal anecdotes of his interactions with prime ministers and presidents, and his own life experiences.

During one of Mrs and Justice Ahmadi's visits to China in his capacity of Chief Justice of India, Jiang Zemin, the President of China, took a liking to Justice Ahmadi. A few months later, when Zemin visited India for official purposes, a dinner was hosted in his honour at the Rashtrapati Bhavan by the President of India. On this particular evening, Zemin and Ahmadi found themselves seated next to each other. In his eagerness to have a conversation with Justice Ahmadi, Zemin dismissed his translator and attempted an animated dialogue in broken English. However, in his enthusiasm to speak, he repeatedly placed his left hand on Ahmadi's right one, inadvertently preventing Ahmadi from eating. Observing this spectacle from his vantage point at the head of the table with a hint of a smile on his face was the President of India, Dr Shankar Dayal Sharma, hugely entertained by the humorous disruption caused by Zemin's earnest attempt at camaraderie. When the time came for Justice Ahmadi to escort President Sharma to his living quarters within the Rashtrapati Bhavan as per protocol, they encountered President Sharma's wife, Vimlaji, standing at the door. Eyes filled with mischief, Dr Shankar Dayal Sharma commented to his wife, *'Chief Justice Saheb ne kuch nahi khaya,'* (Respected Chief Justice has not eaten anything) eliciting a hearty chuckle from the ever-diplomatic and good-humoured Justice Ahmadi.

As the years passed and the weight of time pressed upon them, my grandparents, like a pair of well-worn books, were showing signs of wear. Yet, with each line etched on their faces, their connection deepened. Adversities arrived in the form of my grandmother's battle with uterine cancer, which would leave her with the lifelong effects of radiation, and my grandfather's sudden stroke in 2009. Now, they had begun to rely heavily on Tasneem Ahmadi with whom they shared a home, and would continue to do so for the remainder of their lives. A poignant reversal of roles unfolded as the parents, once the mighty oak that been an umbrella of protection and strength for their daughter, now leaned on her for every need, comfort and support.

And there were joys too. The birth of a third grandchild, Ali Asghar Ahmadi, Huzefa's son became a tremendous source of happiness and delight for the Ahmadi family. Having moved to his own home after Ali was born, Huzefa and his family nevertheless remained within walking distance from our home. Each week, our family congregated around my grandparents' dinner table laden with Bohri delicacies, where we caught up with each other's lives, discussed the latest news and laughed at inside jokes.

But in their sunset years, the Ahmadis would face one last upheaval. This time, it wouldn't originate from the legal sphere but would instead surge from the heart of the Bohra community,

Over the years and decades, as Justice Ahmadi's career flourished with successive achievements, the community's admiration for him had expanded as well. Throughout the 80s and 90s, and even beyond, Ahmadi stood as the preeminent accomplished figure among the Dawoodi Bohras. With his prominent standing came the esteemed title of Sheikh, a recognition that solidified his role as a respected figure and guide. On occasions like Muharram he was regularly graced with the honour of occupying a place on the elevated front row, symbolically seated above the rest of the community. Although he continued to wear the classic white *topi* with gold embroidery for smaller gatherings, he was now entitled to wear the *paagri*, a mark of a prominent member of the community. These threads of respect and recognition were woven intricately into his daily life.

Although not a religious man himself, the pragmatic Ahmadi was often approached for his keen insights and advice by the Bohra leadership. He was consulted by Syedna Mohammad Burhanuddin on all matters of importance, whether a new welfare project they were considering embarking upon, or problems with reformists. His emissaries were routinely sent to Delhi, seeking Justice Ahmadi's advice and counsel.

In many ways, Justice Ahmadi had become a confidant to both Syedna Mohammad Burhanuddin and his half-brother and Mazoon, Khuzaima Qutbuddin, who bestowed upon the family the same love and affection their father had, before them.

But this was all destined to change in 2014, tearing a rift in the community. This seismic shift was going to forever alter personal and community bonds.

The morning of 17 January 2014 brought forth a great sadness to the Bohra community. Ninety-nine-year-old Syedna Mohammad Burhanuddin had passed away. Two figures emerged as claimants to the position of the Dai, a role that held not just spiritual significance, but the weight of generations. The first to declare himself as the next Dai was one of his sons, Muffaddal Saifuddin. His supporters within the family claimed that the *nass* – or conferment of succession – was made in a hospital three years ago when the leader had been hospitalized upon suffering from a stroke. Saifuddin immediately assumed the role of Burhanuddin's successor.

But within mere hours of the news of the Dai's demise, another contender emerged – the figure who had shared in his brother's innermost confidences for years as the *Mazoon-e-Daawat*, a position second only to the Dai himself, one that held its own gravity. As the Dai's trusted second in command, the Mazoon sits to the right of the Dai during religious events and serves as the *Dai's* representative in their absence. Historically, several Dais – including Syedna Mohammad Burhanuddin himself – have been chosen from the rank of Mazoon. While this is indeed common, it need not always be the case. Khuzaima Qutbuddin's presence had been one of quiet strength, loyalty and shared responsibilities, and in early days, the community had grown accustomed to the thought that his hands might one day hold the reins. However, as the Syedna aged and his health declined, gradual shifts in family dynamics began to occur – leading to the gradual sidelining of the Mazoon, and the rising influence of other members of the family. Qutbuddin claimed that the *nass* had been conferred upon him nearly fifty years ago, in 1965. The unalterable aspect of the *nass* prohibits the Dai from reversing his decision; once conferred, it remains binding. This implies that if his claim is substantiated, any future conferment, even if it had indeed occurred, would be invalid. The air was thick with confusion as the grieving community grappled with this information.

Dialogues of speculation and wonderment echoed through the community. The leader's choice, shrouded in mystery, led to a clash of loyalties. In the wake of Syedna Mohammad Burhanuddin's passing, then, the Dawoodi Bohra community found itself standing at a crossroads.

Barely a breath after the passing of Syedna Mohammad Burhanuddin, Khuzaima Qutbuddin's wife, the much loved and respected Sakina Bensaab, dialled Amena Ahmadi's number. Her soft voice echoed through the phone. '*Ben* Ama, *kem chho* (how are you)?' Calling on behalf of her husband, she relayed the message. Khuzaima Qutbuddin would like to speak with Justice Ahmadi. On the other end, Amena guessed instantly what the phone call was regarding and promised to have Ahmadi call Khuzaima Qutbuddin within the hour. Within minutes, the telephone echoed with a shrill ring and a sense of urgency in Khuzaima Qutbuddin's wood-panelled study. The weight of the unsaid hung heavy in the air as Khuzaima Qutbuddin spoke, his voice a mixture of determination and apprehension. '*Bhai* Aziz,' Qutbuddin's words were measured. 'I seek your legal counsel in the matter of succession.'

As the conversation unfolded and Khuzaima Qutbuddin revealed the confidential details of the succession, the evidence he possessed and his intention to pursue the matter legally, Ahmadi's brows met in a deep furrow. His mind raced, his thoughts a churning cauldron of legal implications and moral quandaries. Disturbed at the implications of the community being split into two, Ahmadi offered a hand. 'I will fly to Mumbai,' he said, his voice steady and calm, 'to assess the evidence you possess before rendering my legal opinion.'

Less than twenty-four hours later, Justice Ahmadi landed in the bustling city of Mumbai. Because the Qutbuddins feared for their safety after the death of Syedna Mohammad Burhanuddin, they had been forced to vacate their apartments in the premises of the Saifee Mahal in Mumbai.

This enormous property serves as the headquarters for the Syedna as well as living quarters for his immediate and extended family. The palace complex includes administrative offices, residences and spaces for religious gatherings and ceremonies. The Qutbuddins had relocated to their private property in Thane, a modest home in comparison to the opulence of the Saifee properties.

As he stepped into the Qutbuddin residence, Ahmadi was met with boxes of evidence placed on the floor beside a baithak that had been readied for him. Containing files, papers, objects and photographs, the evidence had been properly categorized, dated and prepared for his visit. For three days, Justice Ahmadi delved into the boxes, his mind navigating the labyrinth corridors of legality. Conversations with the Qutbuddin family were like unravelling the layers of a puzzle, each detail bringing the larger picture into sharper focus. By the time Justice Ahmadi's visit came to an end, he was convinced.

'You possess enough evidence,' Justice Ahmadi's words were firm, 'to substantiate your claim in a court of law.' The two men locked eyes for a moment, heavy with the weight of the challenges they both knew were to come. Then Qutbuddin reached for the telephone. In the presence of Justice Ahmadi, his wife, two sons and one daughter, he dialled his eldest son who lived in the USA and conveyed the decision that they had decided to take the matter to court. Placing the phone back in its cradle, he turned back to Ahmadi and took both his hands, grasping them tightly. Without a word, he slipped off his ruby ring and slid it onto Justice Ahmadi's finger.

The die was cast.

Upon his return to Delhi, Justice Ahmadi sat with his wife at the foot of their bed, the space that had witnessed countless conversations of varying importance over the fifty years of their lives together. In a moment that was both intimate and monumental, he appraised her of his findings in Bombay. 'It is clear that we have to take a side,' he disclosed, his gaze steady, his tone measured. 'You understand the sacrifices . . .' A pause. 'I know,' she interjected, her jaw set, and eyes bright with determination. 'But this is what is just. I will make the calls to convey our solidarity.' In that instant, the lines were drawn, choices crystallizing into a decision that would shape their own lives and reverberate through their community.

The decision made, Amena Ahmadi now stepped to the forefront. In her quiet, resolute way, she made phone call after phone call, reaching out to her brothers, sisters-in-law and other relatives. The matriarch of the family, Amena Ahmadi braced herself for the emotional storm and pressures she knew would follow. Yet, amid the whirlwind of responses, Amena stood with quiet steadiness, unwavering conviction and composure.

The news spread like wildfire. Justice Ahmadi was the community's most accomplished and illustrious member, followed by former Attorney General of India, Goolam Essaji Vahanvaty – who would sadly pass away a mere eight months later. So, when Justice Ahmadi announced his position, all hell broke loose. Ahmadi's daughter, his son, his daughter-in-law – all found themselves navigating the currents of uncertainty.

The pressures were both overt and covert. The very next day, visitors with their own agendas arrived from Bombay, trying to coax Justice Ahmadi to re-evaluate his stand. Others reached out to express how they would be impacted due to their connection with our family. Phone calls, often from friends and relatives, became a constant presence in Amena's life. Voices both familiar and dear, were heavy with anxiety. Begging, imploring, they asked her to consider asking Justice Ahmadi to reconsider his position, to 'return to the fold.' Others disguised their motives in cloaks of worry. What if their cousins turned away? What if they found themselves disinvited from weddings and funerals? The ultimate card, the trump card of the afterlife was laid on the table – a hushed mention of the consequences in the hereafter if they were to be denied a resting place in a Bohra *qabrastan*. The weight of these calls could have been overwhelming for another. But Amena Ahmadi was no stranger to the tempests of life.

Refusing to budge, she simply responded to these with her indomitable will and refusal to engage. 'As Allah wills, so it shall be,' she said, again and again.

On the other hand, several members, encouraged by Justice Ahmadi's stand, deflected immediately. There were other phone calls too – from strangers who wanted to say how heartened they were by Justice *saheb's* courage. These conversations were tinged with wistful longing to do the same, but for many, the journey was fraught with complexities and obstacles that seemed insurmountable.

And so, that is how Amena and Aziz Ahmadi became the flagbearers of the minority. Once again, they found themselves on a road less travelled, that demanded courage and resolute spirit.

Yet, among the two, this path weighed particularly heavily on Ama. The realization that she would be severed from the fabric of community life, woven into her existence since birth was almost too much to endure. But the anguish went deeper. As Muffaddal Saiffuddin announced a social boycott and declared that those who chose to accept Khuzaima Qutbuddin's claim were to be denied access to all community spaces, she was denied a sacred tradition – *ziyarat* – the right to stand before the graves of those who held her heart – her parents and Syedna Taher Saifuddin.

By April 2014, legal proceedings had commenced.

But then, during a visit overseas in 2016, Khuzaima Qutbuddin passed away suddenly and unexpectedly. His son and successor, Taher Fakhruddin, assumed the mantle of spiritual leadership and also stepped into the role of the plaintiff in the lawsuit.

As the days turned into weeks and weeks into months, the storm of concern and coercion began to ebb. But the sacrifices did not. The once familiar rhythm of tradition was shattered. *Ziyarat* was forbidden. Entry to the Bohra Mosque, once welcoming, was now barred. The wider Bohra community united on occasions like Muharram where Justice Ahmadi, a felicitated Sheikh was invited each year to sit in the elevated front row as a depiction of honour; now the family was exiled. Bonds, once unbreakable, became frayed as relatives chose separation to protect themselves from a similar fate. Graver still, the legacy of final resting places came to an end. Access to Bohra graveyards became conditional with humiliating terms imposed – apologize and pledge allegiance to Mufaddal Saifuddin – or be denied a place beside loved ones. And yet, forsaking their principles simply did not occur to them.

Uncapitulating, with every denial Amena and Aziz Ahmadi's resolve only grew. They decided that there would be no plea, no request for a place in the Bohra graveyard when their time came. Their legacy would be marked by a different choice – to lay side by side in a local *qabrastan* in Delhi as a testament to their unyielding unity and faith of conviction. As such, they were prepared to become the first generation of their respective families not to be laid to rest in a bohra *qabrastan*.

On 23 April 2024, a single judge of the Bombay High Court dismissed Qutbuddin's suit, upholding Mufaddal Saifuddin's claim as rightful Dai. However, Fakhruddin Qutbuddin's statements following the verdict remained firm and resolute, as he encouraged his followers to remain steadfast on the path of *sabr* and conviction. He also announced his intention to appeal this judgement, to the full extent of the legal process. 'For truth, for justice, and for the future of the Dawoodi Bohra community, I am duty bound to continue this fight.'[55]

My grandparents were growing visibly older. Slowly shedding the excess weight they had carried in their midlives, they were becoming leaner. And frailer. Turning to each other for support, they now found solace within their family in the midst of life's challenges. After my grandfather was diagnosed with Chronic Lymphocytic Leukemia in 2019, which put him on more lifelong medications, my grandparents became almost inseparable, navigating the complexities of health challenges hand-in-hand. As always, my grandmother looked after his every need, while he was content to just be in the same room as his wife, reading his newspapers or poring over files, preparing for an arbitration. In the familiarity that only a lifetime of shared experiences can cultivate, they seemed to have learnt to read each other's minds. As the sun faithfully rose and set each day, Aziz and Ama's distinguished and remarkable lives gracefully transitioned into the comforting embrace of a quiet and serene peace.

In the final chapter of his life, Justice Ahmadi's thoughts turned to unfinished business. After a lifetime of estrangement came the urgent, irresistible urge to confront the lingering echoes of his familial past, particularly with his sister Zulekha Merchant and, most intensely, with his aged mother, Shirin Ahmadi. The call of blood, that powerful primal force, refused to be silenced and he yearned for reconciliation. While Zulekha and Aziz had made several efforts over the past few years, attempting to rebuild their relationship, his mother was simply too old and frail. Aware that the sands of time were slipping through the hourglass, Justice Ahmadi grappled with the realization that if he wished to meet his mother before the final curtain descended, he would have to traverse the physical and emotional distance that separated them. But my grandfather's health was not as robust as it once was. The Chronic Lymphocytic Leukemia had wreaked havoc, weakening his body considerably. Thin and frail, the shirts which once strained at the belly now hung limply off his shoulders. My grandmother, too, had become tiny and fragile, with the symptoms of the side effects of radiation having become more damaging with age. Worse, she had suffered a fall and was recovering from a fracture.

But in all this, Aziz had lost neither his spirit nor his determination.

And so, it was in July 2022 that my husband Shaurya and I accompanied our grandfather on a journey to Pune with the shared hope of unburdening his mind and alleviating the collective weight that he and his family carried. A pilgrimage of the heart, we were aware that the journey was not merely about reaching a destination; it was about unravelling layers of history, healing wounds and, ultimately, finding closure.

As we landed in Pune and drove to my great aunt Zulekha's home, my grandfather was uncharacteristically quiet. Yet, his sharp, darting eyes betrayed the eager anticipation that brewed beneath the surface.

Blind and almost deaf though she had become, 109-year-old Shirin Ahmadi remained astonishingly alert. Her body bore the marks of a century lived, painfully twisted, with legs that could no longer straighten out, but her spirit and courage – both traits she had passed down to her son in abundance – remained intact. As Zulekha gently placed Aziz's hand in Shirin's and spoke in her ear, it was clear that Shirin Ahmadi knew. It was her son's hand she clasped so tightly in her frail own. 'Aziz?' she called out in a thin, yet surprisingly steady voice, her unseeing eyes looking past his shoulder.

Over the next two days, brother and sister would sit together, their laughter echoing through the room as they shared childhood tales and reminisced about the mischief they had once stirred. Delightedly witnessing this precious moment was Ishaq Merchant, Zulekha's husband. As the visit came to a close, Shaurya and I watched as the weight that had burdened my grandfather's heart for all these years slipped away, making way for a newfound sense of peace, forgiveness and closure. He was visibly lighter, happier, now eager to return to his life. The family had reconciled, but it was the last time they would see each other.

The next few months would prove cruel. Within seven brief months of this emotional reunion, the threads binding Zulekha Merchant, Shirin Ahmadi, Aziz Ahmadi and Amena Ahmadi would be severed – leaving behind no survivors.

It was in the quiet stillness of an ordinary Saturday night in August that my grandmother passed away suddenly and unexpectedly in the hospital she had been admitted to for a seemingly minor ailment – a complication from the side effects of radiation therapy. She would be the first in an avalanche of losses.

Dragging our feet that were suddenly heavy as lead, my mother and I left my mamu and Shaurya in the hospital to navigate the paperwork, knowing that within the walls of our home awaited the heart-wrenching task of delivering the crushing news to Justice Ahmadi that the very essence of his existence had been extinguished. Our hearts sinking, we approached the threshold, steeling ourselves for the gut-wrenching moment.

When my mother uttered those dreadful words, the room seemed to hold its breath. Justice Ahmadi, her father, stared at her uncomprehendingly, his eyes searching hers, as if waiting for her to correct an obvious slip of the tongue. A moment later, as the words sunk in, he drew a sharp, ragged breath.

Tired, emotionally drained, he eventually fell silent, the weight of his shattered world hanging thickly in the air. His once-commanding presence was suddenly fragile and vulnerable. As I sat on a footstool before him, my hands clasping his, he abruptly shook my hands away. 'I have work to do,' he announced, reaching for his walking stick, a desperate attempt to regain control over a world that had suddenly spun out of orbit. Making his way to his study with deliberate steps where a desktop computer stood – the only one intentionally kept without internet access for reasons of security and confidentiality – he sat down.

In that dimly lit room, he stared blankly at a document on the screen, lost in the vast emptiness left by his beloved wife. Over the next few weeks, he ate very little, and spoke even less, spending his time in quiet contemplation before my grandmother's photograph.

The document he was staring at that night is what has become the book you now hold in your hands. In the closing chapter of his life, my grandfather had harboured one more wish – to write his autobiography. Over the course of several years, he had written numerous drafts and passages, with the intention of one day weaving them all together into his life's final project - his *'atma katha'* as he lovingly called it. But without my grandmother, perhaps it was no longer worth it. It remains the only task he ever left unfinished – a testament to the profound impact of love and loss on the human spirit.

Over the next few months, our family dropped everything else and rallied together with a singular focus – to bolster our father and grandfather with the courage to keep going in the absence of his life force. Relatives, arriving from different cities, offered words of solace and courage. But it wasn't a matter of courage. Indeed, if it were, our efforts would not have been needed. He had simply and quietly made up his mind to join the person whose presence was the compass he navigated life by. Surviving his beloved wife by a mere ten days short of six months, it was on the night of 2 March 2023, after a brief hospitalisation, that he ate his favourite Gujarati meal of *kairi no ras* (mango puree) with *chapatti*, lay down in his bed, gently shook off the shackles of earthly life and joined my grandmother.

In the end, my nana jaan died just the way he had lived. On his own terms.

Because, '*Khudi ko kar buland itna ki har taqdeer se pehle khuda bande se khud poochhe, bata, teri raza kya hai.*'

Epilogue

Time and again, Justice Ahmadi's forward-thinking judgements and speeches have reflected his vision for India's future. Whether it was advocating for the rights of marginalized communities, championing democratic and constitutional freedoms or protecting the rights of the individual against the excesses of state power, his eye did not waver from the larger goals of fairness, justice and equality.

While Justice Ahmadi remained optimistic about the Indian judiciary until the end of his days, he did not hesitate to point out the shortcomings of the system when such criticism was warranted. He often highlighted the failings of the lower courts as a young judge, and even the Supreme Court later, especially during the testing times of the National Emergency and the demolition of the Babri Masjid. With the advantage of hindsight, we can now fully appreciate his astute observations then and the ways in which political events and Supreme Court judgements of that time shaped not only present-day politics but also the ways in which social and cultural shifts have played out. As others have pointed out, he had a sound 'common sense' that didn't allow him to lose sight of the larger picture. His fearless speeches holding powerful politicians accountable for the defeat of secularism and loss of harmony in India were, in truth, alarm bells – he had foreseen the religious polarization we live with now long before it had become a reality. Perhaps we might apply that same thinking to present times to better understand the paths upon which we are forced to walk.

Despite this, my grandfather was an optimistic man with an unending faith in the ordinary citizen – the public. 'They are not fools,' he would say before every election, hopeful. Equally, he remained ever optimistic about the Indian judiciary, maintaining the eternal hope that any wrongs could – and would – eventually be righted, and justice would ultimately prevail.

A firm believer in the power and sanctity of the Constitution, he also stressed the importance of the right people being entrusted with its implementation. Often quoting Dr Rajendra Prasad, he cited, *'After all, a Constitution like a machine is a lifeless thing. It acquires life because of the men who control it and operate it, and India needs today nothing more than a set of honest men who will have the interest of the country before them. We can only hope that the country will throw up such men in abundance.'*

But our journey doesn't conclude here. The ideals that Justice Ahmadi stood for are worth preserving for future generations. They are not just memories to cherish but legacies to safeguard. It is with these aims in mind that the Ahmadi Foundation has been established as an institution that seeks to preserve Justice Ahmadi's legacy and the values he held dear. These ideals will be upheld through this institution, with support provided to legal, educational and humanitarian causes aligning with his vision for a more just and equitable society.

As we bid farewell to Justice A.M. Ahmadi, let us honour his memory by continuing the work that he began – by standing for what is right, by fighting for justice and equality, and when we must disagree, let us do so with respect, humility and compassion.

May his legacy inspire us, and his courage fuel ours.

Notes

Foreword

1. S.R. Bommai vs. Union of India, 1994 SCC (3) 1
2. Indra Sawhney vs. Union of India, 1992 supp. (3) SCC 217
3. State of Maharashtra vs. Madhukar Narayan Mardikar, AIR 1991 SC 207.

1. The Black Sheep of the Family

1. A colloquial term used to refer to a native or resident of Surat.
2. Fatemi Dawat | Misaaq – A Covenant with Allah Ta'ala.
3. Imam Ali was Prophet Mohammad's cousin and son-in-law, believed by Shia Muslims to be the first Imam, the rightful religious and political successor to the Prophet.
4. The Dawoodi Bohra belief holds that an Imam, a direct descendant of Prophet Mohammed SA through his grandson Imam Husain AS, serves as the spiritual leader (Imam) in every era. The current twenty-first Imam, Imam al-Tayyib (b. 1130 AD), is in concealment (satr), represented by a vicegerent known as the Dai al-Mutlaq or 'Syedna'.

2. 'I Did Not Choose the Law; the Law Chose Me'

1. Leena Mishra, 'Explained: The History of Lord Jagannath Rath Yatra in Ahmedabad', *Indian Express*, 4 July 2019, https://indianexpress.com/article/explained/explained-the-history-of-lord-jagannath-rath-yatra-in-ahmedabad/.
2. High Court of Gujarat, https://gujarathighcourt.nic.in/.
3. City Civil & Sessions Courts Ahmedabad – Gujarat, https://ahmedabad-ccc.dcourts.gov.in/.

4. Sourced from Justice Ahmadi's private writings, 2015–2019.

4. From Bar to Bench

1. Anuj Aggarwal, 'In Conversation With Former Chief Justice of India, Aziz Mushabber Ahmadi', https://www.barandbench.com/, 7 August 2014, https://www.barandbench.com/interviews/conversation-former-chief-justice-india-aziz-mushabber.
2. Sourced from Justice Ahmadi's personal writings, 2015–2019.
3. High Court of Gujarat, https://gujarathighcourt.nic.in/.
4. Ibid.
5. Anuj Aggarwal, 'In Conversation With Former Chief Justice of India, Aziz Mushabber Ahmadi', https://www.barandbench.com/, 7 August 2014, https://www.barandbench.com/interviews/conversation-former-chief-justice-india-aziz-mushabber.
6. Allauddin Mian & Ors Sharif Mian & Anr vs. State Of Bihar on 13 April, 1989, https://indiankanoon.org/, 13 April 1989, https://indiankanoon.org/doc/1099363/.
7. Shah, G. (1970), 'Communal Riots in Gujarat: Report of a Preliminary Investigation', *Economic and Political Weekly*, 5(3/5), 187–200, https://www.jstor.org/stable/4359550.
8. Anuj Aggarwal, 'In Conversation With Former Chief Justice of India, Aziz Mushabber Ahmadi', https://www.barandbench.com/, 7 August 2014, https://www.barandbench.com/interviews/conversation-former-chief-justice-india-aziz-mushabber.
9. S.T. Desai, https://en.wikipedia.org/wiki/S._T._Desai.
10. Anuj Aggarwal, 'In Conversation With Former Chief Justice of India, Aziz Mushabber Ahmadi', https://www.barandbench.com/, 7 August 2014, https://www.barandbench.com/interviews/conversation-former-chief-justice-india-aziz-mushabber.
11. A.M. Ahmadi, Muljibhai And Anr. vs. United India Insurance Co. Ltd. And Ors. On 21 April, 1982, https://indiankanoon.org/, 21 April 1982, https://indiankanoon.org/doc/950195/.
12. A.M. Ahmadi, Lilaben Udesing Gohel vs. The Oriental Insurance Company Ltd. & . . . on 15 March, 1996, https://indiankanoon.org/, 15 March 1996, https://indiankanoon.org/doc/745697/.
13. Sourced from Justice Ahmadi's private writings, 2015–2019.

14. Ibid.

5. A Fork in the Road

1. Sourced from Justice Ahmadi's personal writings, 2015–2019.
2. Ghanshyam Shah, 'Pulse Of The People', https://www.indiatoday.in/, 29 December 2007, https://www.indiatoday.in/magazine/cover-story/story/20071231-pulse-of-the-people-734871-2007-12-20.
3. G. Shah, 'The Upsurge in Gujarat', *Economic and Political Weekly*, 9(32/34), 1429–1454, https://www.jstor.org/stable/4363918.
4. K. Nayar, 'Beyond The Lines: An Autobiography', Roli Books Private Limited.
5. AIR1974SC2233, (1975)1SCC138, [1975]2SCR330]
6. Ibid.
7. T. Ramakrishnan, 'The 1975 Gujarat Assembly election', *The Hindu*, 5 December 2017, https://www.thehindu.com/elections/gujarat-2017/the-1975-gujarat-assembly-election/article21262462.ece.
8. Parliament of India Official Debates of the Rajya Sabha, 'Re Proclamation Issued By President Relating To the State of Gujarat', 22 March 1976, https://rsdebate.nic.in/bitstream/123456789/437219/1/PD_95_22031976_10_p108_p193_13.pdf.
9. Sourced from Justice Ahmadi's private writings, 2015–2019.
10. T. Ramakrishnan, 'The 1975 Gujarat Assembly election', *The Hindu*, 5 December 2017, https://www.thehindu.com/elections/gujarat-2017/the-1975-gujarat-assembly-election/article21262462.ece.
11. Sourced from Justice Ahmadi's private writings, 2015–2019.
12. Satya Prakash, 'The Court verdict That prompted Indira Gandhi To Declare Emergency', *Hindustan Times*, 26 Januaray 2015, https://www.hindustantimes.com/india/the-court-verdict-that-prompted-indira-gandhi-to-declare-emergency/story-uaDsy0j3B0vSdiPn2md9WO.html.
13. V.R. Krishnaiyer, 'Indira Nehru Gandhi (Smt.) vs. Raj Narain & Anr. on 24 June, 1975', https://indiankanoon.org/ , 24 June 1975, https://indiankanoon.org/doc/1240174/.
14. Sourced from Justice Ahmadi's personal writings, 2015–2019.
15. Life Insurance Corpn. Of India And . . . vs. Prof. Manubhai D. Shah Etc. Etc on 22 July 1992 (indiankanoon.org)
16. Emergency in India during 1975: Atrocities and Acts during Emergency, 26 June 2015, https://www.india.com/education/emergency-in-india-during-1975-atrocities-and-acts-during-emergency-1581724/.

17. Nayar, K. (2012). *Beyond The Lines: An Autobiography*. Roli Books Private Limited.
18. Seema Chishti, The Darkest Hour: ADM Jabalpur Was a Test for SC. Only the Dissenter Passed It, The Indian Express, 29 August 2019, https://indianexpress.com/article/opinion/columns/supreme-court-adm-jabalpur-the-darkest-hour-5945825/.
19. A. N. Ray, 'Additional District Magistrate, Jabalpur vs. Respondent: S.S. Shukla Etc. Etc. on 28 April 1976', https://indiankanoon.org/, https://indiankanoon.org/doc/1735815/.
20. Shanmugham D. Jayan and Raghul Sudheesh, A Chief Justice of India Says "I Am Sorry" But 30 Years Too Late, https://www.firstpost.com/, 16 September 2011, https://www.firstpost.com/politics/a-chief-justice-of-india-says-i-am-sorry-but-thirty-years-too-late-85799.html.
21. Seema Chishti, The Darkest Hour: ADM Jabalpur Was a Test for SC. Only the Dissenter Passed It, The Indian Express, 29 August 2019, https://indianexpress.com/article/opinion/columns/supreme-court-adm-jabalpur-the-darkest-hour-5945825/.
22. Sourced from Justice Ahmadi's personal writings, 2015- 2019.
23. Omens for the summer. India Today
24. Sourced from Justice Ahmadi's personal writings, 2015–2019.
25. HJ/53/19 IN MEMORIAM (himalayanclub.org).
26. Express News Service, March 14, 1976, Forty Years Ago: United We Stand, The Indian Express, 14 March, 2016, https://indianexpress.com/article/opinion/editorials/march-14-1976-forty-years-ago-united-we-stand/.
27. Sourced from Justice Ahmadi's personal writings, 2015–2019.

6. The Citizen's Judge

1. Is Activism of Judiciary Anathema to the Constitutional Structure, A.M. Ahmadi, *The Chief Justice Speaks*, 2016.
2. Sourced from Justice Ahmadi's private writings, 2015–2019.
3. N., D. (1988). Migrant Workers, Super-Exploitation and Identity: Case of Sugarcane Cutters in Gujarat. *Economic and Political Weekly*, 23(23), 1152–1153, https://www.jstor.org/stable/4378575.
4. Sourced from Justice Ahmadi's personal writings, 2015–2019.
5. https://cdn-legacy.iclrs.org/content/events/31/1012.mp3.
6. Sourced from Justice Ahmadi's personal writings, 2015–2019.

7. Ray, Ashutosh, Remembering late Chief Justice of India AM Ahmadi, Bar and Bench, 2023, https://www.barandbench.com/columns/chief-justice-of-india-am-ahmadi-obituary.
8. State Of Gujarat And Another vs. Hon'Ble High Court Of Gujarat on 24 September, 1998 https://indiankanoon.org/, https://indiankanoon.org/doc/199405/.
9. Sourced from Justice Ahmadi's private writings, 2015–2019.
10. State Of Gujarat And Another vs. Hon'Ble High Court Of Gujarat on 24 September, 1998 (indiankanoon.org).
11. Ibid.
12. Team Frontline, 1979: The First PIL Petition, https://frontline.thehindu.com/, 14 August 2022, https://frontline.thehindu.com/social-issues/social-justice/india-at-75-epochal-moments-1979-the-first-pil-petition/article65727193.ece.
13. Ahmadi, A.M., *Flow Of Thoughts: Selected Speeches, Lectures And Writings Of Justice A.M. Ahmadi (Former Chief Justice of India)*, Institute of Objective Studies, 2008, pp 396–407.
14. Fatesang Gimba Vasava And Ors. vs. State Of Gujarat And Ors. on 19 March, 1986 https://indiankanoon.org/, https://indiankanoon.org/doc/1394507/.
15. Ministry of Tribal Affairs, The Kolghas of Gujarat (A Socio-Economic Study And a Development Plan), January 1979.
16. Abhilasha Kumari, Kershi Pirozsha Bhagvagar vs. State Of Gujarat And Anr., https://indiankanoon.org/, 21 June 2007, https://indiankanoon.org/doc/1512604/.
17. Indian Kanoon, Suresh Lohiya vs. State Of Maharashtra And Another on 23 August, 1996 https://indiankanoon.org/, 23 August 1996, https://indiankanoon.org/doc/155648/.
18. A.M. Ahmadi, Megjibhai Khimji Vira vs. Chaturbhai Taljabhai https://indiankanoon.org, 14 February 1977, https://indiankanoon.org/doc/640617/.
19. E.S. Venkataramiah, Gujarat State Road Transport ... vs. Ramanbhai Prabhatbhai & Another, https://indiankanoon.org/, 11 May 1987, https://indiankanoon.org/doc/1541798/.
20. Gadbois, G.H., *Judges of the Supreme Court of India*, Oxford University Press, 2011.
21. Sutlej-Yamuna Link: Dispute Continues For 61 Years After 1st Agreement In 1955, *The Economic Times*, 10 November 2016, https://economictimes.indiatimes.com/news/politics-and-nation/syl-dispute-continues-for-61-years-after-1st-agreement-in-1955/articleshow/55355851.cms?from=mdr.

22. I. Khurana, Politics and Litigation Play Havoc: Sutlej Yamuna Link Canal. *Economic and Political Weekly*, 2006, 41(7), 608–611, https://www.jstor.org/stable/4417835.
23. The Indian Express. (n.d.). *Google Books. The Indian Express*, https://books.google.co.in/books?id=voVlAAAAIBAJ&pg=PA8&dq=eradi+tribunal+haryana&article_id=325.
24. The Indian Express. (n.d.). *Google Books. The Indian Express*, https://books.google.co.in/books?id=voJlAAAAIBAJ&pg=PA8&dq= eradi+tribunal&article_id=1629.
25. The Indian Express. (n.d.). *Google Books. The Indian Express*, https://books.google.co.in/books?id=vYJlAAAAIBAJ&pg=PA6&dq=eradi+ tribunal&article_id=2316.
26. Khurana, I., Politics and Litigation Play Havoc: Sutlej Yamuna Link Canal. *Economic and Political Weekly*, 2006, 41(7), 608–611, https://www.jstor.org/stable/4417835.
27. Himanshu Thakkar, Muddying the Waters, *India Today*, 2 July 2018, https://www.indiatoday.in/magazine/up-front/story/20180702-muddying-the-waters-1266108-2018-06-24.
28. Shiva, V., *The Violence of the Green Revolution: Third World Agriculture, Ecology, and Politics*, 2016, University Press of Kentucky, https://www.jstor.org/stable/j.ctt19dzdcp?turn_away=true.
29. Sutlej-Yamuna Link: Dispute Continues For 61 Years After 1st Agreement In 1955, *The Economic Times*, 10 November 2016, https://economictimes.indiatimes.com/news/politics-and-nation/syl-dispute-continues-for-61-years-after-1st-agreement-in-1955/articleshow/55355851.cms?from=mdr.

7. Gavel and Grit

1. Gadbois, G.H., *Judges of the Supreme Court of India*, Oxford University Press, 2011.
2. Ibid.
3. Sourced from Justice Ahmadi's private writings, 2015–2019.
4. Seema Chishti, Why, 22 Years On, the SC's 'Hindutva Judgment' Remains Elephant In Room, *The India Express*, 3 January 2017, https://indianexpress.com/article/explained/gujarat-riot-nhrc-religion-elections-vote-bank-supreme-court-why-22-years-on-the-scs-hindutva-judgment-remains-elephant-in-room-4456258/.
5. Jagdish Saran Verma, Dr. Ramesh Yeshwant Prabhoo vs. Shri Prabhakar

Kashinath Kunte & Others, https://indiankanoon.org/, 11 December, 1995 https://indiankanoon.org/doc/925631/.

6. Nauriya, A., The Hindutva Judgments: A Warning Signal. *Economic and Political Weekly*, 1996, 31(1), 10–13, https://www.jstor.org/stable/4403638.
7. Seema Chishti, Why, 22 Years On, the SC's 'Hindutva Judgment' Remains Elephant In Room, *The India Express*, 3 January 2017, https://indianexpress.com/article/explained/gujarat-riot-nhrc-religion-elections-vote-bank-supreme-court-why-22-years-on-the-scs-hindutva-judgment-remains-elephant-in-room-4456258/.
8. Narain, A. and John, M., The Hindutva judgments: A comment. *National Law School Journal*, 1997, 9(1), https://repository.nls.ac.in/nlsj/vol9/iss1/36.
9. Ibid.'
10. Md. Ali, Supreme Court Could Have Prevented Babri Demolition: Ex CJI, https://twocircles.net/, 24 October 2010, https://twocircles.net/2010oct24/supreme_court_could_have_prevented_babri_demolition_ex_cji.html.
11. Sourced from Justice Ahmadi's private writings, 2015–2019.
12. Jagdish Singh Khehar, Supreme Court Advocates-On-Record . . . vs. Union Of India, https://indiankanoon.org/, 16 October 2015, https://indiankanoon.org/doc/66970168/.
13. Manoj Mitta, CJI M.N. Venkatachaliah Poised to Radically Alter Entire Judicial System, *India Today*, 31 October 1993, https://www.indiatoday.in/magazine/indiascope/story/19931031-cji-mn-venkatachaliah-poised-to-radically-alter-entire-judicial-system-811736-1993-10-30.
14. Manoj Mitta, M.N. Venkatachaliah Takes An Important Step to Restore Judicial Credibility, *India Today*, 15 October 1993, https://www.indiatoday.in/magazine/nation/story/19931015-m-n-venkatachaliah-takes-important-step-to-restore-judicial-credibility-811668-1993-10-14.
15. Sourced from Justice Ahmadi's private writings, 2015–2019.
16. Ibid.
17. Ibid.
18. Ibid.
19. Bar & Bench, Justice Rohinton Nariman on Free Speech, Slams BBC Ban and IT Raids, 2 March 2023, https://www.youtube.com/watch?v=3nnwaNpCfvs.
20. R. Subrahmanyam, Will Caste-based Surveys Lead to Both Inclusion, Exclusion?, *The Economic Times*, 5 October 2023, https://economictimes.indiatimes.com/news/india/will-caste-based-surveys-lead-to-both-inclusion-exclusion/articleshow/104168240.cms?from=mdr.
21. Planning Commission Government of India New Delhi, Report of the

Committee on India Vision 2020, 5 December 2022, https://py.gov.in/sites/default/files/indiavision2020.pdf.

22. Krishna Ananth, the Bumpy Road of Reservations: the 7 August 1990 Announcement on the Mandal Commission's Recommendations by V.P. Singh, https://www.thepolisproject.com/, 7 August 2021, https://www.thepolisproject.com/read/the-bumpy-road-of-reservations-the-7-august-1990-announcement-on-the-mandal-commissions-recommendations-by-v-p-singh/.
23. B.P. Jeevan Reddy, Indra Sawhney Etc. Etc vs. Union Of India And Others, Etc. Etc. https://indiankanoon.org/, 16 November 1992, https://indiankanoon.org/doc/1363234/.
24. Krishna Ananth, the Bumpy Road of Reservations: the 7 August 1990 Announcement on the Mandal Commission's Recommendations by V.P. Singh, https://www.thepolisproject.com/, 7 August 2021, https://www.thepolisproject.com/read/the-bumpy-road-of-reservations-the-7-august-1990-announcement-on-the-mandal-commissions-recommendations-by-v-p-singh/.
25. Ibid.
26. Ibid.
27. Govt. of India's Orders on Matters Concerning Other Backward Classes Including Issue of Caste Identification Certificates, Ministry of Personal, Public Greivances and Pensions, 13 August 1980, https://anagrasarkalyan.gov.in/documnts/07-07-2017-10-10-16.pdf.
28. 'Storm Created by Mandal Commission Poses Serious Threat to V.P. Singh's Political Survival', India Today, 30 September 2013, www.indiatoday.in/magazine/cover-story/story/19901015-storm-created-by-mandal-commission-poses-serious-threat-to-vp-singh-political-survival-813100-1990-10-14.
29. Krishna Ananth, the Bumpy Road of Reservations: the 7 August 1990 Announcement on the Mandal Commission's Recommendations by V.P. Singh, https://www.thepolisproject.com/, 7 August 2021, https://www.thepolisproject.com/read/the-bumpy-road-of-reservations-the-7-august-1990-announcement-on-the-mandal-commissions-recommendations-by-v-p-singh/.
30. 'Storm Created by Mandal Commission Poses Serious Threat to V.P. Singh's Political Survival', India Today, 30 September 2013, www.indiatoday.in/magazine/cover-story/story/19901015-storm-created-by-mandal-commission-poses-serious-threat-to-vp-singh-political-survival-813100-1990-10-14.
31. Ibid.
32. Team Frontline, 1990: Lal Krishna Advani Embarks on Rath Yatra, https://frontline.thehindu.com/, 15 August 2022, https://frontline.thehindu.com/

politics/india-at-75-epochal-moments-1990-lal-krishna-advani-embarks-on-rath-yatra/article65725588.ece.
33. Case Summary: Indra Sawhney Etc. vs. Union of India and Others 1992, LawLex.Org, https://lawlex.org/lex-bulletin/case-summary-indra-sawhney-etc-vs-union-of-india-and-others-1992/26399.
34. B.P. Jeevan Reddy, Indra Sawhney Etc. Etc vs. Union Of India And Others, Etc. Etc., https://indiankanoon.org/, 16 November 1992, https://indiankanoon.org/doc/1363234/.
35. M.G. Radhakrishnan, Stealing His March, *India Today*, 16 February 2009, https://www.indiatoday.in/magazine/radar/story/20090216-stealing-his-march-738951-2009-02-05.
36. Express News Service, Mandal Report Will Cleave Nation, *The Indian Express*, 3 May 1992, https://books.google.co.in/books?id=goJlAAAAIBAJ&printsec=frontcover&redir_esc=y#v=onepage&q&f=false.
37. B.P. Jeevan Reddy, Para 371 of Indra Sawhney Etc. Etc vs. Union Of India And Others, Etc. Etc., https://indiankanoon.org/, 16 November 1992, https://indiankanoon.org/doc/1363234/.
38. Ibid.
39. Ibid.
40. Express News Service, Mandal Report Will Cleave Nation, *The Indian Express*, 3 May 1992, https://books.google.co.in/books?id=goJlAAAAIBAJ&printsec=frontcover&redir_esc=y#v=onepage&q&f=false.
41. B.P. Jeevan Reddy, Para 277 of Indra Sawhney Etc. Etc vs. Union Of India And Others, Etc. Etc., https://indiankanoon.org/, 16 November 1992, https://indiankanoon.org/doc/1363234/
42. Ibid.
43. Ibid.
44. Ibid.
45. Ahmadi, A. M., Edited by Lokendra Malik and Manish Arora, Empowerment of Muslims Through the Constitution, The Chief Justice Speaks, Universal Law Publishing, LexisNexis, 2016.
46. A.M. Ahmadi, Life Insurance Corpn. Of India And . . . vs. Prof. Manubhai D. Shah Etc. Etc https://indiankanoon.org/, 22 July 1992, https://indiankanoon.org/doc/304068/.
47. Global Freedom of Expression, Life Insurance Corporation of India v. Manubhai - Global Freedom of Expression, https://globalfreedomofexpression.columbia.edu/cases/life-insurance-corporation-of-india-v-manubhai/.

48. Life Insurance Corpn. of India and . . . vs. Prof. Manubhai D. Shah Etc. Etc, https://indiankanoon.org/, 22 July 1992, https://indiankanoon.org/doc/304068/.
49. Ahmadi, A.M., Flow Of Thoughts: Selected Speeches, Lectures And Writings Of Justice A.M. Ahmadi (Former Chief Justice of India), Institute of Objective Studies, 2008, pp 399.
50. Ahmadi, A.M., *Flow Of Thoughts: Selected Speeches, Lectures And Writings Of Justice A.M. Ahmadi (Former Chief Justice of India)*, Institute of Objective Studies, 2008, pp 66.
51. M. Rahman, A.S. Vaidya: The Killing of a General, *India Today*, 31 August 1986, https://www.indiatoday.in/magazine/cover-story/story/19860831-former-army-chief-general-as-vaidya-assassinated-by-sikh-militants-in-pune-801208-1986-08-30.
52. Lalit Maken – Wikipedia, https://en.wikipedia.org/wiki/Assassination_of_Arjun_Dass.
53. Assassination of Arjun Dass – Wikipedia, https://en.wikipedia.org/wiki/Lalit_Maken.
54. Express News Service, SC Confirms Death Sentence on Vaidya Killers, *The Indian Express*, 3 May 1992, https://books.google.co.in/books?id=goJlAAAAI BAJ&printsec=frontcover&redir_esc=y#v=onepage&q&f=false.
55. September 18, 1992 – Sikh Heritage Education.
56. Ibid.
57. Express News Service, Sikh Leaders Petition SC to Save Vaidya Killers, *The Indian Express*, 3 May 1992, https://books.google.co.in/books?id=goJlAAAAI BAJ&printsec=frontcover&redir_esc=y#v=onepage&q&f=false.
58. Indian Kanoon, Karamjeet Singh vs. Union Of India, https://indiankanoon.org/, 8 October 1992, https://indiankanoon.org/doc/530853/.
59. Ibid.
60. Tim McGrik, Protests After Hanging of Sikhs, *The Independent*, 9 October 1992, https://www.independent.co.uk/news/world/protests-after-hanging-of-sikhs-1556488.html.
61. Retired Judges' Lifelong Security: Not a Status Symbol - India Legal (indialegallive.com), https://www.indialegallive.com/viewpoint/retired-judges-lifelong-security-not-a-status-symbol/attachment/justice-chapalgaonkar/.

8. The Ayodhya Matter

1. The Indian Express SC Cautions UP Government on Construction.
2. Mark Tran, Ayodhya: Guardian Coverage of the Babri Mosque Attack, *The*

Guardian, 30 September 2010, https://www.theguardian.com/world/2010/sep/28/ayodhya-mosque-india-guardian-report.
3. Manoj Mitta, BJP Stumps the Court, *India Today*, 15 November 1993, https://www.indiatoday.in/magazine/nation/story/19931115-supreme-court-judges-face-some-awkward-questions-over-babri-masjid-demolition-811772-1993-11-14.
4. Noorani, A.G., 'The Supreme Court and Demolition of the Babri Masjid', *CONSTITUTIONAL QUESTIONS AND CITIZENS' RIGHTS: An Omnibus Comprising Constitutional Questions in India and Citizens' Rights, Judges and State Accountability* (Delhi, 2006; online edn, Oxford Academic, 18 Oct. 2012), https://doi.org/10.1093/acprof:oso/9780195678291.003.0074.
5. Sagarika Ghose., As Most BJP Leaders Celebrated Fall of Babri Masjid, Atal Bihari Vajpayee Was Aghast, *The Wire*, 3 January 2022, https://thewire.in/books/atal-bihari-vajpayee-sagarika-ghose-book-extract.
6. The Wire Staff, Babri Masjid: The Timeline of a Demolition, *The Wire*, 6 December 2021, https://thewire.in/communalism/babri-masjid-the-timeline-of-a-demolition.
7. Sushant Talwar, Oldest Litigant of Babri Case Hashim Ansari Dies of Heart Ailment, https://www.thequint.com/, 20 July 2016, https://www.thequint.com/news/hot-news/oldest-litigant-of-babri-case-hashim-ansari-dies-of-heart-ailment.
8. Manoj Mitta, The judiciary, *India Today*, 21 December 2015, https://www.indiatoday.in/magazine/cover-story/story/20151221-india-today-40th-anniversary-manoj-mitta-the-judiciary-babri-masjid-820986-2015-12-10.
9. Vidya Subrahmaniam, Supreme Court Could Have Prevented Demolition of Babri Masjid, Says Ahmadi, *The Hindu*, 4 December 2021, https://www.thehindu.com/news/national/Supreme-Court-could-have-prevented-demolition-of-Babri-Masjid-says-Ahmadi/article13481392.ece.
10. December 31, 1992, *India Today*, https://www.indiatoday.in/magazine/31-12-1992.
11. Shirish Koyal, This Day 30 Years Ago, the Republic Was Besmirched, *The Wire*, 6 December 2022, https://thewire.in/communalism/this-day-30-years-ago-the-republic-was-besmirched.
12. Manoj Mitta, BJP Stumps the Court, *India Today*, 15 November 1993, https://www.indiatoday.in/magazine/nation/story/19931115-supreme-court-judges-face-some-awkward-questions-over-babri-masjid-demolition-811772-1993-11-14.
13. G.N. Ray, Mohd. Aslam vs. Union of India https://indiankanoon.org/, 24 October 1994, https://indiankanoon.org/doc/782772/.

14. Uday Mahurkar, Orchestrated Onslaught, *India Today*, 25 July 2013, https://www.indiatoday.in/magazine/cover-story/story/19921231-babri-masjid-demolation-was-orchestrated-according-to-an-action-plan-with-key-elements-767335-2013-01-22.
15. Zafar Agha, How Did Rao Blunder?, *India Today*, 31 December 1992, https://indiatoday.in/magazine/cover-story/story/19921231-babri-masjid-demolition-rao-failed-to-evolve-his-own-plans-to-counter-bjps-strategy-767324-2013-05-20.
16. Godbole, M., Ayodhya and India's Mahabharat: Constitutional Issues and Proprieties. *Economic and Political Weekly*, 2006, 41(21), 2072–2076, https://www.jstor.org/stable/pdf/4418261.pdf?refreqid=fastly-default%3A2858d3a25184eb00e882872896fdced3&ab_segments=&origin=&initiator=&acceptTC=1.
17. Sagarika Ghose., As Most BJP Leaders Celebrated Fall of Babri Masjid, Atal Bihari Vajpayee Was Aghast, *The Wire*, 3 January 2022, https://thewire.in/books/atal-bihari-vajpayee-sagarika-ghose-book-extract.
18. Nayar, K., *Beyond The Lines: An Autobiography*. Roli Books Private Limited, 2012.
19. Kuldip Singh, S.R. Bommai And Others Etc. Etc. vs. Union Of India And Others Etc. Etc., https://indiankanoon.org/, 11 March 1994, https://indiankanoon.org/doc/60799/.
20. Ibid.
21. Utkarsh Anand, Bommai Senior and the Legal Foundations of a Historic Verdict, *Hindustan Times*, 29 July 2021, https://www.hindustantimes.com/analysis/bommai-senior-and-the-legal-foundations-of-a-historic-verdict-101627539473703.html.
22. Kuldip Singh, S.R. Bommai And Others Etc. Etc. vs. Union Of India And Others Etc, https://indiankanoon.org/, 11 March 1994, https://indiankanoon.org/doc/60799/.
23. The Hindu Net Desk, What is the S.R. Bommai Case, and Why Is It Quoted Often?, *The Hindu*, 1 December 2021, https://www.thehindu.com/news/national/what-is-the-sr-bommai-case-and-why-is-it-quoted-often/article61834854.ece.
24. Kuldip Singh, S.R. Bommai And Others Etc. Etc. vs. Union Of India And Others Etc. Etc., https://indiankanoon.org/, 11 March 1994, https://indiankanoon.org/doc/60799/.
25. Utkarsh Anand, Bommai Senior and the Legal Foundations of a Historic Verdict, *Hindustan Times*, 29 July 2021, https://www.hindustantimes.com/analysis/bommai-senior-and-the-legal-foundations-of-a-historic-verdict-101627539473703.html.

26. Ibid.
27. Ibid.
28. The Hindu Net Desk, What is the S.R. Bommai Case, and Why Is It Quoted Often?, *The Hindu*, 1 December 2021, https://www.thehindu.com/news/national/what-is-the-sr-bommai-case-and-why-is-it-quoted-often/article61834854.ece.
29. Kuldip Singh, Para 301 S.R. Bommai vs. Union Of India, https://indiankanoon.org/, 11 March 1994, https://indiankanoon.org/doc/60799/.
30. Ibid.
31. Ibid.
32. Ibid.
33. Eastern Book Company - Practical Lawyer, https://www.ebc-india.com/lawyer/digest/.
34. Kuldip Singh, Para 149 S.R. Bommai vs. Union Of India, https://indiankanoon.org/, 11 March 1994, https://indiankanoon.org/doc/60799/.
35. The Hindu Net Desk, What is the S.R. Bommai Case, and Why Is It Quoted Often?, *The Hindu*, 1 December 2021, https://www.thehindu.com/news/national/what-is-the-sr-bommai-case-and-why-is-it-quoted-often/article61834854.ece.
36. Byju's, S.R. Bommai vs. Union of India Case for UPSC Indian Polity & Governance, byjus.com, https://byjus.com/free-ias-prep/bommai-case/#:~:text=SR%20Bommai%20Case%20Significance.
37. Eastern Book Company - Practical Lawyer, https://www.ebc-india.com/lawyer/digest/.
38. Indian Kanoon, Special Reference No. 1 Of 1993 vs. Ram Janma Bhumi-Babri Masjid Matter, https://indiankanoon.org/, 27 January 1993, https://indiankanoon.org/doc/188962496/.
39. Indian Kanoon, M. Ismail Faruqui and Ors. vs. Union of India and Ors., https://indiankanoon.org/, 24 October 1994, https://indiankanoon.org/doc/37494799/.
40. Ajaz Ashraf, RSS Chief's Comment is a Way of Influencing the Supreme Court on Ayodhya Dispute: Justice A.M. Ahmadi, Scroll, 3 December 2017, https://scroll.in/article/859843/rss-chiefs-comment-is-a-way-of-influencing-the-supreme-court-on-ayodhya-dispute-justice-am-ahmadi.
41. V. Venkatesan, The Excavation Order, *The Hindu*, 30 September 2010, https://www.thehindu.com/news/national/other-states/The-excavation-order/article16052940.ece.
42. Para 153 of MANU/SC/0860/1994.
43. Harinder Baweja, Resounding Rebuff, *India Today*, 30 November 1995, https://www.indiatoday.in/magazine/cover-story/story/19951130-resounding-rebuff-754307-1995-11-29.

44. Prabhash K. Dutta, When Congress Brought Ordinance for Ram Mandir at Ayodhya and BJP Opposed it, *India Today*, 30 October 2018, https://www.indiatoday.in/india/story/when-congress-brought-ordinance-for-ram-mandir-at-ayodhya-and-bjp-opposed-it-1378516-2018-10-30.
45. Sourced from Justice Ahmadi's private writings 2015–2019.
46. Para 142 of MANU/SC/0860/1994.
47. Para 144 of MANU/SC/0860/1994
48. S.R. Bommai v. Union of India MANU/SC/0444/1994 as cited in M. Ismail Frauqui & Ors V. Union of India & Ors. MANU/SC/0860/1994 Para 39 stated by B.P. Jeevan Reddy.
49. Para 155 of MANU/SC/0860/1994.
50. Ajaz Ashraf, RSS Chief's Comment is a Way of Influencing the Supreme Court on Ayodhya Dispute: Justice A.M. Ahmadi, Scroll, 3 December 2017, https://scroll.in/article/859843/rss-chiefs-comment-is-a-way-of-influencing-the-supreme-court-on-ayodhya-dispute-justice-am-ahmadi.
51. Sourced from Justice Ahmadi's private writings 2015–2019.
52. Ahmadi, A M., Edited by Lokendra Malik and Manish Arora, Reflections on Democracy, Rule of Law, Press Freedom, *The Chief Justice Speaks*, Universal Law Publishing, LexisNexis, 2016, pp 79.
53. Justice, V. and Prakash (n.d.). Landmark Judgments of the Supreme Court of India *Chairman Law Commission of Madhya Pradesh*, https://nja.gov.in/Concluded_Programmes/2019–20/SE-05_2019_PPTs/6.LANDMARK%20JUDGMENTS%20OF%20THE%20SUPREME%20COURT%20PLAIN.pdf.

9. Triumphs and Trials

1. *Article 124 and Article 217 of the Constitution of India.*
2. Anuradha Mukherjee, Should the Judges Cases Be Revisited? | India Corporate Law, https://corporate.cyrilamarchandblogs.com/, 27 February 2018, https://corporate.cyrilamarchandblogs.com/2018/02/judges-cases-revisited/.
3. P.N. Bhagwati, S.P. Gupta vs. President of India And Ors., https://indiankanoon.org/, 30 December 1981, https://indiankanoon.org/doc/1294854/.
4. Ibid.
5. Prachi Bhardwaj, Remembering Senior Advocate S.P. Gupta and His Crusade for Judicial Independence, https://www.scconline.com/blog/, 18 January 2022, https://www.scconline.com/blog/post/2022/01/18/a-walk-down-the-memory-lane-on-sp-guptas-senior-advocate-90th-birthday/.

6. J.S. Verma, Supreme Court ... vs. Union Of India https://indiankanoon.org/, 6 October 1993, https://indiankanoon.org/doc/753224/.
7. Revisiting the Appointment of Judges: Will the Executive Initiate a Change? on JSTOR.
8. J.S. Verma, Supreme Court ... vs. Union Of India, https://indiankanoon.org/, 6 October 1993, https://indiankanoon.org/doc/753224/.
9. Ibid.
10. Ibid.
11. Ahmadi, A.M., *Flow Of Thoughts: Selected Speeches, Lectures And Writings Of Justice A.M. Ahmadi (Former Chief Justice of India)*, Institute of Objective Studies, 2008.
12. J.S. Verma, Supreme Court ... vs. Union Of India, https://indiankanoon.org/, 6 October 1993, https://indiankanoon.org/doc/753224/.
13. Murali Krishnan, 24 Years and 20 Chief Justices Later, the Collegium Has Taken its First Step Towards Transparency, https://www.barandbench.com/, 7 October 2017, https://www.barandbench.com/columns/24-years-20-chief-justices-later-collegium-taken-first-step-towards-transparency.
14. Ahmadi, A.M., *The Chief Justice Speaks*, 2016, pp 106.
15. Cooke, R. (1998). Where Angels Fear to Tread. *SSRN Electronic Journal*, https://doi.org/10.2139/ssrn.2398661.
16. Seervai, Constitutional Law, p. 2928.
17. Chandrachud, Abhinav, 'The Judges Cases', *The Informal Constitution: Unwritten Criteria in Selecting Judges for the Supreme Court of India* (Delhi, 2014; online edn, Oxford Academic, 19 June 2014), https://doi.org/10.1093/acprof:oso/9780198098560.003.0002.
18. S.P. Bharucha, In Re: Under Article 143(1) of The ... vs. Unknown, https://indiankanoon.org/, 28 October 1998, https://indiankanoon.org/doc/543658/. https://indiankanoon.org/doc/543658/ n Re Special Reference 1 of 1998.
19. Ahmadi, A.M., *Flow Of Thoughts: Selected Speeches, Lectures And Writings Of Justice A.M. Ahmadi (Former Chief Justice of India)*, Institute of Objective Studies, 2008.
20. Sourced from Justice Ahmadi's private writings, 2015–2019.
21. https://www.scconline.com/blog/post/2022/10/26/appointment-of-supreme-court-and-high-court-judges-need-for-a-fresh-look/.
22. Rahel Philipose, Collegium vs. NJAC: What is the renewed Debate Over Appointment of Judges?, *The Indian Express*, 17 December 2022, https://indianexpress.com/article/explained/explained-law-judiciary-appointment-of-judges-collegium-system-njac-debate-explained-8329397/.

23. A saying by Seldon which means to vary from judge to judge.
24. Vijay Hansaria, Why Appointing Supreme Court, High Court Judges Through Closed-Door Collegiums is Flawed | OPINION, *India Today*, 7 February 2022, https://www.indiatoday.in/opinion-columns/story/appointing-supreme-court-high-court-judges-through-closed-door-collegiums-1909740-2022-02-07.
25. Gogoi, Ranjan., Justice for the Judge: An Autobiography. Rupa, 2021.
26. Ahmadi, A.M., *Flow Of Thoughts: Selected Speeches, Lectures And Writings Of Justice A.M. Ahmadi (Former Chief Justice of India)*, Institute of Objective Studies, 2008.
27. Sourced from Justice Ahmadi's private writings, 2015–2019.
28. P-944 Verbatim Report (9.11.15).pdf (nja.gov.in).
29. Amarnath K. Menon, Srisalim Dam: A Forced Exodus, *India Today*, 16 October 2014, https://www.indiatoday.in/magazine/special-report/story/19810731-srisailam-dam-across-krishna-river-displaces-nearly-100000-people-in-andhra-pradesh-773077-2013-11-16.
30. INDEX (upjsa.in).
31. Role of Lok Adalats (allahabadhighcourt.in).
32. Sourced from Justice Ahmadi's private writings, 2015–2019.
33. Eastern Book Company - Practical Lawyer (ebc-india.com).
34. Ahmadi, A.M. (2016). *The Chief Justice Speaks*, pp. 170.
35. https://indiankanoon.org/doc/60046619/.
36. Eastern Book Company - Practical Lawyer (ebc-india.com).
37. Ravindra Kumar Singh, Clinical Legal Educationn—A Robust Instrument for Attainment of Justice: An Indian Perspective, Sage Publications, 22 July 2022, https://journals.sagepub.com/doi/pdf/10.1177/09717218211030784.
38. Ahmadi, A.M., *The Chief Justice Speaks*, 2016, pp 171.
39. History Of National Judicial Academy Final(07-07-17).pdf (nja.gov.in).
40. National Judicial Academy | Department of Justice | India (doj.gov.in).
41. Wajahat Habibullah, *My Kashmir, The Dying of the Light*, Penguin, 22 September 2014.
42. Wajahat Habibullah, Siege: Hazratbal, Kashmir, 1993, India Review, 2002, 1:3, 73-98, DOI: 10.1080/14736480208404634.
43. Refworld | Amnesty International Report 1994 - India, https://www.refworld.org/reference/annualreport/amnesty/1994/en/24050.
44. Sourced from Justice Ahmadi's private writings 2015–2019.
45. Ibid.
46. ASIANOW - Asiaweek (cnn.com).

47. Indian Kanoon, State of J & K vs. J & K High Court Bar Association, https://indiankanoon.org/, 2 November 1993, https://indiankanoon.org/doc/134906887/.
48. Sourced from Justice Ahmadi's private writings, 2015–2019.
49. A.M. Ahmadi and B.L. Hansaria, Supreme Court Legal Aid Committee Representing Undertrial Prisoners v. Union of India and Ors., 7 October 1994, undertrial-prisoners-460682.pdf.
50. Shivendra Srivastava, Exposed: Up's Hell Prison Where Inmates Suffer Viscious Torture and Corruption, *India Today*, 8 September 2016, https://www.indiatoday.in/india/story/exposed-ups-hell-prison-where-inmates-suffer-vicious-torture-and-corruption-339802-2016-09-07.
51. A.M. Ahmadi and B.L. Hansaria, Supreme Court Legal Aid Committee Representing Undertrial Prisoners v. Union of India and Ors., 7 October 1994, undertrial-prisoners-460682.pdf.

10. The Chief's Chair

1. Justice Ahmadi served as India's third Muslim Chief Justice, preceded by Mohammad Hidayatullah in 1968 and Mirza Hamidullah Beg in 1978.
2. The former Chief Justice of India, A.M. Ahmadi interviewed by Bar & Bench (barandbench.com), 7 August 2014, https://www.barandbench.com/interviews/conversation-former-chief-justice-india-aziz-mushabber.
3. Sourced from Justice Ahmadi's private writings, 2015–2019.
4. Thiruvengadam, Arun K. (2015). Tribunals. In Sujit Choudhry, Madhav Khosla and Pratap Bhanu Mehta (eds.). *The Oxford Handbook of the Indian Constitution*. OUP. pp. 412–431, https://ssrn.com/abstract=2872636.
5. Sourced from Justice Ahmadi's private writings, 2015–2019.
6. ADR and Court Automation, Ahmadi, A.M., *The Chief Justice Speaks*, 2016.
7. The former Chief Justice of India, AM Ahmadi interviewed by Bar & Bench, 7 August 2014, https://www.barandbench.com/interviews/conversation-former-chief-justice-india-aziz-mushabber.
8. Hiram E. Chodosh, Stephen A. Mayo, A.M. Ahmadi and Abhishek M. Singhvi, Indian Civil Justice System Reform: Limitation and Preservation of the Adversarial Process, 30 N.Y.U. J. INT'L L. & POL. 1, 1998.
9. Rediff On The NeT: Judicial management essential to reduce case backlog says Justice Ahmadi.

10. Thiruvengadam., Arun K., Tribunals (June 14, 2016). Sujit Choudhry, Madhav Khosla and Pratap Bhanu Mehta (eds.), *The Oxford Handbook of the Indian Constitution* (OUP, 2015), pp. 412-431, https://ssrn.com/abstract=2872636.
11. Sourced from Justice Ahmadi's personal writings, 2015–2019.
12. Ibid.
13. Sourced from Justice Ahmadi's personal writings, 2015–2019.
14. Co-relation Between Mediation and Case Management, https://lawcommissionofindia.nic.in/archive_goto/.
15. Comparison Between Judicial Processes and Various ADR Processes, https://districts.ecourts.gov.in/sites/default/files/Familycourtwrkshopiv.pdf.
16. Sourced from Justice Ahmadi's personal writings, 2015–2019.
17. Nilofer D' Souza, The Make-Up Artist of Indian Courtrooms, *Forbes India*, 7 December 2010, https://www.forbesindia.com/article/real-issue/the-makeup-artist-of-indian-courtrooms/19882/1.
18. P-1198 Report.pdf (thc.nic.in).
19. Development of Mediation in India : A Brief History | Via Mediation Centre.
20. L&L Partners Law Offices, The Evolution of Section 89 C.P.C Through Various Amendments, https://libertatem.in/, 25 August 2020, https://libertatem.in/articles/the-evolution-of-section-89-c-p-c-through-various-amendments/
21. cdn-legacy.iclrs.org/content/events/31/1012.mp3.
22. Table of Contents – Issues 1 & 2 30 *New York University Journal of International Law and Politics 1997-1998* (heinonline.org).
23. cdn-legacy.iclrs.org/content/events/31/1012.mp3.
24. Ahmadi, A.M., *Flow Of Thoughts: Selected Speeches, Lectures And Writings Of Justice A.M. Ahmadi (Former Chief Justice of India)*, Institute of Objective Studies, 2008, pp. 256.
25. Relevance of Technology in Courts System, *The Chief Justice Speaks*, 2016, pp 259.
26. Department of Legal Affairs, (2023). Disposal of Cases Through Mediation Centres. Ministry of Law and Justice, Government of India, 2023, https://legalaffairs.gov.in/sites/default/files/AU3903.pdf.
27. From an interview I conducted with Arun Thiruvengadam, Professor of Law, NLSUI.
28. Indian Kanoon, Constitution Article, https://indiankanoon.org/, https://indiankanoon.org/doc/950881/.
29. Contextualising Ashok Lavasa's dissents: A legal history of T.N. Seshan v Union of India – Law School Policy Review & Kautilya Society.
30. economictimes.indiatimes.com, TN Seshan's Bold Initiatives Led India's Game

Changing Electoral Reforms, *The Economic Times*, 11 November 2019, https://economictimes.indiatimes.com/news/politics-and-nation/tn-seshans-bold-initiatives-led-indias-game-changing-electoral-reforms/articleshow/72002688.cms?from=mdr.

31. Sanya Dhingra, 'Only God or TN Seshan' — Why Politicians Feared the ex-CEC Who Was an Inspiration to Many, *The Print*, 11 November 2019, https://theprint.in/india/only-god-or-tn-seshan-why-politicians-feared-the-ex-cec-who-was-an-inspiration-to-many/319134/.
32. Anand Vardhan, TN Seshan: The Crusader and Newsmaker India Needed in the 1990s, Newslaubdry.com, 12 November 2019, https://www.newslaundry.com/2019/11/12/t-n-seshan-obituary.
33. Sanya Dhingra, 'Only God or TN Seshan' — Why Politicians Feared the ex-CEC Who Was an Inspiration to Many, *The Print*, 11 November 2019, https://theprint.in/india/only-god-or-tn-seshan-why-politicians-feared-the-ex-cec-who-was-an-inspiration-to-many/319134/.
34. T.E. Narasimhan, T. N. Seshan, the Unyielding Force That Cleansed India's Elections (thewire.in), 11 November 2019, https://thewire.in/government/tn-seshan-election-commissioner.
35. Forever courting controversy - India Today
36. Indo-Asian News Service, A No-nonsence Man, TN Sesham Cleaned Up India's Electoral System, *India Today*, 4 April 2022, https://www.indiatoday.in/india/story/tn-seshan-no-nonsense-man-tn-seshan-cleaned-up-india-electoral-system-1617702-2019-11-11.
37. Manoj Mitta, Reined In, For Now, *India Today*, 10 November 2012, https://www.indiatoday.in/magazine/nation/story/19941130-zzz-764879-2012-11-10.
38. Ibid.
39. K.M.Joseph,Anoop Baranwal Versus Union ofIndia,1458_2015_3_1501_42634_Judgement_02-Mar-2023.pdf (sci.gov.in).
40. It takes three to tango, *India Today*.
41. Case Study: T.N. Seshan V. Union Of India, *Desi Kaanoon*.
42. T.N.Seshan Chief Election ... vs. Union Of India & Ors on 14 July, 1995 (indiankanoon.org).
43. Contextualising Ashok Lavasa's dissents: A legal history of T.N. Seshan v Union of India – Law School Policy Review & Kautilya Society.
44. A.M. Ahmadi, T.N.Seshan Chief Election ... vs. Union Of India & Ors, https://indiankanoon.org/, 14 July 1995, https://indiankanoon.org/doc/1890680/.
45. Table of Precedence, 26 July 1979, https://www.mha.gov.in/sites/default/files/

table_of_precedence.pdf.
46. A.M. Ahmadi, T.N. Seshan Chief Election … vs. Union Of India & Ors, https://indiankanoon.org/, 14 July 1995, https://indiankanoon.org/doc/1890680/.
47. Article 319 of the Indian Constitution lays out the rules and regulations regarding the prohibition of holding certain offices by members of a commission once they cease to be members. This provision serves to ensure the integrity and independence of commissions and prevent conflicts of interest.
48. A.M. Ahmadi, Election Commission Of India & … vs. Dr. Subramanian Swamy & Another, https://indiankanoon.org/, 23 April 1996, https://indiankanoon.org/doc/1679128/.
49. Amit Agrahari, The Story of Subramanian Swamy's Friendship With Former CEC TN Seshan, https://tfipost.com/, 12 November 2019, https://tfipost.com/2019/11/the-story-of-subramanian-swamys-friendship-with-former-cec-tn-seshan/.
50. A.M. Ahmadi, Election Commission Of India & … vs. Dr. Subramanian Swamy & Another, https://indiankanoon.org/, 23 April 1996, https://indiankanoon.org/doc/1679128/.
51. T.N.M., When Subramanian Swamy Turned his Attention to an Old Enemy and Friend – J Jayalalithaa, https://www.thenewsminute.com/, 10 May 2015, https://www.thenewsminute.com/tamil-nadu/when-subramanian-swamy-turned-his-attention-old-enemy-and-friend-j-jayalalithaa-30587.
52. Ajith Pillai, By Hook or By Crook, *India Today*, 15 May 1995, https://www.indiatoday.in/magazine/indiascope/story/19950515-jayalalitha-government-pulls-out-all-the-stops-to-get-back-at-subramanian-swamy-807261-1995-05-14
53. Sourced from Justice Ahmadi's private writings, 2015–2019.
54. A.M. Ahmadi, Balaji Raghavan/S.P. Anand vs. Union Of India, https://indiankanoon.org/, 15 December 1995, https://indiankanoon.org/doc/1882300/.
55. Indian Kanoon, Bobby Art International, Etc vs. Om Pal Singh Hoon & Ors, https://indiankanoon.org/, 1 May 1996, https://indiankanoon.org/doc/1400858/.
56. Ahmadi, A.M., *Flow Of Thoughts: Selected Speeches, Lectures And Writings Of Justice A.M. Ahmadi (Former Chief Justice of India)*, Institute of Objective Studies, 2008, pp. 147.
57. A.M. Ahmadi, National Human Rights Commission vs. State Of Arunachal Pradesh & Anr, https://indiankanoon.org/, 9 January 1996, https://indiankanoon.org/doc/767216/.
58. The Question of Citizenship: Chakma and Hajong vs. State of Arunachal

Pradesh | NewsClick.
59. A.M. Ahmadi, State Of Maharashtra And Another vs. Madhukar Narayan Mardikar, https://indiankanoon.org/, 23 October 1990, https://indiankanoon.org/doc/524900/.
60. Spindel, Chewa, et al., With an End in Sight: Strategies from the UNIFEM Trust Fund to Eliminate Violence Against Women, United Nations Development Fund for Women, 2000.
61. Report of the Workshop on Gender Justice : Forging Partnership with Law Enforcement Agencies | National Commission for Women (ncw.nic.in), http://ncw.nic.in/content/report-workshop-gender-justice-forging-partnership-law-enforcement-agencies.
62. Ahmadi, A.M., *Flow Of Thoughts: Selected Speeches, Lectures And Writings Of Justice A.M. Ahmadi (Former Chief Justice of India)*, Institute of Objective Studies, 2008. p. 374.
63. L. Chandra Kumar vs. Union Of India And Others on 18 March, 1997 (indiankanoon.org).
64. Ibid.
65. *Peter Ronald deSouza, Professor at the Centre for the Study of Developing Societies, Delhi.*
66. Sourced from Justice Ahmadi's private writings, 2015–2019.

11. The Bhopal Gas Case: Courage Under Fire

1. S.B. Majumdar, Keshub Mahindra vs. State Of M.P, https://indiankanoon.org/, 13 September 1996, https://indiankanoon.org/doc/1810324/.
2. Ibid.
3. IPC Section 304 - Punishment for culpable homicide not amounting to murder | Devgan.in.
4. Headlines Today, Bhopal gas tragedy: How Warren Anderson got away from our grasp, *India Today*, 1 November 2014, https://www.indiatoday.in/india/north/story/bhopal-gas-tragedy-warren-anderson-union-carbide-dow-chemicals-rajiv-gandhi-congress-arjun-singh-225398-2014-11-01.
5. Liu Chuen Chen, Who is Adil Shahryar and How Does He Know Rajiv Gandhi?, *India Today*, 13 August 2015, https://www.indiatoday.in/fyi/story/who-is-adil-shahryar-and-how-does-he-know-rajiv-gandhi-287985-2015-08-12.
6. Business and Human Rights (ielrc.org).
7. Asian Yearbook of International Law, Volume 3 (Ko Swan Sik et al., eds.;

0-7923-2708-X; © 1994 Kluwer Academic Publishers; printed in Great Britain), pp. 163-179.
8. Ibid.
9. https://www.repository.law.indiana.edu/cgi/viewcontent.cgi?article=3946&context=facpub.
10. R.S. Pathak, Union Carbide Corporation vs. Union Of India And Others, Etc, https://indiankanoon.org/, 14 February 1989, https://indiankanoon.org/doc/654007/.
11. Sabyasachi Mukharji, Charan Lal Sahu Etc. Etc vs. Union Of India And Ors https://indiankanoon.org/, 22 December 1989, https://indiankanoon.org/doc/299215/.
12. Asian Yearbook of International Law, Volume 3 (Ko Swan Sik et al., eds.; 0-7923-2708-X; © 1994 Kluwer Academic Publishers; printed in Great Britain), pp. 163-179.
13. Union Carbide Corporation and Ors. vs. Union of India (UOI) and Ors. (03.10.1991 - SC).
14. Ibid.
15. Ibid.
16. Express News Service, Former Union Carbide CEO Warren Anderson Dies, *The Indian Express*, 1 November 2014, https://indianexpress.com/article/india/india-others/bhopal-gas-tragedy-fugitive-warren-anderson-dies-survivors-say-he-died-unpunished/.
17. S.B. Majumdar, Keshub Mahindra vs. State Of M.P, https://indiankanoon.org/, 13 September 1996, https://indiankanoon.org/doc/1810324/.
18. PTI, Former CJI Defends Verdict in Bhopal Gas Case, *Times of India*, 8 June 2010, https://timesofindia.indiatimes.com/india/former-cji-defends-verdict-in-bhopal-gas-case/articleshow/6024676.cms.
19. Sourced from Justice Ahmadi's private writings 2015- 2019.
20. Gas Tragedy, an Eye Witness, Google Books.
21. Jamal Ayub, Ex-CJI Offers His Services For Bhopal Gas Hospital, *Times of India*, 24 January 2020, https://timesofindia.indiatimes.com/city/bhopal/ex-cji-offers-his-services-for-bhopal-gas-hospital/articleshow/73569385.cms.
22. C.B.I. & Ors. vs. Keshub Mahindra etc. etc. (latestlaws.com), https://www.latestlaws.com/latest-caselaw/2011/may/2011-latest-caselaw-395-sc.
23. ET Bureau, SC to Examine Ahmadi's Bhopal Verdict, *The Economic Times*, 1 September 2010, https://economictimes.indiatimes.com/news/politics-and-nation/sc-to-examine-ahmadis-bhopal-verdict/articleshow/6471691.

cms?from=mdr.
24. Jamal Ayub, Percival Junior Sees No Closure In Bhopal Gas Disaster, *Times of India*, 4 December 2014, https://timesofindia.indiatimes.com/city/bhopal/percival-junior-sees-no-closure-in-bhopal-gas-disaster/articleshow/45369809.cms.
25. Jamal Ayub, Ex-CJI Offers His Services For Bhopal Gas Hospital, *Times of India*, 24 January 2020, https://timesofindia.indiatimes.com/city/bhopal/ex-cji-offers-his-services-for-bhopal-gas-hospital/articleshow/73569385.cms.
26. Swatanter Kumar, Bhopal Gas Peedith Mahila . . . vs. U.O.I. & Ors, https://indiankanoon.org/, 9 August 2012, https://indiankanoon.org/doc/178436640/.
27. Jamal Ayub, Ex-CJI Offers His Services For Bhopal Gas Hospital, *Times of India*, 24 January 2020, https://timesofindia.indiatimes.com/city/bhopal/ex-cji-offers-his-services-for-bhopal-gas-hospital/articleshow/73569385.cms.

12. Beyond the Bench

1. International Commission of Jurists, *Fact-Finding/Needs Assessment Mission to Liberia*, https://www.icj.org/wp-content/uploads/1998/05/Liberia-human-rights-fact-finding-mission-report-1998-eng.pdf.
2. Ibid.
3. Ibid.
4. Sourced from Justice Ahmadi's private writings, 2015–2019.
5. International Commission of Jurists, *Fact-Finding/Needs Assessment Mission to Liberia*, https://www.icj.org/wp-content/uploads/1998/05/Liberia-human-rights-fact-finding-mission-report-1998-eng.pdf.
6. ReliefWeb, Report of the International Commission of Inquiry on East Timor, 31 January 2000, https://reliefweb.int/report/indonesia/report-international-commission-inquiry-east-timor.
7. Sourced from Justice Ahmadi's private writings, 2015–2019.
8. ReliefWeb, Report of the International Commission of Inquiry on East Timor, 31 January 2000, https://reliefweb.int/report/indonesia/report-international-commission-inquiry-east-timor.
9. Sourced from Justice Ahmadi's private writings, 2015–2019.
10. ReliefWeb, Report of the International Commission of Inquiry on East Timor, 31 January 2000, https://reliefweb.int/report/indonesia/report-international-commission-inquiry-east-timor.
11. House of Commons - Foreign Affairs - Appendices to the Minutes of Evidence

(parliament.uk).
12. Zimbabwean Rule of Law in 'Gravest Peril' Say Lawyers, *The New Humanitarian*, 23 April 2001, https://www.thenewhumanitarian.org/news/2001/04/23/zimbabwean-rule-law-%E2%80%98gravest-peril%E2%80%99-say-lawyers.
13. Sourced from Justice Ahmadi's private writings, 2015–2019.
14. Ibid.
15. Zimbabwean Rule of Law in 'Gravest Peril' Say Lawyers, *The New Humanitarian*, 23 April 2001, https://www.thenewhumanitarian.org/news/2001/04/23/zimbabwean-rule-law-%E2%80%98gravest-peril%E2%80%99-say-lawyers.
16. Ibid.
17. Sankar Sen, New Law May Tighten Govt's Control Over NHRC, *The Tribune*, 22 August 2019, https://www.tribuneindia.com/news/archive/comment/new-law-may-tighten-govts-control-over-nhrc-820866#goog_rewarded.
18. Annual Report 1998–99, National Human Rights Commission, https://nhrc.nic.in/sites/default/files/Annual%20Report%201998-99.pdf.
19. Rajindar Sachar, Ignoring Human Rights, *Times of India*, 6 May 2006, https://timesofindia.indiatimes.com/edit-page/ignoring-human-rights/articleshow/1567373.cms.
20. Sankar Sen, New Law May Tighten Govt's Control Over NHRC, *The Tribune*, 22 August 2019, https://www.tribuneindia.com/news/archive/comment/new-law-may-tighten-govts-control-over-nhrc-820866#goog_rewarded.
21. Ibid.
22. Rajindar Sachar, Ignoring Human Rights, *Times of India*, 6 May 2006, https://timesofindia.indiatimes.com/edit-page/ignoring-human-rights/articleshow/1567373.cms.
23. Tahir Mahmood, Tahir Mahmood writes: Chief Justice Aziz Ahmadi, a Gentleman on the Bench, *The Indian Express*, 6 March 2023, https://indianexpress.com/article/opinion/columns/chief-justice-aziz-ahmadi-gentleman-on-bench-8477651/.
24. AMU Minority Status - Supreme Court Observer (scobserver.in).
25. Akhtar, S. (2009). Aligarh Muslim University, a 'Minority Institution' – Agitation, Legislation and the Law Courts, 1965–2009. *Proceedings of the Indian History Congress*, 70, 1169–1180, https://www.jstor.org/stable/44147761.
26. AMU is a Minority Institution: Justice AM Ahmadi, Radiance Weekly, https://radianceweekly.net/amu-is-a-minority-institution-justice-am-ahmadi/.
27. Ahmadi, A.M., *Flow Of Thoughts: Selected Speeches, Lectures And Writings Of*

Justice A.M. Ahmadi (Former Chief Justice of India), Institute of Objective Studies, 2008, pp. 283.
28. Ibid. pp. 319.
29. Tahir Mahmood, Tahir Mahmood writes: Chief Justice Aziz Ahmadi, a Gentleman on the Bench, *The Indian Express*, 6 March 2023, https://indianexpress.com/article/opinion/columns/chief-justice-aziz-ahmadi-gentleman-on-bench-8477651/.
30. Shreeya Sinha, Mark Suppes, Timeline of the Riots in Modi's Gujarat, *The New York Times*, 19 August 2015, https://www.nytimes.com/interactive/2014/04/06/world/asia/modi-gujarat-riots-timeline.html#/#time287_8514.
31. Ghassem-Fachandi, P. (2012). *Pogrom in Gujarat: Hindu Nationalism and Anti-Muslim Violence in India.* Princeton University Press. https://doi.org/10.2307/j.ctt7t0nz.
32. The Fundamentalist Mindset, Google Books.
33. Shreeya Sinha, Mark Suppes, Timeline of the Riots in Modi's Gujarat, *The New York Times*, 19 August 2015, https://www.nytimes.com/interactive/2014/04/06/world/asia/modi-gujarat-riots-timeline.html#/#time287_8514.
34. 'We Have No Orders To Save You': State Participation and Complicity in Communal Violence in Gujarat, Human Rights Watch, April 2002, India0402.pdf, hrw.org.
35. Ibid.
36. Tarushi Aswani, 'They Burnt My Parents Alive': Gujarat Riots Still Haunt Victims, thediplomat.com, 21 April 2022, https://thediplomat.com/2022/04/they-burnt-my-parents-alive-gujarat-riots-still-haunt-victims/#:~:text=He%20explains%20that%20the%20rioters.
37. Praveen Swami, Saffron Terror, https://frontline.thehindu.com/, 16 March 2002, https://frontline.thehindu.com/cover-story/article30244258.ece.
38. Sourced from Justice Ahmadi's private writings, 2015--2019.
39. Shreeya Sinha, Mark Suppes, Timeline of the Riots in Modi's Gujarat, The New York Times, 19 August 2015, https://www.nytimes.com/interactive/2014/04/06/world/asia/modi-gujarat-riots-timeline.html#/#time287_8514.
40. The Wire Staff, 'Wherever Muslims Live . . .': Text of Vajpayee's Controversial Goa Speech, April 2002, The Wire, 17 August 2018, https://thewire.in/communalism/vajpayees-goa-speech-april-2002.
41. Shreeya Sinha, Mark Suppes, Timeline of the Riots in Modi's Gujarat, *The New York Times*, 19 August 2015, https://www.nytimes.com/interactive/2014/04/06/world/asia/modi-gujarat-riots-timeline.html#/#time287_8514.
42. Amy Waldman, Hindu Nationalists Win Landslide Vote in Indian State, *The New York Times*, 16 December 2002, https://www.nytimes.com/2002/12/16/

world/hindu-nationalists-win-landslide-vote-in-indian-state.html.
43. Vinod K. Jose, Narendra Modi's Shadow Lies All Over the Haren Pandya Case, *The Caravan*, 6 July 2019, https://caravanmagazine.in/politics/haren-pandya-narendra-modi-murder-case-supreme-court.
44. Nandini Sundar, Setalvad, Sreekumar's Real 'Crime' Was Raising the Question of Modi's Command Responsibility, the *Wire*, 5 July 2022, https://thewire.in/rights/setalvad-sreekumars-real-crime-was-raising-the-question-of-command-responsibility.
45. 'We Have No Orders To Save You': State Participation and Complicity in Communal Violence in Gujarat, Human Rights Watch, April 2002, India0402.pdf, hrw.org.
46. Ahamdi, A.M., Civil Liberties in Crisis, *The Chief Justice Speaks*, 2016, pp. 165.
47. Ahmadi, A.M., Dimensions of Judicial Activism, *The Chief Justice Speaks*, 2016, pp. 186.
48. Ahmadi, A.M., Minority Rights in India, *The Chief Justice Speaks*, 2016, pp. 72–75.
49. Ahmadi, A.M., *Flow Of Thoughts: Selected Speeches, Lectures And Writings Of Justice A.M. Ahmadi (Former Chief Justice of India)*, Institute of Objective Studies, 2008, pp. 255.
50. Ibid.
51. Ibid.
52. Ibid.
53. NHS Bureau, From the Archives: Politics, Secularism and Democracy, *National Herald*, 7 September 2019, https://www.nationalheraldindia.com/archives/from-the-archives-politics-secularism-and-democracy.
54. Ahmadi, A.M., Civil Liberties in Crisis, *The Chief Justice Speaks.*, 2016, pp. 164.
55. Press Release, Statement to Press Following Bombay High Court Single-Bench Judgement, 25 April 2024, https://www.fatemidawat.com/news/press-releases/statement-to-press-following-bombay-high-court-single-bench-judgement.

Author's Note

When I first embarked upon this project, I was, quite frankly, not prepared for the depth of what I would uncover. I assumed that documenting the life of my grandfather would be easy, almost intuitive. But I had underestimated the richness and complexity of his life, the nature and weight of the decisions he had had to take, and many subtleties of which I had no knowledge at the time. And so, writing this biography has been a journey of discovery for me. As I dove into his life's work, furiously rifling through sheaves of papers and poring over hundreds of pages of judgements, I unearthed not only the legal acumen that defined him professionally but also intricate nuances of his character and beliefs. I found perspectives on matters we never had the chance to discuss when he was alive, and fragments of his personality – poignantly bittersweet in their familiarity. Embedded within his legal writings was also his mettle, unafraid to walk his path alone if necessary, and his refusal to yield to pressure.

I could see that he had approached his role as a jurist not as a mere profession but as a calling, a service – an opportunity to make a difference in the lives of ordinary citizens. An opportunity to make his life count.

With each judgement I read, I was drawn deeper into his world – the world he had inhabited and influenced for thirty-three years. Through his judgements, I met the towering figure revered by the legal community. I glimpsed moments of compassion, empathy and moral fortitude – qualities that had resonated deeply with the grandfather I knew and loved. I hope this book will offer this to you, too.

This story of a man from a minority community starting from humble beginnings and rising to the pinnacle of the Indian judiciary has been pieced together through Justice Ahmadi's personal writings, public speeches, archival research, intimate interviews and family recollections. It is my intention that this biography not only provides an insight into the extraordinary jurist who once lived, but also offers a glimpse into the mind of the man behind the robe.

Now that the final curtain has drawn to a close, let us remember Justice Ahmadi not only for his legal brilliance and fearless integrity, but also for the warmth of his smile, the kindness of his heart and the impact he had on all those who had the opportunity to interact with and learn from him. Let us look not only to the past but also to the future – one in which Justice Ahmadi's ideals of justice, fairness and equality shall prevail. Let us be reminded, also, of the profound impact that one individual can have on the course of history and the lives of those they touch.

May *The Fearless Judge* stay with you long after you've turned the final page.

Acknowledgements

Writing this biography has been far from a solitary endeavour; it has been a collaborative effort over almost a year, enriched by the support and expertise of numerous individuals. As they say, 'It takes a village.'

To my village, to whom I owe a debt of gratitude:

First and foremost, my family. The memories of Justice Ahmadi's children – my mother Tasneem Ahmadi and uncle Huzefa Ahmadi, without whom this book would be only half as rich and meaningful. Their patience, support and legal expertise as they recounted family memories and helped me unravel legal complexities have been invaluable. Without their guidance and input, this book would lack the depth and significance it now holds. My aunt, Insia Ahmadi, ever ready and willing to answer my endless stream of questions. My great uncle and great aunt, Yusuf and Hani Muchhala, through whom I discovered my grandfather's childhood and youth.

To my most ardent supporter and astute critic, my husband, Shaurya Roy, for being my anchor during this emotional journey of chronicling the life of my dear grandfather. And for sharing my passion and sense of purpose in bringing this story to life. Together, we have pored over hundreds of pages of judgements, reports and research, engaged in countless conversations, and discovered the details that have breathed life into this narrative. As I embarked upon this deeply personal project, Shaurya's unexpected research skills too proved a delightful surprise, enriching the story in ways I could not have anticipated.

A special acknowledgement is due to Pragya Rathi, my talented legal research assistant, for her tireless dedication. Her long days and late nights spent immersed in archival research materials are deeply appreciated. Through her meticulous attention to detail, she has safeguarded the accuracy, complexity and integrity of the narrative.

My warm thanks to Dr Arun Thiruvengadam, Professor of Law at NLSUI and India's very first judicial clerk, for his generosity in sharing his memories, time and advice. My heartfelt gratitude, also, to Mr Wajahat Habibullah, India's first Chief Information Commissioner for his insights and recollections of Justice Ahmadi on the bench.

For their invaluable memories and inputs, my great uncles Ishaq Merchant and Ismail Nazir, my great aunts Nafisa Khapra and Sophie Kothari and my great grand aunt Zakia Ahmadi. Esteemed Justices S. P. Bharucha, R.A. Mehta, Manju Goel, Kaushal Thaker and members of the Gujarat Bar, especially Unmesh Shukla, Sudhir Nanavati, Nirupam Nanavati, Shirish Sanjanwala, Kirtikant Nanavati, Suhel Tirmizi, Amar and Priya Bhatt.

Justice Ahmadi's former personal secretaries, Mr Harish Bhateja and Mr Kewal Krishan, for all their assistance, as well as Mr Aziz Siddiqui, former working trustee of the Bhopal Memorial Hospital Trust.

This biography would not have been possible without the collective contributions of each of these individuals. Thank you all for believing in this project and for being part of this journey.

Between us, we have put together a piece of history.

Index

aarti, 68
Acquisition of Certain Area at Ayodhya Act, 153–60
Act 19 of 1986, 219
Act 51 of 1987, 220
Adivasi Forest and Land rights, 93
Adivasis
    bamboo and, 92–3
    to collect forest produce, 92–3
    of Gujarat, 85–94
    Kotwalias, 92–4
    rights of, 92–4
    Vansfodias, 92–4
adjudicatory system, 218–23
Administrative Tribunals Act, 1985 (Act 13 of 1985), 218–19
ADM Jabalpur vs. Shivkant Shukla case, 75
Advani, L.K., 71, 115–16, 136, 141, 143
Agrawal, S.C., 149, 169
Ahmadi, Ali Asghar, 271
Ahmadi, Amena, 24, 26–30, 40, 38, 47–8, 81–2, 123–5, 174, 196, 240, 273–6, 279
Ahmadi, Aziz Mushabber, 1–3, 9–10, 17–20, 32, 99, 117, 149, 153, 163–5, 281–2
    as administrator of temples, 67–70
    agitation against appointment of, 41–2
    on Allauddin vs. State of Bihar case, 46–7
    appointment to Bench, 40
    on Ayodhya matter, 143, 153–61
    on Bandit Queen's certification, 213–14
    on Bhopal gas tragedy case, 230–9
    on binding decisions, 54–5
    birth, 2–3
    boldness, 54–5
    bungalow of, 81–2
    career, 20–4 (*See also specific positions and cases*)
    as case-cracker, 51
    as Chairman of the Advisory Board, 101
    as Chairman of the Bhopal Memorial Hospital Trust, 223
    as Chairman of Third Pay Commission of Gujarat, 101
    as Chairmanship of BMHT, 235–8
    chamber, 23
    as Chancellor of Aligarh Muslim University, 31, 251–5
    as Chief Justice of India, 21, 35, 51, 104–36, 188–224
    childhood memories, 3
    children, 171–5
    chronic lymphocytic leukemia, diagnosed with, 277–8
    as Citizen's Judge, 81–104, 111
    at City Civil Court, 50–1
    civil law, practising of, 37

314 Index

on Collegium system, 163–71
commitment towards women's rights, 216–18
compensation, judgement on, 94–6
competence, establishing his, 50–8
cousins, 6–7
criminal law, practising of, 36–7
cruel practices, witness of, 8
death sentence judgement, 47
delegation to UK, 170
Divan, B.J., meeting with, 59–62
Doctor of Laws (Honoris Causa), honorary degree of, 196
elevated to High Court, 80
to evaluate judicial system in Liberia, 242–3
as Executive Chairman of Lok Adalats, 53–4, 175–9
faced challenges of perception, 50–8
father, 7, 9–10, 198–9
favourite pranks, 10–11
foresight, 89
friends, 20–1, 48
Gandhiji and, 6
grandfather, 6–7
Hindu law, understanding of, 50
as Honorary Government Pleader, 37
on human rights, 248–50
Indo-British Forum Exchanges, participated in, 177–8
international bodies requests for, 241–2
judgements, 43–7, 52–4, 88–9, 92–6, 133–6, 150–2, 210–11, 218–24 (*See also specific cases*)
as judge of Supreme Court, 163–87
judgeship offer to, 39–40
on Judicial Reforms, 195
knowledge from foreign courts and systems, 195–6
at L.A. Shah Law College, Ahmedabad, 19
on L. Chandra Kumar vs. Union of India case, 218–21, 223
lawyer, career as, 20–3
legacy, 222
love for *shayari*, 269–70
meeting with Shelat, J. M., 38–9
on minorities' educational rights, 251–3
mischief, 10–11
in mission for judicial reforms to Bangladesh, 248
mother, 8–9, 199
Muchhala brothers and, 28
Muslim identity, 16, 42, 50, 80, 96, 212, 255
on Narcotics Drugs and Psychotropic Substances Act, 186–7
National Emergency and, 71–6
obsession with cricket, 17–18
opinion on reservations, 113
partition of Indian memories, 13–16
perforated peptic ulcer, diagnosed as, 101–2
pilgrimage of Hajj, 256–7
on PILs of migrant workers exploitation, 84–92
on President's Proclamation under Article 356, 149–52
prestigious events experienced by, 77
on problem of case pendency, 190–6
relationship with his parents, 48, 198–9
retirement, preparation for, 240–51
on rights of Adivasi people, 92–4
as Secretary of the Legal Affairs of

State of Gujarat (1974), 59–72
secular education among Bohras, worked to encourage, 31
on selection of Vice-Chancellor for Jamia Millia Islamia, 250–1
on Seshan's petition, 204–12
Shankar, Shiv visit to, 102–4
shift in career, 18–19
sister, 10, 20
smoking, 10
speech in Toronto (2000), 168–9
Stamp Act case and, 44–5
stance on secularism, 107
success, 37–8
as Supreme Court Judge, 104–36
on Supreme Court Legal Aid Committee Representing Undertrial Prisoners vs. Union of India case, 186
teachings, 31
on temple's affairs, 67–70
Thakkar, M.P. and, 37, 83–4
thoughts on fundamental rights, 120–4
travels, 195–6
United Bohra Club and, 19–20
views on CEC's powers, 205–12
views on legal education system in India, 179–82
visits to China, 270
wedding of daughter, 96–8
welfare schemes, 31
in Zimbabwe, 246–8
Ahmadi, Huzefa, 74, 83, 97, 125, 135, 171–5, 223, 238, 240–1, 271
Ahmadi, Imran Ali, 6–7, 32, 198
Ahmadi, Mushabber Imran, 7
Ahmadi, Rehana, 6
Ahmadi, Shirin, 8–9, 29, 32, 34–5, 199, 277–9
Ahmadi, Tasneem, 32, 34, 40, 83–4, 96–8, 124–5, 171–5, 238, 240–1, 270
Ahmed, Altaf, 117, 184
Ahmed, Fakhruddin Ali, 71
Ahmed, S. Saghir, 213, 220
Ahmedabad, 1, 6, 12, 14–15, 20, 22, 28, 45–6, 49
   Hindus and Muslims, communal tensions between, 14–16
   riots in, 258–64
   violence in, 49
AIJS, *See* All India Judicial Service
Akali Dal (L), 100
Ali, Imam, 4
Aligarh Muslim University Act, 1920 (AMU Act), 252
Aligarh Muslim University (AMU), 31, 251–3
   Ahmadi's views on, 253–5
   AMU (Amendment) Act, 1965 and, 252–3
   as minority institution, 252–3
   protection under Article 30 (1), 253
Allah, 265
Allahabad High Court, 71, 253–4
All Arunachal Pradesh Students Union (AAPSU), 215
Allauddin vs. State of Bihar case, 46–7
All India Judicial Service (AIJS), 222
Alternative Dispute Resolution (ADR) method, 193–4
AMU, *See* Aligarh Muslim University
AMU (Amendment) Act, 1965, 252
Anand, A. S., 163, 166
Anderson, Warren M., 226–7
Andhyarujina, T. R., 149
Ansari, Mohammad Hashim, 141
anti-Sikh riots (1984), 132
apex court, 95–6, 105, 141–3, 209, 254
appeasement of Muslims, 261–5
Article 14 of Constitution, 187

Article 15(4) of Constitution, 114
Article 16(1) of Constitution, 118
Article 16(2) of Constitution, 117–18
Article 16(4) of Constitution, 117–19
Article 18 of Constitution, 212–13
Article 19 of Constitution, 187
Article 20 of Constitution, 71
Article 21 of Constitution, 71, 187, 215
Article 23 of Constitution, 90
Article 30 (1) of Constitution, 253
Article 30 of Constitution, 251–2
Article 32 of Constitution, 133, 211, 219–21
Article 39A of Constitution, 177
Article 46 of Constitution, 118
Article 124(2) of Constitution, 163, 165
Article 143 (1) of Indian Constitution, 153
Article 192 (2) of Constitution, 210–11
Article 192 of Constitution, 209
Article 217(1) of Constitution, 163, 165
Article 226 of Constitution, 110, 219–21
Article 319 of Constitution, 208
Article 323A of Constitution, 218–19
Article 324 (1) of Constitution, 204
Article 324 of Constitution, 200, 206–7, 210
Article 340 of Constitution, 114
Article 352 of Constitution, 71
Article 356(1) of Constitution, 147–9
Article 356 of Constitution, 67, 143–5, 147
Article 359 of Constitution, 71, 75
Asia Pacific Advisory Forum on Judicial Education on Equality Issues, 218

assassinations, 131–4
Attah, Judith Sefi, 245
Ayodhya, 137–61
    Babri Masjid, demolition of, 116, 137–41, 144, 146
    kar sevaks (religious volunteers) in, 138–43, 146
    mediation to resolve dispute over, 194–5
    President's Rule in, 143
    symbolic *kar seva*, 138–41
Azad Hind Fauj, 5

Babri Masjid, demolition of, 116, 136, 137–41, 144–6, 153–4, 185, 281
Backward Class, 113
backwardness, 119
Bajrang Dal, 140
bamboo, 92–3
bamboo products, 92–3
Bandit Queen film, 213–14
Banerji, Milon, 139, 141, 149
ban on Hindu extremist organizations, 145–7
Bar Council examination, 181
Bar Council of India, 181–2
Bar Councils of the States, 182
Bar judge, 106
Barnala, Surjit Singh, 100
Basha, S. Azeez, 252–4
Beg, M. H., 75
Benares Hindu University (BHU), 254
Bensaab, Shirin, 8–9
Beyond Genocide, 120–1
Bhagwati, P. N., 75–6, 91
Bharati, Uma, 141
Bharatiya Janata Party (BJP), 108, 115–6, 135–6, 138, 140, 143–147, 202, 207, 260
Bharatiya Jan Sangh, 70
Bharatiya Lok Dal, 70

Bharat Ratna, 212–13
Bharucha, S. P., 153–7, 163, 166, 206, 220
Bhatt, Niranjan, 21, 48, 57, 190, 193
Bhopal Gas Leak Disaster (Processing of Claims) Act, 228, 230
Bhopal Gas Tragedy, 120–1, 225–39
　Ahmadi's involvement in multifaceted case, 230–9
　Anderson released on bail, 227
　arresting of employees, 226–7
　birth defects as consequence of, 226
　case in India's judicial system, 229–30
　compensation claim for, 228–39
　consequence of, 226
　deaths in, 226–7
　FIR on UCIL, 226
　Gandhi, Rajiv secret deal with Reagan, Ronald on, 227
　genetic abnormalities as consequence of, 226
　legal proceedings on, 228
　Methyl Isocyanate (MIC) gas leaking, 225–6
　rejection of India's claim in USA, 229
　Union of India filed claim for USD 3.3 billion against, 228–9
Bhopal Memorial Hospital, 236
Bhopal Memorial Hospital Trust (BMHT), 235–6, 312
Bhushan, Prashant, 231
Bhushan, Shanti, 75, 149, 231
Bilkis, 49–50
BJP, *See* Bharatiya Janata Party
'Black Days' of Indian democracy, *See* National Emergency
BMHT, *See* Bhopal Memorial Hospital Trust
Board of the Ghalib Institute, 269

Bohras community, 3
　Aziz worked to encourage secular education, 31
　connections in India, 13–14
　cultural practices, ties with, 5
　customs of, 4
　demographic change in 1940s, 5
　education, focused on, 5
　entrepreneurship, focused on, 5
　food of, 3–4
　loyalty, 13–14
　mealtimes, 4
　peace-loving, 5
　public wealth and, 5
　in sports, 17
　as trading community, 13
　tradition, ties with, 5
　traditional dress of, 4
　women, 4
Bohra Welfare Society, 19
Bombay High Court, 22, 93
Bommai, S. R., 147–9
Bose, Subhash Chandra, 5
British, 1–2
Burhanuddin, Syedna Mohammad, 30, 271–3

Calcutta Bohras, 5
capital punishment, 45, 268
case pendency, problem of, 190–207
caste-based discrimination, 56
caste system, 117–18
censorship, 71
Central Law Department, 72–3
Chagla, M. C., 252
Chakma and Hajong vs. State of Arunachal Pradesh case, 214–16
Chandosh, Hiram E., 194
Chandrachud, D. Y., 76, 253
Chandrachud, Y. V., 66, 75
Charan Lal Sahu Etc. vs. Union Of

India And Ors, 230
charity/donation box in temple, 68
Chief Election Commissioner and other Commissioners (Condition of Service) Act, 1991, 203
Chief Election Commissioner (CEC), 200–12
Chief Justice of India, 21, 35, 104–36, 167–9
Chitale, 99
City Civil and Sessions Court, 22, 41, 52
Civil Procedure Code (CPC), 192–3
Claims Tribunals, 54
Code of Civil Procedure, 21
Collegium system, 163–71
    Ahmadi on, 163–71
    concerns about, 168–9
    criticism, 171
    Gogoi's autobiography about, 171
Commission on Human Rights, 244
Committee for the appointment of Section Officers, 55
communal riots (1969), 48
communal violence, 145
Communist Party of India, 43
compensation cases, 53–4, 94–6
Conferment of Decoration on Persons (Abolition) Bill, 1969, 212
confiscation, 72
Congress party, 78, 117, 135, 143, 144, 203
Conservation of Foreign Exchange and Prevention of Smuggling Activities Act (COFEPOSA), 101
Constitution of India, 167
Cooke, Robin, 169–70
CPC (Amendment) Act (1999), 193
creamy layer, 118, 119
cricket, 17
customs of Bohras, 4, 31

Dai, 4, 9, 14, 29–32, 272, 277

Dai-e-Mutalaq (high priest), 4–5, 14, 29–30
Daruwala, Bejan, 21
Dawoodi Bohras, 2–4, 13, 32, 271, 273, 277
Dayal, Yogeshwar, 149, 163, 166
De, Niren, 75, 79
death sentence judgement, 47, 132
Delhi High Court, 54, 213
Delhi University, 254
Desai, Morarji, 70–1, 113–14
Desai, P. D., 92–3
Desai, S.T., 50
Devi, Phoolan, 213
Devi, Rabri, 153
Dhanoa, S. S., 203
dheda, 56
Divan, B.J., 51, 59
Divecha, Akbar, 258
Doordarshan, 121–2
Durrani, Salim, 57
Dwarka Temple, 69

East Timor, 244–5
    Commission's report recommendations, 246
    forced displacement in, 244
    human rights violations in, 244
    International Inquiry Commission in, 244–6
    violence in, 244
education, 5–6, 31, 179–82, 223, 250–2, 265
Election Commission of India (ECI), 200–12
electoral reforms, 205
Eradi, V. Balakrishna, 99
Eradi Tribunal, 99–100
execution application, 51
execution brief, 21
Executive Chairman of Lok Adalats,

53–4, 175

Faruqui, Ismail, 153
Fatal Accidents Act, 1855, 94
firkis, 58
First Judges Case, 162–3
forced labour, 89–90
Forest Department, 92
Fourth Judges Case, 162, 170
freedom of speech and expression, 74, 120–4
fundamental rights, 120–4

Gandhi, Indira, 71, 74, 131
Gandhi, Mahatma, 6, 48, 152
Gandhi, Rajiv, 98–9, 117, 133, 148, 227
Gandhi ashram, 49
gangrape in Delhi, 267–9
General Insurance Corporation of India, 232
Gill, M.S., 203–4
Ginsburg, Ruth Bader, 192
Godbole, Madhav, 144, 207
Godhra riots, 257–8, 261
Gogoi, Ranjan, 171
Gokhala, Vijay, 226
Gokulakrishnan, P.R., 105
Golden Temple in Amritsar, 131
Goldsmith, Peter, 247
Goswami, Rajiv, 115
Gubbay, Anthony, 246
Gujarat, 6, 48, 257
    Adivasis of, 84–104
    exploitation of impoverished migrant workers in sugar industry, 84–92
    mass agitation in, 61
    Panchayat elections suspended, 64–5
    President's rule in, 61, 65, 77–8
    riots, 257–64

sugarcane harvesting in, 85
Gujarat Club, 37–8
Gujarat High Court, 22–3, 37, 42, 59–60, 79–80, 85–6, 90, 93, 95–6, 99
Gujarat Panchayats (Amendment) Act 8 of 1974, 65
Gujjar, Babu, 213

Habibullah, Wajahat, 183, 184, 185
halwas, 4
haraam, 29
Haryana, 98–100
Hazratbal incident, 248
Hazratbal shrine, 183–4
Hegde, Ramakrishna, 147
High Court judges, transfer of, 109, 168–9
Himachal Pradesh, 145–7, 151
Hindu law, 50
Hindu–Muslim clashes, 14–16, *See also* riots
Hindu-Muslim harmony, 48
Hindu nationalism, 48, 112
Hindus, 14–15
    religious structure, 153–4
    violence against, 138
Hindutva, 48, 107–8, 116, 135–6, 260–4
Hindutva judgements, 107–8, 159
Honorary Government Pleader, 37
human migrations, 13–14
Husain, Zakir, 266

Ige, Tokunbo, 242
imperialism, 229
INC(O), 70
Indian Army, 183–5
Indian Forest Act, 93
Indian independence movement, 5–6
Indianization, 107
Indian Penal Code, 45, 155

Indira Sawhney vs. Union of India case, 113
Indo-US national legal exchange programme, 192–3, 196
Institute for Arbitration Mediation Legal Education and Development (AMLEAD), 193
Institute for the Study and Development of Legal Systems (ISDLS), 192
International Bar Association (IBA), 241, 246, 248
International Commission of Inquiry, 244
International Commission of Jurists (ICJ), 241–2
intra-court appeal, 92
Ismail Faruqui vs. Union of India case, 152–5
Iyer, Krishna, 71, 91

Jafri, Ehsan, 258
Jaising, Indira, 231
Jamalpur, 49–50
Jammu and Kashmir Liberation Front (JKLF), 183–4
Janata Dal, 114–16, 147, 205
Janata Front, 70, 77
Janata Party, 147, 260
Jayalalitha, J., 209–11
Jethmalani, Ram, 149, 152
Jinda, 47, 132–4
JKLF, *See* Jammu and Kashmir Liberation Front
judicial clerkship programme, 197
judicial culture, 60
Judicial Reforms, 21, 195–6, 241, 248
Judicial Service Commission, 243
judicial system in Liberia, 242–3
Jung, Ali Yavar, 252

Kadri, M.H., 57, 258
Kaka Kalelkar Commission Report (1955), 113
Kakata Circuit Court, Margibi County, 243
Kania, M.H., 117, 132–3, 180
Kapi, Mari, 245
Kaptai Hydel Power Project, 215
Kareem Nagar, 176
Karnataka, 147–51, 176
Kar seva, 108, 137–40
kar sevaks (religious volunteers), 138–41
Kesavananda Bharti case, 163
Keshub Mahindra vs. State of Madhya Pradesh case, 232–3
Kesri, Sitaram, 202
Khaira, Manjit Singh, 100
Khalistan, 131
Khan, Syed Ahmed, 252
Khanna, H.R., 75, 161
Khurana, Madan Lal, 115–16
Kidwai, Akhlaqur Rahman, 250
Kirpal, B.N., 180–1, 213
Kisan Mazdoor Lok Paksha (KMLP), 70, 77
Kotwalias, 92–4
koytas, 85–6
Krishnamoorthy, K., 176
Krishnamurthy, G.V.G., 203–4
kurta-pajama-saaya (tunic, trousers, overcoat) set, 4

L. Chandra Kumar vs. Union of India case, 218–21, 223
L.A. Shah Law College, Ahmedabad, 19
law clerks, 196
Law Department of Gujarat, 62–80
and Central Law Department, 72–4
as 'dumping ground', 63

efficiency, 64
'level jumping' approach for routine files, 64
library, 64
on MISA, 71–4
working conditions of, 62–3
legal education system in India, 179–82
Legal Study Group, 192
Leutheusser-Schnarrenberger, Sabine, 245
Liberia, 242–3
   Judicial Service Commission, 243
   judicial system in, 242–3
   post-war challenges, 243
LIC Insurance Corporation of India vs. Prof Manubhai D. Shah case, 120
Life Insurance Corporation of India, 232
Lok Adalats, 53–4, 175–9
Lok Dal, 147
Longowal, Harchand Singh, 98–9

Madhya Pradesh, 145–7, 151
Madras High Court, 54
Maharashtra, 6, 108
Mahindra, Keshub, 226, 232–3
mahram, 29
mahram by milk, 29–30
mahram relationships, 29–30
Maintenance of Internal Security Act (MISA), 71, 72, 75
Majumdar, S.B., 233
Maken, Lalit, 132
Malimath Committee, 193–4, 221
Mandal, B.P., 113–14
Mandal Commission, 112–19
Mann, Simranjit Singh, 132
Manohar Joshi vs. Nitin Bhaurao Patil case, 108
MAO College, *See* Muhammadan Anglo-Oriental College
Mardikar, M.N., 216
Mayo, Stephen A., 192, 194
Mazoon-e-Daawat, 30, 272
Mediation Act, 195
Meghalaya, 148, 150, 151
Mehmood, Tahir, 251–2, 255
Mehta, R.A., 87, 92–3
Menon, P.C. Balakrishna, 99
Merchant, Mahomedaali Jivaji, 20–1
Merchant, Zulekha, 10, 12, 20, 29, 32, 277–9
Methyl Isocyanate (MIC) gas, 225–6
Miabhoy, N.M., 42, 60
militants, 183–4
minorities' educational rights, 251–3
MISA, *See* Maintenance of Internal Security Act
misaaq, customs of bohras, 4
Misra, R., 231
Model Code of Conduct, 201, 204
Modi, Narendra, 257–64
Moi-e-Muqqadas, 183
Molakery, K.R., 147
Motor Accident Claims Tribunal, 94
Motor Vehicles Act (1939), 54, 94
Motor Vehicles Act (1988), 95
Muchhala, Fatema, 30
Muchhala, Taher, 19–20
Muchhala, Yusuf, 19–20
Muchhala brothers, 24–8
   Aziz and, 28–9
   as charitable family, 25
   investments, 25
   jute industry, 25
   Muchhala, Hatim, loss of, 25–6
   Partition and, 26
   as prosperous Surti Bohra families, 25
   yearly earnings, 25
Mugabe, Robert, 246–7

Muhammadan Anglo-Oriental
   College (MAO College), 252
Muharram, 271
Mukharji, S., 231
Mulla & Mulla, 50–1
Mulla & Mulla (Desai), 50
Mumbai, bloody riots and bomb blasts,
   138, 160
Munshi, Aziz, 20–1
Muslims, 13–14
   appeasement of, 257–65
   Bohras (*See* Bohras community)
   Hindu–Muslim clashes, 14–16,
      257–65 (*See also* riots)
   identity, 16, 42, 50, 80, 96

Nagaland, 148, 150, 151
Nanavati, I.M., 67
Nanavati, Sudhir, 111–12
Narayanan, K.R., 259
Narcotic Drugs and Psychotropic
   Substances Act, 186–7
Nariman, Fali, 169, 231
National Awards, 212–13
National Commission for Backward
   Classes Act of 1993, 119
National Emergency, 71–6
National Human Rights Commission
   (NHRC), 215, 248–50
national judicial academy, 182
National Judicial Appointment
   Commission Act (2014), 170
National Law Colleges, 181
National Law Universities, 181–2
Nav Nirman movement, 61
Nayar, Kuldip, 72, 144
Nehru, Jawaharlal, 77
NHRC, *See* National Human Rights
   Commission
non conveniens, 228

Ojha, N.D., 231

Okudzeto, Sam, 242
129th Law Commission, 193–4
Operation Blue Star, 131, 185
Other Backward Classes (OBCs), 114,
   119
otlas (quintessential Surat style
   porches), 3

P.J. Reddy Commission, 49
Padma awards, 212–13
Palkhivala, Nani, 71, 117
Pandian, S.R., 105, 117, 119, 149, 163,
   166
Parasaran, K., 117, 119, 149
partition of India, 13–16
patawaalas, 2
Patel, Babubhai Jasbhai, 70, 77
Patel, Chimanbhai, 61, 70, 77
Patel, Jasubhai, 57–8
Pathak, R.S., 106, 229
Patwa, Sunder Lal, 146
Personal Security Officers (PSOs),
   127–8
Picado, Sonia, 244–5
Poti, P.S., 116
poverty, 119
Prabhoo, R.Y., 107
Prasad, Rajendra, 282
President's Rule, 145, 147–9, 151
   in Gujarat, 61, 65, 70, 77–8
   in Himachal Pradesh, 146
   in Karnataka, 147–8
   in Madhya Pradesh, 146–7
   in Punjab, 98–9
   in Rajasthan, 145
   in Uttar Pradesh, 142–3
Prevention of Black Marketing
   and Maintenance of Supplies of
   Essential Commodities Act, 101
Prevention of Sexual Harassment at
   Workplace, 218

Prophet Muhammad, 4, 183
Protection of Human Rights Act (1993), 248–50
Public Interest Litigations (PILs) in deliverance of social justice, 84–92
pujari, 67–8
Punchhi, M.M., 163–4, 165, 166, 168–69, 220
punishment for Smaller Offences, 45
Punjab, 98–100, 131
Punjab Reorganisation Act of 1966, 98

Qarz-e-Hasana, 31
Qur'an, 265
Qutbuddin, Khuzaima, 30, 271–4, 276–77

R. Y. Prabhoo vs. P. K. Kunte case, 107
Rai, Kalpnath, 202
Rajasthan, 98–100, 145, 147, 149, 151
Rajiv-Longowal accord (1985), 98–9
Ramaswamy, K., 132–3, 149, 151–2, 220
Ram Rath Yatra (chariot journey), 116
Ram Temple, 116, 138, 140, 153–4
Rana, Chandrakant Chanalal, 41
Rao, M. Jagannadha, 180
Rao, P. P., 99, 117
Rao, P. V. Narasimha, 112, 117, 143–4, 185, 189, 203
rapes, 268–9
Rashtriya Swayamsevak Sangh (RSS), 145–6, 257
Ravi-Beas water dispute, 98–100
Ray, A. N., 75, 163, 169
Ray, G. N., 138, 153, 163, 166
Ray, S. S., 106
Reagan, Ronald, 227
Reddy, B. J., 117
Reddy, B. P. Jeevan, 149, 213
Reddy, S. Obul, 80

refugees, 14–15
Representation of People Act (India) 1951, 107
reservations, 112–19
rida, 4
right to freedom of speech and expression, 74, 120–4
Right to Legal Aid, 177–8
Right to Life and Personal Liberty, 71
riots, 14, 48, 112, 116, 131–2, 138, 160, 257, 260–4
Robinson, Mary, 243–4
Roy, Shaurya, 269
RSS, *See* Rashtriya Swayamsevak Sangh

S.P. Gupta vs. Union of India and Ors case, 163
S.P. Sampath Kumar vs. Union of India case, 219–20
S.R. Bommai vs. Union of India case, 145, 147, 152
Sahai, R. M., 117, 119
Saifuddin, Muffaddal, 272, 276
Saifuddin, Syedna Taher, 30–3, 40, 276
Saikia, K. N., 105, 193
Sakshi, feminist NGO, 217–18
Salem Advocates Bar Association vs. Union of India case, 194
Sangh Parivar, 108, 116, 262
Sarela, Akbar Sharafali, 42
Sarin, H.C., 77–9
Sarkaria, R.S., 66
Sarvajanik Law College, 19
Sawant, P.B., 117, 149
Sawhney, Indra, 116–17
Scalia, Antonin, 192
Scheduled Castes (SC), 85, 118–19, 170, 177
Scheduled Tribes (ST), 85, 118–19, 170, 177

schools for girls, 31
Scott, Gloria M., 242
Second Backwards Class Commission, 113–14
Second Judges Case, 109, 162–3, 169–70, 206
Secretary of the Legal Affairs of State of Gujarat (1974), 59–70
Section 89, in Civil Code Procedure, 190–1
Section 123 (3) of Representation of the People Act, 1951, 152
Section 235 (2), Code of Criminal Procedure, 47
Section 302, Code of Criminal Procedure, 88
Section 303A, Panchayat Act, 64–7
Section 313, Code of Criminal Procedure, 43
secularism, 107, 113, 118, 143, 151–2, 158–61, 266, 281
Seervai, H.M., 169
Seshan, Tirunellai Narayanaiyer, 200–12
Shankar, Shiv, 102–4
Sharma, O.P., 139
Sharma, Shankar Dayal, 153, 185–6, 189, 250–1, 270
Shekhar, Chandra, 112, 115–17, 202
Shelat, J.M., 38–39, 42
Shiromani Akali Dal, 99–100
Shukla, Dhruvkumar Harshadrai, 23, 48, 88
Sibal, Kapil, 99
Siddiqui, Aziz, 236
Sikh community, 131–2
Singh, Arjun, 202
Singh, K., 117
Singh, K. N., 231
Singh, Kalyan, 138–9, 142–3
Singh, Kuldip, 105–6, 109, 119, 149, 163, 166, 197, 213
Singh, M. P., 54
Singh, Manmohan, 264
Singh, Moti, 227
Singh, N.P., 206, 213
Singh, V.P., 112, 114–18
Singhvi, Abhishek M., 194
Singhvi, L.M., 178
Sinha, Jagmohan Lal, 71
Smaller Offences, punishment for, 45
socialism, 84
Socialist Party, 70
Socially and Educationally Backward Classes (SEBCs), 114–15, 118
Sock, Raymond C., 242
Solanki, Madhavsingh, 79
Sorabjee, Soli, 21, 75, 116, 149, 231
Srikrishna Commission, 160
Srisailam Dam project, 175–6
Stamp Act, 44–5
State of Maharashtra And Another vs. Madhukar Narayan Mardikar case, 216–17
Sukha, 132–3
Sukumaran, S., 116
Supreme Court-Advocate-on-Record vs. Union of India case, 109
Supreme Court Advocates on Record Association vs. Union of India (1993) case, 163
Supreme Court Legal Aid Committee Representing Undertrial Prisoners vs. Union of India case, 186
Supreme Court of India, 42, 75, 95–6, 104, 138–42, 204
Surat, 3
  baked goods, 3
  Bohras of, 3
  diamonds, 3
  food, 3
  namkeens, 3

undhiyu, 3
Surtis, 3
Sutlej Yamuna Link canal, 99
Swamy, Subramanium, 208–12
Swaraj, Sushma, 227
Syedna, 4–5
SYL canal, 100
symbolic *kar seva*, 138–41

TADA, 248–9
Tarkunde, V. N., 75
Taylor, Charles Ghankey, 242
temple
    Ahmadi's on affairs of, 67–70
    charity/donation box in, 68
    collections, 67–70
    Dwarka, 69–70
    funds collected for maintenance of, 68
    pujaris of, 67–8
    renovation, 69–70
    safety of devotees, 69–70
    widen entry passage of, 69
thaal, 4
Thaker, Jayendra Mohanlal, 23, 37, 48
Thackeray, Bal, 107
Thakkar, Manharlal Pranlal, 23, 37, 48, 57, 83–4, 95–6
Third Judges Case, 162, 169–70
Thiruvengadam, Arun, 197
Thomas, K.T., 220
Thommen, T.K., 105, 117, 119
Togadia, Pravin, 260
Training Programme for law graduates, 181
transfer policy for High Court judges, 109
typhoid, 26

Union Carbide Corporation of India vs. Union of India, 231
Union Carbide India Limited (UCIL) pesticide plant, 225–39
United Bohra Club, 19–20
Uttar Pradesh, 137–61

Vahanvaty, Goolam Essaji, 275
Vahanvaty, Murtaza, 96–8
Vaidya, A.S., 131–2, 134
Vaidya, Arun, 47
Vajpayee, Atal Bihari, 71, 144, 260
Vakil, Nassarwanji, 22
Vansfodias, 92–4
Venkatachaliah, M. N., 106–10, 117, 138–43, 153, 189, 194–5, 231, 248
Venkatasubbaiah, Pendekanti, 147
Venkataswami, K., 220
Venugopal, K.K., 116–17, 141
Verma, J.S., 106–10, 149, 153, 163–4, 166, 170, 197
Vice-Chancellor for Jamia Millia Islamia, selection of, 250–1
violations of human rights by security forces in Jammu and Kashmir, 248–50
violence, 48–9, 100
Vishakha guidelines, 218
Vishwa Hindu Parishad (VHP), 138, 140, 146, 260

Wallace, Clifford, 192, 194
white crocheted caps, 4
Wisner, Frank, 192
women, 4
    independence, 31
    rights, Ahmadi's commitment towards, 216–18
Woolf, Harry, 194
Woolfe, Baron Harry, 178–9
World War II, 1

Zimbabwe's legal and judicial system, 246–8
ziyarat, 276
Zulekha, 10, 20, 29